Editor in Chief **Dana L. Blatt, J.D., Esq.**

Managing Editor **Marie H. Stedman**

Written By **Mark Melo, J.D., Esq.**
Tony Thompson, J.D., Esq.
Brian Arnold, J.D., Esq.
Krista Stevenson, J.D., Esq.

Memory Graphics **Norman Vance**

Page Design **Terri Asher**

Chief Administrator **Richard A. Strober**

Adaptable to Courses Utilizing Dukeminier and Krier's Casebook on Property, 5th Edition

Published by **WEST GROUP**
610 Opperman Drive
Eagan, MN
55123

610 Opperman Drive
P.O. Box 64526
St. Paul, MN 55164-0526

ISBN 0-314-14166-9

Printed in the United States of America

3rd reprint 2003

A Message from Dana L. Blatt, J.D., Editor In Chief West Group High Court Case Summaries

As Editor in Chief of West Group's High Court Case Summaries, I am pleased to be associated with West Group and its tradition of providing the highest quality law student study aids such as Nutshells, Hornbooks, the Black Letter Series, and Sum and Substance products. I am also pleased that West Group, as the new publisher of High Court Case Summaries, will continue its tradition of providing students with the best quality student briefs available today. When you use these High Court Case Summaries, you will know that you have the advantage of using the best-written and most comprehensive student briefs available, with the most thorough analyses. Law students cannot afford to waste a minute of their time. That's why you need High Court Case Summaries. You'll find that with High Court you not only save time, but also have the competitive edge with our exclusive features such as memory graphics, "party lines," overview outlines, and case vocabulary. The following two pages will introduce you to the format of a High Court Brief.

Dana L. Blatt, J.D., Editor In Chief

FORMAT FOR A HIGH COURT BRIEF

THE HEADNOTE

Like a headline in a newspaper, the headnote provides you with a brief statement highlighting the importance of the case to the course.

"PARTY" LINE

A quick memory aid. For instantaneous recollection of the names of the parties and their relationship to each other.

MEMORY GRAPHIC

"A picture is worth a thousand words." Our professional cartoonists have created an entertaining "picture of the facts." To assist you in remembering what a particular case is about, simply glance at the picture.

INSTANT FACTS

Another great memory aid. A quick scan of a single sentence will instantly remind you of all of the facts of the case.

BLACK LETTER RULE

This section contains the single most important rule of the case (determined by reference to the chapter of the casebook where the case can be found). Read together with instant facts, you have a perfect mini brief.

CASE VOCABULARY

Every new or unusual legal, Latin or English word found in the original case is briefly defined in this section. This timesaver eliminates constant references to separate dictionaries.

PROCEDURAL BASIS

In a single sentence we summarize what happened, procedurally, to cause the case to be on appeal.

FACTS

"Just the facts ma'am..." Our facts are clearer and easier to understand than the original case. In fact, you can have a complete understanding of the original case without ever having to read it. Just read our brief.

ISSUE

Utilizing our I.R.A.C. format (Issue, Rule, Application, Conclusion), we put it all in focus by simply stating the single most important question of every case.

DECISION AND RATIONALE

We know you need to understand the rationale of every case to learn the law. In a clear, concise, and meticulous fashion we lay it all out for you. We do the work of separating what is important from what is not. Yet, we provide you with a thorough summary of every essential element of every case. Every concurrence and dissent is summarized as well.

ANALYSIS

We provide you with an extensive analysis of every single case. Here you will learn what you want to know about every case. What is the history or background of the litigation? What do authorities say about the opinion? How does it fit in with the course? How does each case compare with others in the casebook? Is it a majority or minority opinion? What is the importance of the case and why did the casebook author choose to include it as a major opinion in the casebook? What types of things will the professor be asking about the case? What will be said about the opinion in class? Will people criticize or applaud it? What would you want to say about the case if called upon in class to brief it? In other words, what are the "secret" essential things that one must know and understand about each case in order to do well in the course? We answer these and many other questions for you. Nobody else comes close to giving you the in-depth analysis that we give!

A Great All-Around Study Aid!

IMPLIED WARRANTIES OF MERCHANTABILITY SURVIVE EXPRESS CONTRACTUAL PROVISIONS TO THE CONTRARY

Henningsen v. Bloomfield Motors, Inc.

(Auto Purchaser) v. (Auto Dealer)

32 N.J. 358, 161 A.2d 69 (N.J. 1960)

M E M O R Y   G R A P H I C

Instant Facts

An automobile purchaser sued the dealer and manufacturer for breach of an implied warranty of merchantability, although the express contractual terms of the sale disclaimed all implied warranties.

Black Letter Rule

A contract of adhesion does not trump statutory implied warranties of merchantability.

Case Vocabulary

CAVEAT EMPTOR: Let the buyer beware.

CONTRACT OF ADHESION: A contract between parties of unequal bargaining position, where the buyer must "take it or leave it."

IMPLIED WARRANTY OF MERCHANTABILITY: A warranty that means that the thing sold must be reasonably fit for the general purpose for which it is manufactured and sold.

Procedural Basis: Certification to New Jersey Supreme Court of appeal of judgment awarding damages for breach of implied warranty.

Facts: Mr. Henningsen purchased a car from Bloomfield Motors Inc. (D), a retail dealer. The car had been manufactured by Chrysler Corporation (D). Mr. Henningsen gave the car to his wife for Christmas. Mrs. Henningsen (P) was badly injured a few days later when the steering gear failed and the car turned right into a wall. When he purchased the car, Mr. Henningsen signed a contract without reading the fine print. The fine print contained a "warranty" clause which disclaimed all implied warranties and which granted an express warranty for all defects within 90 days or 4000 miles, whichever came first. Mrs. Henningsen (P) sued Bloomfield (D) and Chrysler (D). The trial court dismissed her negligence counts but ruled for Mrs. Henningsen (P) based on the implied warranty of merchantability. Bloomfield (D) and Chrysler (D) appealed.

Issue: Does a contract of adhesion trump statutory implied warranties of merchantability?

Decision and Rationale: (Francis, J.) No. A contract of adhesion does not trump statutory implied warranties of merchantability. In order to ameliorate the harsh effects of the doctrine of caveat emptor, most states have imposed an implied warranty of merchantability on all sales transactions. This warranty simply means that the thing sold must be reasonably fit for the general purpose for which it is manufactured and sold. The warranty extends to all foreseeable users of the product, not merely those in privity of contract with the seller. In order to avoid the implied warranty obligations, many manufacturers, including Chrysler (D) and all other automobile manufacturers, include an express warranty provision which disclaims all statutory implied warranties. We must determine what effect to give this express warranty. Under traditional principles of freedom of contract, the law allows parties to contract away obligations. However, in the auto sales context, the fine-print disclaimer of implied warranties is a contract of adhesion. It is a standardized form contract, and the purchaser has no opportunity to bargain for different terms. He must "take it or leave it," and he cannot shop around to different dealers because all of them use the same standard contract. Because the purchaser and seller occupy grossly inequal bargaining positions, we feel that justice must trump the principle of freedom of contract. Chrysler's (D) attempted disclaimer of an implied warranty of merchantability is so inimical to the public good as to compel an adjudication of its invalidity. Affirmed.

Analysis:

This well-written opinion presents an excellent exegesis of several areas of law, ranging from products liability to various contract principles. The opinion notes several conflicting interests and principles which the court must weigh. First, the traditional principle of caveat emptor faces the modern doctrine of implied warranties of merchantability. The court has little difficulty in holding that modern commercial transactions require protection for purchasers. An implied warranty of merchantability is imposed in all auto sales transactions in order to protect the buyer. Second, the requirement of privity of contract is weighed against an implied warranty. The court notes that, in modern sales transactions, a warranty safeguards all consumers of a product, not merely those in direct contractual privity with the seller. Third, the principle of freedom of contract is weighed against this implied warranty. Freedom of contract is one of the fundamental tenets of the law. Parties should be free to contract for any provisions, and generally parties are bound by the terms of their contract. However, an important exception exists when a contract is one of adhesion. Contracts of adhesion typically involve terms in fine print, written by a powerful seller to limit liabilities or impose responsibilities upon an unsuspecting buyer. No bargaining occurs for these terms, and indeed the buyer is in no position to bargain. If the buyer attempts to change the terms of the contract, the seller simply will not complete the transaction. In order for a contract to be considered "adhesive" or "unconscionable," the buyer usually has nowhere else to go. As in the case at bar, all sellers of a particular type of goods may include similar terms in their adhesive contracts. Weighing all of these factors, a court may rule that the express contractual terms are invalid, notwithstanding the principle of freedom of contract. The arguments for and against this approach are easy to see. On one hand, a buyer should not be allowed to benefit from his failure to read the terms of a contract or to attempt to change some unwanted terms. On the other hand, social justice requires that the buyer be protected from an all-powerful seller, especially where the buyer has no other option but to accept the contract as written. All in all, public policy, and not traditional law, shapes this court's opinion.

Table of Contents

Alphabetical Table of Cases

Chapter 1

The acquisition of property is a fundamental pursuit of many individuals. Therefore, the rules of property acquisition are crafted so as to encourage certain types of behavior while discouraging other types of behavior. Also, these rules embody many values present in our society.

Property may be acquired by discovery. The principle is that he who is first in time to discover hitherto undiscovered property owns it. Before the modern era, this rule was intended to encourage the discovery of new lands. But it also embodied the notion that it is somehow fairer to give title to whoever is first in time.

Property may also be acquired by conquest. Unfortunately, this principle encouraged the physical taking of much land. Yet, it also has philosophical justifications. For example, in the case of the European conquest of the Americas, many philosophers approved of this conquest because the Europeans made productive use of the land while the Indians allegedly did not. Indeed, the notion that land should be used productively is a powerful one in the law of property. It appears in the law of adverse possession, nuisance, and eminent domain.

Title to property may also be gained by the capture of wild animals. Title goes to the person who captures the animal rather than to the one who merely pursues it. This rule promotes competition among hunters and increases the amount of wild animals caught for the benefit of society. However, it is possible that the practices of a particular industry are more efficient at capturing wild animals. In such a case, the law will defer to the local custom.

Title to property may also be acquired by creation. First and foremost, this embodies the notion that it is only fair to give title to the creator. Also, however, the law wishes to encourage the creation of new property for all of society to benefit. Thus, there are many forms of common law and statutory protection for the creators of property. Note that this property is often intangible, such as a computer program.

Property can also be acquired by purchase, gift and contract. But these common approaches are largely outside the scope of this chapter.

Chapter Overview Outline
Acquisition of Property by Discovery, Capture and Creation

Chapter 1

NOTE: THE PURPOSE OF THIS OUTLINE IS TO ORGANIZE THE CASES SO THAT ONE CAN QUICKLY UNDERSTAND THE RELEVANCE OF EACH CASE TO THE COURSE. NO ATTEMPT IS MADE IN THIS OVERVIEW TO ADDRESS EVERY CONCEPT THAT MUST BE STUDIED. BE SURE TO READ THE ENTIRE CASEBOOK AND/OR OTHER MATERIALS TO GAIN A FULL UNDERSTANDING OF ALL CONCEPTS.

I. Acquisition by Discovery
   A. Discovery of land in America by a European power gives absolute title subject only to the Indian right of occupancy. *Johnson v. M'Intosh.*

II. Acquisition by Capture
   A. In order to gain title to a wild animal, a hunter must either trap the animal or mortally wound it. *Pierson v. Post.*
      a. Exception: Title to a wild animal is acquired when a hunter apprehends the beast in accordance with custom. *Ghen v. Rich.*
   B. The law wants to encourage the capture of wild animals.
      1. Example: A person may not maliciously prevent another from capturing wild animals in the pursuit of his trade. *Keeble v. Hickerongill.*
   C. Property rights, such as the right to capture wild animals, are adjusted so as to eliminate externalities. These changes in property rights promote a more efficient allocation of resources. *Harold Demetz, Toward a Theory of Property Rights.*

III. Acquisition by Creation
   A. The law wants to encourage the efficient use of property by as many people as possible; consequently, not all creations are given legal protection. Unless the common law or the patent or copyright statutes give protection from appropriation, a person's property interest is limited to the chattels which embody his creation. *Cheney Brothers v. Doris Silk Corp.*
   B. Competition increases social welfare. Imitation increases competition. Therefore, the law should not protect intangible property, but allow others to copy an inventor's creation, only if this freedom to imitate does not destroy the incentive to create. *Intellectual Property and the Legacy of* International News Service v. Associated Press.
      1. Example: If a company has a legal right to copy a competitor's product, it may inform consumers that its product is equivalent to its competitor's product. *Smith v. Chanel.*
   C. Excised body parts belong to the doctor removing them. *Moore v. Regents of University of California.*
   D. Punitive damages may be awarded for intentional trespass to land. *Jacque v. Steenberg Homes, Inc.*
   E. Property rights may not be exercised so as to endanger the well-being of others. *State v. Shack*

Johnson v. M'Intosh

(Successor to Indian Title) v. (Successor to United States Title)
(1823) 21 U.S. (8 Wheat) 543

MEMORY GRAPHIC

Instant Facts

M'Intosh (D) acquired title to land under grant from the United States; Johnson (P) acquired title to the same land by purchase from the Painkeshaw Indians.

Black Letter Rule

Discovery of land in America by a European power gives absolute title subject only to the Indian right of occupancy.

Case Vocabulary

ABSOLUTE TITLE: Perfect title; unencumbered title.
CEDE: To transfer, usually from one government to another.
CONVEY: To transfer realty to another person.
CONVEYANCE: The transfer of land from one person to another.
EJECTMENT: An action to recover the possession of land.
OCCUPANCE: Same as possession.
PATENT: A grant of public property by the United States.
REGAL GOVERNMENT: The state.
SOVEREIGN: A state which has supreme authority.
VEST: To give a right to.

Procedural Basis: Appeal from judgment in action to eject.

Facts: Johnson (P) purchased land from the Chiefs of the Piankeshaw Indians. The Chiefs were duly vested by the tribe to represent those rights that the Indians had. M'Intosh (D) acquired title to this same piece of land by grant from the United States. The United States obtained this land by grant from Virginia.

Issue: Is title by grant from a discovering nation superior to title obtained by purchase from those that the nation conquered?

Decision and Rationale: (Marshall). Yes. Upon the discovery of America, the nations of Europe agreed that discovery would vest title in the discovering nation against all other powers of Europe. The discoverer governed its relations with the natives as it deemed fit. In the establishment of these relations, the Indians were given the right to occupancy. However, their right to absolute title was divested and taken by the discoverer. This principle, that title vests in the European nation that discovers the land, was especially recognized by England. As early as 1496 the King of England commissioned an explorer to take title to all land discovered by the explorer, except land previously discovered by Christian people. After the revolution, title to all land passed from Great Britain to the colonies. As mentioned, this title was absolute subject only to the Indian right of occupancy. The colonies affirmed the principle that title traced to a discovery is superior to Indian title. Virginia, for example, declared the "exclusive night of pre-emption from the Indians." The land which is at controversy in this case was granted from Virginia to the United States. The United States has also affirmed the principle that title traced to a discovery is superior to Indian title. The title which discovery has given is as follows: Discovery gives an exclusive right to extinguish an Indian right of occupancy either by purchase or by conquest. This court will not decide whether it is just to expel the Indians. "Conquest gives a title which the courts of the conqueror cannot deny, whatever the private and speculative opinions of individuals may be." Usually the principles of human relations dictate that conquered peoples be allowed to assimilate with the conqueror. However, since the Indians were fierce savages, they could not be assimilated. In consequence, the Indians were driven out by the sword. Those that were not warlike retained the right to occupancy. However they did not have the right to grant land. Consequently, the Piankeshaw Indians did not have the right to sell the land to Johnson (P). Judgment affirmed.

Analysis:

Discovery and conquest, in international law, are two means of acquiring land. Discovery means the finding of hitherto unknown territory. Of course, the Americas were not unknown when the Europeans "discovered" it. The Indians knew the land very well. Why then didn't the land belong to them? The answer is disturbing: The Indians were viewed by men of the times as savages who were incapable of owning land. Aside from this, the doctrine of discovery has important foundations. It comes from the notion that being first in time justifies ownership: If you discover something, you own it because you are first in time. (The reasons for this rule will be discussed in the section on finders.) Conquest is the taking of land by force. In actuality, this is how the Europeans came to own much of the Americas. Though this doctrine may disturb many, it again has very relevant doctrinal underpinnings. The reasoning comes from John Locke's labor theory, and goes something like this: A man owns his own body. He also owns the work and labor of his body. Therefore, when he mixes his labor with a parcel of land, by cultivating it for example, he owns that piece of land. Since the Indians were savages and did not build roads and houses on the land and did not improve the land, they could not own it. The Europeans owned the land because they worked it. Whether the reasoning is faulty or not, the idea is important because the following principle dominates much of property law: One of the goals of property law is to encourage the efficient and productive use of land. This principle appears, for example, in the law of adverse possession, nuisance, and eminent domain.

COURT DECLARES THAT A HUNTER MUST EITHER TRAP OR MORTALLY WOUND A WILD ANIMAL BEFORE HE ACQUIRES TITLE TO IT

Pierson v. Post

(Killer of Fox) v. (Pursuer of Fox)
(1805) 3 Cal. R. 175; 2 Am. Dec. 264

MEMORY GRAPHIC

Instant Facts

While Post (P) was pursuing a fox, Pierson (D) killed the fox and took possession it.

Black Letter Rule

A hunter must either trap or mortally wound a wild animal in order to acquire title to it.

Case Vocabulary

BODILY SEISIN: Actual physical possession of some body, e.g., a wild animal.
CERTIORARI: A writ issued by a superior court ordering an inferior court to produce a record of a case tried in the inferior court; the writ is a process by which the superior court may review the proceedings below.
CONSTRUCTIVE POSSESSION: Dominion and control over an object, though not physical possession.
FERAE NATURAE: A wild animal.
HOSTEM HUMANI GENERIS: Enemies of the human race.
INSTITUTE: A textbook containing principles of law.
PANDECTS: A compilation of Roman law, consisting of the chief ideas of the most authoritative jurists.
PURSUER: One who attempts to capture property.
RATIONE SOLI: Because of the land; in the context of title to animals this refers to ownership because of the presence of the wild animal on the claimant's land.

Procedural Basis: Writ of Certiorari after judgment in action for damages for trespass on the case.

Facts: Post (P) discovered a fox on wild and uninhabited land. In an attempt to capture the fox Post (P) began to hunt and pursue the fox with his dogs. Even though Pierson (D) knew that Post (P) was hunting the fox, he killed the fox and took possession of it. Post (P) contends that he acquired title to the fox because he was the first to hunt it. Pierson (D) maintains that he acquired title to the fox because he killed the fox.

Issue: Does mere pursuit of a wild animal vest title in the pursuer?

Decision and Rationale: (Tompkins). No. Since a fox is a wild animal, a property right can be acquired in it only if the hunter "occupies" it. Some authorities feel that a hunter can occupy a wild animal only if he traps it. Other authorities feel that a hunter can occupy a wild animal if he mortally wounds it and remains in pursuit. This is because a hunter in pursuit of a mortally wounded animal has effectively captured the animal. But all authorities agree that mere pursuit of a wild animal is insufficient to vest title in the hunter. This is to prevent litigation. If mere pursuit were to vest title, it would be very difficult to determine who was the first to pursue. Since Post (P) was in mere pursuit of the fox, he acquired no title to it. Judgment reversed.

Dissent: (Livingston). Since foxes are a public nuisance, the killing of foxes is in the public interest. Therefore, the rule that this court should adopt would encourage the destruction of these animals. The following rule accomplishes this: A pursuer acquires title to a wild animal if he is in reach of the animal or if he has a reasonable prospect of capturing the animal. Since it is nearly certain that Post (P) would have captured the fox, the judgment below should be affirmed.

Analysis:

There are two justifications advanced for the rule that capture is required to vest title. First, this rule advances society's goal of capturing wild animals (the desire to make "efficient use" of property). Society rewards the captor only because this rule fosters competition. More competition means more hunters. More hunters results in the more efficient capturing of wild animals. The second reason for this rule is that it is easy to administer. While it is easy to determine who has captured a wild animal, it would be very difficult to determine who was the first to pursue a wild animal. Alternatively, one may use the principle of first in time to understand this case: "He who first occupies a wild animal owns it." Of course, the fight is over whether one must be the first to chase a wild animal or the first to capture it. The majority rules that one must be the first to capture it for the reasons given above.

Interestingly, the majority here went against the established custom, which recognized hot pursuit as vesting a right of ownership in the pursuer. In looking at all of the obscure legal authorities, the majority ignored this custom. Keep this in mind as you read the next case, Ghen v. Rich, which seems to exalt custom over formal legal rules.

Ghen v. Rich

(Hunter) v. (Finder)
(1881) 8 F. 159

MEMORY GRAPHIC

Instant Facts

Ghen (P) shot and killed a whale, which sank to the bottom of the sea. Three days later, Ellis found the whale on the shore and sold it to Rich (D).

Black Letter Rule

Title to a wild animal is acquired when a hunter apprehends the beast in accordance with custom.

Case Vocabulary

APPROPRIATION: The act of making a particular thing one's own.
DECEIT: A misrepresentation of the truth so as to induce another person to act in a particular manner.
FRAUD: A misrepresentation of the truth so as to induce another person to act in a particular manner.
LIBEL: In maritime law, the equivalent of a lawsuit.
LIBELLANT: In maritime law, the equivalent of a plaintiff.
MARITIME LAW: That system of law which pertains to the sea and commerce thereon.
Respondent: Defendant
STATUTE OF LIMITATIONS: The time period that a person must possess an object before he takes title to it.
USAGE: A local custom which is so well-established that all are presumed to act with reference thereto.

Procedural Basis: Suit in trial court for damages for conversion of property.

Facts: Ghen (P) shot and killed a whale in Cape Cod, which sank to the bottom of the sea. Three days later Ellis found the whale on the shore and sold it to Rich (D). In killing the whale, Ghen (P) followed the local custom of Cape Cod. The custom is as follows: Fishermen kill the whales with bomb-lances. Each fisherman's lance leaves a unique brand so that the killer of the whale can be known. When the whales are killed, they sink to the bottom, but rise again to the surface in two to three days. The whales then float out to sea or float ashore. When a whale floats ashore, the finder usually sends word to the killer. The killer retrieves the whale and usually pays a small fee to the finder. This business and custom is practiced by few people since it requires great skill, experience, and capital. Ghen (P) contends that title may be acquired when the hunter apprehends a beast in accordance with custom. Rich (D) contends that custom does not govern the acquisition of title.

Issue: Is title to a wild animal acquired when a hunter apprehends the beast in accordance with custom?

Decision and Rationale: (Nelson). Yes. Other cases have held that title may be acquired by a hunter if he apprehends the beast in accordance with custom. This is because a custom usually embraces an entire industry. When a custom embraces an entire industry, there is no need for the court to fashion a judge-made rule. Rather, the custom is good enough. Custom is compelling in this case for several reasons: the custom affects few people; it has been relied upon for many years; it requires the hunter to perform all that is possible given the circumstances of whale hunting in Cape Cod; it gives a reasonable fee to the finder; without this custom, this industry would die, since no person would engage in the industry if his labor could be appropriated by a chance finder. Since Ghen (P) captured the whale in accordance with the custom of Cape Cod, title has vested in him. Judgment for Plaintiff.

Analysis:

One of the ways to understand this case is to recall one of the goals of property law: Property law should promote the efficient capture of wild animals. The custom of a local hunting trade is often more efficient than the general rule that wild animals must be captured. This is because a hunting custom has been refined to fit the particular needs of that trade. In this case, for example, it is more efficient to award the whale to the killer, even though he does not immediately capture it, because the killer ship can go off and look for other whales without waiting for the dead whale to rise to the surface. In *Pierson v. Post* it was custom to award the wild fox to the man first in hot pursuit. In that case, however, the custom did not promote the efficient capture of wild animals, or at least the majority did not think that the custom promoted this goal. Thus, custom did not prevail.

COURT DECLARES THAT AN INDIVIDUAL MAY NOT MALICIOUSLY PREVENT ANOTHER FROM CAPTURING WILD ANIMALS IN PURSUIT OF HIS TRADE

Keeble v. Hickeringill

(Hunter) v. (Duck Frightener)

(1707) 11 East 574; 103 Eng. Rep. 1127; 1 1 Mod. 74, 130 (as Keble v. Hickringill); 3 Salk. 9 (as Keeble v. Hickeringill)

M E M O R Y G R A P H I C

Instant Facts

When Keeble (P) lured wildfowl to his land with decoys, Hickeringill (D) frightened the wildfowl away by firing a gun.

Black Letter Rule

A person may not maliciously prevent another from capturing wild animals in the pursuit of his trade.

Case Vocabulary

ACTION UPON THE CASE: A general term for a lawsuit.
FIRST IN TIME: The principle that he who first takes possession to unclaimed property takes title.
LAWFUL: Authorized by the law; sanctioned by the law.
MALICIOUS: Having evil motives.
THITHER: Toward a particular place.
VIVARY: A place for keeping wild animals.

Procedural Basis: Appeal from judgment in action for damages for interfering with the capture of wild animals.

Facts: Keeble (P) owned a pond. Keeble lawfully (P) placed decoys and other equipment near the pond to lure and catch wildfowl. Keeble (P) hunted the wild animals in pursuit of his trade. With the purpose of frightening away the wildfowl, Hickeringill (D) fired a gun three times near the pond. The wildfowl were permanently frightened away.

Issue: May a landowner, in pursuit of his trade, lawfully capture wildfowl free of the malicious interference of another?

Decision and Rationale: (Holt). Yes. There are two public policy reasons why a landowner may, in pursuit of his trade, lawfully capture wildfowl free of the malicious interference of another. First, every man should be able to enjoy the use of his land as he sees fit so long as the use is lawful. Second, the capture of wildfowl in pursuit of a trade is profitable; it creates wealth for the tradesman, for employees, and for the nation at large. There are cases where an individual may interfere with another in the pursuit of his trade. For example, if Hickeringill (D) had lured the wildfowl away from Keeble's (P) land by setting up decoys on his own land, there would be no action. This is because Hickeringill (D) also has the right to enjoy his land as he sees fit. But Hickeringill (D) did not lure the wildfowl away by placing decoys on his own land. He maliciously frightened the wildfowl away by firing a gun. Therefore, he is liable for damages. Judgment affirmed.

Analysis:

Again, this case may be understood by appealing to the goal that the law promote the efficient capture of wild animals. A man cannot scare off wild animals about to be captured by another out of spite. This is inefficient. However, man may engage in competition to capture a wild animal. When two men compete to capture a wild animal, it is more likely that the wild animal will be caught. Note, however, that in modern times the goals of society may have changed. In the case of endangered species the law (often statutory) will want to prevent the capture of wild animals. Another way to understand this case is with the doctrine of ratione soli. This doctrine asserts that an owner of land owns the wild animals on that land. Note, however, that this rule may discourage the efficient capturing of wild animals if the owner refuses to capture them. On the other hand, it discourages trespassing. Were it not for this rule, individuals may be tempted to trespass on another's land to be the first to capture a wild animal. This doctrine had little influence on the Court's decision, however. The doctrine is nevertheless important because it serves to protect a landowner's constructive right to possession as against a trespasser. As an interesting side note, at least one court faced with a dispute over ownership of oil and gas used the rules set forth in the wild animal cases to resolve the dispute, likening fugitive natural resources like oil and gas to wild animals. [The case was Hammonds v. Central Kentucky Natural Gas Co.] This approach has been strongly criticized, though, and has not been followed. The capture rule has been identified as similar to the first in time, first in right rule of prior appropriation in western water law.

U. S. SUPREME COURT DECLARES THAT NEWLY PRINTED NEWS IS PROTECTED FROM COPYING

International News Service v. Associated Press

(Copier) v. (Creator)
(1918) 248 U.S. 215

M E M O R Y   G R A P H I C

Instant Facts

International News Service (D) copied news that Associated Press (P) gathered.

Black Letter Rule

Where a company has expended resources in creating news and information, the creator can exclude others from copying it until its commercial value as news has passed away.

Case Vocabulary

APPROPRIATING: To take for oneself.
MISAPPROPRIATION: The improper taking of another's property for the sole purpose of capitalizing on the good name of the property owner.
PIRATING: The illegal reprinting or stealing of copyrighted material.
UNFAIR COMPETITION: Dishonest rivalry in commerce; the misappropriation for commercial gain of another's property.

Procedural Basis: Appeal from judgment in action for injunction to prevent the copying of news.

Facts: The Associated press (P) gathered news from several member newspapers. This collection of news was then made available to all of the members of Associated Press (P). International News Service (D) copied news from one of the papers and published it.

Issue: Is there a property interest in freshly printed news that allows the creator to prevent others from copying it?

Decision and Rationale: Yes. Since Associated Press (P) has invested time and resources into the creation of the news, it can prevent others from copying the news until the commercial value of the news has passed away. If the court allowed the copying of fresh news, no news service could manage to stay in business.

Analysis:

This case can be viewed in two possible ways. First, we can understand the case as attempting to encourage the creation of property. In this case, AP (P) created a collection of news. This property can be viewed as intangible, that is, as intellectual property. So the court enjoined INS (D) from copying AP's (P) collection of news to encourage the creation of such news. Without such protection, the court reasoned, such collected news would not be created. Another way to view this case is to see it not as protecting intangible, intellectual property, but as protecting tangible property. In this view, the court is protecting the chattels (the words) themselves, not merely protecting the intellectual concept from being copied. After all, INS (D) was copying the words, not the business idea. This view is consistent with Chenev Brothers v. Doris Silk Corp. In that case, Doris Silk (D) was not appropriating the actual clothes but merely the intellectual idea. Since Cheney Brothers (P) had not patented the idea, they were not protected. Had Doris Silk (D) physically taken the chattels, as INS (D) had done in this case, it would have been held liable. But, it may be impossible to reconcile Cheney with INS except on policy grounds.

Cheney Brothers v. Doris Silk Corp.

(Creator) v. (Copier)
(1930) 35 F.2d 279, cert. denied, 281 U.S. 728

M E M O R Y   G R A P H I C

Instant Facts

Doris Silk Corp. (D) copied a fashion design from Cheney Brothers (P). All such designs have a short life.

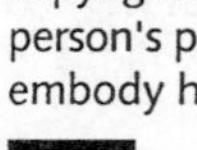

Black Letter Rule

Unless the common law or the patent or copyright statutes give protection from appropriation, a person's property interest is limited to the chattels which embody his creations.

Case Vocabulary

AMENDMENT: An improvement.
DESIGN PATENT: A grant of privilege by the government allowing the holder to exclude others from producing his invention.
EPHEMERAL: Short-lived.
FIRST POSSESSION: Acquisition of property by discovery, capture, and creation.
PRIMA FACIE: Presumed to be true. Evidence, unless rebutted, which is sufficient on its face to establish a given.
REDRESS: To compensate for a wrong.
SOLECISM: A violation of conventional usage.

Procedural Basis: Appeal from sustaining of demurrer to complaint for declaratory relief for appropriation of design.

Facts: Cheney Brothers (P) creates new fashion designs. These designs have a very short life. These new designs are not sufficiently original to support a patent. They cannot be copyrighted under the copyright act either. Since Cheney Brothers (P) has neither patent nor copyright protection, Doris Silk Corp. (D) copied one of Cheney Brother's (P) designs. The parties stipulate that Doris Silk Corp. (D) knew that the design was created by Cheney Brothers (P). Cheney Brothers (P) contends that the Supreme Court created a common law patent protection in the case of *International News Service v. Associated Press* [issue of whether there was a property interest in newly printed news] and that such protection is applicable in this case. Doris Silk Corp. (D) contends that there is no such common law patent protection.

Issue: Is there a generic common law patent protection which lasts for the commercial life of a creation?

Decision and Rationale: (Hand) No. There can be no common law patent protection because it would be too difficult to define the boundaries of such protection. For example: would such protection extend to trade secrets? It is incorrect to suppose that the Supreme Court created a common law patent protection in *International News Service v. Associated Press*. This is because only congress may create patent protection. Therefore, the ruling in *International News Service v. Associated Press* must be limited to the facts of that case and cannot be applied here. Unless there is some pre-existing protection at common law or patent or copyright protection, a person's property interest is limited to the chattels which embody his invention. Since Cheney Brothers (P) has not shown protection under a recognized common law protection or patent protection or copyright protection, its creation may be copied. Order affirmed.

Analysis:

First, it is important again to recall one of the goals of property law: Property law should encourage the efficient creation of property. To achieve these ends, there is common law and statutory protection for the creators of tangible and intangible property. Why then did Cheney Brothers (P) fail to get protection for its creation? The reason lies in another of the goals of property law: Property law should encourage the efficient use of property. In order for society to enjoy the benefits of innovation and creation, competitors must be allowed to imitate the products of others. This is why patents expire after some fixed amount of time. Unfortunately, Cheney Brothers (P) was the victim of this second goal of property law. Notice how easily the court here dispenses with the International News Service ("INS") case, which preceded this case. In INS, the U.S. Supreme Court granted the Associated Press ("AP") protection for its proprietary interest in being the first to report on newly printed news. How is this different than a proprietary interest in newly designed clothes? It isn't. [Best you learn now that not all distinctions in law are easily justified!] Some have tried to explain the two inconsistent results as being a matter of public policy: in INS the court is trying to protect the news service business, while in this case, it is trying to protect competition. Others have tried to explain the inconsistencies by pointing out that in INS, it was not so much an idea that was being copied, but actual words that AP had a first right to, being the first to appropriate them, while in the instant case, it was the idea behind the design that was being copied. The underlying theory being ideas cannot be protected by common law property or copyright laws. Neither explanation is very persuasive. Perhaps the best result is that taken by the court here: to limit INS to the facts before the Supreme Court there and perceive its ruling as an aberration of the general rule, the general rule being that applied in the instant case. The problem becomes more complex when modern day issues, such as those arising from the use of the Internet, are brought before the courts. How these rules apply to those types of issues is the focus of the next case, Virtual Works v. Volkswagen of America.

Virtual Works, Inc. v. Volkswagen of America, Inc.

(Domain Name Owner) v. (Corporation Wanting Domain Name)
238 F.3d 264 (4th Cir. 2001)

MEMORY GRAPHIC

Instant Facts

Virtual Works, Inc. (P) registered the domain name *vw.net* with the intent of selling it to Volkswagen of America, Inc. (D).

Black Letter Rule

Registering a domain name that is identical or confusingly similar to a trademark with the bad faith intent to profit by selling that name to the trademark owner constitutes cybersquatting under the law and will result in liability for monetary damages and transfer or cancellation of the domain name.

Case Vocabulary

CYBERSQUATTING: The Internet version of a land grab, where a party deliberately and in bad faith registers a well-known brand name as a domain name in violation of the rights of trademark owners and in order to force the rightful owners of the marks to pay for the right to engage in electronic commerce under their own brand name.

DE NOVO: A standard of review wherein the appellate court looks at the evidence in the record as if it were the trial court.

DOMAIN NAME: A web address consisting of two parts, a top level and secondary level, which serves like a street address telling people where they can find a given company or subject on the internet.

PRINCIPAL: In business law, refers to an officer or primary owner of a business or corporation.

SUMMARY JUDGMENT: A finding by the trial court on briefs submitted prior to trial that there are no material issues of fact and, based on those facts, one party is entitled to judgment as a matter of law.

TRADEMARK: A trademark is a word or symbol that indicates the source of a product or service; statutory law against infringement or dilution protects such marks by others.

Procedural Basis: Appeal from judgment entered in favor of Volkswagen (D) requiring Virtual Works (P) to relinquish its rights to the domain name.

Facts: In October 1996, Virtual Works, Inc. ("Virtual") (P) registered the domain name *vw.net* with Network Solutions, Inc. ("NSI"). At that time, NSI was the only company authorized to register domain names. At the time Virtual registered the domain name, two of its principals were aware that some users would think *vw.net* was affiliated with Volkswagen of America, Inc. ("Volkswagen") (D). In fact, the two discussed the issue and decided to use the domain name for Virtual (P) but to sell it to Volkswagen (D) for "a lot of money" should Volkswagen (D) offer to purchase the domain name. They made this decision despite the fact that many other domain names were still available, including *vwi.net, vwi.org, virtualworks.net and virtualworks.org*. Virtual (P) used the *vw.net* address for approximately two years. In December 1998, various Volkswagen dealerships contacted Virtual (P), expressing an interest in purchasing the rights to the *vw.net* domain name. Virtual (P), in turn, contacted Volkswagen (D) offering to sell those rights. The terms of the offer, however, were somewhat unusual, in that Virtual (P) stated that unless Volkswagen (D) bought the rights, it would sell the rights to the highest bidder. Virtual (P) gave Volkswagen (D) 24 hours to respond. Perceiving the offer as a threat to Volkswagen's (D) VW trademark, Volkswagen (D) initiated dispute resolution proceedings with NSI. As a result of those proceedings, Virtual (P) was told that it would lose the rights to the *vw.net* domain name unless it filed a declaratory judgment action in the courts. Virtual (P) complied, and Volkswagen (D) counterclaimed for trademark dilution, infringement and cybersquatting under the Anticybersquatting Consumer Protection Act ("ACPA").

Issue: May a party register a domain name that is confusingly similar to a trademark without incurring liability?

Decision and Rationale: (Wilkinson) No. Congress enacted the ACPA in 1999 in response to the proliferation of cybersquatting. It was Congress' view that cybersquatting was harmful insofar as it threatened the continued growth and vitality of the Internet. New legislation was required because existing law did not adequately address the problem. Hence, the ACPA. Under the ACPA, a person alleged to be a cybersquatter is liable to the owner of a protected mark if that person (1) has a bad faith intent to profit from that mark and (2) registers or uses a domain name that (a) in the case of a mark that is distinctive, is identical or confusingly similar to that mark or (b) in the case of a famous mark, is identical or confusingly similar to or dilutive of that mark. The statute goes on to provide numerous factors that a court may consider in determining whether someone has acted in bad faith, including the trademark or other rights of the person in the domain name, the extent to which the domain name consists of the legal name of the person, the person's prior use, if any, of the domain name, the person's fair use of the domain name for offering goods and services, the person's intent to divert customers from the trademark's owner, the person's offer to sell or transfer the domain name to the trademark owner, the person's provision of material and misleading false contact information when applying for the domain name, the person's registration or acquisition of multiple domain names that the person knows are identical or similar to other trademarks and the extent to which the mark incorporated in the person's domain name is or is not distinctive or famous. In addition, the Second Circuit has articulated other factors that may be used, including the unique circumstances of the case that do not fit neatly into the specific factors enumerated in the act. The ACPA also has a safe harbor provision, however, that precludes a finding of bad faith intent in a case where the court determines that the person believed and had reasonable grounds to believe that the use of the domain name was fair or otherwise lawful. The remedies available to a trademark owner that is the victim of cybersquatting as defined by the ACPA, depend on when the violation occurred. If the violation occurred after the date of enactment, the violator is liable for monetary damages and transfer or cancellation of the domain name. If the violation occurred prior to enactment of the ACPA, however, as is the case here, the sole remedy is the transfer of the domain name to the rightful trademark owner. Having detailed the statutory framework, we must now decide whether Virtual (P) violated the ACPA when it registered the *vw.net* domain name. The trial court found that a number of the specifically enumerated factors supported Volkswagen's (D) claim that Virtual (P) had violated the ACPA. For instance, the trial court found that Virtual (P) had never done business or been identified as "VW", nor had it any right to or interest in the letters. Finally, the trial court found that the disparaging remarks posted on Virtual's (P) website and the famousness of the VW mark, also pointed to a violation. Therefore, the trial court entered summary judgment in favor of Volkswagen (D). Because this appeal comes from an order granting summary judgment to Volkswagen (D), we review this matter de novo. The first issue under the ACPA is whether Virtual (P) acted with a bad faith intent. The trial court found that it did and Virtual (P) argues that this finding was erroneous. Because the nine factors set forth in the ACPA are permissive and not exclusive, we need not address each individual factor. However, in this case, there is both circumstantial and direct evidence that supports the trial court's conclusion that Virtual (P) acted in bad faith, including the famousness of the VW mark, the similarity of the *vw.net* domain name to that mark, the admission that Virtual (P) never does business as VW or identifies itself as such and the availability of other suitable domain names. We do not suggest that in every case these four facts alone will resolve an issue of bad faith intent under the ACPA. The mere fact that a domain name resembles a famous mark is hardly in and of itself dispositive. Here, unlike a situation where the domain name is similar, there is also evidence that two principals at Virtual (P) recognized the similarity, discussed it and even went so far as to state they would sell it to Volkswagen (D) should a dispute arise prior to the time they registered the domain name. Thus, the evidence establishes that Virtual (P) had a dual purpose in selecting *vw.net* as its domain name: one to establish an internet site for the company and two, to potentially profit from selling that name to Volkswagen (D). Furthermore, the evidence in the record regarding the offer Virtual (P) made to Volkswagen (D) also supports a finding of bad faith intent. Finally, Virtual's (P) argument that it is not liable by virtue of the safe harbor provision is not persuasive. The safe harbor is only available when the defendant both believed and had reasonable grounds to believe that its use of the name was fair and reasonable. Here, Virtual (P) openly admitted and hoped that it would profit by registering this domain name because of its similarity with Volkswagen's trademark. We do not read the safe harbor provision as broadly as Virtual (P). We believe the provision was meant to apply only in those rare circumstances where there is a clear lawful motive for the registration, not merely to those situations, like here, where there may be a dual purpose. Here, the evidence establishes that at the time Virtual (P) registered the *vw.net* domain name, it was motivated by a bad faith intent to profit from the famousness of the VW trademark. The next inquiry requires us to determine whether Virtual (P) registered or used a domain name that is identical or confusingly similar to a distinctive mark or that is identical or confusingly similar to or dilutive of a famous mark. There is no dispute here as to the famousness of the VW mark. Virtual (P) argues, however, that its domain name is not identical or confusingly similar to or dilutive of that mark. We disagree. It is Virtual's (P) position that the mark is not identical, similar or dilutive because the .net secondary level domain name was reserved for internet service provides, like Virtual (P) and that at that time, Volkswagen (D), who is not an internet service provider, could not have registered the name itself. This argument is undermined, however, by the fact that NSI stopped enforcing its distinction between secondary level domain names, such as .com or .net, a year before Virtual (P) registered the domain name. Additionally, Virtual (P) has admitted it recognized the potential confusion of the domain name with Volkswagen's (D) trademark. Therefore, the trial court was correct in holding that the *vw.net* domain name is confusingly similar to the VW trademark owned by Volkswagen (D). Volkswagen (D) is thus entitled to the remedy it seeks, to use the *vw.net* name for itself. Affirmed.

Analysis:

The importance of this opinion comes from its discussion of the ACPA and the requirement of bad faith intent. As technology has advanced, so too have the laws regarding property rights. Thus, while we are hardly ever concerned with who holds title to a wild animal, as was the case in Pierson v. Post and its progeny, new issues have forced new legislation and, in some cases, distorted interpretations of existing law. The birth of the Internet has been the main culprit in recent times for bringing property issues back to the forefront of American jurisprudence. Generally, there are three practices that have led to litigation. First, is cybersquatting, which was the focus of this opinion and has been addressed by the ACPA. Second, is the registering of domain names similar to well-known trademarks for use in ways that tarnish the marks, like promoting a site with sexual content that is similar to Toys-R-Us. People who practice this are known as "parasites". The third practice is known as poaching. Poachers are those that register domain names that use the name of other organizations in order to disseminate unfavorable information about those organizations. Regardless of the practice that results in litigation, courts have taken the same approach. Basically, courts will strive to protect innocent trademark holders from those with evil or bad faith intent, such as Virtual (P) in the instant case. In the absence of a wrongful intent, however, courts will apply the law stringently before finding liability. For your purposes, the key is to recognize the evolution of property law concepts and their application to current issues, such as those raised by the birth and growth of the Internet.

Moore v. Regents of the University of California

(Spleen Source) v. (Spleen Exploiter)

(1990) 51 Cal. 3d 120; 793 P.2d 479; 271 Cal. Rptr. 146; cert. denied, 111 S.Ct. 1388

M E M O R Y G R A P H I C

Instant Facts

The Regents (D) removed Moore's (P) spleen and retained it for research purposes. As a result of this research, the Regents (D) established a cell line from Moore's (P) cells and obtained a patent for it.

Black Letter Rule

A doctor has a duty to disclose the extent of his research and economic interests in a patient's body parts. Human body parts are not property such that they may be converted.

Case Vocabulary

BUNDLE OF RIGHTS: A collection of rights which taken together characterize property ownership.
CONSENSUAL PEDIGREE: The history of consent.
CONVERSION: The taking of the right of ownership to property from another.
DECEIT: An intentional distortion of the truth.
DELIBERATIVE FORUM: A place where ideas are debated, such as a legislature.
DEMURRER: An answer by a defendant alleging that a plaintiff has alleged nothing that entitles him to a remedy.
FIDUCIARY DUTY: The duty to act in the interest of another.
FRAUD: An intentional distortion of the truth.
INTENTIONAL INFLICTION OF EMOTIONAL DISTRESS: Purposely causing another to be emotionally distressed.
INTER ALIA: Among other things.
NEGLIGENT MISREPRESENTATION: Not taking care, as a reasonable person would, to represent the facts accurately.
PATENT: A grant of a privilege.
POST MORTEM: After death.
RIGHT OF POSSESSION: The right to occupy land.
STRICT LIABILITY TORT: A cause of action where the defendant must pay for damages whether or not he was negligent or at fault.
SUI GENERIS: Unique; one-of-a-kind.

Procedural Basis: Appeal from an order by the appellate court reversing a demurrer to a complaint for damages for conversion.

Facts: After undergoing tests, Moore (P) was told by the Regents (D) that he had hairy-cell leukemia and that his spleen should be removed. The Regents (D) did not tell Moore (P) that his cells were unique and that access to them was of great scientific value. After the splenectomy, Moore (P) underwent some seven years of follow-up tests that he was led to believe were important to his treatment. During these tests blood and tissue were removed from Moore (P). Additionally, the Regents (D) retained Moore's (P) spleen for research without his knowledge or consent. Eventually, he was informed that his bodily substances were being used for research, but he was never informed of the Regent's (D) commercial interest in them. Subsequently, the Regents (D) created a cell line from Moore's (P) cells, received a patent for it, and commercially marketed these items for a great deal of money. Moore (P) sues for tortious conversion of his body parts.

Issue: (1) Does a doctor have a duty to disclose the extent of his research and economic interests in a patient's body parts? (2) Are human body parts property such that they may be converted?

Decision and Rationale: (Panelli) (1) Yes. (2) No. A doctor must disclose the extent of his research and economic interest in a patient's body parts. This is so that a patient's interests are not compromised for the sake of the doctor's interests. The existing law of conversion does not give Moore (P) a cause of action. To establish a conversion Moore (P) must show either interference with his ownership or his right of possession. Since Moore (P) did not retain possession of his body parts after their removal, he must show an ownership interest in them. There are three reasons why we conclude that Moore (P) did not retain an ownership interest. First, there is no case law to support the contention that a person retains an ownership interest in excised body parts. This lack of authority is not surprising, since the law of property interests in human organs, dead bodies, fetuses, etc., is unique. The law of property interests in human organs, etc., has been crafted to meet policy goals rather than to comport with normal property law. The second reason why Moore (P) did not retain a property interest in his body parts is as follows: California statutes limit a patient's control over excised body parts. Health & Safety Code §7054.4 restricts the use of excised parts and requires their ultimate destruction. This so severely restricts the enjoyment of body parts that it is hard to call them property that can be owned. Finally, the patent cannot possibly be Moore's (P) property. This is because the patent is simply (factually and legally) a different object than the organs. Moore (P) argues, along with the appeals court, that nonetheless an ownership interest should be found. He relies on cases that find a proprietary interest in one's likeness or photograph. The analogy is inappropriate, however, because one's likeness is unique, whereas the patent and the cell line creates lymphokines which are the same in every human. Pushing yet farther, the court of appeals concluded that there must be an ownership interest to protect the privacy and dignity of the patient. But this is unnecessary since the duty to disclose protects these interests. Having decided that existing conversion law does not support Moore's (P) claim, we next consider whether conversion law should be expanded. We conclude that conversion liability should not be extended for three reasons. The first reason comes from a weighing of policy considerations. On the one hand is the patient's right to make an informed decision. On the other hand is the fact that conversion is a strict liability tort. To allow an action for conversion to be extended to cases like this would expose innocent researchers (who may have unwittingly obtained the body parts) to liability. This would make companies unlikely to invest in such research and slow scientific progress. Since the duty to disclose adequately protects a patient's right to informed consent, the social policy of fostering scientific progress requires that conversion liability not be extended. The second reason why conversion liability should not be extended is because the problems involved in this area are better suited to the legislature. Finally, the duty of the doctor to disclose his research and economic interests in the patient's body parts adequately protects the patient's right to determine the fate of his body parts. If he does not like what the doctor proposes to do with his body parts, he may seek another doctor. Since Moore's (P) claim for conversion of his body parts is not supported by existing law, he cannot maintain a claim. Order of the appellate court reversed.

Concurrence: (Arabian). I concur in the majority's opinion. I write separately to emphasize that the human body is sacred and that it should not be treated as property which can be bartered in a free market.

Concurrence and Dissent: (Broussard). I concur in the majority's opinion with respect to a doctor's duty to disclose. However, I dissent from the view that Moore (P) has no cause of action for conversion. If a plaintiff consents to the removal of his organ for research purposes, I agree that he has no cause of action. However, if a plaintiff is misled and thereby deprived of the opportunity to determine the disposition of his body parts after removal, he has a cause of action. This cause of action is the traditional common law action of conversion. This is because the Uniform Anatomical Gift Act [a donor has the authority to make a gift of his body parts upon his death] supports the notion that a patient retains a property interest in excised body parts. Moreover, the Uniform Anatomical Gift Act gives this property interest (the right to designate the use of the excised body part) to patients and not to doctors. The tort of conversion protects a plaintiff from interference with his night to designate the use of his property. Since the Regents (D) have deprived Moore (P) of the opportunity to determine the disposition of his body parts, they are converters. Finally, I think that the majority's and Justice Mosk's reasoning that it is immoral to create a market place for human body parts is flawed. It appears to me that the majority has created a marketplace for body parts. It has merely barred Moore (P) and other plaintiffs from participating in the markets, while it has given such a right to the Regents (D) and other defendants.

Dissent: (Mosk). It is true that there are many restrictions on the use of property. However, what remains after these restrictions is still property. As such, Moore (P) had at least as much right to dispose of his body parts as the Regents (D) did. Therefore, Moore (P) has stated a claim for conversion. I also disagree with the majority's reasoning in deciding whether to extend the tort of conversion for two reasons. First, I feel that the specter of slavery and the like haunts our biotechnology industry. This specter comes to light whenever scientists claim the right to exploit a person's body for profit. Second, I feel that it is unfair for the Regents (D) to take all of the gain from Moore's (P) body parts, while Moore (P) gets nothing. Yet by failing to recognize a tort of conversion, the majority gives a windfall to the Regents (D). Moore (P) and the Regents (D) should be allowed to bargain for the right to his organs. When the majority suggests that patients like Moore (P) cannot sell organs, it is wrong. Contrary to the suggestions of the majority, The Uniform Anatomical Gift Act [whether an individual may sell excised body parts or not] allows individuals to sell body parts. They may simply not sell body parts for use after they die. Since the Act recognizes a right to sell body parts, there should be an action for conversion. Also, the duty of a doctor to disclose is no protection for the plaintiff because it may be difficult to prove the elements of this cause of action. Moreover, the duty to disclose only protects the patient's right to refuse to sell. It does not grant him the right to sell. Finally, the duty to disclose gives Moore (P) an action against his doctor. It does not reach a second class of defendants: research laboratories. These may well be the true exploiters.

Analysis:

This case demonstrates how the goals of society influence the law of property. In particular, social goals have determined that the Regents (D) have acquired title to Moore's (P) excised body parts. The goal that guides the majority is as follows: Property law should encourage the efficient research of medical technologies. To implement this goal the court rules that unless there was a prior agreement to the contrary, Moore (P) loses title to his excised body parts. Also influencing the majority is the following: Property law should not debase human dignity. To give effect to this goal, the court curtails trade in human body parts as much as possible. There is a goal of property law pulling in the opposite direction: The law should promote the alienability of property. Freely alienable property promotes an efficient market economy. The goal that property should be freely alienable appears in the law of future interests, for example. In this case, the court found the competing goals listed above more compelling. As a side note, notice that Moore (P) argued that his case was similar to those in which courts have recognized a property interest in one's own name and likeness, known as the "right of publicity" cases. The Court here quickly dispensed with this argument, concluding that body parts, like the spleen at issue here, is not unique to each individual, but rather is common to all humans. This is consistent with the underlying basis for the right of publicity cases, in which the rationale for recognizing a property right is the work the individual put into making a name for oneself to the extent that his/her likeness becomes marketable. It can hardly be said that one can put an effort into making one's organ, an organ all others have, so unique as to be marketable. Additionally, note that this case is also important because of its discussion of the "bundle of rights", sometimes referred to as the "bundle of sticks". Under the law, property is not so much about things but rather about rights over things: the right to use, to possess, to exclude and to transfer/sell. At its barest, property law is all about these four rights and who has them. Thus it is in this case that the discussion turns, at least in part, on who has the right to sell or gift the spleen, or excised body parts in general. This bundle of rights concept is one with which you should become familiar, as it will be an underlying concept throughout your study of property law [and one you no doubt will get tired of hearing!].

Jacque v. Steenberg Homes, Inc.

(Landowner) v. (Developer)
563 N.W.2d 154 (Wisc. 1997)

M E M O R Y   G R A P H I C

Instant Facts

A landowner sought punitive damages after a developer delivered a mobile home across the landowner's property without permission.

Black Letter Rule

Punitive damages may be imposed for intentional trespass to property.

Case Vocabulary

NOMINAL DAMAGES: A small sum awarded when a legal wrong has occurred but when there is no substantial loss or injury to be compensated.
PUNITIVE DAMAGES: Damages intended to punish and deter certain wrongful conduct.

Procedural Basis: Review of decision affirming denial of punitive damages in action for intentional trespass to property.

Facts: Steenberg Homes (D) desired to travel across the property of Harvey and Louis Jacque (P) in order to deliver a mobile home. Steenberg (D) sought the Jacques' (P) permission and offered to pay for the inconvenience, but the Jacques (P) refused to grant permission. Nevertheless, Steenberg (D) plowed a path through the Jacques' (P) snow-covered field and delivered the mobile home via that path. The Jacques (P) sued Steenberg (D) for intentional trespass. The jury awarded the Jacques (P) $1 in nominal damages and $100,000 in punitive damages. However, the circuit court overturned the punitive damage award. The court of appeals confirmed, concluding that an award of nominal damages would not sustain a punitive damage award. The Jacques (P) appealed to the Wisconsin Supreme Court.

Issue: May punitive damages be imposed when nominal damages are awarded for an intentional trespass to land?

Decision and Rationale: (Justice Not Stated) Yes. Punitive damages may be imposed when nominal damages are awarded for an intentional trespass to land. An individual landowner has a strong interest in protecting his land from trespass. He has the right to exclude others from his own land and to exclusively enjoy his own property for any purpose which does not invade the rights of another person. In addition, a series of intentional trespasses can even threaten the individual's ownership of land. Thus, the Jacques (P) have the right to tell Steenberg Homes (D) and anyone else that they cannot cross the Jacques' (P) land. But that right has no practical meaning unless protected, and a nominal damage award would not deter any trespasser. Private landowners should feel confident that wrongdoers who trespass upon their land will be appropriately punished. In addition, this will make private landowners less likely to resort to self-help remedies.

Analysis:

This case highlights one of the most fundamental rights to property, the right to use and enjoy one's own land and to exclude potential trespassers. The court reaches a common-sense holding, as a nominal damage award would be insufficient to deter trespassers like Steenberg (D) and would, in effect, strip the Jacques' (P) of their property rights. But should property owners necessarily have the absolute right to exclude others? What if there was no possible way Steenberg (D) could relocate the mobile home except through the Jacques' (P) land? Should the Jacques (P) be allowed to stop commerce just because they don't want their land to be disturbed? Apparently so, according to this court. The opinion raises another interesting point in support of this position. As will be detailed later in the casebook, the continuing presence of trespassers on land can threaten the true owners' property rights. If the trespassing occurs for a long enough period and if certain other conditions are met, the trespasser can actually gain title to the property via the doctrine of "adverse possession." Apparently the Jacques (P) learned about adverse possession the hard way in an unrelated prior action. This may explain why they were so adamant in denying the seemingly innocuous request by Steenberg (D).

State v. Shack

(State) v. (Good Samaritan)
(1971) 58 N.J. 297; 277 A.2d 369

MEMORY GRAPHIC

Instant Facts

Shack (D) entered Tedesco's property to give legal aid to a migrant farm worker. Shack (D) refused to depart upon Tedesco's demand and is prosecuted for trespass.

Black Letter Rule

Property rights may not be exercised so as to endanger the well-being of others.

Case Vocabulary

AMICUS CURIAE: Literally, friend of the court; a brief submitted to a court by a party who has a strong interest in a case, but is not a party to that case.
DE NOVO: From the beginning; all over again.
FEDERAL STATUTES: Laws passed by the Congress of the United States.
MAXIM: A rule of conduct; a principle.
PENUMBRA: Something implied from the Constitution based on what is explicitly said there.
TENANT: One who possesses the land of another. One who has the temporary use and occupation of land owned by another (called the "landlord"). The terms of the occupation are usually specified in a lease.
TRESPASS: To unlawfully enter upon another's land.
UNFAIR LABOR PRACTICE: A labor practice contrary to the National Labor Relations Act.
VESTED: To take control of. One is vested of an estate in land when he has an immediate right to present or future enjoyment; the possibility of the right to future enjoyment is not good enough to be vested.

Procedural Basis: Appeal from an order sustaining a conviction for trespass.

Facts: Shack (D) and Tejeras, employees of the U.S. Office of Economic Opportunity, entered the private land of Tedesco. Pursuant to an act of Congress, they entered the land for the purpose of delivering legal and medical advice to migrant farm workers. These workers were housed on Tedesco's property. Tedesco insisted that Shack (D) and Tejeras meet the migrant farm workers in his presence. Shack (D) and Tejeras insisted that they had the right to see the migrant farm workers in privacy. Thereupon, Tedesco filed a formal criminal complaint for trespass. The state (P) contends that the trespass statute is valid because it merely embodies the notion that a landowner may exclude others from his land. Shack (D) contends that no land may be used in a manner that endangers the well-being of others.

Issue: May a landowner use land in a manner that endangers the well-being of others?

Decision and Rationale: (Weintraub). No. Shack (D) first argues that the first amendment allows him to enter Tedesco's property to distribute information. In *Marsh v. Alabama*, a private corporation owned a town. However, except for the fact that the town was owned by a private corporation, it was identical to any other town. Thus, the court held that the first amendment allowed a Jehovah Witness to distribute literature on this land without being held a trespasser. Though there may be some migrant camps with similar attributes to the town in *Marsh v. Alabama*, that is not true in this case. Next, Shack (D) argues that the Supremacy Clause of the Constitution allows him to enter. This is because the state law of trespass, which protects private property, conflicts with the federal law which authorizes Shack (D) to aid the migrant workers. Various other Constitutional arguments are presented by Shack (D). However, we need not resort to the United States Constitution because our state law of property bars Tedesco from using his land in a manner that endangers the well-being of others. This is because property rights serve the needs of society and public policy. Congress, in authorizing Shack (D) and Tejeras to deliver social aid to migrant farm workers, has declared a public policy of aiding the migrant farm workers, who are poor and disenfranchised. Our property law must accommodate this public policy. Since it is difficult to reach the migrant farm workers, who are isolated from the rest of the community, Tedesco's right to exclude others from his property must yield to society's desire to aid the farm workers. Since Shack (P) was attempting to deliver legal and social services to migrant farm workers, he committed no trespass. Conviction reversed and dismissed.

Analysis:

The case introduces how the law controls the usage of property. Limitations on the use of property appear in the law of nuisance, easements, and covenants, for example. The rules formulated are designed to achieve certain goals. In this case, the land usage at issue is the right of a landowner to exclude others from entering his land. Ordinarily, this right to exclude is fundamental. For many, it is an essential characteristic of property. However, as this case demonstrates, social goals limit the right to exclude. However, there is a line of reasoning that suggests that the power to exclude should be absolute. The reasoning is as follows: The absolute right to exclude establishes only the initial conditions of access to property. Subsequent market transactions will adjust these conditions in the most efficient manner. For example, if the government wishes access to a parcel of land, it need only buy it. In fact, the law of eminent domain forces the government to pay for that land that it takes. In this line of reasoning, market imperfections allow for the courts to adjust the right to exclude.

Chapter 2

Adverse possession is a method of acquiring land. If an owner of property fails to protect his property, another person may acquire his land by simply possessing it for a long enough time. The adverse possessor in effect says, "I now own this property because I have been here and you have not been here."

Like acquisition by conquest, adverse possession divests title from one person and vests it in another. At a basic level, this process of divestment occurs when one person occupies the property of another for a long enough time. Thus, the law of adverse possession has much to do with the law of possession. Since possession is so prominent, there are many similarities to the law of finders. For example, an adverse possessor who is in possession of land may be said to have title good against all the world except the true owner.

Though at first acquiring title by adverse possession may seem like theft, it serves many important social policies. Moreover, these policies have parallels to other areas of property law. For example, one of the goals of adverse possession is to encourage the productive use of land. This goal of the law also appears in the law of easements, the rules promoting alienability, and the law of concurrent interests. Another goal of adverse possession is to stabilize uncertain boundaries. This allows property owners the security of knowing what they own so that they can make plans regarding their land and use it efficiently. Finally, it is sometimes said that the law of adverse possession means to punish the landowner who is not diligent in using his land. In this respect, it is similar to the justification the Europeans advanced for the acquisition of foreign land by conquest.

So as to ensure fairness to the title holder, a person must meet several requirements before he may acquire title by adverse possession. There must be actual possession of the land. This is an attempt to ensure that the adverse possessor uses the land productively. The possession must be open and notorious. This is an attempt to place the title holder on notice that someone else claims his property and that he should act; if he is not diligent, the law will not protect him. The possession must be adverse and under claim of right. If the possessor is on the land with the owner's permission, the possession is not adverse. One of the purposes of this requirement is to prevent the possessor from lulling the true owner into believing that he will make no claim against him. Imagine what it would be like if a tenant could acquire title to the property that he is renting by adverse possession. Finally, possession must be continuous for the statutory period. This is merely to give the property owner a fair amount of time to assert his rights. It is also a statute of limitations.

Chapter Overview Outline
Acquisition of Property by Find, Adverse Possession, Gift

Chapter 2

NOTE: THE PURPOSE OF THIS OUTLINE IS TO ORGANIZE THE CASES SO THAT ONE CAN QUICKLY UNDERSTAND THE RELEVANCE OF EACH CASE TO THE COURSE. NO ATTEMPT IS MADE IN THIS OVERVIEW TO ADDRESS EVERY CONCEPT THAT MUST BE STUDIED. BE SURE TO READ THE ENTIRE CASEBOOK AND/OR OTHER MATERIALS TO GAIN A FULL UNDERSTANDING OF ALL CONCEPTS.

I. One way a person may acquire property is by finding it.
   A. The finder of lost property has a title superior to all but the true owner. *Armory v. Delamirie.*
   B. However, there are exceptions to this general rule.
      1. If the finder also loses the property [this property is hard to keep track of!], a subsequent finder will have title superior to all but the true owner *and* the previous finder. The previous finder's loss of the property does not diminish his right to possession; it remains superior to all but the true owner. Thus, in the hierarchy of claims the previous finder's right to possession is superior to that of the subsequent finder because he found the property first.
      2. A person who has possession of property, even if he has achieved it by theft rather than finding, has good title against all but those who have better title. *Anderson v. Gouldberg.*
         a. However, some scholars say courts only invoke the prior possessor rule on behalf of honest claimants.
      3. If the owner of property has never occupied his land, the finder of property on this land has a superior title against the land owner. *Hannah v. Peel.*
      4. A finder has no title to property which was mislaid in a shop rather than lost. The shopowner has a duty to safeguard the property for the true owner. *McAvoy v. Medina.*
      5. At English common law treasure trove belonged to the king. In America, courts treat hidden treasure as any other found property and try to determine whether it was lost, mislaid, or abandoned.
      6. Under federal law, any abandoned shipwreck embedded in the submerged land of a state belongs to that state, and the law of finds does not apply. *Abandoned Shipwreck Act of 1987.*

II. Another way to acquire property is by adverse possession.
   A. Adverse possession is a means of transferring title to land without the permission of the prior owner. Statutes of limitations fix the time beyond which the prior owner can bring an action to recover possession of his land. Once the statute has run, the adverse possessor may acquire title. *Richard R. Powell, The Law of Real Property § 91.01.*
      1. The purpose of these statutes of limitations is more to automatically quiet titles which are openly and consistently asserted than, as some argue, to reward a trespasser for making use of the land or to punish the owner for sleeping on his rights. *Henry W. Ballantine, Title by Adverse Possession.*
         a. Oliver Wendell Holmes argues that the most important justification for these statutes is that after a person has used a thing for a long time, he instinctively begins to feel that he owns it. Given this instinct, he argues that when the owner knows an adverse possessor is establishing such a connection, justice requires that he either take steps to warn or stop him, or risk losing the property. *Oliver Wendell Holmes, The Path of the Law.*
      2. To acquire title by adverse possession, possession must be actual and under claim of title, and the land must be either enclosed or sufficiently improved. *Van Valkenburgh v. Lutz.*

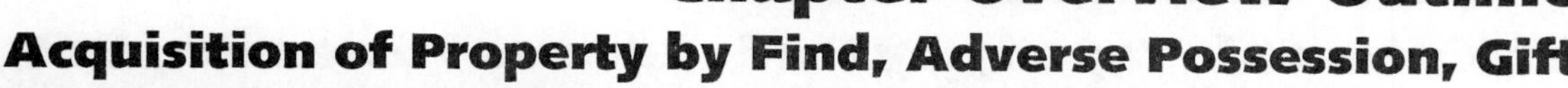

a. As in *Lutz*, most jurisdictions have case law as well as statutes of limitations governing adverse possession. These cases generally require actual, exclusive possession that is open and notorious, adverse or "hostile," under a claim of right, and continuous for the statutory period.

b. An adverse possessor's use of the property is sufficiently actual and exclusive if it is the type of use an ordinary owner would make of the property under the circumstances. *Ewing v. Burnet.*

c. Open possession of a cave part of which underlies another's property is not notorious for purposes of adverse possession. *Marengo Cave Co. v. Ross.*

d. There are three approaches to the claim of right element of adverse possession, sometimes called claim of title.

(1) England and some states use the *objective standard*, under which the adverse possessor's state of mind is irrelevant.

(2) Many states use the *good-faith standard*, under which the adverse possessor must have thought he owned the property when he took possession.

(3) Other states use the *aggressive trespasser* standard, under which the adverse possessor knows he does not own the property but intends to make it his, or at least to stay unless a better owner forces him to leave.

3. A claim under color of title [different from claim of title] is a claim based on a written instrument or court judgment which is invalid due to some defect.

(1) England and most states do not require a claim under color of title, but a few states do.

(2) Claims under color of title can have the advantage of giving the adverse possessor constructive possession of the entire property covered by the writing or judgment, not only the portion he actually possesses.

4. Adverse possession cases often involve border disputes. Adverse possession must be open and notorious enough to give the true landowner notice. In the case of minor border encroachments the court will not presume notice; the landowner must have actual knowledge of the encroachment. *Mannillo v. Gorski*.

a. Courts also use the doctrines of agreed boundaries, acquiescence, and estoppel to address cases of mistaken boundaries.

(1) Where neighbors are uncertain about a boundary line, their oral agreement as to the boundary will be enforceable if they accept it for a long time.

(2) Similarly, a long period of acquiescence to a boundary line is evidence of an agreement between the parties even if the period is shorter than the statutory period.

(3) Under the doctrine of estoppel, if one neighbor makes changes in reliance upon the conduct or representations of another neighbor about their boundary line, the other neighbor will be estopped to deny that boundary.

b. Where a person makes improvements on another's property by mistake, the modern trend is to force a conveyance of the improvement at market value. The conveyance will generally be to the improver, but courts will sometimes give the landowner the option to buy the improvement.

B. The law of adverse possession includes special rules for certain circumstances.

1. If an adverse possessor uses the land in a customary manner, courts will deem his use continuous for purposes of adverse possession. Tacking is permissible where there is a reasonable connection between successive adverse possessors. *Howard v. Kunto*.

2. All states extend their statutes of limitations for adverse possession cases when the owner suffers from a disability, such as insanity, minority, or imprisonment.

3. Following the common law, most states do not permit adverse possession against the government. Some do, however, some under the usual terms, some only after a longer statutory period, and some only where the government held the land in a proprietary capacity.

C. A person may also acquire chattels by adverse possession.

1. However, if the owner of stolen chattels, upon discovery of the theft, makes diligent efforts to locate and recover the chattels, the statute of limitations is tolled. *O'Keeffe v. Snyder*.

a. New York has rejected the rule in *O'Keeffe*. Rather than look to the efforts of the owner, New York requires the good faith purchaser to investigate the chain of ownership before making his purchase. The statute does not begin to run until the owner demands the return of the chattels and the good faith purchaser refuses. *Solomon R. Guggenheim Found. v. Lubell*.

2. Under the Native American Graves Protection and Repatriation Act of 1990, a museum must return Native American sacred and cultural objects to the descendants of their owners unless it can show a "right of possession," which it would have if it could show that prior Native American owners voluntarily gave it possession. Adverse possession does not suffice to give a right of possession under the Act.

III. [Perhaps best of all], a person may acquire property by gift. To make a gift of personal property, the donor must manifest an intent to give the property to the donee and must transfer possession of the property to him. Constructive or symbolic delivery might suffice if actual delivery of the property is not practicable.

A. In some states, symbolic delivery of a gift is not effective, but constructive delivery is allowed if it is impractical to deliver actual possession. *Newman v. Bost*.

B. A gift causa mortis, which a person makes when he is expecting to die shortly, is revoked if the donor lives. Courts have applied the requirements for these gifts more strictly than for inter vivos gifts. They have also added requirements, such as redelivery if the donee already has possession of the gift.

C. A party may give a future interest in chattels as a gift while reserving a life estate in himself. *Gruen v. Gruen*.

COURT DECLARES THAT THE FINDER OF LOST PROPERTY HAS A TITLE SUPERIOR TO ALL BUT THE TRUE OWNER

Armory v. Delamirie

(Finder) v. (Subsequent Possessor)
(1722) 1 Strange 505

M E M O R Y   G R A P H I C

Instant Facts

Armory (P) found a jewel and took it to Delamirie's (D) jewelry shop. Delamirie (D) refused to return the jewel.

Black Letter Rule

The finder of lost property has a title superior to all but the true owner.

Case Vocabulary

TROVER: A suit to recover the value of the plaintiff's chattel that the defendant has converted.

Procedural Basis: Appeal from judgment in action to recover property found by plaintiff.

Facts: Armory (P) found a jewel and took it to Delamirie's (D) jewelry shop to have it appraised. Delamirie's (D) apprentice removed the stones. Delamirie (D) offered three half pence to Armory (P) for the jewel. Armory (P) refused this offer and demanded the jewels to be returned to him. Delamirie (D) refused to return the stones. Armory (P) sues.

Issue: Does the finder of lost property have a title superior to all but the true owner?

Decision and Rationale: Yes. A finder of property does not acquire an absolute title; the true owner has absolute title. However, the finder does acquire a title superior to the rest of the world. Since Armory (P) found the jewel, and since Delamirie (D) is not the true owner, Armory (P) has a superior title. Judgment affirmed.

Analysis:

The rule announced in this case is called the prior possessor rule. It achieves several social goals: 1) It protects an owner who cannot prove that he is the true owner. Imagine how difficult it would be to prove that you own the blow dryer that you lent to your neighbor yesterday; 2) It protects individuals who entrust goods to others. Entrusting goods to others promotes social welfare. For example, an individual may entrust his clothes to the laundry without worrying that he may not get them back. Since he is the prior possessor, he will prevail over the laundry; 3) It protects the expectations of prior possessors, who expect to prevail; 4) It promotes peaceable possession. Were prior possessors not to prevail, individuals might begin to steal property, hoping that the law would protect them.

COURT DECLARES THAT A PROPERTY OWNER DOES NOT NECESSARILY HAVE TITLE TO ALL THAT IS FOUND ON HIS PROPERTY

Hannah v. Peel

(Finder) v. (Property Owner)
(1945) [1945] K.B. 509

MEMORY GRAPHIC

Instant Facts

Hannah (P) found a brooch on Peel's (D) property. Peel (D) never lived on this parcel of property.

Black Letter Rule

If the owner of property has never occupied his land, the finder of property on this land has a superior title against the land owner.

Case Vocabulary

CHATTELS: Personal property, as distinct from real property, or land
DEMISE: To transfer property from one to another. The conveyance of an estate in property from one person to another.
FREEHOLD: An estate in land that entitles one to current possession, sale, etc.
FREEHOLDER: Owner of land.
LOCUS IN QUO: The area under consideration.
PARCEL: An item of personal property; also used to mean a plot or area of land.
WRIT: A judicial order to perform some act.

Procedural Basis: Action to recover money found by plaintiff.

Facts: In 1938 Peel (D) purchased a home. He never lived in this home. In July of 1940 Peel's (D) home was requisitioned by the government. In August of 1940 Hannah (P) was stationed at this home of Peel's (D). While stationed there, Hannah (P) found a brooch in a room being used for a sick bay. The room was in a remote place of the house. At this point, Peel (D) had no knowledge of the brooch. Hannah (P) gave the brooch to the police. Two years later, since the true owner was not found, the police awarded the brooch to Peel (D). Hannah (P) sues for damages or replevy. Hannah (P) contends that he has superior title, since he is the finder. Peel (D) contends that he has title, since he owned the land where the brooch was found.

Issue: If a landowner has never lived on a parcel of land, does a finder of property on that land have superior title to the landowner?

Decision and Rationale: (Birkett). Yes. The case authority gives support to the contentions of both parties. There are three principle cases in this area. First, *Bridges v. Hawksworth*. In that case, a bag of money was left in a shop. The bag was left in that area of the shop accessible to the general public. The principle issue in that case was whether superior title lay in the finder or in the shop owner. The court applied the old rule: superior title goes to finder. The court ruled this way because the shop owner never possessed the bag and because the place where the bag was found was open to the public. In *South Staffordshire Water Co. v. Sharman*, a servant found two rings on the landowner's land while working for the landowner. The issue in that case was whether superior title lay in the finder or the landowner. They applied a new rule: superior title goes to the landowner. The court ruled this way because the finder worked for the landowner. By employing the servant, the landowner was exercising control over that part of the land where the rings were found. In *Elwes v. Briggs Gas Co.*, a prehistoric boat was found in land that was leased to the defendant. The issue was whether the boat belonged to the lessor or lessees. The court ruled that the boat belonged to the lessor. From these cases the following is evident: 1) A landowner possesses everything attached to or under his land and 2) a landowner does not necessarily possess that which is unattached to his land. In this case, since the brooch was not attached to the land, neither *Bridges v. Hawksworth* or *South Staffordshire Water Co. v. Sharman* governs. This court chooses to follow *Bridges v. Hawksworth* in this case. It is noted that this result rewards Hannah (P) for meritorious conduct, such as giving the brooch to the police. Judgment for Plaintiff.

Analysis:

This case cites the prior possessor rule and two exceptions to that rule. First, lost property goes to the finder. This is the prior possessor rule. This protects owners who cannot prove title, it encourages the entrusting of goods to others, and protects the expectations of possessors, and it promotes peaceable possession. Second, if an employee finds a lost article on the employer's premises, the property goes to the owner. One reason for this is the view that the employee is acting on behalf of the employer. There is a criticism of this rule, however. It discourages finders from reporting found articles. If they do not report the lost article, they keep it. If they do report it, they lose it. Reporting lost articles is a social goal because it helps return lost property to the true owner. Finally, lost property found under the soil or embedded in the soil belongs to the landowner. The reason for this rule is that owners of land expect that they own not just the surface, but all that lies underneath it. It also discourages trespassers from coming onto land in search of treasure.

McAvoy v. Medina

(Finder) v. (Shop Owner)
(1866) 93 Mass. (I 1 Allen) 548

MEMORY GRAPHIC

Instant Facts

A customer of the shop owner placed his wallet on the counter, but neglected to remove it. McAvoy (P) found the wallet.

Black Letter Rule

A finder has no title to property that is mislaid.

Procedural Basis: Appeal from judgment in action to recover money found by plaintiff.

Facts: A customer of a shop placed his wallet on the counter but neglected to remove it; the customer had mislaid his wallet. McAvoy (P) found the wallet and gave it to the shop owner Medina (D) to keep until the true owner should claim it. If the true owner did not claim it, McAvoy (P) requested that Medina (D) advertise the lost money. The true owner was never found and Medina (D) refused to turn the money over to McAvoy (P).

Issue: Does the finder of mislaid property have title to that property?

Decision and Rationale: (Dewey). No. The ordinary rule is that a finder of lost property has title superior to all the world except the true owner. Here, however, the property was mislaid, not lost. When property is mislaid in a shop, the shop owner has a duty to safeguard the property until the true owner returns. Therefore, a finder can never gain title to mislaid property. *Bridges v. Hawkesworth* is distinguishable. In that case, the property was not voluntarily placed somewhere and then forgotten. Rather, in that case, the property was lost. In this case, since the property was not lost but mislaid, McAvoy (P) can claim no title. Judgment affirmed.

Analysis:

Lost property goes to the finder. Mislaid property goes to the shop owner. One way to understand this rule is to look to one of the goals of property law: Property law should promote the return of lost property to its true owner. If property is mislaid, the true owner will likely retrace his steps and return to the shop where he mislaid it. Thus, the rule that places mislaid property in the hand of the shop owner will more efficiently return mislaid property to the true owner. There are two criticisms to this rule. First, it is difficult to determine whether property has been mislaid or lost. For example, a wallet found on the floor could easily have fallen through a person's pocket and been lost. However, it also could have been mislaid on a counter and knocked to the floor by another customer. The second criticism is that individuals retrace their steps for both lost and mislaid property.

COURT MAKES IT DIFFICULT TO OBTAIN LAND BY ADVERSE POSSESSION: THE POSSESSOR MUST ACTUALLY BE ON THE LAND, HE MUST BELIEVE THAT IT IS HIS, AND HE MUST ENCLOSE IT OR SUBSTANTIALLY IMPROVE IT

Van Valkenburgh v. Lutz

(Title Holder) v. (Adverse Possessor)

(1952) 304 N.Y. 95; 106 N.E.2d 28

M E M O R Y   G R A P H I C

Instant Facts

The Lutzes (D) occupied the Van Valkenburgh's (P) land by building a one-bedroom shack on it, by cultivating a garden on it, and by storing rubbish on it. In another action to establish a right of way across the land, the Lutzes (D) admitted that the land belonged to the Van Valkenburghs (P).

Black Letter Rule

In order to acquire title by adverse possession, possession must be actual, it must be under claim of title, and the land must be either enclosed or sufficiently improved.

Case Vocabulary

DISSEIZED: To dispossess.
DIVEST: To take a right of ownership away from.
EASEMENT: The right to use land.
EASEMENT BY ADVERSE POSSESSION: The right to use the property of another acquired under the doctrine of adverse possession.
ORAL DISCLAIMER: Oral repudiation of ownership..
PRESCRIPTIVE RIGHT: An easement obtained by adverse possession.
VEST: To give a present right to ownership.

Facts: In 1912 the Lutzes (D) bought lots 14 and 15 in a large subdivision. Instead of climbing a steep grade to get to their lot, the Lutzes (D) crossed lots 19-22, which they did not own, to get to their lot. With regard to lots 19-22, the Lutzes (D) cleared it, built a one-bedroom shack on it, and grew vegetables on it. The vegetables were sold. In 1937 the Van Valkenburghs (P) purchased a lot near the Lutzes (D). In 1947, the Van Valkenburghs (P) purchased lots 19-22, the lots that the Lutzes (D) had been using. Soon after, the Van Valkenburghs (P) sent a letter to the Lutzes (D) informing them that they, the Van Valkenburghs (P), now owned the property. The letter also requested that the Lutzes (D) remove their property from the land. The Lutzes (D) removed only part of their property, but claimed a prescriptive right of way across the land. Later, the Van Valkenburghs (P) erected a fence across the land, preventing the Lutzes (D) from crossing the land. The Lutzes (D) sued the Van Valkenburghs (P), admitting that the Van Valkenburghs (P) owned the land, but claiming a right of way across the land. The Lutzes (D) prevailed on this issue. The Van Valkenburghs (P) sue here to gain possession of the lots. The Lutzes (D) contend that they acquired title to the lots by adverse possession.

Issue: (1) Must possession be actual in order to acquire title by adverse possession? (2) Where a person claims title not founded upon a written instrument, must a person either protect land by a substantial enclosure or cultivate or improve land to be deemed to be in possession? (3) Must land be possessed under a claim of title to acquire it by adverse possession?

Decision and Rationale: (Dye). Yes. Yes. Yes. New York Civil Practice Act § 39 [requirements to acquire title by possession] clearly states that land must be actually possessed. This requirement is not met here for two reasons: 1) The garden occupied only a small portion of lots 19-22, and 2) the Lutzes' garage encroached on the land by only a few inches. New York Civil Practice Act § 40 [requirements to acquire title by adverse possession] clearly states that where a person claims title not founded upon a written instrument, he must show that the land was protected by a substantial enclosure or that he cultivated or improved the land. This requirement is not met here. Concededly, the land was not enclosed. The land was not sufficiently improved for two reasons: 1) The shack was too small ; 2) The garden was insubstantial; and 3) placing rubbish on the land is not an improvement. New York Civil Practice Act § 39 clearly states that land must be possessed under claim of title. Since Lutz (D) testified that he knew that the land belonged to the Van Valkenburghs (P) in this action and in the prior action by Lutz (P) to establish a right of way, he fails to prove the "claim of title" element of the adverse possession statute. (Judgment reversed)

Dissent: There is substantial evidence to indicate that the land was substantially improved. Second, the land need not be completely occupied. It need be occupied only to the extent necessary to put the true owner on notice. There was enough evidence to support this element. Finally, in order to satisfy the "claim of right" element of the statute, it is not necessary that the Lutzes (D) believed that the property was theirs. It is sufficient only that they intended to acquire and use the land as their own. The fact that the Lutzes (D) admitted that they did not have title is only evidence of whether or not they intended to acquire and use the land as their own. This is true because this admission was made after the statute had run.

Analysis:

Though acquisition of title by adverse possession seems like stealing, it serves many policy goals, which are illustrated nicely in the majority and dissenting opinions. As we have encountered in prior cases, and as we shall continue to encounter, one of the goals of property law is to encourage the efficient use of property. This is why acquisition of title by adverse possession requires actual possession and (sometimes) improvement of the land. The majority felt that the Lutzes (D) did not satisfy these requirements. Related to the goal of efficient use of property is the notion that owners who are lazy should be punished. Thus, if an owner knows that another is possessing his land adversely, but does nothing, he loses title. This is the view that the dissent takes in requiring that actual possession means only possession that will put the owner on notice. Finally, another goal of the law is to encourage honesty. This is one way to explain why the majority requires that an adverse possessor acquire title only under "claim of right." If a possessor honestly believes that it is his, he is eligible to receive title to it.

Mannillo v. Gorski

(Landowner) v. (Encroacher)
54 N.J. 378, 255 A.2d 258 (1969)

MEMORY GRAPHIC

Instant Facts

A property owner sought to enjoin the alleged trespass of an adjoining landowner whose pathway encroached 15 inches and who claimed title to the strip by adverse possession.

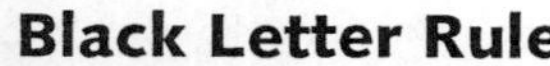

Black Letter Rule

Possession need not be knowingly and intentionally hostile, but it must be notorious enough to give the true owner actual or constructive notice of the encroachment.

Case Vocabulary

DICHOTOMY: Division into two contradictory parts.

Facts: Mannillo (P) and Gorski (D) owned adjacent lots. For a period of over 20 years, steps and a concrete walk leading from Gorski's (D) house encroached upon Mannillo's (P) land some 15 inches. As a result, Mannillo (P) filed a complaint seeking to enjoin Gorski's (D) alleged trespass. Gorski (D) counterclaimed for a declaratory judgment to the effect that Gorski (D) had gained title to the 15-inch strip of land by adverse possession. Mannillo (P) contended that Gorski (D) did not gain title by adverse possession because her taking was not of the requisite hostile nature. According to Mannillo (P), encroachment must be accompanied by an intention to invade the rights of another. Gorski (D) was not aware that the steps and path encroached onto Mannillo's lot, but rather operated under the mistaken belief that she owned the land. The trial court accepted Mannillo's (P) argument and entered judgment for Mannillo (P). Gorski (D) appealed.

Issue: (1) Must possession be accompanied by a knowing intentional hostility for adverse possession? (2) Does a minor border encroachment satisfy the "open and notorious" requirement for adverse possession?

Decision and Rationale: (Haneman, J.) (1) No. Possession need not be accompanied by a knowing intentional hostility for adverse possession. Entry and continuance of possession under the mistaken belief that the possessor has title to the lands involved may exhibit the requisite hostile possession to sustain the obtaining of title by adverse possession. If knowing intentional hostility were required, as the Maine doctrine suggests, we would be rewarding the possessor who entered with a premeditated and predesigned hostility and we would be punishing the honest, mistaken entrant. Rather, we choose to follow the Connecticut doctrine and hold that mistake does not negate the hostility requirement. The key to adverse possession is the true owner's neglect to recover possession of his land, which does not hinge on whether the adverse entry is caused by mistake or intent. (2) No. A minor border encroachment does not satisfy the "open and notorious" requirement for adverse possession. Generally when possession of land is clear enough to be immediately visible, the true owner may be presumed to have knowledge of the adverse occupancy. However, a border dispute such as the instant action does not create a clear situation of adverse occupancy. Indeed, the only way that Mannillo (P) could have determined that Gorski (D) was encroaching was to have a survey performed. Landowners should not be required to bear the expense of a survey every time the adjacent landowner makes some improvement. Thus, we hold that no presumption of knowledge arises from a minor encroachment along a common boundary. Only where the true owner has actual knowledge of the encroachment may it be said that the possession is open and notorious. Nevertheless, we realize that this may impose an undue hardship on the adverse possessor who mistakenly encroaches on his neighbor's property while making an improvement. Equity may require that the court force the true owner to convey the land upon payment of the fair value by the adverse possessor. We remand this case for a determination of whether Mannillo (P) had actual knowledge of the encroachment and, if not, whether Mannillo (P) should be required to convey the strip of land to Gorski (D).

Analysis:

This case addresses two key requirements for adverse possession: hostility and notoriousness. Overall, according to this court, adverse possession requires entry and possession for some requisite period of time which is exclusive, continuous, uninterrupted, visible, and notorious. The court abandons the requirement that the possession be openly and knowingly hostile. On one hand, the court's adoption of the Connecticut doctrine makes sense, because it does not award an intentional wrongdoer over an honest, mistaken entrant. In another light, however, the Maine doctrine makes more sense. The Maine doctrine rewards only the person who actually desires to take possession of land. If a person mistakenly erects a fence beyond his boundary with no intention to claim title if he later finds out that he is encroaching on his neighbor's land, why should this person be rewarded? With regard to the "open and notorious" requirement, the court states a simple but important concept. Possession must be of such a degree that the true owner has actual knowledge, or should have knowledge, of the intrusion. Minor border encroachments are often insufficient to provide actual knowledge, and the court justly holds that they do not provide constructive knowledge either. Finally, the court's discussion of its equitable powers is interesting. If the encroacher does not meet the requirements for adverse possession, he can nevertheless have a court force the true owner to sell the land if the court determines that this is the most equitable result.

COURT MAKES IT EASIER TO ACQUIRE TITLE BY ADVERSE POSSESSION: CUSTOMARY USE NOW SATISFIES THE REQUIREMENT OF CONTINUITY AND THERE NEED BE ONLY A REASONABLE CONNECTION BETWEEN SUCCESSIVE OCCUPANTS TO TACK

Howard v. Kunto

(Title Holder) v. (Adverse Possessor)
(1970) 3 Wash. App. 393; 477 P.2d 210

MEMORY GRAPHIC

Instant Facts

Kunto (D) had a house on and occupied land to which Howard (P) had title.

Black Letter Rule

Land that is used in a customary manner is deemed to be used continuously. Tacking between successive adverse possessors is established if there is a reasonable connection between them.

Case Vocabulary

CLAIM OF RIGHT: In the law of adverse possession, possession of land while claiming it as one's own.
COLOR OF TITLE: The appearance of title.
PREDECESSOR IN INTEREST: The person who has possessed or owned land before the current occupant or owner.
PRIVITY: A relationship between two people of such quality so as to have legal consequences.
PRIVITY OF ESTATE: In the law of adverse possession, that relationship between successors in interest that is required for tacking.
QUIET TITLE: The determination of who owns property.
SQUATTER: One who has possession.
TACKING: When a person adds the time that he has possessed property to the time that his predecessor has possessed.

Procedural Basis: Appeal from judgment in action to quiet title.

Facts: Howard (P) was in possession of a lot in a resort area. Just east of Howard, Moyer was in possession of a lot in the same resort area. Just east of Moyer, Kunto (D) was in possession of a lot in the same resort area. However, the title that Howard (P) had was to the land occupied by Moyer. The title that Moyer had was to the land occupied by Kunto (D). The title that Kunto (D) has was to the lot just west of him. Kunto (D) obtained his title by deed from his predecessor. Howard (P) conveyed the deed to the land that Moyer occupied to Moyer. In return, Moyer conveyed the deed to the land that Kunto (D) occupied to Howard (P). Howard now sues to quiet title to the lot occupied by Kunto (D).

Issue: (1) Is land that is used in a customary manner, even though it is not possessed continuously, sufficient to vest title by adverse possession? (2) Is a reasonable relationship between successive adverse possessors all that is required to tack?

Decision and Rationale: (Pearson). Yes. Yes. It is not necessary that land be occupied continuously to vest title by adverse possession. All that is required is that the possession be of such quality that a third party would believe that the actual owner was occupying it. An adverse possessor may add the time that his predecessor occupied the land onto his own time if he is in privity with him. This is called tacking. Normally, privity is furnished by the deed transferring title. Moreover, the normal case involves a plaintiff claiming more land than that described in the deed. Howard (P) contends that there was no privity between Kunto (D) and his predecessor because the deed contained no mention of the land that Kunto (D) occupies. He claims, in effect, that there was no transfer of "claim of title", but transfer of possession only. This argument is not persuasive. The requirement of privity was developed merely to prevent trespassers, who had no "claim of right," from tacking. Therefore, we construe privity to mean nothing more than a judicial recognition of some reasonable connection between successive occupants. Since Kunto (D) believed in good faith that he was receiving good title to the land he occupies, there is privity. Judgment reversed.

Analysis:

As an aid to understanding why the court ruled that there need be only a reasonable relationship between successive possessors, consider the following two goals of property law: 1) After a long time has passed, uncertain titles should be stabilized and 2) Persons who have acquired land from an adverse possessor in good faith reliance upon his apparent ownership should be protected. In this case, there had been many decades between the mistaken survey and the time that Kunto (D) took possession. This is certainly long enough for society to expect that the title should be settled. The doctrine of adverse possession ensures that titles are settled so that people can rely on them and put the land to efficient use. Also, since Kunto (P) relied in good faith upon the apparent title of his predecessor, it is fair that he gain title. One way to understand the ruling that an adverse possessor need only use the land in a customary manner is to consider that the law of property wants to encourage the efficient use of land. If an adverse possessor uses land according to custom, he is deemed to be using the land in an efficient manner. The law does not require more of an adverse possessor (who may believe in good faith that he has title) than it does of a true owner.

O'Keeffe v. Snyder

(Title Holder) v. (Adverse Possessor)
(1980) 83 N.J. 478; 416 A.2d 862

M E M O R Y   G R A P H I C

Instant Facts

Three of O'Keeffe's paintings were stolen from an art gallery. The thefts were not reported to anyone.

Black Letter Rule

The statute of limitations is tolled if the owner of stolen chattel makes diligent efforts to locate and recover the lost chattel.

Case Vocabulary

CONVERSION: To take property from another.
DISCOVERY RULE: The rules by which one may obtain title to chattels by adverse possession. It provides that the statute of limitations does not run if the true owner uses diligence to discover the possessor of his property.
IMPLEAD: To bring a third party into a lawsuit on the ground that such third party is liable to the defendant.
INTERROGATORY: A formal set of questions propounded to a party designed to elicit the facts.
LEGATEES: A person who takes property under a will.
PLENARY HEARING: A complete hearing of a case to fully determine the facts.
REPLEVIN: An action to regain possession.
REPLEVY: To take or get back by a right for replevin.
SUMMARY JUDGMENT: Judgment rendered in a case based only on consideration of the law, where there is no dispute of the facts.
VOIDABLE TITLE: Title which remains valid until the true owner asserts ownership.

Procedural Basis: Appeal from an order by the appellate court reversing an order of summary judgment for defendant in action to replevy chattels.

Facts: In 1946 three paintings by O'Keeffe (P) were stolen from an art gallery operated by her husband, Stieglitz. O'Keeffe (P) suspected that Estrick may have stolen the paintings. However, she did not confront him about it; neither did she report the theft to the police. O'Keeffe explains that she did not pursue her efforts to find the paintings because she was settling her deceased husband's estate. Finally, in 1972 O'Keeffe (P) authorized Bry to report the theft to the Art Dealers Association of America, which maintains a registry of stolen paintings. It is not clear whether such a registry existed in 1946. In 1976 O'Keeffe (P) discovered that Frank had sold her paintings to Snyder (D). Frank acquired the paintings from his father. Frank does not know how his father acquired the paintings, but he recalls seeing them in his father's house as early as 1941. This is inconsistent with O'Keeffe's allegation of theft. For the purposes of this appeal, Snyder (D) concedes that the paintings are stolen. Frank claims continuous possession for over 30 years through his father and claims title by adverse possession.

Issue: If possession of chattels is obtained by theft, and the true owner makes diligent efforts to locate and recover the chattels, is the statute of limitations for adverse possession tolled?

Decision and Rationale: (Pollock). Yes. In no circumstances can a thief transfer good title. However, if Frank acquired a voidable title from his father, who may have been a thief, Frank has the power to transfer good title to a good faith purchaser under the U. C. C. If Snyder (D) was not a good faith purchaser, or if Frank did not have a voidable title, Snyder (D) may still acquire title by adverse possession. However, in certain situations, the statute of limitations is tolled to avoid harsh results. Unlike land that is adversely possessed, the owner of chattels may not know that her property has been stolen, or she may not know who the adverse possessor is. This is especially true with stolen art, which is often concealed. O'Keeffe (P) contends that nothing short of public display should suffice to put the true owner on notice. However, this rule is harsh to good faith purchasers who wish to display art in the privacy of their homes. The following compromise, called the discovery rule, balances these interests. Upon discovery of theft the statute of limitations is tolled if the true owner of the chattels makes diligent efforts, under the circumstances, to locate and recover the chattels. Depending upon the circumstances, this may include reporting the theft to the police or registering the lost chattels with a registry so as to notify potential buyers that it may be stolen. Reversed and remanded for a finding of whether O'Keeffe (P) used diligence in discovering who had the lost paintings.

Analysis:

The policy goals motivating the doctrine of adverse possession include: 1) after a long time titles should be settled; and 2) encouraging the efficient use of land. In this case, we see the converse of these principles: A true owner who is not at fault in failing to recover his property should not be divested of title. This is based on simple notions of justice. Notice, however, that this rule may harm a good faith purchaser who had the bad luck to buy stolen property. The court does not give this concern much weight. It reasons that a purchaser may always learn whether property is stolen or not. In practice, however, a good faith buyer may not be able to learn this.

COURT MAKES IT MORE DIFFICULT TO GIVE GIFTS: SYMBOLIC DELIVERY IS NOT ALLOWED

Newman v. Bost

(Donee) v. (Administrator of Donor's Estate)
(1898) 122 N.C. 524; 29 S.E. 848

MEMORY GRAPHIC

Instant Facts

After giving the keys to much of the furniture in the house to Newman (P), the decedent pointed to the furniture and said to Newman (P) that he was giving it all to her. In one of the pieces of furniture was a life insurance policy.

Black Letter Rule

Symbolic delivery of a gift is not effective. Constructive delivery is allowed only when it is impractical to deliver actual possession.

Case Vocabulary

ADMINISTRATOR: A person appointed by a testator to carry out the directions in his will.
DONATIO CAUSA MORTIS: A gift made when death is impending.
ESTATE: The accumulated property and legal rights of a deceased person.
EXPRESS: Made clear, usually by verbal or written communication, as contrasted with implied.
GIFT CAUSE MORTIS: A gift made when death is impending.
GIFT INTER VIVOS: A gift made while alive and healthy.
IN EXTREMIS: Near death.
INTESTATE: One who has died without a will; the estate of one who has died without a will.
ISSUE: The children of a testator
STATUTE OF WILLS: The statute enacted in England which allowed persons to dispose of their property at death as they desired.
TESTATOR: One who has made a will.

Procedural Basis: Appeal from judgment in action for damages for conversion.

Facts: After decedent was stricken ill, he gave to Newman (P) all that was in his home. He did this as follows: In the presence of Houston, he had Newman (P) summoned. He asked Newman (P) to give him his keys. Decedent then handed the keys to Newman (P), saying that he wanted her to have everything in his house. He then pointed to specific pieces of furniture including a locked bureau. Among the keys given to Newman (P) was a key that unlocked his bureau. This was the only key to the bureau. In this bureau was a life insurance policy covering the life of the decedent. Bost (D), administrator of decedent's estate, sold all of the property in the decedent's home. Newman (P) sues for the value of the life insurance policy as well as for the value of the other goods in the home.

Issue: Is symbolic delivery sufficient to make a gift good? Is constructive delivery sufficient when delivery of actual possession is impractical?

Decision and Rationale: (Furches). No. Yes. First, in order to make a valid gift, the donor must intend to make the gift. In this case it is not clear whether the decedent intended to give only the bureau that he pointed to or its contents or both. Thus, the life insurance, which was in the bureau, was not a good gift. Second, in order to make a valid gift, the donor must deliver actual possession. This rigid rule was made for a time when few could read. As time passed, written conveyances became acceptable, as the statute of frauds and wills makes clear. Accordingly, when actual delivery is impractical, constructive delivery will suffice. However, we are still mindful of fraud so we do not allow symbolic delivery. Constructive delivery is the handing over of the means of obtaining possession and control. An example is the handing over of keys to a car. Regarding the life insurance, actual delivery of possession is not impractical. The decedent could have easily had someone else get the life insurance policy and hand it over to Newman (P). Thus, there can be no constructive delivery. Since there was neither actual or constructive delivery, there was no gift of the life insurance policy. However, since the furniture in the house to which Newman (P) had the keys was heavy and impractical to deliver, the handing over of the keys was good constructive delivery. Also, the furniture in Newman's (P) own bedroom was actually delivered to her, since she exercised control over it. The other furnishings in the house, to which Newman (P) did not have keys, were not constructively or actually delivered. Affirmed in part, reversed in part, and remanded for a new trial.

Analysis:

In this case there are two competing policy goals in operation. The first goal is to protect owners of property from being defrauded. The second goal is to promote the free alienability of property. This court has reconciled these competing goals with a compromise. Symbolic delivery will not be allowed; constructive delivery will be allowed only if actual delivery is impractical under the circumstances. This compromise between the desire to make property freely alienable and the desire to protect the owner from being defrauded also appears in the law of concurrent interests.

COURT MAKES IT EASIER TO GIVE GIFTS: A PARTY MAY GIVE A REMAINDER TO ANOTHER WHILE RESERVING A LIFE ESTATE IN HIMSELF

Gruen v. Gruen

(Donee) v. (Possessor)

(1986) 68 N.Y. 48, 496 N.E.2d 869, 505 N.Y.S.2d 849

MEMORY GRAPHIC

Instant Facts

The elder Gruen gave Gruen (P) a painting but reserved a life estate for himself. Gruen (P) has never had possession of the painting.

Black Letter Rule

A party may give a future interest in chattels as a gift while reserving a life estate in himself.

Case Vocabulary

CONSTRUCTIVE DELIVERY: Delivery of the means by which property may be possessed.
DECEASED: Dead person.
DELIVERY: To give over possession.
DISPOSITIVE: Of such a nature or quality as to by itself determine the outcome of a case.
IRREVOCABLE: Incapable of being taken back.
LIFE ESTATE: A possessory estate in property that has one's life as the measure of duration.
REMAINDER INTEREST: An interest in property that is not currently possessory, but will become possessory in the future.
RESERVE: To keep for oneself rather than conveying to another.
ROYALTIES: Proceeds from the earnings of property or business.
SYMBOLIC DELIVERY: Delivery in the eyes of the law; the performing of some act that represents delivery, such as executing a writing.
TESTAMENTARY: Pertaining to a will.
VEST: To give a present right to ownership.
WILL: An instrument by which one disposes of his property and legal rights upon his death.

Procedural Basis: Appeal from an order of the appellate division reversing a judgment in an action for delivery of chattels.

Facts: Gruen's (P) father wrote a letter to him giving him a painting for his birthday. However, the elder Gruen reserved a life estate for himself. The original letter was destroyed on the instructions of the elder Gruen. The elder Gruen felt this was necessary for tax reasons. However, he did send a second letter to Gruen (P) giving him the painting, though not mentioning that he reserved a life estate in himself. Seventeen years later, the elder Gruen died. Gruen (D), the defendant's stepmother, now has possession of the painting and refuses to deliver it to Gruen (P). Gruen (D) contends that the purported gift is invalid because title vests only after the death of Gruen. That is, she contends that the gift was testamentary and did not satisfy the formalities of a will. Alternatively, Gruen (D) contends that a donor may not make a valid gift of a chattel while reserving a life estate in himself because possession is not delivered.

Issue: May a valid inter vivos gift be made where the donor reserves a life estate in the chattel and the donee has never taken possession?

Decision and Rationale: (Simons). Yes. An inter vivos gift requires that the donor intend to make a present transfer of title. If the intention is to make a transfer of title only after death, the gift is invalid unless made by a will. Gruen (D) errs in maintaining that the elder Gruen intended to make a transfer of title only at his death. On the contrary, he intended to make a present transfer of a future interest. Title to this future interest, which is a remainder, vested at the time of the gift. It is irrelevant that possession is not taken until some time in the future. As to Gruen's (D) contention that the gift was invalid because possession was not delivered, we note that the rule that possession must be delivered to consummate a gift is flexible. This is a better statement of the rule: The delivery that is required is that delivery that is best under the circumstances. In this case, since Gruen (P) had only a remainder, it was impossible to deliver such an interest until the elder Gruen had died. Moreover, it would be silly to have the elder Gruen deliver possession merely to take it back so that he could enjoy his life estate. Judgment affirmed.

Analysis:

One of the principle goals of property law is to promote the alienability of property. This goal is of such importance that the court in *Gruen v. Gruen* allowed the elder Gruen to make a gift of a future interest, even though it was not possible to deliver possession of this interest, and even though the possibility of fraud was great. The possibility of fraud is great in the area of future interests because a person may easily claim that he was given a gift, but that he was not given possession because he was given a future interest. The tension between the possibility of fraud and the desire to make property freely alienable appears throughout the law of estates and concurrent interests.

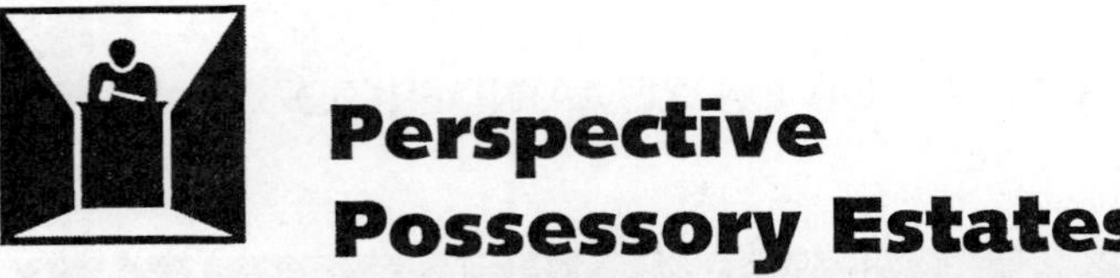

Perspective
Possessory Estates

Chapter 3

The ordinary person thinks of real property as something tangible that can be located, measured, and built upon. This is the way that our predecessors viewed property as well – a tangible asset that was to be worked to the benefit of one's Lord. While vestiges of the English feudal system can still be seen in modern property law, the modern lawyer thinks of property in the abstract. Today, property is conceived of as a bundle of rights that attach to a parcel of land. A person can have full rights in the land to sell, develop, or change it. However, a person can also have more limited rights, such as the right of mere possession, or the right to use the land subject to preserving it for some future owner. To the American lawyer, these rights characterize property more so than the physical boundaries of the land itself. Thus, to understand the law of property, one must understand the collection of rights that go along with any parcel of land.

The guiding principal of real property law in the United States is the free alienability of land. That is the guarantee that the present owners of land will be reasonably free to sell or alter land and will thereby have the ability and the incentive to put the land to its economically most productive use. Free alienability is accomplished by a legal preference for land passing in fee simple; that is, by passing the land without restricting its future use. Thus, land is not forever bound up in one family. Each transferee must individually decide whether to sell the land or pass it on to the next generation.

However, the law also recognizes that it is not desirable for every transfer of land to be completely unfettered. People seem to have the age-old desire to see their possessions passed down from generation to generation. In some instances, one generation may doubt the ability of the next to properly care for and use the land. Thus, the law allows people the ability to pass less than complete control of the land to another in certain limited circumstances.

This chapter addresses the rights, responsibilities and limitations of the possession and transfer of real property.

Chapter Overview Outline Possessory Estates

Chapter 3

NOTE: THE PURPOSE OF THIS OUTLINE IS TO ORGANIZE THE CASES SO THAT ONE CAN QUICKLY UNDERSTAND THE RELEVANCE OF EACH CASE TO THE COURSE. NO ATTEMPT IS MADE IN THIS OVERVIEW TO ADDRESS EVERY CONCEPT THAT MUST BE STUDIED. BE SURE TO READ THE ENTIRE CASEBOOK AND/OR OTHER MATERIALS TO GAIN A FULL UNDERSTANDING OF ALL CONCEPTS.

I. Historical Basis for Modern Property Law. The law of real property in the United States has roots going back to the Norman Conquest of England in the 11th century, which was the beginning of the feudal system of property ownership and transfer. Thus, in order to understand the rules and the rationale behind the modern real property law we must first get a sense of where the rules came from.

A. In the feudal system, land, not commerce, was power.

1. Lords who held great estates could muster great armies to garner favor with the King.

a. Each Lord raised the armies by granting each knight a certain amount of land.

b. The knights in turn could grant some or all of the land to others in exchange for further military, economic, or religious service.

2. Thus, the feudal system was a system of "layers," where the King granted land to Lords in exchange for services (military, economic, and religious.)

3. The Lords in turn granted their land to others in exchange for services, and the others granted the land to still others.

4. This system of getting land from a Lord and then granting it to another (thereby becoming a Lord yourself) was known as subinfeudation.

B. The feudal system depended upon the personal relationship between Lord and tenant.

1. The Lord would naturally only grant the land to the tenant who the Lord thought to be the most capable of providing service to the Lord.

2. Due to the personal nature of tenancy upon land, the Lord was entitled to a return of the land when the tenant died.

a. However, it was commonly thought that the best replacement for a tenant was the tenant's eldest son, who presumably knew best how to carry out the tenant's service to the Lord.

3. Over the years, this developed into a system where the eldest son had the right to inherit his father's interest in the Lord's land. The system came to be known as primogeniture.

C. In 1290, the parliament passed the statute of *Quia Emptores*, which began the decline of the feudal system and was the beginning of the modern concept of the free alienability of land.

1. *Quia Emptores* prohibited the "layering" that was essential to the feudal system.

2. Under this statute, a tenant could transfer his interest in land to another tenant, even without the Lord's permission.

3. However, the tenant could no longer grant the land to others and become a Lord himself.

D. Another important statutory development for modern real property law was the *Statute de Donis*, which was passed by parliament in 1285.

1. This statute more or less formalized the primogeniture system.

2. Where property was granted "to A and his heirs," the land passed, as of right, from generation to generation in the same family until A had no more descendants.

3. No action by A or any of his sons could prevent the passing of the land to the next generation (except, of course, refusing to have children.)

4. This system of limitation on land ownership is called fee tail.

E. Since feudal times, society has been evolving from dependence on family ties (or dependence on ties to a Lord) to dependence on individual obligation.

1. In other words, our society has been shift-

Chapter Overview Outline
Possessory Estates

ing emphasis from status to contract. *Ancient Law*.

a. Thus, it is the exchange of things, rather than the relationship of persons, that is now of primary economic importance. *The Growth of English Industry and Commerce*.

2. This explains how the function of land has changed from a method of defining interpersonal relationships in feudal times to a medium or object of exchange today.

II. Freeholds and Ownership in Fee Simple. The systems of primogeniture and fee tail became a means whereby a hereditary, landed aristocracy could develop. Therefore, the early state legislatures abolished these systems after the American Revolution.

A. The principle of free alienability is so strong that in the law today there is a presumption that when there is a transfer of rights in real property, a transferor intends to transfer all of his interest in the land to the transferee, absent a clear indication to the contrary. *White v. Brown*.

B. There are four main objections to restraints upon alienation of property:

1. Restraints make the property unmarketable, and thus unavailable for its most economically valuable use;

2. Restraints perpetuate the concentration of wealth by not allowing the land owner to sell the land and spend the money;

3 Restraints act as a disincentive for improvement on land, as the owners are not likely to spend money to improve and increase the value of land that they cannot sell; and

4 Creditors are less likely to borrow against and take a security interest in land if they cannot hold absolute title in the land.

III. Methods of Transferring Less than all Rights. While primogeniture and fee tail (also known as "dead hand" control over land) will never be enforceable, not every transfer of interest in real property must be the transfer of a fee simple. Certain lesser restraints on alienation are honored in deference to a person's ability to do a[s] he or she pleases with his or her own propert[y]. *Mountain Brow Lodge No. 82, Independen[t] Order of Odd Fellows v. Toscano*.

A. Life Estate

1. A life estate means that the grantee ma[y] hold and use the property for his or her lif[e] after which the property goes to anothe[r] person.

2. The life estate gave grantors a limited abilit[y] to control inheritance.

B. Trust Res

1. Life estates in property may not be we[ll] suited to modern society, in which land [is] simply another asset.

2. The trust is another legal devise that allow[s] the grantor to control the future use of th[e] property, yet allow enough flexibility t[o] change with the times.

3. In short, the trustee holds the property i[n] fee simple, yet has a strict duty to use th[e] trust property to the best advantage of th[e] trust beneficiaries.

4. Thus, unlike the life estate holder, th[e] trustee has the power to sell, lease, o[r] mortgage the land, or to exploit the natur[al] resources found on the land – whichever [is] most beneficial for the beneficiaries.

C. Leaseholds

1. Leases are not strictly interests in real prop[-]erty, but were historically regarded as [a] personal property interest in the lessee.

2. As a result, in a lease the landlord continue[s] to hold all of the interests of ownership.

3. In feudal times this meant that the tenan[t] of a leasehold did not owe the Lord any o[f] the duties (such as military service) or inc[i]dents that went with the land.

4. In modern times, this means that the land[-]lord, not the tenant, is ultimately respons[i]ble for taxes and assessments on the lan[d].

D. Defeasible Estates

1. The fee simple comes in two varieties.

a. A fee simple absolute means that th[e] owner holds the property outright an[d] cannot be divested of any property inte[r]est unless he transfers it.

(1) However, the fee simple may also be made defeasible. A defeasible fee simple is not absolute ownership.

b. A defeasible fee might or might not endure forever. If some pre-specified event occurs, the owner is divested of his interest in the land.

2. There are two types of defeasible fees.

a. Fee Simple Determinable

(1) The possessory interest in property ends automatically upon the occurrence of some specified event.

(2) For example, A grants land to B "to be used for school purposes only." B has a fee simple determinable estate in the land. This fee simple has the potential to endure forever. However, if B uses the land for some other purpose, the school's fee simple interest automatically ends and goes to someone else. *Mahrenholz v. County Board of School Trustees.*

b. Fee simple subject to condition subsequent

(1) Here, the fee simple estate may end upon the occurrence of some specified event *if* the grantor elects to terminate and retake the estate.

(2) Example: A grants land "to school, but if school fails to teach Algebra, grantor has a right of entry." This fee simple has the potential to endure forever. However, if the school does not teach Algebra, the school's fee simple interest may end. It will end if A elects to terminate and retake the estate.

/. Present versus Future Interest Holders

A. There is an inherent tension between the holders of a present interest in land (e.g., life estate or fee simple defeasible) and the holders of a future interest (e.g., those who get the land after the life estate holder dies.)

1. The present interest holder has an interest in getting as much as he can from the land while he still has an right to use the land.

2. The future interest holder has an interest in preserving as much of the value of the land as possible until the day that he can take possession.

B. Waste

1. The holder of a present possessory interest in land is prohibited from committing waste – he may not use the land in a way that unreasonably diminishes its value to the future interest holder.

2. Affirmative Waste

a. The present interest holder may not actively participate in activities that diminish the value of the land.

b. Such actions have historically included cutting mature trees, putting the land to a different agricultural use, mining the land (unless the mine was already open at the time he came into possession), and tearing down existing buildings.

3. Passive Waste

a. The present interest holder also has the duty to take reasonable steps to prevent a deterioration in the value of the land.

b. This includes the duty to repair structures, to pay taxes, and to pay interest on any mortgage that may exist on the land.

C. Dividing Proceeds from a Sale

1. Where property is subject to both present and future interests, the general rule is that it cannot be sold unless all interest holders consent. A court may order a sale of such property only if it is in the best interest of all parties. *Baker v. Weedon.*

a. Such a sale then leaves the question of the value of the interest that each party holds.

2. Upon sale of land, the proceeds should be divided – some going to the future interest holders and some going to the present interest holders. *Ink v. City of Canton.*

3. In the context of a life estate, the valuation of present and future interests in property is calculated using life expectancy tables.

a. The longer the life tenant is expected to live, the more value the land has to the life tenant and the less value the land has to the future interest holder.

COURTS PRESUME THAT A CONVEYANCE OF REAL PROPERTY IN A WILL WAS INTENDED TO CONVEY A FEE SIMPLE ESTATE, UNLESS CONTRARY INTENT IS DEMONSTRATED

White v. Brown

(Heir) v. (Heir)
(1977) 559 S.W.2d 938

MEMORY GRAPHIC

Instant Facts

Jessie Lide died leaving a will stating "I wish Evelyn White (P) to have my home to live in and not to be sold. . . . My house is not to be sold."

Black Letter Rule

Unless a contrary intention appears by the terms of the will and its context, a will conveys a testator's entire interest.

Case Vocabulary

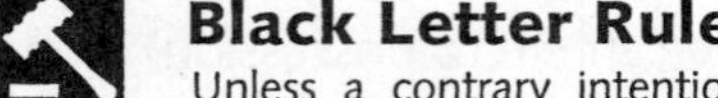

ALIENATION OF PROPERTY: The principle that the owner of a piece of property should be able to sell or use the land as he or she sees fit, without limitation by the former owner.
ESTATE: The extent or nature of one's interest in property. Also, the sum total of all of one's property at death.
FEE SIMPLE: The largest estate in land that one may own.
INTESTATE: To die without a will.
LIFE ESTATE: An estate that lasts either for the life of the owner or the life of another person.
REMAINDER: The future interest that becomes possessory after the expiration of some intervening estate.
RESTRAINT ON ALIENATION: A restriction on the sale or conveyance of property.

Procedural Basis: Appeal from judgment in action to construct a will.

Facts: White (P), along with her husband and daughter, lived in Jessie Lide's house for 25 years. When Jessie Lide died, she left a holographic will which read in part: "I wish Evelyn White (P) to have my home to live in and not to be sold. . . . My house is not to be sold." White (P) contends that the will conveyed a fee simple interest in the house. Brown (D) contends that the will merely conveyed a life estate to White (P). The trial court ruled that the will, on its face, unambiguously conveyed a life estate. Since the trial court found that the will was facially unambiguous, it did not consider extrinsic evidence.

Issue: Unless a contrary intention appears by the terms of the will and its context, does a will convey a testator's entire interest?

Decision and Rationale: (Brock). Yes. At common law, there was a presumption that a testator conveyed only a life estate. However, the legislature has enacted a rule of construction which reverses this presumption: A will shall convey all the real estate belonging to the testator unless a contrary intention appears by the terms of the will and its context. Several cases demonstrate the strength of the presumption that a testator conveys his entire interest. In *Green v. Young*, testatrix left her property to her husband "to be used by him for his support and comfort during his life." Yet, the will was held to pass a fee simple to the husband. In *Williams v. Williams*, the testator devised real property to his children "for and during their natural lives." Yet, the will was held to pass a fee simple. Therefore, it is clear that if the only language in Lide's will was that the home was for White (P) to "live in", a fee simple would pass. However, the language "not to be sold" complicates matters. We must look to the context to determine if Lide intended to convey only a life estate. Where there is ambiguity, we construe a will to dispose of the testator's entire estate, which would be a fee simple in this case. In this case, it appears that Lide attempted to pass a fee simple to White (P) and further attempted to restrain her from alienating the property. This attempt to restrict alienation is clear: "My house is not to be sold." A restraint on alienation is void as against public policy, leaving White (P) with a fee simple. Judgment reversed.

Dissent: (Harbison). Lide's will is not ambiguous. It is clear that she intended to pass only a life estate: ". . . to have my home to live in and not to be sold." *Green v. Young* is distinguishable because in that case the testatrix bequeathed all of her real and personal property to her husband, so it is reasonable to presume that a fee simple was intended. Here, Lide bequeathed to White (P) only real property. *Williams v. Williams* is not applicable because it contains other clauses which indicate a clear intent to pass a fee simple: the children of the testator "were to have all the residue of my estate." In this case, the testatrix knew how to convey all her property. She demonstrated this when she left all her personal property to her niece. As to White (P), she merely wished that she "live in" her home; she intended to convey a life estate.

Analysis:

This case illustrates a fundamental policy of property law: The law promotes the free alienability of property. It seems odd, in a country founded on the economic principles of "freedom of contract" that the law would (or could) restrict the conditions that people can put on the transfer of their own property. However, remember the historical background in which property laws developed. Under the laws of England at the time of the American Revolution, property could perpetually be bound up in the hands of a single family. The only way to free the property was to go through complicated and expensive legal proceedings. This resulted in the creation of a landed aristocracy, which the Founders were loathe to replicate here in the United States. There are also sound economic reasons for limiting the "dead hand" control of property that forces land to be used in ways that are outmoded and inefficient.

Baker v. Weedon

Remaindermen) v. (Life Tenant)
1972) 262 So. 2d 641; 57 A.L.R.3d 1183

MEMORY GRAPHIC

Instant Facts

John Weedon left a life estate to Weedon (P) and a remainder to the Bakers (D). Weedon (D) wishes to sale the land now to reap its value; Baker (P) wishes to retain ownership of the land to allow its value to increase.

Black Letter Rule

A trial court shall order a judicial sale only if it is in the best interest of both the freehold tenant and the holder of the future interest.

Case Vocabulary

ECONOMIC WASTE: To allow land to depreciate in value; to not put land to its best and most valuable use.
FUTURE INTEREST: An interest in land that is not currently possessory.
INHERITANCE: Property which descends to another upon the death of someone.
REMAINDERMEN: Those persons who have an interest in property that will not become possessory until some intervening estate has expired.
TRUST: A legal entity created by one person for the benefit of another; usually, the trustee has legal title to the property, and the beneficiary is entitled to the income from the trust.

Procedural Basis: Interlocutory appeal from ruling of the trial court ordering the sale of land.

Facts: John Weedon's first marriage to Lula Edwards resulted in two children, Florence Weedon Baker and Delette Weedon Jones. Florence Weedon Baker mothered three children, Henry Baker (P), Sarah Baker Lyman (P) and Louise Virginia Baker Heck (P). These children were the plaintiffs in the trial court and are the appellants here. After a second marriage, John Weedon finally married Anna Plaxico (D), 38 years his junior. Anna (D) and John had no children together. Anna Plaxico, now Anna Plaxico Weedon (D), was the defendant in the trial court and the appellee here. In his will, John Weedon left to Anna Plaxico a life estate and left to his grandchildren a contingent remainder: "I give to . . . Anna Plaxico Weedon (D) all of my property . . . during her life . . . and in the event she dies without issue then . . . I give . . . all of my property to my grandchildren." John Weedon died in 1932. Anna (D) ceased to farm the land in 1955 due to her age and began to rent to property. It is undisputed that this rental income and Anna's (D) other income is insufficient to support her. In 1964, just as the commercial value of the land was increasing rapidly, the state sought a right-of-way through the property. At trial, the property was worth $168,500. However, the property's estimated value in four years is placed at $336,000. Although Anna (D) now lives in a new home, she is in economic distress and prays that the land be sold so that she can reap her share of the property value. The Bakers (P) wish to allow the property to increase in value before it is sold. The trial court ordered the land sold because it felt that the land was being wasted. The Bakers (P) appeal.

Issue: Shall a trial court order a judicial sale only if it is in the best interest of all parties?

Decision and Rationale: (Patterson). Yes. Trial courts have jurisdiction to order the sale of land for the prevention of waste if the facts so merit. However, the trial court can order a sale only if it is in the best interest of all the parties. This rule has the necessary flexibility to meet unique situations and to yield equitable solutions. In this case, though it is true that a sale would benefit Weedon (D), it would bring great financial loss to the Bakers (P). Thus, a judicial sale is not in the best interest of all parties. We suggest, however, that a sale of part of the land may be equitable under the circumstances. Ordered reversed.

Analysis:

This case illustrates how the preference for free alienability is complicated when land is divided into a present interest and a future interest. The law prefers that property be alienable because it maximizes the value of land. When land is divided into present and future interests, however, the land is often worth more to the freehold tenant if it is not sold and more to the future tenant if it is sold. Thus, the law must make a choice. Several rules have developed in an attempt to maximize the value and equities to both the freehold tenant and the future tenant. Note, however, that no solution will make all parties happy. In order to avoid the problems created by a legal life estate followed by a remainder, a grantor can create a trust. In a trust, a trustee holds the legal fee simple to the property. The trustee must manage the fee simple for the benefit of all parties. He may allow the life tenant into possession or he may pay income from the fee simple to the life tenant, but in any case, he must do what is equitable for both the life tenant and the future tenant. Since the trustee holds the legal fee simple, he may easily sell the fee simple if it is in the best interests of both parties. Thus, it is far more flexible than a legal life estate followed by a remainder.

Mahrenholz v. County Board of School Trustees

(Holder of Future Interest) v. (Holder of Defeasible Fee Simple)

(1981) 93 Ill. App. 3d 366; 417 N.E.2d 138

MEMORY GRAPHIC

Instant Facts

The Huttons conveyed land to the School Board (D) "to be used for school purposes only." Subsequently, the school used the land for storage.

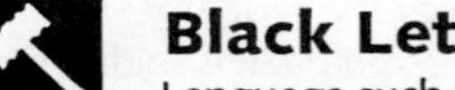

Black Letter Rule

Language such as "to be used for school purposes only" creates a fee simple determinable.

Case Vocabulary

DEFEASIBLE FEE SIMPLE: A fee simple estate in land which can be divested if a pre-determined condition subsequent actually occurs.

FEE SIMPLE DETERMINABLE: A fee simple which is divested from the owner and reverts back to the grantor upon the occurrence of a pre-determined condition subsequent.

FEE SIMPLE SUBJECT TO CONDITION SUBSEQUENT: A defeasible fee which gives the grantor the right to re-take the land from the grantee if a pre-specified condition subsequent actually occurs.

INTER VIVOS CONVEYANCE: A conveyance made while the grantor is alive.

POSSIBILITY OF REVERTER: The future interest that corresponds to the fee simple determinable. If the pre-specified condition subsequent occurs, the property automatically reverts to the grantor (who is the holder of the possibility of reverter).

Procedural Basis: Appeal from demurrer in action to quiet title.

Facts: In 1941 the Huttons conveyed property to the Trustees of School District No.1. The deed stated: "This land to be used for school purposes only; otherwise to revert to grantors herein." Also in 1941 the Huttons conveyed their reversionary interest in this property to Jacqmain. In 1959, Jacqmain conveyed this reversionary interest to Mahrenholz (P). When Mr. and Mrs. Hutton died, their only legal heir was Harry Hutton. In 1977 Harry Hutton conveyed any possibility of reverter or right of entry that he may have had in the land to Mahrenholz (P). Later in 1977 Hutton disclaimed any interest he had in the land to the School Board (D). The property that the Huttons conveyed to the school was used for classes until 1973. Since then, the school has used the property for storage. Mahrenholz (P) contends that the deed conveying the land to the school board created a determinable fee simple followed by a possibility of reverter. The school board (D) contends that the deed created a fee simple followed by right of entry.

Issue: Does language such as "to be used for school purposes only" create a fee simple determinable?

Decision and Rationale: (Jones). Yes. First, since neither a right of entry nor a possibility of reverter can be transferred by will or inter vivos conveyance, Mahrenholz (P) could not have acquired the land from Jacqmain. Thus, we must determine what interest, if any, Mahrenholz (P) acquired from Harry Hutton. To determine whether a fee simple on condition subsequent or a fee simple determinable was created, we need to examine the words in the deed. Words such as "so long as the land is used for school purposes" or "while it was used for school purposes" or "until the land ceased to be used for school purposes" create a fee simple determinable. Words such as "on the condition that the land be used for school purposes" or "provided that the land be used for school purposes" create a fee simple subject to condition subsequent. Upon examination of the language in the deed, it appears that the Huttons conveyed a fee simple determinable. The phrase "for school purpose only" suggest that Huttons wanted to give the land only as long as it was needed and no longer. The second phrase, "otherwise to revert to grantors," seems to trigger an automatic return of the property to the Huttons. Thus, the grant indicates a fee simple determinable. There are many cases where similar language was held to create a fee simple determinable. For example, in *U.S. v. 1119.15 Acres of Land*, "when said land cease to be used for school purposes it is to revert to the above grantor" was held to create a fee simple determinable. *Latham v. Illinois Central Railroad Co.* is distinguishable because in that case land was granted to the grantee "their successors and assigns *forever* . . . in case of non-use of said land for the above purposes, title shall revert back to grantors." In contrast, Hutton did not grant land forever, but only so long as it was used for school purposes. In *McElvain v. Dorris*, the grantor granted land "to be used for mill purposes, and if not for mill purposes the title reverts back to the former owner." The court held that this created a fee simple on condition subsequent. This case in not applicable for two reasons: (1) It is not clear whether the court held that this language created a fee simple on condition subsequent or whether it was referring to an earlier provision in the deed; (2) the court's holding may simply reflect the parties' agreement as to what the provision meant. A more appropriate case is *North v. Graham*. There, "said land . . . to revert to the party of the first whenever it ceases to be used . . ." was held to create a fee simple determinable. Therefore, the 1941 deed from the Huttons to the School Board (D) created a fee simple determinable. Reversed.

Analysis:

The case illustrates how significantly different legal outcomes can turn on the wording of a deed. If a deed is construed to create a fee simple determinable, the title *automatically* reverts to the grantor or his successor in interest if the condition subsequent is broken. If a deed is construed to create a fee simple on condition subsequent, the title reverts to the grantor or his successor only if he retakes the land. If he fails to retake the land, the grantee may acquire fee simple absolute by adverse possession or abandonment.

A CONDITION WHICH PROHIBITS THE SALE OF LAND IS A RESTRAINT ON WHO MAY USE THE LAND AND IS VOID UNLESS A FEE SIMPLE SUBJECT TO CONDITION SUBSEQUENT IS INTENDED

Mountain Brow Lodge No. 82, Independent Order of Odd Fellows v. Toscano

(Holder of Fee) v. (Possible Holder of Future Interest)
(1968) 257 Cal. App. 2d 22; 64 Cal. Rptr. 816

MEMORY GRAPHIC

Instant Facts

A deed provided that a lot shall revert back to the grantor if the grantee, a lodge (P), either failed to use the lot or attempted to sell it.

Black Letter Rule

The use of land may be restricted in a conveyance.

Case Vocabulary

HABENDUM CLAUSE: That portion of a deed which describes the restrictions or limitations that go along with the property being conveyed.

Procedural Basis: Appeal from final judgment in action to quiet title.

Facts: Toscano, an active member of the Mountain Brow Lodge (P), deeded property to the Lodge (P). The deed state that the land was conveyed in consideration of "love and affection." The deed provided that the lot shall revert back to Toscano if the Lodge (P) either failed to use the lot or attempted to sell or transfer it. The Lodge (P) contends that this language is a restraint on who may use the land. As such, the Lodge (P) contends, it is a restraint on alienation and is void. Toscano's heirs (D) contend that the language creates a fee simple subject to a condition subsequent.

Issue: May the use of land be restricted in a conveyance?

Decision and Rationale: (Gargano). Yes. Clearly, a condition which prohibits the sale of land is a restraint on who may use the land and as such is void. The remaining question, then, is whether the condition which requires that the Lodge (P) use the land created a defeasible fee or whether it is a void restraint on alienation. Considering that Toscano (D) was an active member of the lodge and that he conveyed it in "loving consideration," the clause which reads "the land is restricted for the *use* of the second party" meant that the land be used for Lodge purposes. It did not mean or intend to restrict alienation. Thus, this clause created a fee simple subject to condition subsequent. Even though a restraint on how land may be used can possibly be a restraint on who may use the land, such restraints are still allowed in California. Restraints on the use of land are also allowed in other jurisdictions. Judgment declaring the restriction on the sale of land reversed. Judgment declaring the restriction on the use of land affirmed.

Dissent: (Stone). The clause which requires that the Lodge (P) use the land is a restraint on alienation because it effectively prohibits the sale to another person.

Analysis:

This case again replays a fundamental theme of property law: The law should promote the free alienability of land. In this case, however, the court struggles to accommodate another principle of property law: The owner of property should be able to use his land as he desires, and he should be able to restrict the use of his land in a conveyance. As the dissent points out, these two goals often come into conflict. When the goals do come into conflict, courts will often weigh the two policy goals and choose that which yields the most equitable result.

COURT RULES THAT PROCEEDS FROM EMINENT DOMAIN PROCEEDING ARE TO BE DIVIDED BETWEEN THE HOLDER OF THE FEE SIMPLE DETERMINABLE AND THE HOLDER OF THE REVERTER

Ink v. City of Canton

(Holder of Reverter) v. (Holder of Fee Simple Determinable)

(1965) 4 Ohio St. 2d 51; 212 N.E.2d 574

M E M O R Y G R A P H I C

Instant Facts

The descendants of Harry Ink conveyed to The City of Canton (P) land to be used for park purposes only. Subsequently, the state of Ohio instituted eminent domain proceedings against the land.

Black Letter Rule

The proceeds from an eminent domain proceeding are to be divided between the holder of the fee simple on condition subsequent and the holder of the reverter.

Case Vocabulary

EMINENT DOMAIN: The right of a state to take private property for public use (the state, however, must pay for the property).

Procedural Basis: Appeal from judgment in action for declaratory judgment.

Facts: In 1936, the descendants of Harry Ink (P) conveyed land to the City of Canton (D). The land was for use as a park and for no other use. The City of Canton (D) used the land as restricted until 1961 when the state of Ohio condemned it using its power of eminent domain. The state paid $130,822 into an account to be paid to those with interests in the land. Ink (P) claims the right to retake the premises (and take the entire $130,822) since the land is no longer being used as a park. The City of Canton (D) claims that it gets the entire sum since it has not voluntarily elected to stop using the land for a park.

Issue: Should the proceeds from an eminent domain proceeding be divided between the holder of the fee simple on condition subsequent and the holder of the reverter?

Decision and Rationale: Yes. Where property is conveyed with a use restriction, it would seem reasonable that the land revert to the grantor when eminent domain proceedings prevent that use. This rule seems harsh to the grantee. On the other hand, the great weight of authority holds that there is no reverter when eminent domain proceedings prevent the land from being used as restricted. There are two justifications given for this. First, it is said that the grantor's interest is too remote to value. However, valuation of a reverter is often possible. Second, it is said that the grantee should be excused from using the land as required since the law (eminent domain) has made performance impossible. No reasoning is offered for this justification. To the contrary, this rule seems unfair for two reasons. First, the grantor's reverter is destroyed. Second, the grantee gets more than the original grant: He is given land without a use restriction. Originally, he was only given land with a use restriction. Where are grantee has paid for a fee simple on condition subsequent, we feel that the following division of the eminent domain proceeds seems logical: The grantee should be entitled to value of the land with a use restriction. The grantor should be entitled to the value of the land with no restriction *less* the value of the land with a use restriction. The grantor should get this because this is what he refrained from conveying to the grantee. In this case, The City of Canton (D) paid nothing for the fee. Also, The City of Canton (D) has a fiduciary duty to use the land for a park. Thus, the rule stated above as applied to this case yields the following result: The City of Canton (D) gets the value of the land with a use restriction. Ink (P) gets the value of the land with no restriction *less* the value of the land with a use restriction. If The City of Canton (D) fails to use its proceeds for park purposes, this money shall revert to Ink (P).

Analysis:

In *Baker v. Weedon*, the issue was whether to sell the land and divide the proceeds between the owner of the freehold and the holder of the future interest. The solution crafted by the court was that the land be sold if it is in the best interest of both parties. Here, the issue is not whether to sell the land, but how to divide the proceeds. Again, the court simply does what is fair: Divide the proceeds in proportion to the interests held by the respective parties.

Chapter 4

Future interests are called future interests for one simple reason: the owner of the estate is not entitled to possess the land today.

There are five types of future interests: reversion, possibility of reverter, right of entry, remainder, and executory interest. A reversion is a future interest that remains in a grantor when he grants a lesser estate than the one that he owns. For example, suppose that A has a fee simple and grants to "B for life." A has given B less than a fee simple, so A has a reversion. B has a life estate. When B dies, the property will revert to the ownership of A. Notice that a reversion is certain to become possessory at some point in the future.

A possibility of reverter is a future interest that remains in a grantor when he grants a fee simple determinable. For example, A grants land "to school so long as the school teaches Algebra." The school has a fee simple determinable estate in the land. A has a possibility of reverter. If the school does not teach Algebra, the estate reverts to A. Notice that the possibility of reverter is a future interest that may or may not become possessory at some point in the future.

A right of entry is a future interest that remains in a grantor when he grants a fee simple subject to a condition subsequent. For example, A grants land "to school, but if school fails to teach Algebra, grantor has a right of entry." The school has a fee simple on condition subsequent. A has a right of entry. If the school does not teach Algebra, A may elect to enter and retake the estate. Notice that the right of entry is a future interest that may or may not become possessory at some point in the future.

A remainder is a future interest created in a *grantee* that may become possessory upon the expiration of some preceding estate. There are two types of remainders: vested remainders and contingent remainders. A vested remainder is a remainder that is not subject to a condition precedent. For example, A grants "to B for life, then to C in fee simple." B has a life estate which entitles him to present possession. C has a vested remainder. He gets what remains after B's life estate ends. Notice that unlike the reversion, possibility of reverter and right of entry, the remainder is not a future interest in the grantor, but in a grantee. A vested remainder may be defeased by a third party. For example, A grants "to B for life, then to C, but if C does not learn Algebra in one year, then to D." C has a vested remainder because he has a future interest that may become possessory upon the termination of B's estate. However, B's interest will be divested if he does not learn Algebra in one year. The second type of remainder is a contingent remainder. A contingent remainder is a remainder that is subject to a condition subsequent. For example, A grants "to B for life, then to C in fee simple if C learns Algebra." B has a life estate which entitles him to present possession. C has a contingent remainder. He gets what remains after B's life estate if he learns Algebra. Notice that a remainder is a future interest that may or may not become possessory at some point in the future.

An executory interest is a future interest in a grantee. There are two types of executory interests: springing executory interests and shifting executory interests. A springing executory interest springs out of the grantor at some future date. The springing executory interest divests the grantor of ownership. For example, A grants "to B when she learns Algebra." A has a fee simple. When and if B learns algebra, B will gain a fee simple that will spring out of A's interest. A will be divested. A shifting executory interest divests a preceding grantee of ownership. For example, A grants "to B, but if C learns Algebra, then to C." B, a grantee, has a fee simple. When and if C learns Algebra, C will gain a fee simple. This fee simple will *shift* from B to C. Notice that executory interests are future interests that may or may not become possessory at some point in time.

Perspective (Continued)
Future Interests

As has been mentioned many times before, there is a general policy in the law to make land freely alienable. In consequence, certain restraints on alienation are void. For example, in a transfer of a freehold estate, any language which purports to limit the grantee's ability to transfer the estate *to another person* is void. But, restrictions on the alienation of freehold estates are not alone in prohibiting the free alienability of property. The mere *existence* of a future interest may inhibit the alienation of property. For example, suppose that A grants "to B for life, then to C in fee simple." B has a present life estate and C has a remainder in fee simple. Further, suppose that B wishes to sell the parcel of land. He will have a difficult time finding a buyer for the land because he cannot sell absolute ownership. Any owner who buys B's interest will have to turn over the land to C when B dies. The purchaser will not be inclined to do this, especially if he intends to build structures on the land. In order for the land to be sold, it will likely require B and C to come together and agree on mutually acceptable terms. This will be difficult. Thus, the mere *existence* of future interests can inhibit the alienability of land. In consequence, the law has developed many rules that void certain types of future interests.

One such rule destroys certain types of contingent remainders. A contingent remainder is destroyed if it does not vest before or at the time the immediately preceding freehold estate ends. For example, suppose that A grants "to B for life, then to C when he finishes college." Further, suppose that B dies while C is still in college. When B dies, C's contingent remainder does not vest if and until he finishes college. After B dies but before C finishes college no person is seised of the land (that is, no person has possession). As a result, since C's contingent remainder does not vest either before or at the time the preceding estate ends, it is destroyed. When the contingent remainder is destroyed, the land reverts to the grantor in fee simple. Clearly, the land in the hands of the grantor in fee simple is more alienable than the land waiting for C to finish college before vesting. Thus, this rule makes land more alienable.

No gap in seisin can precede an executory interest. Therefore, the destructibility rule cannot destroy executory interests. Therefore, the common law Rule Against Perpetuities was created to control limitations on the alienability of land caused by the executory interests. The Rule Against Perpetuities applies to both contingent remainders and executory interests.

The Rule Against Perpetuities is simply stated: no interest is valid unless it *must* vest, *if at all*, not later than 21 years after some life in being at the creation of the interest. For example, in 1995 A grants "to B when B finishes college." B has a springing executory interest in fee simple. Her interest will spring from the grantor when she finishes college. However, her executory interest is voided by the Rule Against Perpetuities. B's interest may vest the following year, if she finishes college the following year. B's interest may vest in four years if she finishes college by then. Her interest may vest 30 years later if it takes her that long to finish college. Or B may die tomorrow. It is clear that it is not true that B's interest *must* vest within 21 years. Thus, it is void. On the other hand, suppose that in 1995 A grants "to B, but if B does not finish college, to C." B is alive when the grant is made. B's interest is valid because it *vests* when it is created. The Rule Against Perpetuities does not apply to vested interests. C's interest is valid because it will either vest or not vest within 21 years of B's life. If B finishes college, then C's interest will fail to vest during B's life. If B dies before finishing college, then C's interest will vest upon B's death (which is within 21 years of B's life).

Chapter Overview Outline
Future Interests

Chapter 4

NOTE: THE PURPOSE OF THIS OUTLINE IS TO ORGANIZE THE CASES SO THAT ONE CAN QUICKLY UNDERSTAND THE RELEVANCE OF EACH CASE TO THE COURSE. NO ATTEMPT IS MADE IN THIS OVERVIEW TO ADDRESS EVERY CONCEPT THAT MUST BE STUDIED. BE SURE TO READ THE ENTIRE CASEBOOK AND/OR OTHER MATERIALS TO GAIN A FULL UNDERSTANDING OF ALL CONCEPTS.

I. Introduction
  A. A future interest is a legal right to own and enjoy property at a future time—it is a present interest that has the potential to become possessory at a later date. For example:
    1. A party may have, in the form of a future interest, the right to own and enjoy a piece of property after its current owner passes away.
  B. The law of future interests allows a property owner to determine what will happen to certain property not only at his or her death, but at the death of future persons as well.
  C. There are two general categories of future interests: future interests retained by the grantor and future interests created in a transferee. These categories, in turn, contain five types of future interests: the reversion, possibility of reverter, right of entry, remainder, and executory interest.

II. Future Interests Retained by the Transferor
  A. Reversion
    1. A reversion is a future interest that remains in a grantor when he or she gives another person a lesser estate than the one that the grantor owns and does not specify who is to take the property when that lesser estate expires.
      a. Example: If an owner of a fee simple grants to another a life estate without specifying what is done with the property after the transferee dies, the grantor has a reversion.
    2. For a grantor to retain a reversion, there need not be any guarantee that the reversion will become possessory in the future.
      a. For example, if the grantor conveys a life estate to a transferee and specifies that the property is then to go to a second transferee if that transferee survives the first, the grantor retains a reversion which will become possessory only if the second transferee dies before the first.
    3. Reversions can be both transferred during life and devised upon death.
  B. The Possibility of Reverter
    1. A possibility of reverter is a future interest that remains in a grantor when he or she gives to another a fee simple determinable estate.
    2. For example, if a grantor gives the state a piece of property "so long as that property is used for educational purposes," the grantor retains a possibility of reverter. Such a grant is a grant of a fee simple determinable estate.
  C. The Right of Entry
    1. A right of entry is a future interest retained by a grantor when he or she grants a fee simple that is subject to a condition subsequent.
    2. A right of entry only exists when the grantor specifically retains the power to terminate the granted estate.

III. Future Interests Created in the Transferee
  A. Remainders
    1. A remainder is a future interest created in a grantee that holds the possibility (not the certainty) of becoming possessory upon the expiration of some preceding estate.
    2. There are two general types of remainders:
      a. A *vested remainder* is a remainder that is given to an ascertainable person and is not subject to any sort of condition precedent other than the natural termination of a prior estate.
        (1) For example, if a grantor grants an estate "to X for life, and then to Y and his heirs," Y has a vested remainder because Y is an ascertainable person and no conditions precedent exist to hinder the transfer.
        (2) A vested remainder that is certain to become possessory is referred to as an indefeasibly vested remainder. One not certain to become possessory is a vested remainder subject to divestment.
      b. A *contingent remainder* is one that is given to an unascertainable person or is subject to the happening of a specified condition precedent.
        (1) For example, if a grantor grants an estate "to X for life, and then to Y's heirs," and Y is still alive, Y's heirs are not ascertainable at the time of the grant (since Y has no heirs until he is dead) and the remain-

der is therefore a contingent remainder.

(2) A contingent remainder also exists when a grantor grants "to X for life, and then to X's heirs if X graduates from college before Y," because X's graduation from college before Y does so is a condition precedent.

c. The law often favors vested remainders over contingent remainders because vested remainders are more flexible and more alienable than contingent remainders. *Swanson v. Swanson*.

B. Executory Interests

1. The Basics of Executory Interests

a. An executory interest is a future interest created in a transferee that has the ability to cut short or divest a preceding estate and must do so in order to take effect.

(1) For example, if a grantor gives a piece of property "to X so long as he remains employed in the education field, then to Y," Y has an executory interest.

b. There are two basic types of executory interests: shifting executory interests and springing executory interests.

(1) A springing executory interest is one which springs out of the grantor at some future date and thereby divests the grantor of ownership.

(a) For example, if X makes a grant "to Y and his heirs, to take possession in January of 2003," X has created a springing executory interest.

(2) A shifting executory interest is one which divests a prior grantee of ownership.

(a) If instead X were to make a grant "to Y, but if Y dies without any surviving children, to Z," X has created a shifting executory interest.

IV. Trusts

A. Another type of estate is the trust. In the trust, a trustee holds the legal title to trust property and is charged with managing the property for the benefit of the beneficiaries, who own equitable title in the trust property.

B. Trusts are frequently the subject property of future interests. *Swanson v. Swanson*.

1. For example, X may convey a fee simple estate to Y, to be held in trust, the income from the property to go to Z for the duration of her life and the principal to pass to Z's heirs upon her death. In such a situation, Y holds legal title to the property, Z owns an equitable life estate, and Z's heirs own an equitable contingent remainder.

V. Destruction of Contingent Future Interests

A. Introduction

1. Contingent future interests started to gain widespread use in 16th and 17th century England. Despite their popularity, however, the judiciary were not fond of these contingent interests because their existence often made land unmarketable.

2. As such, several common law rules were developed which sought to preclude parties from creating contingent future interests. Among these are the rules regarding the destructibility of contingent remainders, the Rule in Shelly's Case, the Doctrine of Worthier Title, and the Rule against Perpetuities (some of the more complicated subjects studied in law school).

B. The Destructibility of Contingent Remainders

1. The doctrine of the destructibility of contingent remainders holds that a contingent remainder in real property is destroyed if it fails to vest either at or before the natural termination of the prior estate.

a. The destructibility doctrine does not apply to contingent remainders in trust property. Nor does it apply to executory interests, which is why some English courts created a preference for construing a limitation as a contingent remainder instead of an executory interest.

2. A majority of American jurisdictions have abolished the doctrine of the destructibility of contingent remainders.

C. The Rule in Shelly's Case

1. The Rule in Shelly's Case holds that if a grantor gives a person a life estate and in the same instrument gives a remainder to that person's heirs, and the life estate and the remainder are either both legal or both equitable, the remainder becomes a remainder in fee simple.

2. At that point, the life estate generally merges into the remainder to become a vested remainder in fee that belongs to the owner of the original life estate. The estate can then be

transferred or sold when it previously could not be so transferred.

3. Most American jurisdictions have abolished the Rule in Shelly's Case.

D. The Doctrine of Worthier Title

1. The Doctrine of Worthier Title holds that where a grantor making an inter vivos transfer of land to another leaves his own heirs either a remainder or an executory interest, the resulting future interest transforms into a reversion in the grantor.

2. Designed as a way of furthering the alienability of land (a reversion can be transferred while a remainder or executory interest may not be transferrable), the Doctrine of Worthier Title has largely been abolished in the United States.

E. The Rule Against Perpetuities

1. The Rule Against Perpetuities at Common Law

a. The Rule against Perpetuities holds that "[n]o interest is good unless it must vest, if at all, not later than twenty-one years after some life in being at the creation of the interest." *John C. Gray, The Rule Against Perpetuities.*

(1) To put it another way, if a future interest such as a contingent remainder is not absolutely certain to vest within a life in being plus twenty-one years, it is void.

(2) For example, if a grantor leaves an estate "to X for life, then to X's first grandchild to reach age 24r," the second part of the grant will be found to violate the Rule against Perpetuities because it is not certain that the first grandchild to reach the age of 24 will do so within the lifetime of X plus 21 years.

b. The purpose of the Rule against Perpetuities is to invalidate future interests that might vest too far in the future.

(1) When a particular future interest violates the Rule against Perpetuities, the Rule requires that the violating interest be erased and the remaining interests stand as if the stricken interests never existed.

(2) Thus, in the above example, the "then to X's first grandchild to reach the age of twenty-four" portion of the transfer is stricken, X receives a life estate, and there exists a reversion in the grantor.

c. The Rule against Perpetuities considers what might happen at the time the interest is created—when applied in its purest form, it does not wait to see if the interest actually vests during the perpetuities period. *Jee v. Audley.*

d. The Rule against Perpetuities does not apply to reversions, possibilities of reverter, and rights of entry (the three future interests retained by the grantor), because these rights are deemed to have vested as soon as they arise.

(1) It does, however, apply to all other types of future interests, as well as to other land-related agreements, such as commercial option agreements. *Symphony Space v. Pergola Properties.*

e. When a gift is to a class of persons (such as "to X's daughters"), vesting cannot occur until the class is closed (i.e., until X can no longer have any daughters (i.e., X is dead!)).

2. The Wait-and-See Doctrine

a. An alternative to the traditional application of the Rule against Perpetuities that so often strikes down interests not certain to vest within the perpetuities period.

b. There are two general approaches to the wait-and-see doctrine.

(1) The first approach holds a contingent interest valid if it actually vests within the common law perpetuities period (a life in being plus twenty-one years).

(2) The second view, promoted by the Uniform Statutory Rule Against Perpetuities (USRAP), holds that if the contingent interest vests within a certain predetermined period of time (90 years under USRAP), it is valid (i.e., there is no need to find a life in being from which to measure the perpetuities period).

3. The Abolition of the Rule Against Perpetuities

a. In recent years, many American jurisdictions have completely done away with the Rule against Perpetuities.

b. Others have created a way around the Rule by permitting the creation of perpetual trusts, or trusts that can endure forever without interference from the Rule.

(1) Under the current American system, perpetual trusts can provide significant tax advantages / tax avoidance advantages.

WORDS OF SURVIVORSHIP SHOULD BE CONSTRUED SUCH THAT REMAINDERS ARE DEEMED VESTED RATHER THAN CONTINGENT

Swanson v. Swanson

(Decedent's Wife & Children) v. (Decedent's Daughter-In-Law)
(1999) 270 Ga. 733, 514 S.E.2d 822

Instant Facts

A lawsuit arose when a decedent's daughter-in-law attempted to claim assets left by his will to her deceased husband–the decedent's son.

Black Letter Rule

When a court must determine whether a remainder is contingent or vested, the law favors construing conditions to be subsequent and remainders to be vested.

Case Vocabulary

CONDITION PRECEDENT: A condition that must occur before a future interest can become possessory.
CONDITION SUBSEQUENT: A condition that will terminate a future interest if the condition occurs.
CONTINGENT REMAINDER: A remainder that is either given to an unascertainable person or is subject to the happening of a specified condition precedent.
DEFEASANCE: The termination of a property interest.
LIFE BENEFICIARY: One who receives the benefit of something (such as a trust) during the life of a measuring person.
LIFE ESTATE: An estate that terminates upon the death of some specified person.
REMAINDER: A future interest created in a grantee that has the possibility (not the certainty) of becoming possessory upon the expiration of some preceding estate.
TESTATE: Having left a will (i.e., to die having left a will).
TRUST CORPUS: The trust principal, or the property that makes up the principal of the trust (as differentiated from the interest or income of the trust).
VEST: To become possessory.
VESTED REMAINDER: A remainder that is given to an ascertainable person and is not subject to any sort of condition precedent other than the natural termination of a prior estate.
VESTED SUBJECT TO DEFEASANCE: A vested remainder that is potentially subject to termination (i.e., a remainder that is not certain to take effect).

Procedural Basis: Appeal to the Supreme Court of Georgia of a trial court's decision to grant summary judgment in favor of the family (D) of a deceased man whose daughter-in-law (P), under protest by the family, was attempting to claim some assets under his will.

Facts: When he died in 1970, George Swanson left a will that created two trusts in which his wife, Gertrude, had a life estate, the remainder to go to George's nine children. George was predeceased by one of his sons, Bennie, who left everything he had to his wife, Peggy Swanson (P). After George's death, Peggy (P) attempted to lay claim to her deceased husband's remainder interests in the two trusts. George's wife and other children (D) objected, and a lawsuit was filed for the purpose of determining who had what rights under the trust.

Issue: Does the law create a preference for vested remainders over contingent remainders?

Decision and Rationale: (Fletcher, J.) Yes. To distinguish between vested and contingent remainders, courts must determine whether, at the time an instrument of transfer takes effect, there exists a person who would take all of the transferred property if the life estate were to end immediately. If there is such a person, the remainder is vested subject to either partial or complete defeasance. If no such person can be identified, then the remainder is subject to a condition precedent and is a contingent remainder. In making a determination between contingent and vested remainders, Georgia law has followed two common law principles: (1) the law favors construing conditions to be subsequent, and (2) the law favors vested remainders when there is any doubt as to the nature of a remainder. The first trust at issue in this case provides that Gertrude Swanson, George's wife, can dispose of the corpus of the trust either during her life or in her will, and if she fails to do so, then the corpus passes to George's nine children in equal shares; the trust further provides that if any of the children "should not be in life at the time of death of my said wife, the share of such deceased child shall go to his or her surviving children, per stirpes." Following George's death, there were immediately identifiable persons who would take the property if Gertrude's life estate ended: George's nine children. Therefore each child, including Bennie, had a vested remainder interest. Additionally, there were two conditions subsequent attached to the vested remainder. These conditions, which carried with them the possibility of bringing about the total defeasance of the vested remainder, were: (1) Gertrude's exercise of her power of appointment, and (2) a child predeceasing Gertrude but leaving children who survived her. Neither of these conditions occurred, so therefore Bennie's interest remained fully vested and passed to his wife (P) under his will. Holding these remainders to be vested and not defeased by the occurrence of a condition subsequent is consistent with our prior decisions. The second trust also provides for equal distribution among George's nine children. As with the first trust, then, Bennie's remainder was vested and therefore passed to his wife (P) upon his death. In conclusion, we hold that Bennie's one-ninth interest in the trusts passed to his wife (P) because his remainder had vested and no condition subsequent occurred prior to the termination of the life estate. This holding is supported by both case law and common law principles. Reversed.

Analysis:

Swanson v. Swanson teaches two significant principles of law with respect to future interests. First, it shows how trust property can be the subject of future interests. In most law school property law classes, future interests are taught with examples involving the transfer of land, such as the classic "O to A for life, then to B and his heirs." However, as this case teaches, land is not the only property that can be the subject of a future interest—personal property can also be the subject of a future interest. In this case, it was the trust corpus that invoked the future interest rules. While the opinion does not state what property made up the trust corpus, it is entirely possible that it could have been made up of solely personal property (stocks, bonds, cash, etc.) The second principle of law taught by *Swanson* is the law's preference for vested remainders over contingent remainders. The reason the law favors vested remainders is they are often more flexible and more readily transferrable than contingent remainders. Vested remainders are remainders given to ascertainable persons that are not subject to any conditions precedent other than the natural termination of a prior estate. Because this is so, a person can immediately transfer his or her vested remainder upon the making of the grant. For example, if a grantor grants an estate "to X for life, and then to Y," Y has a vested remainder because Y is an ascertainable person and no conditions precedent exist to hinder the transfer. In other words, Y is certain to get the property, and he therefore has an interest that he can transfer immediately, before X's life estate even ends—i.e., he can sell his vested remainder. Contingent remainders, on the other hand, are remainders that are either given to an unascertainable person or are subject to the happening of a specified condition precedent. Because this is so, the parties must wait to see what happens before anyone is certain to take the property, meaning no one has the ability to immediately transfer or sell a contingent remainder. For example, if a grantor grants an estate "to X for life, and then to Y's heirs," and Y is still alive, Y's heirs are not ascertainable at the time of the grant (Y has no heirs until he is dead) and the remainder is therefore a contingent remainder. Because at the time of the grant it is unclear who will receive the property after X, no one has the immediate ability to transfer that interest. Instead, the involved parties must again wait to see what happens, meaning the interest lays stagnant and cannot be sold until ownership becomes clear. Because the law favors the alienability of land, the law favors the remainder that does not hinder that alienability—the vested remainder.

COURT RULES THAT IT WILL NOT WAIT AND SEE IF AN INTEREST VESTS DURING THE PERPETUITIES PERIOD; INSTEAD, IT WILL LOOK TO SEE WHAT MIGHT HAPPEN

Jee v. Audley

(Holder of Executory Interest) v. (Grantor's Estate)

(1787) 1 Cox 324; 29 Eng. Rep. 1186

M E M O R Y   G R A P H I C

Instant Facts

Edward Audley bequeathed an executory interest to the Jee daughters (P). John and Elizabeth Jee were too old to have more children.

Black Letter Rule

The rule against perpetuities considers what might happen at the time an interest is created.

Case Vocabulary

AFTER-BORN: An individual born after the death of a testator.

Procedural Basis: Action to declare a future interest as nonviolative of the rule against perpetuities.

Facts: Edward Audley bequeathed an interest in 1000 Pounds to his wife for life. Upon his wife's death, Audley willed the principal to his niece, Mary Hall, in fee tail. If Mary Hall dies without issue, than the principal is to go to the daughters then living of John and Elizabeth Jee. Edward Audley's wife predeceased him. When Edward Audley died, John and Elizabeth Jee were 70 years old; Mary Hall was 40 and without children. The Jee daughters (P) sue to have the principal secured to them in the event Mary Hall dies without issue. The Jee Daughters (P) contend that since John and Elizabeth Jee are so old, they are unlikely to have more daughters; since John and Elizabeth Jee are unlikely to have more daughters, the Jee daughters (P) contend that the class of Jee daughters is fixed and determined; finally, since the class of Jee daughters is fixed and determined, the Jee daughters (P) contend that the interest is not remote and does not violate the rule against perpetuities. On the other side, the Audley estate (D) contends that the interest held by the Jee daughters is void because it violates the letter of the rule against perpetuities.

Issue: Does the rule against perpetuities consider what might happen at the time the interest is created rather than wait and see if an interest actually vests during the perpetuities period?

Decision and Rationale: (Kenyon). Yes. It would be unwise to hold as a matter of law that John and Elizabeth Jee are too old to have children. If this path were followed in this case, perhaps a future court would hold as a matter of law that a 25-year-old couple could not have children. This path is too dangerous to follow. Moreover, we must look to see whether the interest was valid when created, not whether it is valid now. In this case, the interest created in the Jee daughters was void when created because John and Elizabeth Jee might have children 10 years after Edward Audley died, and then Mary Hall might die without issue 50 years afterwards. Thus, the interest might vest far in the future. It is void. Judgment for Audley (D).

Analysis:

This case establishes the what-might-happen test: The court considers what might happen *at the time the interest is created.* The rule is sometimes justified because it gives certainty to title. When an interest is created, the rule against perpetuities can be immediately applied to either validate or void an interest. However, as this case illustrates, the what-might-happen test sometimes belies reality. The alternative is the wait-and-see test. In this test, the court will wait and see if the interest vests within the perpetuities period. The virtue of this test is that it conforms to reality. However, this rule makes it difficult to determine whether an interest will be void or not; it increases uncertainty.

The Symphony Space, Inc. v. Pergola Properties, Inc.

(Property Owner) v. (Holder of Buy-Back Option)
(1996) 88 N.Y.2d 466, 669 N.E.2d 799, 646 N.Y.S.2d 641

MEMORY GRAPHIC

Instant Facts

A property owner filed a declaratory judgment action when the holder of a buy-back option notified the owner of its intent to buy back the property covered by the agreement.

Black Letter Rule

There is no exception to the Rule Against Perpetuities for commercial option agreements.

Case Vocabulary

BUY-BACK OPTION AGREEMENT: A commercial agreement which gives one party a right to purchase property from its current owner but carries with it no obligation to do so.
PREEMPTIVE RIGHTS: The right to purchase something before it is sold to someone else (a right of first refusal).
RULE AGAINST PERPETUITIES: Common law rule which holds that no contingent interest will be permitted unless that interest must vest, if at all, within a certain period of time determined by a life in being at the creation of the contingent interest plus twenty-one years.
WAIT AND SEE DOCTRINE: Alternative to the stringent application of the Rule against Perpetuities under which contingent interests are only voided when they do not actually vest during the perpetuities period—the possibility that a contingent interest might vest outside the period is irrelevant.

Procedural Basis: Appeal to the Court of Appeals of New York (New York's highest court) of two lower court decisions refusing to exempt commercial option agreements from the purview of New York's version of the Rule against Perpetuities.

Facts: In 1978, Broadwest Realty Corp. sold a two-story building in Manhattan to Symphony Space, Inc. (P), a non-profit entity devoted to the arts. The sale price of the building, which contained both a theater and office space, was $10,010, well below the property's market value. The deal included a lease-back provision under which Broadwest leased the office-space portion of the building from Symphony (P) for $1 per year. It also included a 25-year mortgage with Broadwest serving as mortgagee, and, finally, for an additional sum of $10, Broadwest was granted the option to repurchase the building "at any time after July 1, 1979, so long as the Notice of Election specifies that the Closing is to occur during any of the calendar years 1987, 1993, 1998, and 2003." The deal was advantageous to both sides for tax reasons. In 1981, three years after the initiation of the sale/lease-back, Broadwest sold and assigned its interest in the lease, option agreement, and mortgage to another party for $4.8 million. That party then transferred its newly-acquired interest to Pergola Properties, Inc., and four other entities (D's) as tenants in common. Because the value of the property had increased significantly since the original deal had been signed, Pergola (D) decided to exercise the option to buy back the premises. Hoping to keep ownership of the building, Symphony (P) filed a declaratory judgment action arguing that the option agreement that it originally entered into with Broadwest was void under New York's version of the Rule against Perpetuities. The trial and intermediate appellate courts agreed with Symphony (P), and Pergola (D) appealed to New York's highest court.

Issue: Are options to purchase commercial property exempt from the Rule against Perpetuities and its prohibition of remote vesting?

Decision and Rationale: (Kaye, C.J.) No. New York has recognized the Rule against Perpetuities since 1830. As with the common law rule, the purpose of our version is (1) to limit control of title to real property by dead landowners who seek to reach into future generations; and (2) to "ensure the productive use and development of property by its current beneficial owners by simplifying ownership, facilitating exchange and freeing property from . . . impediments to alienabilty." *Metropolitan Transp. Auth. v. Bruken Realty Corp.* Our current statutory version of the rule, found in EPTL 9-1.1, contains two subsections important for today's action. First, subsection (a) voids any estate in which the conveying instrument suspends the absolute power of alienation for longer than lives in being at the creation of the estate plus twenty-one years. Second, subsection (b) prohibits remote vesting by invalidating any interest not certain to vest within the specified time period. In addition to these statutory formulas, New York also retains the common law rule against unreasonable restraints on alienation. It is against this background that we consider the validity of the option agreement in the present case. Pergola (D) proffers three grounds for upholding the option: the statutory prohibition against remote vesting does not apply to commercial options; the option here cannot be exercised beyond the statutory period; and this Court should adopt the "wait and see" doctrine. We will consider each in turn. Under the common law, options to purchase land are subject to the rule against remote vesting. Under New York law, the same is true even when options to purchase are part of an arms-length commercial transaction and not a family disposition of land. In reaching the conclusion that EPTL 9-1.1(b) applies to commercial option agreements, this court has placed emphasis on the fact that the legislature specifically intended to incorporate the American common-law rules governing perpetuities into the New York statute. Furthermore, because the common law prohibition against remote vesting applies to both commercial and noncommercial options, it likewise follows that the legislature intended EPTL

9-1.1(b) to apply to commercial purchase options as well. Consequently, any creation of a general exception to EPTL 9-1.1(b) for all commercial purchase options would remove an entire class of contingent future interests that the legislature intended the statute to cover. Such a statutory change would require legislative action. Pergola (D) cites *Metropolitan Transp. Auth. v. Bruken Realty Corp.* in support of its position. However, *Bruken* applies only to preemptive rights, and because preemptive rights only minimally affect alienability of land, they are treated differently from option agreements. In the present case, the option agreement creates precisely the sort of control over future disposition of the property that we have previously associated with purchase options and that the common law rule against remote vesting seeks to prevent. The option grants its holder absolute power to purchase the property at the holder's whim and at a token price. The property owner is thus discouraged from investing in improvements to the property. Furthermore, the option's existence significantly impedes the owner's ability to sell the property, thereby rendering it practically inalienable. If the option is exercisable beyond the statutory perpetuities period, refusing to enforce it would thus further the purpose and rationale underlying the statutory prohibition against remote vesting. Pergola (D) alternatively claims that the agreement does not permit exercise of the option after expiration of the statutory perpetuities period, meaning there is no conflict with the Rule against Perpetuities. Where the parties to a transaction are corporations and no measuring lives are stated in the instruments, the perpetuities period is simply 21 years. The agreement at issue here allows the option holder to exercise the option "at any time during any Exercise Period" set forth in the agreement. Moreover, the agreement provides that the option may be exercised "at any time after July 1, 1979," so long as the closing date is scheduled during 1987, 1993, 1998, or 2003. Even factoring in the requisite notice, the option could potentially be exercised as late as July 2003—more than 24 years after its creation. Pergola's (D) contention that the agreement does not permit exercise of the option beyond the 21-year period is thus contradicted by the plain language of the instrument. Nor can New York's "saving statute," which creates a presumption that a grantor intended to create a valid estate, be invoked to shorten the duration of the exercise period under the agreement. While the saving statute obligates reviewing courts to avoid constructions that frustrate the parties' intended purposes, it does not authorize courts to rewrite instruments that unequivocally allow interests to vest outside the perpetuities period. The rules of construction of EPTL 9-1.3 apply only if a contrary intention does not appear in the instrument. The unambiguous language of the agreement here expresses the parties' intent that the option be exercisable at any time during a 24-year period. Thus, the instrument does not permit a construction that the parties intended the option to last only 21 years. For this reason, the saving statute is inapplicable. Pergola (D) next urges that we adopt the "wait and see" doctrine, which holds that an interest is valid if it actually vests during the perpetuities period, irrespective of what might have happened. The option here would survive under the "wait and see" approach since it was exercised in 1987, well within the 21-year limitation. This court, however, has long refused to "wait and see" whether a perpetuities violation in fact occurs. The very language of EPTL 9-1.1, moreover, precludes us from adopting that approach. Under the statute, an interest is invalid "unless it must vest, if at all, not later than twenty-one years after one or more lives in being." Because the option here could have vested after expiration of the 21-year perpetuities period, it offends the rule. We therefore conclude that the option agreement is invalid. Finally, Pergola (D) argues that, if the option fails, the contract of sale conveying the property from Broadwest to Symphony (P) should be rescinded due to the mutual mistake of the parties. Such a rescission is inappropriate. A contract entered into under mutual mistake of fact is generally subject to rescission. However, the mistake here is one of law, and rescission is therefore not required. The Rule against Perpetuities reflects the public policy of the State. Granting the relief requested by Pergola (D) would thus be contrary to public policy since it would compel performance of contracts violative of the rule. Affirmed.

Analysis:

Symphony is an instructive case because it provides a good example of how the common law Rule against Perpetuities works to limit a prior owner's control of property. Additionally, it provides the reader with some introduction to a current alternative version or reading of the common law rule that is gaining some acceptance in American law. One of the more difficult subjects studied in law school, the Rule against Perpetuities holds that "[n]o interest is good unless it must vest, if at all, not later than twenty-one years after some life in being at the creation of the interest." *John C. Gray, The Rule Against Perpetuities*. To put it another way, if a future interest such as a contingent remainder (the Rule does not apply to reversions, possibilities of reverter, and rights of entry) is not absolutely certain to vest within a life in being at the time of the creation of the instrument plus twenty-one years, it is void. In determining whether an interest is void under the Rule, one must first identify the measuring life, or the "life in being." The measuring life can be anyone alive at the time of the creation of the future interest, though it generally is found to belong to someone who has the power to control the time at which the future interest will vest. Thus, the measuring life may be that of a prior life tenant, the party who is to take the contingent interest, any person who has the ability to affect the identity of that taker, or anyone who has the power to affect a condition precedent attached to the interest. Once the measuring life is determined, an interest's validity is ascertained by looking to whether the interest must vest within the perpetuities period, which, again, is the life in being plus twenty-one years. If the interest is not certain to vest within that period of time, the interest is deemed void and is stricken from the grant. For example, if a grantor leaves an estate "to X for life, then to X's first grandchild to reach age twenty-four," the second part of the grant will be found to violate the Rule against Perpetuities. This is because it is not certain that the first grandchild to reach the age of twenty-four will do so within the lifetime of X plus twenty-one years (it is possible that X will die before the birth of his first grandchild). Under the Rule, the invalid interest will then be stricken, leaving the grant to read simply "to X for life," meaning X receives a life estate and the grantor gets a reversion. The purpose of the Rule against Perpetuities, as the *Symphony* opinion states, is to both further alienability and marketability of land and to encourage landowners to make improvements to their land. Without the Rule against Perpetuities, dead landowners would have that ability to control what happens to property for generations into the future. Furthermore, because landowners down the chain of control would have

no ability to sell the land (since the dead landowner had essentially prohibited it), there would thus be less incentive to improve the land. For example, as Judge Kaye points out in *Symphony*, if Symphony were found to not be able to sell the building at issue to anyone but Pergola, and it further was only able to receive a nominal purchase price upon sale, it would have no incentive to make major renovations to better the property. Again, the law favors improving property. *Symphony* is also instructive because it provides the reader with an introduction to one of the current alternative theories to the common law Rule against Perpetuities—the wait-and-see doctrine. In recent times, many lawmakers, judges, and commentators have begun to argue that the application of the Rule against Perpetuities to certain grants of future interests creates too harsh of a result in that it invalidates many future interests and the grantor's intent to create those future interests. To lessen this effect, doctrines such as the wait-and-see doctrine—an alternative to the traditional application of the Rule against Perpetuities that so often strikes down interests not certain to vest within the perpetuities period—was created. Under the wait-and-see doctrine, as described in *Symphony*, a court will not automatically strike down a future interest simply because it might vest outside the perpetuities period, but will instead wait to see whether it actually vests outside the period. In the case of *Symphony*, that would have meant that the interest was valid (thus the reason for Pergola's argument that the court adopt the doctrine). New York did not adopt the less-restrictive alternative in *Symphony*, but other jurisdictions have. Each jurisdiction is different, so one dealing with a perpetuities issue will have to look to the law of the particular state to determine what rules apply. Today the Rule against Perpetuities is no longer as widely accepted as it once was—many American jurisdictions have either limited the power of the rule (such as by adopting the wait-and-see and other related doctrines) or abolished it altogether, but it still remains an important principle of property law that must be studied and understood by students of the law.

Perspective
Co-ownership and Marital Rights

Chapter 5

This chapter discusses the legal relationship between two or more people who arrange to own a piece of property together. This type of ownership arrangement is known as co-ownership. Co-ownership is only present when two or more people have rights of possession that exist at the same time.

Two important types of co-ownership are explained in this chapter. The first type includes three different forms of concurrent interests. The first is a tenancy in common. When two or more people own property this way, and one of the tenants (owners) dies, the dead person's right to the property does not go to the other tenants. The dead tenant's interest in the property gets passed on by a will. The second form of concurrent interest is called a joint tenancy. Here, when one tenant dies, the tenant or tenants who are still alive get the other tenant's interest in the property. The third type that is covered in the chapter is a tenancy by the entirety. This arrangement can only be held by a married couple. Like a joint tenancy, this allows a surviving husband or wife to take the property if the other one dies. This chapter discusses the responsibilities that these different co-owners have to each other, and the rights each co-owner has against co-owners and other people.

The second type of co-ownership that is included in the chapter is marital property. The laws of marital property have changed a lot over the years. Although courts used to say that a husband owned all the wife's property, the laws now treat husbands and wives more equally. Also, laws that have said which person owned property that the couple received while married, and who gets what property in case the couple gets a divorce are constantly changing. This chapter discusses how the laws for married couples and their property are different from before, and how they are different from state to state.

Chapter Overview Outline
Co-ownership and Marital Rights

Chapter 5

NOTE: THE PURPOSE OF THIS OUTLINE IS TO ORGANIZE THE CASES SO THAT ONE CAN QUICKLY UNDERSTAND THE RELEVANCE OF EACH CASE TO THE COURSE. NO ATTEMPT IS MADE IN THIS OVERVIEW TO ADDRESS EVERY CONCEPT THAT MUST BE STUDIED. BE SURE TO READ THE ENTIRE CASEBOOK AND/OR OTHER MATERIALS TO GAIN A FULL UNDERSTANDING OF ALL CONCEPTS.

I. Common Law Concurrent Interests
  A. Severance of Joint Tenancies
    1. A joint tenant can unilaterally sever a joint tenancy without the use of an intermediating third party by conveying his or her property interest to himself or herself. *Riddle v. Harmon.*
    2. A mortgage given by one tenant on his or her interest in property held in a joint tenancy does not sever the joint tenancy. *Harms v. Sprague.*
    3. A surviving joint tenant can take the interest of a deceased joint tenant without having it encumbered by a mortgage or other lien upon that interest. *Harms v. Sprague.*
  B. Relations among Concurrent Owners
    1. Partition
      a. If co-owners cannot agree on a division of property or of proceeds from its sale, partition is required.
      b. A partition by sale should only be ordered if the physical attributes of the land in question are such that a partition is impracticable or inequitable, and the interests of the owners would be promoted by a partition by sale. *Delfino v. Vealencis.*
      c. A partition by sale is justified if it appears to the court that the value of the land in question when divided into shares is significantly less than its value when owned by only one party. *Johnson v. Hendrickson.*
    2. Sharing Benefits and Burdens of Co- ownership
      a. In the absence of an agreement to pay rent, a cotenant in possession is not liable to his or her cotenants for the value of his or her use and occupation of the property unless there is ouster of a cotenant. *Spiller v. Mackereth.*
      b. A joint tenant, during the existence of a joint estate, has the right to convey or mortgage his or her interest in the property, even if the other joint tenant objects. *Swartzabugh v. Sampson.*

II. Marital Interests
  A. The Common Law Marital Property System
    1. During Marriage
      a. An estate by the entirety is not subject to the claims of creditors of only one of the spouses because neither spouse acting alone can transfer his or her interest. *Sawada v. Endo.*
      b. A tenant by the entirety has the right to possess and use the whole property during his or her lifetime and the right to obtain title in fee simple absolute if his or her cotenant predeceases him or her, and is also protected against a levy on the property by any of the cotenant's creditors. *United States v. 1500 Lincoln Avenue.*
    2. Termination of Marriage by Divorce
      a. Every common law property state has enacted rules of equitable distribution of marital property upon divorce.
      b. Some states hold that an educational degree is not property, and therefore is not subject to division upon divorce. *In re Marriage of Graham.*
      c. Other states hold that the working spouse should be awarded "reimbursement alimony." *Mahoney v. Mahoney.*
      d. New York also holds that an increase in the value of one spouse's career, when it is the result of the efforts of the other spouse, constitutes marital property and is thus subject to equitable distribution. *Elkus v. Elkus.*
      e. It has been suggested that in treating professional degrees and licenses as property, and by valuing them in terms of the spouse's lifetime earning capacity, New York, in effect, counts a professional's accumulations twice and possibly penalizes the holder of the degree. *Putting Asunder in the 1990s.*
  B. The Community Property System
    1. Community property consists of all earnings and property bought with earnings during marriage. Property acquired by either spouse during marriage is strongly presumed to be community property.
  C. Status and Contract
    1. Contracts between Unmarried Cohabitants
      a. Express and implied contracts and agreements between non-marital partners should be enforced except to the extent that the contract is explicitly founded on the consideration of meretricious sexual services. *Marvin v. Marvin.*
      b. Stanford University, as well as other universities and corporations, have extended health insurance coverage and other institutional benefits to partners of gay faculty and employees. *Stanford to Provide Benefits for Partners of Gays.*

CALIFORNIA APPELLATE COURT HOLDS THAT A JOINT TENANT MAY SEVER A JOINT TENANCY BY CONVEYING HIS OR HER INTEREST IN THE PROPERTY TO HIMSELF OR HERSELF WITHOUT THE USE OF A THIRD PERSON "STRAWMAN"

Riddle v. Harmon

(Husband) v. (Wife's Executrix)

(1980) 102 Cal. App. 3d 524, 162 Cal. Rptr. 530

MEMORY GRAPHIC

Instant Facts

Mrs. Riddle did not want her husband to get their land automatically when she died, so she tried to sever the joint tenancy without him.

Black Letter Rule

A joint tenant can unilaterally sever a joint tenancy without the use of an intermediating third party by conveying his or her property interest to himself or herself.

Case Vocabulary

FEOFFEE: The person to whom a fee, or interest in land, is conveyed; the grantee.

FEOFFMENT: The granting of an interest in land under English common law.

FEOFFOR: The person who conveys a fee to another person; the grantor.

JUS ACCRESCENDI: The right of the surviving joint tenant or tenants to take the whole estate upon the death of one or more of the other joint tenants; the right of survivorship.

LIVERY OF SEISIN: Element of the common law ceremony of feoffment by which a feoffor would hand over a symbol of the land being conveyed, such as a lump of the soil or a branch, to the feoffee as a means of transferring possession of the land.

STRAWMAN: A third party who receives property from a joint tenant with the intent to convey the property right back to the joint tenant with the purpose of helping to sever the joint tenancy.

Procedural Basis: Appeal from summary judgment to quiet title.

Facts: Mr. (P) and Mrs. Riddle, husband and wife, purchased some real estate and took title as joint tenants. Several months before she died, Mrs. Riddle had an attorney plan her estate. This attorney told her that her property was held in joint tenancy and thus, upon her death, it would pass to her husband (P). After learning this, Mrs. Riddle wished to sever the joint tenancy so she could pass on her interest in the land by the use of a will. Her attorney prepared a deed which allowed Mrs. Riddle to grant an undivided one-half interest in the property to herself. This document also explicitly stated that its purpose was to "terminate those joint tenancies formerly existing" between Mr. and Mrs. Riddle. Mrs. Riddle's attorney also prepared a will disposing of her interest in the property. Both the grant deed and will were executed on December 8, 1975. Mrs. Riddle died on December 28, 1975. The trial court denied her plan to sever the joint tenancy and quieted title to the property to her husband. Harmon (D), executrix of Mrs. Riddle's will, appeals from that judgment.

Issue: Can a joint tenant unilaterally sever a joint tenancy without the use of an intermediary by conveying his or her interest to himself or herself?

Decision and Rationale: (Poche) Yes. One joint tenant may unilaterally sever a joint tenancy without the use of an intermediary device. In *Clark v. Carter* (1968) 265 Cal. App. 2d 291, 70 Cal. Rptr. 923 [transfer of property requires two parties, a grantor and grantee] a similar wife's actions of conveying her interest to herself were found to be insufficient to sever a joint tenancy. This idea of requiring two separate parties to transfer property was rooted in the English common law ceremony of livery of seisin. In this ceremony, the feoffor (grantor) would hand a symbol of the land, whether a branch or some of the earth, to the feoffee (grantee), and then relinquish possession of the land. Of course, one could not hand oneself a clod of dirt; two parties were needed. Here, however, the archaic rule that one cannot convey an interest in property to oneself is discarded. The rationale of the *Clark* case is rejected because the use of clods of earth as the means of transferring title has been replaced with grant deeds and title companies. Many attorneys have created several methods to get around the *Clark* case and its rule that one cannot be both grantor and grantee simultaneously. Examples of such means can be found in *Burke v. Stevens* (1968) 264 Cal. App. 2d 30, 70 Cal. Rptr. 87 [permitted wife's use of associate of her attorney as third party in property transfer used to sever joint tenancy] and *Reiss v. Reiss* (1941) 45 Cal. App. 2d 740, 114 P. 2d 718 [wife severed joint tenancy by transferring interest to son as trustee of a trust for her use and benefit]. Mrs. Riddle could have terminated the joint tenancy through any number of means. Judgment reversed.

Analysis:

In essence, the Court used the reasoning of the state legislature regarding the creation of a joint tenancy and flipped it around. The California legislature stated in its Civil Code §683 that a joint tenancy could be created not only by two or more persons receiving a title from another person, but also, among other means, by "the transfer from a sole owner to himself and others." As the state deemed a strawman unnecessary to the creation of a joint tenancy, the Court extended that loosened requirement to the termination of a joint tenancy, as well.

ILLINOIS SUPREME COURT HOLDS THAT A MORTGAGE GRANTED BY ONE JOINT TENANT DOES NOT SEVER THE JOINT TENANCY AND DOES NOT SURVIVE THE DEATH OF THE MORTGAGOR AS A LIEN ON THE PROPERTY

Harms v. Sprague

(Surviving Brother) v. (Dead Brother's Executor)
(1984) 105 Ill. 2d 215, 473 N.E. 2d 930

M E M O R Y G R A P H I C

Instant Facts

As a favor to Sprague, John mortgaged his and William's land, without telling William, and later devised everything to Sprague when he died.

Black Letter Rule

A mortgage does not sever a joint tenancy, and the surviving joint tenant takes the interest of a deceased joint tenant without being encumbered by the mortgage.

Case Vocabulary

LIEN: A claim secured by property for payment of a debt.
MORTGAGE: An interest in land which provides security for the payment of a debt, such as a loan, or the performance of a specific duty.
MORTGAGEE: Person that loans money to another in exchange for that person's title to the land being used as the security for the loan; the person who "receives" the mortgage.
MORTGAGOR: Person who gives legal title or a lien to a mortgagee in order to secure a mortgage loan; the borrower, or debtor, in a mortgage transaction.
PROMISSORY NOTE: A written promise to pay a specific sum of money at a given time, or on demand, to a specific person.
REDEMPTION: The right to repurchase land and free it from the foreclosure of a mortgage.
TITLE THEORY: Theory of mortgage law that states that until a mortgage is satisfied, or foreclosed, a mortgagor retains the right to possession of the property and legal title to the property belongs to the mortgagee.

Procedural Basis: Appeal from complaint to quiet title and for declaratory judgment.

Facts: William Harms (P) and his brother, John Harms, took title to real estate on June 26, 1973, as joint tenants, with full rights of survivorship (first property). Years later, in a separate transaction, Charles Sprague (D) wished to purchase other property (second property) from the Simmonses (D) for $25,000, but had to sign a promissory note for $7,000. On June 12, 1981, John Harms and Sprague (D) executed a promissory note for $7,000 payable to the Simmonses (D). The note states that it was to be paid from the proceeds of the sale of John Harms' interest in the first property, but no later than six months from the date the note was signed. The last of five monthly interest payments on the note was recorded November 6, 1981. John Harms also executed a mortgage, in favor of the Simmonses (D), on his undivided one-half interest in the (first property) joint tenancy property to secure payment of the note. William Harms (P) (co-tenant in the first property) was unaware of the mortgage. John Harms died on December 10, 1981, and devised his entire estate to Sprague (D). The mortgage from John Harms to the Simmonses was recorded on December 29, 1981. The trial court held that the mortgage severed the joint tenancy and survived John Harms' death. The appellate court reversed and found the property unencumbered by the mortgage.

Issue: (1) Is a joint tenancy severed when one joint tenant mortgages his or her interest in the property? (2) Does such a mortgage become a lien on the property after the death of the mortgagor?

Decision and Rationale: (Moran) (1) No. A lien on a joint tenant's interest in property will not effectuate a severance of the joint tenancy, absent the conveyance by deed following the repayment of a mortgage debt. This rule is reflected in *Peoples Trust and Savings Bank v. Haas* (1927) 328 Ill. 468 [judgment lien secured against one joint tenant did not sever joint tenancy], and *Van Antwerp v. Horan* (1945) 390 Ill. 449 [levy upon interest of a debtor joint tenant does not destroy unity of interest and does not sever joint tenancy]. In a mortgage situation, the title of the mortgagee (lender) really only exists between the mortgagee and mortgagor (borrower), so no title transfer occurs between them. Thus, a mortgage is, in essence, a lien, and a lien on the mortgagor's interest in property does not sever the joint tenancy. Because the mortgage did not sever the joint tenancy, the inherent right of survivorship still exists. William Harms' (P's) right of survivorship became operative upon the death of his brother. (2) No. A surviving joint tenant acquires the share of the deceased joint tenant through the conveyance which granted the joint tenancy in the first place. The property right of the deceased joint tenant, John Harms, was extinguished at the moment of his death. At that moment, the lien of the mortgage ceased to exist as well. Judgment affirmed.

Analysis:

Not all jurisdictions follow this logic. Some courts hold that a surviving joint tenant would have to take on the deceased joint tenant's interest subject to any mortgage against it. This position would be fair to the mortgagee, who would otherwise lose the financial security in the transaction.

CONNECTICUT SUPREME COURT HOLDS THAT WHERE THE HOME AND GARBAGE BUSINESS OF A TENANT IN COMMON ARE LOCATED ON CONCURRENTLY OWNED PROPERTY, A PARTITION BY SALE CANNOT BE ORDERED AS IT WOULD NOT BE IN THE BEST INTERESTS OF ALL PARTIES INVOLVED

Delfino v. Vealencis

(Building Developers) v. (Garbage Lady)
(1980) 181 Conn. 533, 436 A.2d 27

M E M O R Y   G R A P H I C

Instant Facts

The Delfinos owned 99/144 of the property and wanted a residential development, while Vealencis owned 45/144 and wanted to keep her garbage business on it.

Black Letter Rule

A partition by sale should only be ordered if the physical attributes of the land in question are such that a partition is impracticable or inequitable, and the interests of the owners would be promoted by a partition by sale.

Case Vocabulary

PARTITION BY SALE: A court-ordered division of land held by joint tenants or tenants in common by which the land is sold and the proceeds are divided among the tenants according to the size of their interests in the land.

PARTITION IN KIND: A court-ordered, physical division of land held by joint tenants or tenants in common by which each tenant's interest is converted into a parcel taken from the whole, and each tenant then takes exclusive possession of their share of the land.

Procedural Basis: Appeal from hearing in action seeking a partition of property by sale.

Facts: Angelo and William Delfino (Ps) and Helen Vealencis (D) own real property as tenants in common. The property is a rectangular 20.5 acre parcel of land with Vealencis' (D's) house on the extreme western end of it. The Delfinos (Ps) own an undivided 99/144 interest in the land, and Vealencis (D) owns a 45/144 interest. They (Ps and D) are the sole owners of the property. Vealencis (D) also runs a garbage removal business on a portion of the land. None of the people involved is in actual possession of the remainder of the property. The Delfinos (Ps) want to develop the property into forty-five residential lots. In 1978, the Delfinos (Ps) brought an action in the trial court seeking a partition [dividing of the lands resulting in individual ownership of the interests of each joint tenant] of the property by sale. They (Ps) also wanted the proceeds of the sale divided according to their (P's) and Vealencis' (D's) respective interests. Vealencis (D) moved for a judgment of in-kind partition [physical division of the property into separate tracts] . After a hearing, the trial court concluded that a partition in kind would result in "material injury" to both the Delfinos (Ps) and Vealencis (D). The court then ordered the property to be sold at auction by a committee and that the proceeds be paid into the court and redistributed to the tenants. Vealencis (D) appealed.

Issue: Can a partition by sale be ordered when a physical partition is possible, and a partition by sale would protect the interests of the owner of a larger share of the property over the owner of the other share?

Decision and Rationale: (Healey) No. Under Connecticut General Statutes §52-500 [statute governing sale of real or personal property owned by two or more persons] a court is not required to order a physical partition even in cases of extreme hardship. A partition by sale, however, should only be ordered when the physical attributes of the land make a partition in kind impracticable or inequitable, and when the interests of all the owners, not just one, would better be promoted by such a sale. Here, the property is essentially rectangular, and Vealencis' (D) dwelling is located on the extreme western side of it. There are only two competing ownership interests, the Delfinos' (P) and Vealencis' (D) shares, as well. These facts demonstrate that a physical partition of the property into two separate tracts is clearly practicable here. Moreover, the lower court's failed to consider that a partition by sale would force Vealencis (D) to surrender her home and business, both of which were located on the property. Vealencis (D) had been in actual and exclusive possession of the property for some time. Though Vealencis' (D) business might possibly cause difficulty for the Delfinos (Ps) in their attempt to develop residential lots, the interests of all the tenants in common must be considered. The potential economic gain of one tenant or group of tenants alone cannot justify a partition by sale. The trial court erred in ordering a partition by sale. Judgment set aside and case remanded.

Analysis:

Although courts usually say that partition in kind is preferred, more often than not it is the opposite that occurs. The present trend has been to order sale in partition in a great majority of cases. This is usually done in deference to the wishes of all parties involved, or because the courts believe that sale of the property is actually the fairest means of ending any conflict between them.

ALABAMA SUPREME COURT HOLDS THAT WHERE NO AGREEMENT EXISTS BETWEEN COTENANT TO PAY RENT, A COTENANT IN POSSESSION IS NOT LIABLE FOR RENT TO OTHER COTENANT UNLESS OUSTER IS ESTABLISHED

Spiller v. Mackereth

(Warehouse Occupant) v. (Other Tenant)

(1976) 334 So. 2d 859

M E M O R Y G R A P H I C

Instant Facts

After another tenant vacated their building, Spiller used it as a warehouse, and Mackereth demanded he pay rent or vacate half of the building.

Black Letter Rule

In the absence of an agreement to pay rent, a cotenant in possession is not liable to his or her cotenants for the value of his or her use and occupation of the property unless there is ouster of a cotenant.

Case Vocabulary

OUSTER: The beginning of the running of the statute of limitations in cases of adverse possession; the liability of an occupying cotenant for rent to other cotenants.

PER MY ET PER TOUT: "By the half and by the whole;" term used to describe how each tenant in a tenancy in common or a joint tenancy holds a whole share of the property with regard to survivorship, but holds a share equal to other tenants with regard to the right to occupy.

Procedural Basis: Appeal from action awarding rent to nonpossessing cotenant.

Facts: John Spiller (P) and Hettie Mackereth (D) owned a building as tenants in common. A lessee, Auto-Rite, was renting the building but later vacated, and when moving out Auto-Rite removed the locks. Spiller (P) began using it as a warehouse and acquired new locks to secure the merchandise he (P) stored inside. Mackereth (D) then wrote a letter dated November 15, 1973 demanding that Spiller (P) either vacate half the building or pay half the rental value. When Spiller (P) did neither, Mackereth (D) brought suit. The trial court awarded Mackereth (D) $2,100 in rent. Spiller (P) appealed.

Issue: Is a cotenant in possession of property liable to other cotenants for rent when there is no evidence the cotenant in possession has done anything to exclude the other cotenant from the property?

Decision and Rationale: (Jones) No. The general rule is that in absence of an agreement to pay rent or ouster of a cotenant, a cotenant in possession is not liable to cotenants for the value of use and occupation of the property. The key here lies in the definition of the word "ouster." Ouster can refer to either the beginning of the running of the statute of limitations for adverse possession or the liability of an occupying cotenant for rent to other cotenant. The adverse possession aspect of the word is precluded here as Spiller (P) has acknowledged the existence of the cotenant relationship by filing a bill for partition. With regard to liability for rent, ouster is evidenced when an occupying cotenant refuses a demand of other cotenants to be allowed into use and enjoyment of the land. Here, Mackereth's (D) letter only demanded that Spiller (P) vacate or pay rent, and did not state any desire of Mackereth (D) to enter the premises. The letter was insufficient because Spiller (P), as an occupying cotenant holds title to the whole property and may rightfully occupy it until Mackereth (D), another cotenant, asserts possessory rights. Mackereth (D) claims Spiller's (P) use of new locks amounts to ouster. However, there is no evidence that the locks were used to do anything other than secure Spiller's (P) merchandise inside. There is also no evidence that Mackereth (D) or any other cotenants asked for the keys to the locks or were prevented from entering the building because of the locks. Without evidence that he (P) intended to exclude the other cotenants, Spiller (P) is not liable for rent. Judgment reversed.

Analysis:

Some jurisdictions take the view that a cotenant in exclusive possession must pay rent to cotenants out of possession even when no ouster is established. This view may seem more fair to cotenants out of possession. When a cotenant occupies the property in question, it is essentially kept "off the market" and thus potential rent from a prospective renter is lost. However, the majority rule here would seem to encourage constructive use of property, as opposed to leaving it vacant and possibly unimproved until a new renter occupies the premises.

CALIFORNIA APPELLATE COURT HOLDS THAT EACH TENANT IN A JOINT TENANCY HAS THE RIGHT TO POSSESSION OF THE WHOLE PROPERTY, AND THUS CAN LEASE OUT OR TRANSFER HIS OR HER RIGHT TO OCCUPY OR USE AS HE OR SHE SEES FIT

Swartzbaugh v. Sampson

(Lessor's Wife) v. (Boxing Pavilion Lessee)
(1936) 11 Cal. App. 2d 451, 54 P. 2d 73

MEMORY GRAPHIC

Instant Facts

Mr. Swartzbaugh leased part of some land for a boxing pavilion, but Mrs. Swartzbaugh, the joint tenant, never signed the lease and wants to cancel it.

Black Letter Rule

A joint tenant, during the existence of a joint estate, has the right to convey or mortgage his or her interest in the property, even if the other joint tenant objects.

Case Vocabulary

MECHANIC'S LIEN: A claim created by state law which attaches to property and enables persons to have priority in receiving payment for work they performed in building, improving, or repairing a building or structure on that property.
MOIETY: Half of something; extent to which a joint tenant is said to hold an interest in property ("hold by moieties").
NONSUIT: Judgment against a plaintiff when he or she has failed to prove his or her case; a dismissal.
OPTION: Contract made for the purpose of keeping an offer of another contract open for a specified period of time.
PRESCRIPTION: A person's acquisition of the right to use property by virtue of his or her continuous use of that property.

Procedural Basis: Appeal from granting of motion for nonsuit in action to cancel leases.

Facts: Mr. and Mrs. Swartzbaugh (D and P, respectively) owned sixty acres of land containing walnut trees. They owned this land as joint tenants with the right of survivorship. In December, 1933, Sampson (D) began negotiations with Mr. and Mrs. Swartzbaugh (D and P) to lease a fraction of the land in order to build a boxing arena. Mrs. Swartzbaugh (P) objected to making such a lease at all times. An option for a lease, dated January 5, 1934, was executed by Sampson and Mr. Swartzbaugh (D). Mrs. Swartzbaugh (P) was injured in February, 1934, and was confined to her bed for some time. The lease was executed by Mr. Swartzbaugh and Sampson (D) on February 2, 1934, and a second lease for property adjoining the boxing pavilion site was also signed after this date. Mrs. Swartzbaugh's (P) refused to sign these documents and her name does not appear on any of them. The walnut trees were removed from the leased premises against Mrs. Swartzbaugh's (P) wishes. Sampson (D) then went into possession and built the pavilion. Mrs. Swartzbaugh (P) filed suit on June 20, 1934. At trial she testified that she received no part of the $15 monthly rent, a rate which she considered too low when compared to the $10,000 needed to build the arena. She (P) also claimed that she did not want the arena on her land because "women and liquor followed." Sampson (D) filed for nonsuit and the motion was granted. Mrs. Swartzbaugh (P) appealed.

Issue: Can one joint tenant, who has not joined in the leases executed by a cotenant and a lessee in exclusive possession of the leased property, maintain an action to cancel the leases?

Decision and Rationale: (Marks) No. In a joint tenancy, each joint tenant owns an equal interest in, and has an equal right to possession of, the whole property. This court has held that each joint tenant has the right convey or mortgage an equal share of the property, and can also pledge his or her interest in the property to another person. In addition, a joint tenant can make a lease to his or her share of the property, and such a lease would be valid as to his or her share. Even a lease to all of the joint property by one joint tenant would be a valid and supportable contract as far as the lessor in the joint property is concerned. Thus, the leases from Mr. Swartzbaugh (D) to Sampson (D) are valid and existing contracts which give Sampson (D) the same right of possession of the leased property that Mr. Swartzbaugh (D) had. A joint tenant cannot recover exclusive possession of joint property from a cotenant. Because Sampson (D) has effectively the same rights to the leased property that Mrs. Swartzbaugh (P) had prior to the transaction, she (P) cannot cancel the leases. Mrs. Swartzbaugh (P) may fear that she may lose her interest in the premises by prescription. This fear is unfounded because a lessee cannot generally dispute a landlord's title or claim adverse possession while holding the property under the conditions of a lease. There is no evidence that Sampson (D) is holding adversely to her, nor that Mrs. Swartzbaugh (P) ever demanded entry into the premises. Judgment affirmed.

Analysis:

The rule of this case is pretty straightforward. Although Mrs. Swartzbaugh could attempt to prove ouster if Sampson resists her attempts to enter, she would only be entitled to one-half the reasonable rental value of the land. This may result in more money for Mrs. Swartzbaugh, but she would not be able to remove him or the boxing arena from the land. This would also lead to questions of who would be responsible for paying her the full value of rent; should it be Sampson, or Mr. Swartzbaugh, for agreeing to such a low monthly rent in the beginning? She may also consider trying a partition action as a remedy, but such measures would, in the end, give her a smaller parcel of land than the one she started with.

HAWAII SUPREME COURT HOLDS THAT THE CONVEYANCE OF MARITAL PROPERTY BY A HUSBAND AND WIFE TO THEIR SONS DID NOT DEFRAUD THE HUSBAND'S JUDGMENT CREDITORS BECAUSE A TENANCY BY THE ENTIRETY IS NOT SUBJECT TO THE CREDITORS OF ONE SPOUSE

Sawada v. Endo

(Judgment Winner) v. (Judgment Debtor)

(1977) 57 Hawaii 608, 561 P.2d 1291

M E M O R Y G R A P H I C

Instant Facts

Kokichi and Ume Endo conveyed their property to their sons the same day that Kokichi got into an auto accident that injured the Sawadas.

Black Letter Rule

An estate by the entirety is not subject to the claims of creditors of only one of the spouses because neither spouse acting alone can transfer his or her interest.

Case Vocabulary

COVERTURE: Earlier status of married women under common law, when a wife possessed only the right of survivorship, and not the right to use and enjoyment and exercise of ownership, in the marital estate.

Facts: Kokichi (D) and Ume Endo, husband and wife, owned a parcel of real property as tenants by the entirety. On November 30, 1968, Masako and Helen Sawada (Ps) were injured when struck by car driven by Kokichi Endo (D). On June 17, 1969, Helen Sawada (P) filed her complaint against Kokichi Endo for damages. Mr. (D) and Mrs. Endo conveyed the property to their sons by a deed dated July 26, 1969. Masako Sawada (P) filed her suit against Kokichi Endo (D) on August 13, 1969. The complaint and summons in each suit was served on Kokichi Endo on October 29, 1969. The deed from Mr. (D) and Mrs. Endo to their sons was recorded on December 17, 1969. The sons paid no consideration for the conveyance. Both sons were aware at the time of conveyance that their father (D) had been in an auto accident and carried no liability insurance. Mr. (D) and Mrs. Endo continued to reside on the premises they conveyed to their sons. On January 19, 1971 judgment was entered in favor of Helen Sawada (P) against Kokichi Endo (D) for the sum of $8,846.46. Judgment was also entered in favor of Masako Sawada (P) for the sum of $16,199.28. Ume Endo died ten days later, and was survived by Kokichi Endo (D). The Sawadas (P) brought suit to set aside the conveyance of the marital property and satisfy their judgment. The trial court refused, and the Sawadas appealed.

Issue: Is the interest of one spouse in real property, held in tenancy by the entireties, subject to levy and execution by his or her creditors?

Decision and Rationale: (Menor) No. Under the Married Women's Property Act, the interest of a husband or wife in an estate by the entireties is not subject to the claims of his or her individual creditors during the joint lives of the spouses. This is apparently the prevailing view of the lower courts of this jurisdiction. This jurisdiction has long recognized the tenancy by the entirety and its basis upon the legal unity of husband and wife and their single ownership of the estate. Tenants by the entirety are each considered to take the whole estate, so each spouse can have all the privileges that ownership confers. Despite this, however, neither spouse has a separate divisible interest in the property that can be conveyed or reached by execution of a judgment. While a joint tenancy may be severed by such a process, a tenancy by the entirety cannot. The estate is indivisible and this is an indispensable feature of the tenancy by the entirety. The estate can only be created with a married couple, and thus can only be destroyed by the actions of a married couple. There is nothing to prevent a creditor from insisting that a property held in such a tenancy be subject to levy before extending credit, of course. Also, tenancy by the entirety cannot be entered to defraud creditors. But if the tenancy already exists, the creditor presumably has notice of the characteristics of the estate which would limit the ability to reach the property. With regard to public policy, the property held by spouses in a tenancy by the entirety is often the single most important asset of the family unit. To allow third parties to become a joint tenant with a couple would severely hinder the use of this asset as security for loans on education and other family expenses. For these reasons, the conveyance of marital property by Mr. (D) and Mrs. Endo to their sons is not subject to the claims of the Sawadas (P), and moreover did not defraud the judgment creditors.

Dissent: (Kidwell) The majority's interpretation of the Married Women's Act equalizes the positions of the spouses by taking away the husband's right to transfer his interest. This position prevents the wife from exercising the same right that the husband once enjoyed for the sake of equality. It would have been better to say either spouse may levy and execute upon their rights of survivorship. Accordingly, the separate interest of Kokichi Endo (D) should be alienable by him and subject to attachment by his separate creditors. A voluntary conveyance by him (D) should be set aside when it is done to defraud his (D) creditors.

Analysis:

The majority of states do not allow a creditor of one spouse to reach a tenancy by the entirety because one spouse acting alone cannot assign his or her interest. This aspect of the tenancy effectively protects the family home as well as other property from unwise transfer by one spouse or from creditors of that one spouse. It is likely that this condition is one of the main reasons the tenancy by the entirety has endured.

UNITED STATES APPELLATE COURT HOLDS THAT AN INNOCENT TENANT BY THE ENTIRETY WHO CO-OWNED A PHARMACY WHERE CRIMES WERE COMMITTED IS ENTITLED TO EXCLUSIVE USE OF THE PROPERTY IN HER LIFETIME

United States v. 1500 Lincoln Avenue

(Government) v. (Pharmacy Owners)

(1991) 949 F.2d 73

MEMORY GRAPHIC

Instant Facts

The government wanted forfeiture of Leonard and Linda Bernstein's pharmacy after Leonard's conviction for drug crimes, but Linda was an innocent owner and challenged them.

Black Letter Rule

A tenant by the entireties has the right to possess and use the whole property during his or her lifetime and the right to obtain title in fee simple absolute if his or her cotenant predeceases him or her, and is also protected against a levy on the property by any of the cotenant's creditors.

Case Vocabulary

FORFEITURE: The loss or destruction of a right, such as a right to property, as the penalty for an illegal act.

LIS PENDENS: A pending lawsuit; notice of this is often filed in public records in order to warn prospective buyers of property that the title is involved in litigation, and that they may be responsible for any adverse judgment that results.

Procedural Basis: Appeal from order dismissing complaint seeking civil forfeiture of property.

Facts: A. Leonard Bernstein and his wife, Linda M. Bernstein (D), came into possession of property on 1500 Lincoln Avenue in Pittsburgh, Pennsylvania on October 1979. From 1984 to 1987, Mr. Bernstein (D) used the property, site of the Pentown Pharmacy, Inc., for the illegal distribution of prescription drugs. Mr. Bernstein (D) was indicted for numerous offenses by a federal grand jury. He (D) eventually pled guilty to nine counts and was convicted. The government (P) filed a civil forfeiture complaint for the property containing the pharmacy under 21 U.S.C. §881 [property used in furtherance of a drug crime is to be forfeited unless owner had no knowledge of crime or gave no consent]. In her (D) answer to the complaint, Mrs. Bernstein (D) stated that she (D) had no knowledge of the illegal activity that occurred at the pharmacy, and that she (D) did not occupy the premises. The government (P) claimed that Mr. Bernstein's (D) illegal activity severed the entireties estate and that Mrs. Bernstein (D) was thus entitled to keep only a one-half interest in the property. The district court dismissed the complaint, and the government (P) moved to alter or amend the judgment. The district court denied the motion but noted that the government (P) could file a lis pendens [notice that a lawsuit is pending against the property in question] against the property and preserve its ability to seek forfeiture of Mr. Bernstein's (D) interest in the event of his wife's (D) death or the severance of the tenancy. The government (P) appealed.

Issue: Can the action of one tenant by the entirety in subjecting property to forfeiture extinguish the property rights of the other tenant?

Decision and Rationale: (Alito) No. There were two goals that 21 U.S.C. §881 was intended to promote. One was the forfeiture of the property used in committing drug offenses, and the other was the protection of property rights of innocent owners. Here, Mrs. Bernstein (D), the innocent owner, held title as a tenant by the entireties. As such, she (D) has the right to possess and use the whole property during her life and the right to obtain title in fee simple absolute if her husband predeceases her. Moreover, she (D) is protected against any levy upon her husband's former interest or any action to force her to relinquish title without her consent. A denial of forfeiture, as Mrs. Bernstein (D) advocates, completely disregards the strong interest in forfeiture of property used in drug offenses. To follow the lower court's suggestion of a lis pendens would frustrate the innocent owner's property rights. Furthermore, the use of a lis pendens would complicate forfeiture proceedings by requiring the government (P) to wait until Mr. Bernstein acquires an interest in the property. Such an event may not occur for years, making the use of evidence problematic. The lower court erred in dismissing the complaint. The lower court should determine whether Mr. Bernstein's interest is subject to forfeiture. If it is, then it should be forfeited, but Mrs. Bernstein's (D's) interest should nonetheless be preserved. Case remanded.

Analysis:

While it would appear that Mrs. Bernstein has succeeded in maintaining her property rights, her rights are not completely unencumbered by this decision. She can devise the property or give it as a gift. However, her ability to sell the property is affected, for if she does not survive her husband, any subsequent buyer of the property would have to relinquish title to it. In addition, her ability to enter a long-term lease is similarly affected by this condition. Mrs. Bernstein is left in a position of needing to negotiate with the government if she wishes to transfer her interest.

COLORADO SUPREME COURT HOLDS THAT A MASTER'S DEGREE IN BUSINESS ADMINISTRATION AND THE INCREASED EARNING POWER IT PROVIDES DOES NOT CONSTITUTE MARITAL PROPERTY AND THUS IS NOT SUBJECT TO DIVISION UPON DIVORCE

In re Marriage of Graham

(Stewardess Wife and Business Graduate Husband)

(1978) 574 P.2d 75

M E M O R Y   G R A P H I C

Instant Facts

Flight attendant supports husband through business school, covering seventy percent of their expenses, and after he graduates they get a divorce.

Black Letter Rule

An educational degree is not property, and therefore is not subject to division upon divorce.

Case Vocabulary

MAINTENANCE: Financial support or assistance paid by one spouse to another after divorce; alimony.

PLEDGE: The use of personal property as security for the payment of a debt.

Procedural Basis: Appeal from ruling in divorce action.

Facts: Anne Graham (P) and Dennis Graham (D) were married on August 5, 1968. Throughout the six-year marriage, Anne Graham (P) was employed full-time as a flight attendant and continues in that profession. Dennis Graham (D) worked part-time for most of the marriage, and devoted his time to his education. He (D) attended school for about three and one-half years of the marriage, acquiring a bachelor's degree in engineering physics and a master's degree in business administration. After graduation, he obtained a corporate position at a starting salary of $14,000 per year. During the marriage, Anne Graham (P) contributed roughly seventy percent of the total income, which was used for family expenses and for Dennis Graham's (D) education. The couple accumulated no marital assets during the marriage. Anne Graham (P) also did the majority of the cooking and other housework. Both persons filed jointly for divorce on February 4, 1974. Anne Graham (P) made no claim for maintenance [request for her husband to provide her with financial support] or for attorney fees. The trial court found that, as a matter of law, an education obtained by one spouse during a marriage is jointly-owned property to which the other spouse has a property right. Anne Graham (P) was awarded $33,134 of Dennis Graham's (D) future earnings. The court of appeals reversed.

Issue: Does a person's education constitute property which can be divided between spouses in the event of a divorce?

Decision and Rationale: (Lee) No. The purpose of the division of marital property is to give to each spouse the property that fairly belongs to him or her. There is no rigid formula that the court must follow in doing so. However, there are limits on what actually constitutes property. An educational degree is not encompassed even by very broad views of the concept of property. A degree is of personal value to the holder. The degree itself terminates on the death of the holder and is not inheritable. It cannot be assigned, sold, transferred, conveyed, or pledged. The degree is an intellectual achievement that may assist in the future acquisition of property, but it is not property in and of itself. A spouse who provides financial support while the other spouse acquires an education will have that contribution taken into consideration when marital property is to be divided. Here, though, no marital property has been accumulated by the Grahams. Judgment affirmed.

Dissent: (Carrigan) In a practical sense, the most valuable asset acquired during the Grahams' marriage was the husband's (D) increased earning capacity. This was undeniably the result of Dennis Graham's (D) obtaining the two degrees while married. In fact, Anne Graham's (P) earnings amounted to an investment in that she took on the brunt of financial responsibilities so Dennis Graham (D) would have the time and funds necessary to get a degree. In cases such as this, where the wife works to educate her husband but is rewarded with a divorce after the husband attains a degree, the court should go beyond narrow concepts of property in order to promote equity. The law of torts recognizes that the deprivation of future earnings is something that can be compensated for when impaired or destroyed. Thus, Anne Graham should be compensated for the loss of future earnings of her husband, which were made possible by her investment in his education.

Analysis:

A number of other states agree with the decision of the New Jersey court in *Mahoney v. Mahoney*, 91 N.J. 488, 453 A.2d 527 (1982) [professional degree too speculative in value to be considered marital property]. The court held that the working spouse should be awarded "reimbursement alimony." With this ruling, the working spouse would be repaid for covering the costs of the spouse's education, travel expenses to and from school, household expenses, and any other means of support he or she provided while the other spouse earned a degree. Some states have overruled this decision by the enactment of statutes specifically mandating a division of educational benefits. One problem, however, is whether or not to reimburse the working spouse for the income the other spouse might have contributed if he or she had not devoted all their time to education.

NEW YORK SUPREME COURT, APPELLATE DIVISION, HOLDS THAT AN INCREASE IN THE VALUE OF ONE SPOUSE'S CAREER, WHEN BROUGHT ABOUT BY THE CONTRIBUTIONS OF THE OTHER SPOUSE, CONSTITUTES MARITAL PROPERTY

Elkus v. Elkus

(Opera Singer Wife) v. (Voice Coach Husband)
(1991) 169 A.D.2d 134, 572 N.Y.S.2d 901

M E M O R Y   G R A P H I C

Instant Facts

Beginning opera singer marries a voice coach, and after her career skyrockets while he coaches her during marriage, he wants his share upon divorce.

Black Letter Rule

An increase in the value of one spouse's career, when it is the result of the efforts of the other spouse, constitutes marital property and is thus subject to equitable distribution.

Procedural Basis: Appeal from order in divorce action.

Facts: Frederica von Stade Elkus (P), a beginning opera singer, and her husband (D), a singer and teacher, were married on February 9, 1973. During the marriage, Mrs. Elkus (P) achieved tremendous success. Her (P) income went from $2,250 in 1973 to $621,878 in 1989. She (P) became an internationally known recording artist and performer, won numerous awards, and performed for the President of the United States. During the marriage, Mr. Elkus (D) traveled with her, attending and critiquing her (P) many performances and rehearsals throughout the world. He (D) photographed her for album covers and magazine articles. He (D) also served as her (P) voice coach and teacher for ten years of the marriage, and took care of their (P and D) two children. Mr. Elkus (D) claimed that he (D) sacrificed his own career as a singer and teacher to devote his time to her (P) career and to the children. Mrs. Elkus (P) claimed her career and celebrity status are not licensed, but rather are the products of her talent, and thus do not constitute property. However, because Mrs. Elkus' (P) celebrity status and career level increased in value in part because of his (D) efforts, Mr. Elkus (D) claimed he (D) was entitled to equitable distribution of this marital property (her career and/or celebrity status). The Supreme Court disagreed with Mr. Elkus (D), and Mr. Elkus (D) appealed.

Issue: Does an increase in the value of one spouse's career, when brought about by the efforts of the other spouse, constitute marital property which can be equitably divided?

Decision and Rationale: (Rosenberger) Yes. Things of value that are acquired during marriage are marital property even if they do not fit the traditional definitions of property. Moreover, the property may be tangible or intangible. Such was the case in *O'Brien v. O'Brien*, 66 N.Y.2d 576, 498 N.Y.S.2d 743, 489 N.E.2d 712 [medical license constitutes marital property as it increases one's earning capacity]. There, the court also referred to New York Domestic Relations Law §236 in its decision. That law states that when making an equitable distribution of marital property, the court shall consider any direct or indirect contribution a spouse makes "to the career or career potential of the other [spouse]." Thus, an interest in one's career counts as marital property, and this may be represented by contributions of the other spouse, including financial and non-financial contributions, such as caring for the home and family. The fact that Mrs. Elkus' (P's) career is not a licensed profession like medicine is irrelevant. It is not the license or degree, but rather the increased earning capacity, that constitutes marital property. Here, it is clear that Mr. Elkus (D) made direct and concrete contributions to Mrs. Elkus' (P's) career, and gave support through his time with the children. Though Mrs. Elkus (P) came into the marriage with her own genuine talent, and with a position in the Metropolitan Opera, her career had barely begun at that time. Mr. Elkus (D) was actively involved in her (P's) career through his critiquing, teaching, and coaching of her (P). Thus, to the extent the appreciation in Mrs. Elkus' (P's) career was due to Mr. Elkus' (D's) efforts, this appreciation constitutes marital property. Judgment reversed.

Analysis:

Some may find this decision to be unfair to Mrs. Elkus. Mr. Elkus claimed that, during the marriage, he served as Mrs. Elkus' voice coach and teacher, and sacrificed his own career to do so. The problem with this position is that Mr. Elkus already was a teacher at the time of the marriage. In essence, then, Mr. Elkus was able to keep his career, but then later enjoy a (presumably) comfortable lifestyle as he accompanied his only student all over the world for concerts and other performances. It would seem that Mr. Elkus has already enjoyed considerable acclaim and other benefits, not only as the husband, but as the teacher of an internationally known opera singer. The court's decision allowed him to continue reaping those benefits even though he no longer fills the role of husband or teacher. Other courts have found that an entertainer has "good will" which is a marital asset, regardless of the contributions of the other spouse.

Baker v. State

(Same-sex Couple) v. (State Government)
170 Vt. 194, 744 (1999)

M E M O R Y   G R A P H I C

Instant Facts

Three same-sex couples denied marriage licenses sued the State claiming that the State Constitution guarantees them the same privileges and benefits provided to opposite-sex couples.

Black Letter Rule

The Common Benefits Clause of the Vermont Constitution guarantees same-sex couples the same rights, benefits, and protections provided to married opposite-sex couples.

Case Vocabulary

EMOLUMENT: Something gained or earned as a result of a certain status or position.

Procedural Basis: Appeal to the State Supreme Court after the trial court ruled that the State's denial of marriage licenses to same-sex couples was constitutional.

Facts: Baker (P) is the named Plaintiff out of three same-sex couples who have lived together in committed relationships for several years. Each couple applied for a marriage license, but was denied as ineligible under Vermont's (D)(the State) marriage laws. Baker (P) sued, seeking a declaratory judgment that the refusal to issue the marriage license violates the Vermont Constitution.

Issue: Does the refusal to issue marriage licenses to same-sex couples unconstitutionally deny them the common benefit, protection, and security afforded married opposite-sex couples?

Decision and Rationale: (Amestoy, C.J.) Yes. The Common Benefits Clause of the Vermont Constitution states that "government is...instituted for the common benefit, protection, and security of the people...and not for the particular emolument or advantage of any single person, family, or set of persons, who are a part only of that community." The issue before the court is whether Vermont's (D) exclusion of same-sex couples from the benefits and protections its laws provide to opposite-sex married couples may be squared with the Common Benefits Clause. We hold that the State is constitutionally required to extend to same-sex couples the common benefits and protections that flow from marriage under Vermont law. Baker (P) claims that denial of a civil marriage license excludes same-sex couples from a broad array of legal benefits and protections incident to the marital relation, such as spouse's medical, life, and disability insurance, intestate succession, etc. The State (D) asserts that the current scheme furthers the link between procreation and child rearing, thus promoting permanent commitment between couples who have children to ensure that their offspring are considered legitimate and receive ongoing parental support. Also, that sanctioning same-sex unions "would diminish society's perception of the link between procreation and child rearing," thus advancing the notion that "fathers and mothers are mere surplusage to these functions." Baker (P) notes, however, that the large number of married couples without children, and the increasing incidence of same-sex couples with children, undermines the State's (D) rationale. Further, that the State's (D) guarantee of the right of same-sex parents to adopt children renders the current scheme illogical. Chief among the principles advanced by the Common Benefits Clause is that of inclusion. This was a result of the framers' resentment of political preference of any kind. When a statute is challenged under the Common Benefits Clause, we must first define the community disadvantaged by the statute. Here, the marriage statute applies to opposite-sex couples, thus excluding same-sex couples. Next we must identify the asserted governmental purpose. As stated above, the State's (D) purpose is to further the link between procreation and child rearing. It is beyond dispute that the State (D) has a legitimate and long-standing interest in promoting a permanent commitment between couples for the security of their children. However, many opposite-sex couples marry for reasons that do not include the raising of children. As such, given the asserted purpose, the statute is underinclusive. Moreover, many children today are being raised, and even conceived, by same-sex parents. The State (D) has not only recognized this reality, but has removed legal barriers in order to allow same-sex couples to adopt and raise children. The exclusion of same-sex couples from the legal protections incident to marriage exposes their children to the precise risks that the State (D) argues are dealt with by the marriage laws. In other words, parties similarly situated for purposes of the law are treated differently. It is true that same-sex couples must either adopt or use technology to conceive. But the simple fact that same-sex couples cannot conceive on their own does not mean they do not feel the same sense of parental responsibility or foster the sense that they are mere "surplusage" to the conception and parenting of their children, and the State (D) does not claim this. Indeed, there is no reasonable basis to make this conclusion. On the other side, it is clear that the right to marry and enjoy its legal protections and benefits significantly enhances the quality of life in our society. [The court lists a number of rights and protections extended on the basis of marriage.] These rights and benefits can be withheld only upon public concerns of sufficient weight, cogency and authority that the justice of the deprivation cannot be seriously questioned. Given the extreme logical disjunction between the classification and the stated purpose of the law, the exclusion falls well short of this standard. Furthermore, the long history of official intolerance of intimate same-sex relationships cannot justify the denial of equal protection of the laws. Also, many states and the federal government have enacted laws prohibiting discrimination in many contexts on the basis of sexual orientation. We therefore conclude that none of the interests asserted by the State (D) provides a reasonable and just basis for the exclusion of same-sex couples from the benefits and protections incident to a civil marriage. By way of clarification, we hold only that same-sex couples are entitled to obtain the same benefits and protections afforded by Vermont law to married opposite-sex couples. However, it is up to the legislature to craft an appropriate means of addressing this mandate, and we hold that the current scheme shall remain in place for a reasonable period in order to allow the legislature to do so. Reversed.

Concurrence: and Dissent: (Johnson, J) I would grant the requested relief and enjoin defendants from denying a marriage license based solely on the gender of the applicants. This is a straightforward case of sex discrimination. Classifications based on sex should be analyzed under our common-benefits jurisprudence which until today, has been very similar to the federal equal protection analysis under the Fourteenth Amendment. Therefore, the classification must be narrowly tailored to further important, if not compelling, governmental interests. The rationalizations asserted by the State (D) fail to pass heightened scrutiny, or even the standard rational-basis test.

Analysis:

Normally, one would expect to find this case in a family law text. However, it is included in your property law text because of the court's reasoning behind its newly enunciated rule: that drawing legal distinctions based on a couple's gender, without at least a rational basis for doing so, unconstitutionally deprives citizens of the full protection of the law. Under this new precedent, same-sex couples may rely on the protections and enjoy the benefits, of the law that are provided on the basis of marriage, a form of civil union. This is not the case in the vast majority of other states, where a same-sex spouse does not possess the rights that married couples take for granted. Beside the standard objections to legal recognition of same-sex couples are objections that making such a recognition will make the cost of doing business rise dramatically. The argument is that such recognition will force employers to extend the full panoply of employee benefits to domestic partners. Is this a valid point? Perhaps the majority of same-sex partners already receive such benefits through their own employer, and will thus not need to rely on their spouse's benefit plan. This objection is similar to those asserted when Congress was considering the Family and Medical Leave Act in the early 1990s. As evidenced by the economic boom of the 1990's, the extension of a right to a leave of absence to employees in that context has certainly not crippled American businesses. Why should it be any different in this context?

Chapter 6

Before attempting a study of leasehold estates, it is important to understand how a leasehold differs from other interests in property. A leasehold is a right to possession of land by the permission of another. Contrast this with profits, easements, and licenses, which involve only the right to use land, not the right to possess it. Also contrast this with freehold interests such as a life estate or a fee simple. Freehold estates are possessory interests which the owner holds absolutely with the permission of no one, while leasehold estates are possessed by the tenant with the permission of the landlord. The distinction is important because certain rights and duties arise when a leasehold has been created that do not arise when either a freehold has been conveyed or when a right to use has been created.

There are four types of leaseholds. First, a tenancy for years is a lease for a fixed period, such as 6 months or 10 years. Second, a periodic tenancy is renewed at the option of landlord and tenant, such as a lease that is renewed every month. Third, a tenancy at will is a lease that exists so long as landlord and tenant both desire. Finally, a tenancy at sufferance, or a hold-over tenancy, exists when a tenant wrongfully remains in possession at the end of a lease. When a tenant holds-over, a landlord may either treat him as a trespasser and evict him or elect to hold him to a new term. Once he chooses either to evict the tenant or to hold him to a new lease, he cannot change his mind.

It is also important to appreciate that a lease is both a conveyance and a contract. In the early development of landlord tenant law, the leasehold was viewed as a conveyance. This was because the land was seen as the essence of the transfer; the dwelling was of secondary importance. Land was the essence because a lease was undertaken primarily to grow crops, not for a residence. Since the law viewed a leasehold as a conveyance, the covenants in a lease were independent. This meant that a breach by the landlord of any term in the lease did not excuse the tenant from paying rent. Conversely, a breach by the tenant did not excuse the landlord from performing his duties. Another consequence of viewing the lease as a conveyance was that the tenant took possession without warranty as to the condition of the premises. The rule was *caveat emptor,* or let the buyer beware. This meant that the buyer entered a lease at his peril. Again, the reason for this was that the tenant entered into a lease primarily to farm land, not for a dwelling.

In modern times, however, a tenant leases land primarily for a place to live. As a result, he bargains not so much for land to farm but for a habitable place to live. In order to make the law more fair to tenants, the law of leaseholds began to view a lease more and more as a contract. With this shift to contract, new rights and duties arose. For example, a landlord has a duty not to interfere with the tenant's quiet enjoyment of the premises. If a landlord interferes with the tenant's quiet enjoyment, he will be held to have constructively failed to deliver possession to the tenant. This is called the doctrine of constructive eviction. If a landlord constructively evicts a tenant, the duty of the tenant to pay rent is extinguished. Thus, a landlord constructively evicts a tenant if he habitually enters the premises without permission because such behavior interferes with the tenant's quiet enjoyment of the premises. A landlord also has a duty to deliver the premises in a condition fit for habitation. This is called the implied warranty of habitability. If the conditions are unfit for habitation, the landlord has breached the implied warranty of habitability and the tenant is excused from paying rent. Finally, if a tenant has abandoned the premises, the landlord has a duty to make best efforts to re-let the land so that damages do not unnecessarily accrue.

Though many duties of the landlord and tenant are based on contract, other important rights and duties are based on property law. For example, a landlord has the duty to deliver possession to the tenant, though jurisdictions differ over whether the landlord must deliver either the right to possession or actual possession. The tenant, since he has a property interest in land, has the right to sublease or assign his leasehold.

Finally, the legislature has attempted to modify the rights and duties of landlords and tenants. For example, apartment owners may not refuse to lease to another based on race or ethnicity. Also, many local ordinances require that rent be limited in amount.

Chapter Overview Outline
Landlord-Tenant Law

Chapter 6

NOTE: THE PURPOSE OF THIS OUTLINE IS TO ORGANIZE THE CASES SO THAT ONE CAN QUICKLY UNDERSTAND THE RELEVANCE OF EACH CASE TO THE COURSE. NO ATTEMPT IS MADE IN THIS OVERVIEW TO ADDRESS EVERY CONCEPT THAT MUST BE STUDIED. BE SURE TO READ THE ENTIRE CASEBOOK AND/OR OTHER MATERIALS TO GAIN A FULL UNDERSTANDING OF ALL CONCEPTS.

I. The Leasehold Estates
   A. A *tenancy for years* is an estate that lasts for a fixed period of time, such as six months or ten years.
   B. A *periodic tenancy* continues from period to period until either the landlord or tenant elects to terminate it.
   C. A *tenancy at will* is terminable at the will of either landlord or tenant.
      1. If a lease is terminable at the will of only one party and the lease is for the life of that party, a determinable life tenancy is created. *Garner v. Gerrish*.
   D. A *hold-over tenancy* or a *tenancy at sufferance* occurs when a tenant wrongfully stays in possession after his lease has expired
      1. Once a landlord elects either to treat a holdover as a trespasser or to hold him to a new term, he may not change his mind. *Crechale & Polles v. Smith.*

II. Selection of Tenants
   A. Discrimination on the basis of race, sex, disability, or familial status in the rental of housing, or advertisements which express a preference for a particular race, sex, or familial status, are prohibited by the federal Fair Housing Act. *42 U.S.C. § 3604.*
      1. Housing providers can defeat discrimination claims by showing legitimate reasons for refusing to rent, and factfinders are allowed to inquire into the providers' subjective intent in questioning prospective applicants. *Soules v. U.S. Department of Housing & Urban Development.*
   B. "Discrimination" includes a refusal to make reasonable accommodations in rules an[d] policies when such accommodations may b[e] necessary to afford the tenant equal opportunity to use and enjoy a dwelling. *42 U.S.C. [§] 3604(f)(2).*
      1. The factfinder must determine the "reasonableness" of the accommodations base[d] on a cost-benefit analysis that takes bot[h] parties' needs into account. *Bronk v. Ineichen.*

III. Delivery of Possession
   A. Some jurisdictions, following the English Rul[e], require that a landlord deliver actual possession. *Hannan v. Dusch.*
   B. Other jurisdictions, following the America[n] Rule, require only that a landlord deliver th[e] legal right to possession.

IV. Subleases and Assignments
   A. The modern rule is that in determining whether an assignment or a sub-leasing has occurred, the court looks to the intentions of th[e] parties. *Ernst v. Conditt.*
   B. If the lease contains a clause that subjec[ts] assignment or subleasing to the landlord['s] approval, the landlord may not unreasonab[ly] and arbitrarily withhold his or her consen[t]. *Kendall v. Ernest Pestana.*

V. Defaulting Tenants
   A. If the tenant breaches a term of the lease an[d] remains in possession, the landlord may evi[ct] the tenant. Some states prohibit self-help an[d] require the landlord to resort to the judici[al] process to evict a tenant. *Berg v. Wiley.*
   B. If a tenant wrongfully abandons possessio[n], the landlord has two options.
      1. The landlord may accept the tenant's surrender and terminate the lease.
      2. The landlord may choose not to accept th[e] tenant's surrender and leave the premis[es] vacant. He may then sue for the rent as [it] comes due.
         a. Some jurisdictions require that a landlo[rd] mitigate damages by making reasonab[le]

efforts to re-let an apartment wrongfully vacated by the tenant. *Sommer v. Kridel.*

VI. Duties Concerning the Condition of the Premises

A. If a landlord interferes with a tenant's right to quiet enjoyment of the premises--which constitutes a constructive eviction--the tenant may vacate the premises and terminate the lease. *Reste Realty Corp. v. Cooper.*

B. If a landlord breaches the implied warranty of habitability, the tenant may withhold rent or cancel the lease, depending upon the jurisdiction. *Hilder v. St. Peter.*

C. If the purpose for which a lease was created is frustrated or made extremely impractical, the tenant may cancel the lease. *Albert M. Greenfield v. Kolea.*

VII. Affordable Housing

A. Many local townships have passed ordinances, including rent control and government-assisted housing, that attempt to make housing more affordable.

B. Rent Control

1. A rent control ordinance must guarantee a fair rate of return to the landlord. *Cromwell Associates v. Mayor and Council of Newark.*

2. A rent control ordinance which makes minor re-allocations of rights between landlords and tenants is reasonably related to a legitimate public goal. However, the relation is often tenuous. *Chicago Board of Realtors v. City of Chicago.*

D. Government-Assisted Housing

1. If the market for housing were perfect, income subsidies would make housing affordable for all. However, since the market is not perfect, the government must intervene. When the government does intervene, however, some commentators feel that it should provide income subsidies and not provide new housing developments. *Privatizing Federal Low Income Housing Assistance: The Case of Public Housing.*

COURT REVERSES OLD COMMON LAW AND ALLOWS PARTIES TO CREATE A DETERMINABLE LIFE TENANCY

Garner v. Gerrish

(Landlord) v. (Tenant)

(1984) 63 N.Y.2d 575; 473 N.E.2d 2

M E M O R Y   G R A P H I C

Instant Facts

Donovan leased house to Gerrish (D) for as long as Gerrish (D) wished.

Black Letter Rule

If a lessee has the option of terminating a lease when he pleases, a determinable life tenancy is created.

Case Vocabulary

LESSEE: One who leases land from another.

LESSOR: One who leases land to another.

QUIET ENJOYMENT: A covenant, implied if not expressly incorporated into a lease, which states that a lessor shall not interfere with the lessee's ability to enjoy the premises.

SUMMARY PROCEEDING: An expedited procedure for evicting a tenant.

TENANCY AT WILL: One who may possess land so long as both he and the landlord desire.

Procedural Basis: Appeal from an order by the appellate court affirming a judgment in action to eject.

Facts: In 1977 Donovan leased land to Gerrish (D) for $ 100 per month. The lease stated that Gerrish (D) had the option of terminating the lease at a date of his choice. Gerrish lived there without incident until 1981. In 1981, Donovan died, and Garner (P) became the executor of his estate. Garner (P) requested Gerrish (D) to quit the premises. When Gerrish (D) refused, Garner (P) commenced this action. Garner (P) contends that the lease created a tenancy at will since the length of the lease was indefinite. Gerrish (D) contends that the lease, by its language, created a determinable life tenancy.

Issue: If a lessee may terminate a lease when he pleases, is a determinable life tenancy created?

Decision and Rationale: (Wachtler). Yes. At common law, the rule was that a lease for so long as the lessee shall please is a lease at will of both lessee and lessor. This rule had its origin in the ancient ritual of livery of seisin. Livery of seisin, the transfer of a clod of dirt, was required to create a life estate. Therefore, the common law did not allow the creation of a determinable life tenancy without livery of seisin. Hence the old rule: A lease for so long as the lessee shall please is a lease at the will of both lessee and lessor. In modern times, livery of seisin has been abandoned because it is out of step with the realities of modern life. In modern times, the courts look to the terms of the agreement to determine what type of lease has been created. In this case, the terms of the agreement clearly indicate that Donovan and Gerrish (D) agreed that Gerrish (D) would have a determinable life tenancy. Judgment reversed.

Analysis:

This case introduces the tension between property law and contract law that is present throughout all of landlord-tenant law. At early common law, a leasehold was viewed as an interest in property. Since it was a property interest, all of the rules of property law, not contract law, applied. For example, the premises were conveyed without warranty as to the condition of the premises and breach of the agreement by the landlord did not excuse the tenant from paying rent. The view of a lease as a conveyance of an estate rather than as a contract has come under pressure because of the changing nature of society. As the next several cases demonstrate, courts have responded to this by incorporating many contract principles into the law of property. Thus, the law of leaseholds is a mixed bag of property law and contract law. A crucial question in all of these cases is how much should be property law and how much should be contract law.

COURT LIMITS A LANDLORD'S OPTIONS: ONCE A LANDLORD ELECTS TO EITHER HOLD A TENANT OVER OR TREAT HIM AS A TRESPASSER, HE MAY NOT CHANGE HIS MIND

Crechale & Polles, Inc. v. Smith

(Landlord) v. (Tenant)

(1974) 295 So. 2d 275

Smith's
CRECHALE & POLLES
EVICT HIM, OR LET HIM STAY?

MEMORY GRAPHIC

Instant Facts

When Smith (D) held over past the expiration of his lease, Crechale (P) decided to treat Smith (D) as a trespasser. Later, he decided to hold him over to a new term.

Black Letter Rule

Once a landlord elects either to treat a hold-over as a trespasser or to hold him to a new term, he may not change his mind.

Case Vocabulary

EVICT: A legal proceeding to remove a non-owner from possession.
HOLDOVER: One who stays in possession of leased premises longer than he is entitled.
MONTH-TO-MONTH LEASE: A lease that has a term of one month, but which may be renewed for a month if both parties agree.
QUIT: To give up possession.
TENDER THE PREMISES: To give over possession.

Procedural Basis: Appeal from judgment in action for damages for breach of lease agreement.

Facts: In 1964, Crechale (P) entered into a lease with Smith (D). The term of the lease was for 5 years. As the end of the lease approached, Smith (D) learned that the new building he intended to occupy would not be immediately available. Smith (D) notified Crechale (P) that he wished to hold over on a month-to-month basis. Crechale (P) refused this offer and told Smith (D) that he would have to vacate at the end of the lease. Subsequently, Smith (D) held over. Crechale (P) accepted payment for the first month over. Now, Crechale (P) wants to bind Smith (D) for a full-lease term.

Issue: If a landlord elects to treat a holdover tenant as a trespasser, may he subsequently change his mind and hold him to a new term?

Decision and Rationale: (Rodgers). No. The landlord may elect one of two options when a tenant holds over. He may either (1) treat him as a trespasser or (2) hold him over for a new term. However, once a landlord elects one option or the other, he may not change his mind. Since Crechale (P) initially elected to treat Smith (D) as a trespasser, he cannot hold him over to a new term. Since Crechale (P) accepted rent for the first month over, he has effectively held Smith (D) over on a month-to-month basis. However, he cannot hold Smith (D) over for a new term. Judgment affirmed.

Analysis:

This case hints at the struggle for power between landlords and tenants. On the one hand, there is the desire to let landlords make as efficient use of the land as possible. By allowing landlords free rein in deciding whether to hold over a tenant or evict him, a landlord has great flexibility. However, it is unfair to a tenant to allow a landlord to change his mind, since a tenant will be unable to plan. Thus, the following compromise: A landlord may elect to hold over a tenant to a new term or he may evict him. However, once he chooses one option, he may not change his mind. Note that the two options given to the landlord do not maximize his flexibility. If there is a third party tenant who is willing to pay more for the immediate possession of the premises, the landlord may be unable to gain this increase in rent. If the landlord elects to hold the current tenant over, he will lose the increase in rent. If he elects to evict the tenant, he may still lose the increase in rent because the third party tenant may not be willing to wait for the time consuming eviction process to run its course. Thus, land may not be put to its most efficient use. To remedy this problem some states have enacted an expedited eviction process.

Soules v. U.S. Department of Housing & Urban Development

(Prospective Tenant) v. (Government Agency)
967 F.2d 817 (2nd Cir. 1992)

MEMORY GRAPHIC

Instant Facts

A single mother sued for discrimination after being denied the opportunity to apply for an apartment based on her family status.

Black Letter Rule

Housing providers can defeat discrimination claims by showing legitimate reasons for refusing to rent, and factfinders are allowed to inquire into the providers' subjective intent in questioning prospective applicants.

Case Vocabulary

DE NOVO: Anew, as if it had not been heard before.
PRETEXTUAL: Relating to an excuse; ostensible.
PRIMA FACIE: On the face of it.

Procedural Basis: Petition for review of order dismissing claims for discrimination in renting apartment.

Facts: Sherry Soules (P) was a single woman looking for a three bedroom apartment for herself, her twelve-year-old daughter, and her mother. Soules (P) responded to an advertisement published by Mary Jean Downs (D), a Realtor who listed, managed, and rented properties. The three bedroom apartment was on the second floor of a building on Bird Avenue in the Richmond area of Buffalo, New York. During the initial telephone interview, Downs asked how old Soules's (P) child was and whether the child was noisy. Soules (P) became irritated and asked why Downs needed to know the information. Downs responded that two elderly persons lived in the first floor unit, and that they did not want an upstairs resident who would make too much noise. Following the unpleasant conversation, Soules (P) contacted Housing Opportunities Made Equal, Inc. ("HOME") (P), a non-profit organization that seeks to ensure all persons receive equal housing opportunities. HOME investigated the discrimination allegations by having two "testers" call regarding the apartment. Downs agreed to show the apartment to the tester who had no children (Marjorie Murray) but not to the tester who had a seven-year-old son (Robin Barnes). Soules (P) subsequently met with Downs but was only shown a less appealing apartment. Downs lied and said that there were no apartments in the Richmond area available. Downs thereafter showed the Bird Avenue apartment to a family with children. The apartment was eventually rented to a single woman with no children. Soules (P) and HOME (P) brought suit based on two sections of the Fair Housing Act ("FHA"). One section made it unlawful to refuse to rent after the making of a bona fide offer a dwelling to any person based on familial status. The other section made it unlawful to advertise (in print or orally) an apartment that indicates any preference based on familial status. "Familial status" was defined to include families with children. An Administrative Law Judge denied Soules's (P) and HOME's (P) claim, ruling that Downs did not unfairly discriminate in violation of either section of the FHA. The ruling became a final order of the U.S. Department of Housing & Urban Development ("HUD"). Soules (P) and HOME (P) brought a petition for review before the Court of Appeals.

Issue: (1) Can a housing provider defeat a rental applicant's prima facie showing of discrimination by proving a legitimate, nondiscriminatory reason for refusing to rent? (2) May a factfinder inquire as to a housing provider's discriminatory intent in questioning prospective renters about family status?

Decision and Rationale: (Meskill, J.) Yes. (1) A housing provider can defeat a rental applicant's prima facie showing of discrimination by proving a legitimate, nondiscriminatory reason for refusing to rent. Soules (P) established a prima facie case of discrimination by proving that Downs denied the Bird apartment to Soules (P) knowing of the familial status. Downs asserted two legitimate reasons for denying to rent to Soules (P): Soules's (P) combative attitude and the fact that Downs had to frequently be out of town caring for a sick relative, making it impossible to monitor the status of the Bird apartment. Soules (P) contended that these were mere pretexts for Downs' discrimination against Soules (P) and Barnes as compared to Murray and the woman who eventually rented the apartment, both of whom had no children. We find that substantial evidence supports the Judge's conclusion that Downs had legitimate reasons for not renting to Soules (P). In particular, the treatment of Perry indicates that Ms. Downs was willing to rent to a family with children. Petition for review denied. (2) Yes. A factfinder may inquire as to a housing provider's discriminatory intent in questioning prospective renters about family status. While overt discriminatory statements (in print or orally) violate the FHA, it is not necessarily impermissible to ask whether a prospective renter has children and whether they are noisy. Rather, it is a question of fact whether such interrogation has a discriminatory purpose. Thus, it was proper for the Judge to determine whether Downs' questions were egitimate or merely pretext for discrimination. The Judge concluded hat there was a non-pretextual reason for asking questions about ;oules's (P) daughter's age and if she was noisy. As to age, local ıousing codes require that each child over age five have his or her own bedroom. As to noise, a housing provider is not precluded from attempting to ascertain whether prospective tenants will be noisy, because noisy tenants can be deemed a nuisance and can be evicted. The Judge concluded that Downs asked about the child's noise in order to guarantee that the elderly tenants continued to live in a quiet environment. Her questions were not pretextual, especially in light of Downs' offer to rent to Perry, a person with children. We conclude that substantial evidence supported the Judge's determination. Petition for review denied.

Analysis:

The Fair Housing Act codifies the common-sense legal principle that housing providers cannot discriminate on the basis of race, religion, sex, handicap, or familial status. As this case indicates, application of the FHA can be quite complicated. The need to prevent discrimination must be balanced against a housing provider's legitimate concerns in renting to appropriate persons. A housing provider is not obligated to rent to anyone and everyone. Rather, applications can be refused if a family is not financially qualified, for example, or if the family is too large to meet the local housing code requirements. Having said this, it does appear that Downs' behavior was nevertheless discriminatory. Downs refused to show the Bird Avenue apartment to two families with children. She agreed to show it to the Perrys only because she had a pre-existing relationship with that family. Certainly Downs had a legitimate right to protect the elderly tenants, but she refused even to give the applicants with children the opportunity to show that they could be appropriate tenants. It is somewhat surprising that the Administrative Law Judge overlooked these facts. His approach indicates a restrictive interpretation of the FHA. Apparently, as long as the discrimination is not overt or racially repugnant, it is acceptable.

COURT RULES THAT A LANDLORD NEED NOT PLACE A TENANT IN POSSESSION; THE LANDLORD NEED ONLY GIVE A RIGHT OF POSSESSION

Hannan v. Dusch

(Tenant) v. (Landlord)

(1930) 154 Va. 356; 153 S.E. 824; 70 A.L.R. 141

M E M O R Y   G R A P H I C

Instant Facts

When Hannan's (P) lease was to begin, Dusch (D) failed to evict a hold-over tenant.

Black Letter Rule

A landlord only has a duty to deliver the right to possession of the premises to a tenant, not actual possession.

Case Vocabulary

OUST: To remove from possession.

Procedural Basis: Appeal from the sustaining of a demurrer in action for damages for failure to deliver possession.

Facts: Hannan (P) leased land from Dusch (D). When the lease was to begin, the tenant then in possession failed to vacate. Dusch (D) failed to put Hannan (P) in possession. Hannan (P) contends that Dusch (D) must deliver actual possession and that he should have evicted the holdover tenant. Dusch (D) contends that he need only deliver the legal right to possession. There is no covenant in the lease to the effect that Dusch (D) must put Hannan (P) in possession.

Issue: Must the landlord deliver actual possession to the tenant?

Decision and Rationale: (Prentis). No. It is clear that a landlord must at least provide the legal right to possession. It is also clear that once the tenant takes possession, he is responsible for ejecting a trespasser. Were there a covenant in the lease stating either that the landlord did or did not have the duty to put the tenant in possession, that covenant would prevail. Where there is no covenant, there are two rules: (1) The English rule says that the landlord must place the tenant in possession and (2) The American rule says that the landlord must only give the tenant the right to possession. We must pick the one that we believe is better supported by reason. There are a couple of reasons why the English rule is good: (1) A tenant contracts for possession and not for a lawsuit to evict a hold-over; (2) The landlord is in a better position to assess whether a current tenant will in fact hold-over. However, we chose the American rule because it is unfair to hold the landlord liable for the wrong of another. Judgment affirmed.

Analysis:

One way to understand this case is to view a lease as an estate in land. Under that view, the landlord has conveyed an interest in land. As with any other interest in land, the landlord must deliver only the title to the land. As is apparent throughout the law of landlord/tenant, whether one views a lease as a contract or as a property interest greatly affects the rights and duties of the landlord and tenant. Treating a lease like an estate seems more proper if the tenant is a large corporation and the land will be used for commercial purposes. In that case, the corporation seeks more than just possession but also some form of title, albeit not a freehold title. Moreover, a corporation has more resources to vindicate its rights. However, if the tenant is a family and the land will be used as a residence, the primary concern of the tenant is possession. In this case, the lease is more properly viewed as a contract where the landlord has the duty to deliver possession.

Ernst v. Conditt

(Lessor) v. (Assignee)
(1964) 54 Tenn. App. 328; 390 S.W.2d 703

MEMORY GRAPHIC

Instant Facts

Rogers, the original lessee, transferred his interest to Conditt (D).

Black Letter Rule

In determining whether an assignment or a sub-leasing has occurred, the court looks to the intentions of the parties.

Case Vocabulary

ASSIGN: To give to another one's entire interest in a lease.
PRIVITY OF CONTRACT: A relationship between parties that arises because they have entered into a contract with one another.
PRIVITY OF ESTATE: A relationship between parties that arises because they share an interest in property.
SUBLET: To transfer a portion of a lessee's interest in a lease to another.

Procedural Basis: Appeal from judgment in action for damages for breach of lease agreement.

Facts: Ernst (P) leased land to Rogers for a term of 1 year, 7 days. After Rogers operated a race track for a short time on the premises, he entered into negotiations with Conditt (D) for the sale of the business. The original lease was modified. The modified lease contained the following provisions: (1) The term of the lease was extended to 2 years; (2) Rogers was given the right to "sublet" the premises to Conditt (D) on the condition that Rogers remain personally liable for the performance of the terms of the lease. Subsequently, Rogers leased the premises to Conditt (D). In the contract between Rogers and Conditt (D), the term "sublet" was used. After Conditt (D) took possession, he operated the race track for a short time. Soon, however, Conditt (D) quit paying rent, but he remained in possession. Ernst (P) sues Conditt for rent owed. Ernst (P) contends that the agreement between Rogers and Conditt (D) is an assignment of the lease, which would render Conditt (D) liable to Ernst (P). Conditt (D) contends that the agreement between Rogers and him was a subletting.

Issue: In determining whether an assignment or a sub-leasing has occurred, must the court look to the intentions of the parties?

Decision and Rationale: (Chattin). Yes. An assignment allows the land owner to recover from the assignee. A sublease does not allow the land owner to recover from sub-lessees. At common law, the following rule was used to determine whether a lessee assigned or sublet the premises: An assignment conveyed the entire interest in a lease; it left nothing to the original lessee. A sublease granted an interest that was less than that owned by the original lessee; the original lessee retained a reversionary interest. The modern method of determining whether there has been an assignment or sublease is to ascertain the intention of the parties. Under the common law rule, Conditt (D) is liable to Ernst (P) because he took Rogers' entire interest in the land. The fact that the modified contract between Rogers and Ernst (P) held Rogers to be personally liable to Ernst does not matter for the following reason: The liability of Rogers to Ernst (P) is not determined by an agreement between Rogers and Conditt (D). Also, the fact that the modified agreement between Rogers and Ernst (P) contained the word "sublet" does not matter. Ernst's consent to "sublet" has been held to be only a consent to one other than the original lessee to go into possession; it authorizes both a subletting and an assignment. In any case, Conditt (D) is liable to Ernst (P) under the modern rule. By the terms of the agreement between Rogers and Conditt (D), Rogers retained no reversionary interest; he conveyed all that he had. Thus, Rogers has assigned his lease. Judgment affirmed.

Analysis:

This case illustrates and introduces the interplay between contract and property law. The lease between the lessor and lessee creates duties for both parties. Many of these duties, as will become apparent, have derived from contract law. On the other hand, a lease is an interest in property, and as such it may be conveyed. However, when it is conveyed, often the rights and duties follow it, as when a lessee assigns a lease. This binds the original lessor into a landlord tenant relationship with the lessee. The terms of this lease are the same terms as those between the original lessor and lessee. Notice that the landlord did consent to the new tenant. Many landlords reserve the right to refuse an assignment. The next case illustrates under what circumstances a landlord may do this.

COURT DECLARES THAT LESSOR MUST ACT REASONABLY: A LESSOR MAY NOT ARBITRARILY WITHHOLD CONSENT TO AN ASSIGNMENT

Kendall v. Ernest Pestana

(Assignee) v. (Lessor)

(1985) 40 Cal. 3d 488; 709 P.2d 837; 220 Cal. Rptr. 818

M E M O R Y G R A P H I C

Instant Facts

Ernest Pestana (D) demanded increased rent in exchange for consent to assign a lease.

Black Letter Rule

A lessor may not unreasonably and arbitrarily withhold his or her consent to an assignment.

Case Vocabulary

APPROVAL CLAUSE: A clause requiring the lessors approval before a lease can be assigned or sub-let.
FORFEITURE RESTRAINT: A restraint on the alienation of property which, if breached, causes the breacher's entire interest to be forfeited.
MITIGATE DAMAGES: To prevent the accrual of damages.
SURETY: One who will respond in damages if another person causes the damages. An insurance company acts as a surety.

Facts: The city of San Jose leased a hangar to Perlitch. Perlitch sublet the premises to Bixler for a term of 25 years. The lease provided that written consent of the lessor was required before the lessee could assign his interest. Bixler was to run an airplane maintenance business. Subsequently, Perlitch assigned his interest to Ernest Pestana (D). Later, Bixler attempted to sell his interest to Kendall (P). Kendall (P) was more financially sound than Bixler. As per the terms of the original lease between Bixler and Perlitch, Bixler requested consent from Ernest Pestana (D) for the sublease. Ernest Pestana (D) demanded an increase in rent in exchange for consent. Ernest Pestana (D) contends that he may arbitrarily refuse consent. Kendall (P) contends that this provision is against public policy since it is an unreasonable restraint on alienation.

Issue: May a lessor unreasonably and arbitrarily withhold his or her consent to an assignment?

Decision and Rationale: (Broussard). No. The law favors the free alienability of property, including a leasehold. However, alienability may be restricted by contract so as to protect the lessor. Such contracts are construed against the lessor, especially when the act of assigning terminates the lease. The majority rule allows the lessor to arbitrarily withhold consent. Even in the majority states, however, the lessor may waive his right or be estopped from asserting it. A growing trend asserts the following rule: A lessor may withhold consent only when he has a commercially reasonable objection to the assignment. We adopt this rule for the following reasons: (1) Public policy favors free alienability; (2) The relationship between lessor and lessee has become more and more impersonal. As a result, the lessor is just as likely to find a high quality tenant in the assignee as the lessee; (3) The lessor's interests are protected by the fact that the lessee remains contractually liable to the lessor; (4) A lease is increasingly viewed as a contract. As a result, since the lessor has discretion in withholding consent, the lessor can withhold consent only in good faith. The lessor may withhold consent in the following circumstances, for example: (1) The property is ill-suited for the proposed use; (2) The proposed use is illegal; (3) The proposed use requires altering the premises. The lessor cannot withhold consent solely on the basis of personal taste. Nor may he demand higher rent in exchange for consent. This is because the original lease already exhibits an agreement between lessor and lessee, and lessor may not attempt to get more than he bargained for. There are four reasons advanced for allowing arbitrary withholding of consent: (1) Lessor has picked his tenant and he should not have to look elsewhere for the rent. This is unpersuasive because lessor may still refuse consent if it is reasonable. If an assignee is a poor financial risk, lessor may reasonably withhold consent. Moreover, the original lessee is still liable to the lessor; (2) The lessee could have bargained for a contract clause that provided that consent could be withheld only if reasonable; the court should not place this clause in the contract. This is rejected because the fact that the parties agreed to a consent requirement must mean that they contemplated that the lessee give some reason for withholding consent; (3) The court must follow the rule because of stare decisis. Rejected, because the court has never ruled on this issue; (4) The lessor has a right to realize the increased value of his property by demanding higher rent. Rejected because the lessee took the risk that property prices would fall. He is also entitled to any gain should prices rise. The lessor, as well as the lessee, must live with the risk incurred as a result of the contract made. Judgment reversed.

Dissent: The terms of the contract should be honored. There was no requirement in the contract that withholding of consent had to be reasonable. Moreover, the legislature has already adopted the rule that consent may be withheld arbitrarily.

Analysis:

This case continues the development of contract doctrine in the law of property. In this case, the doctrine of good faith is applied. A lessor may withhold his or her consent to an assignment only with good reason. Notice that in this case, the contract doctrine of good faith helps achieve one of the goals of property law. It promotes the free alienability of property.

Berg v. Wiley

(Tenant) v. (Landlord)

(1978) 264 N.W.2d 145

MEMORY GRAPHIC

Instant Facts

Wiley (D) changed the locks on property that he leased to Berg (P).

Black Letter Rule

A landlord may not use self-help to regain possession of his land.

Case Vocabulary

ABANDON: To give up possession.
BREACH OF PEACE: The eruption of violence.
RE-ENTRY: To retake possession.
RESTRAINING ORDER: A judicial order preventing a person from performing some act.
SELF-HELP: Vindicating one's rights without going to a court.
SUMMARY PROCEDURE: An expedited method to evict one in possession.
SURRENDER: To give up possession.
UNLAWFUL DETAINER STATUTE: Statute detailing the procedures that must be followed to evict a tenant.

Procedural Basis: Appeal from directed verdict in action for damages for wrongful eviction.

Facts: Wiley (D) leased land to Phillip Berg for a term of five years. The lease provided that no changes in the building structure should be made without Wiley's (D) consent. Wiley (D) reserved the right to retake possession should Phillip Berg fail to meet the terms and conditions of the lease. Subsequently, Phillip Berg assigned his lease to Berg (P). Without securing Wiley's (D) permission, Berg (P) began to remodel the premises to make them suitable for a restaurant. A dispute arose between Berg (P) and Wiley (D) as a result of Berg's (P) continued remodeling of the restaurant without permission and operation of the restaurant in violation of the health code. Wiley (D) demanded that the health code violations be remedied and that Berg (P) complete the remodeling within two weeks. At the close of two weeks, Berg (P) closed the restaurant, dismissed her employees, and placed a sign on the premises that read, "Closed for Remodeling." Also after two weeks, Wiley (D) attempted to change the locks on the doors, but ceased this attempt when Berg (P) arrived. Three days later, without Berg's (P) knowledge, Wiley (D) changed the locks. Berg (P) contends that she was wrongfully evicted. Wiley (D) raises the defense of abandonment. The trial court ruled Wiley's (D) entry was forcible.

Issue: May a landowner use self-help to retake possession of his property?

Decision and Rationale: (Rogosheske). No. Though the testimony is in conflict, there is ample evidence to support the jury's finding that Berg (P) did not abandon the premises. At common law, a landlord could use self help if: (1) The landlord is legally entitled to possession, such as when a tenant is a hold-over; and (2) the landlord's means of entry are peaceable. On the first requirement, Wiley (D) contends that he was entitled to possession since Berg (P) breached the lease. However, it is for the courts, not Wiley (D), to determine if a landlord is entitled to possession. Turning to whether entry was peaceable, Wiley (D) contends that only actual or threatened use of violence should give rise to liability. We are not convinced. There has been a public policy in this state, expressed by both the courts and the legislature, aimed at discouraging self-help. To discourage self-help, the legislature has created summary proceedings to help the landlord regain possession quickly. To further discourage self-help, the legislature has provided treble damages for forced entry. In consideration of this policy, Wiley's (D) entry was not peaceable. Given the historical relations between Berg (P) and Wiley (D), the only reason violence did not erupt was because Berg (P) was not present when the locks were changed. Indeed, any use of self-help has the potential for violence. Therefore, unless the tenant has abandoned or surrendered the premises, a landlord may not use self-help. The landlord must resort to the judicial process to regain possession. Judgment affirmed.

Analysis:

Does this case illustrate a maxim of the law: Possession is nine tenths of the law? Because Berg (P) had possession of the premises, the law gave her much protection. There are many reasons for protecting possessors on rented land: (1) As the court mentioned, it discourages the forcible taking of possession. The law always wants to deter violence; (2) It protects families from being left with no-where to go. Note, however, that protection of possessors comes at the expense of the landlord, who may be legally entitled to possession. As a compromise, some states forbid self-help to evict a residential tenant, but allow self-help for the eviction of a commercial tenant.

COURT MAKES LEASE MORE LIKE A CONTRACT: LANDLORD NOW HAS DUTY TO MITIGATE DAMAGES

Sommer v. Kridel

(Landlord) v. (Tenant Who Has Abandoned)
(1977) 74 N.J. 446; 378 A.2d 767

M E M O R Y   G R A P H I C

Instant Facts

Sommer (P) failed to make efforts to re-let an apartment when Kridel (D) abandoned it.

Black Letter Rule

A landlord is under a duty to mitigate damages by making reasonable efforts to re-let an apartment wrongfully vacated by the tenant.

Case Vocabulary

DEFAULTING TENANT: A tenant who abandons or does not do some other act required under a lease (including the failure to pay rent).
MITIGATE DAMAGES: To attempt to reduce the damages that occur as a result of a breach or abandonment.
REASONABLE DILIGENCE: That amount of diligence that an ordinary man would exercise under the circumstances.
RE-LET: To lease to another.
SECURITY DEPOSIT: A sum of money paid by a lessee to insure against damage to the premises.

Procedural Basis: Appeal from an order by the appellate court reversing judgment in action for damages to recover back rent.

Facts: Sommer (P) leased apartment 6-L to Kridel (D) for a term of 2 years. Kridel (D) paid the first month's rent plus a security deposit. Before Kridel (D) went into possession, however, he informed Sommer (P) by letter that he could no longer afford the lease. Sommer (P) did not respond to the letter. Subsequently, a third party inquired about apartment 6-L. Though the third party was ready, willing, and able to rent apartment 6-L, she was refused because it had already been rented to Kridel (D). Over a year later, the apartment was finally re-let for terms and conditions similar to those negotiated with Kridel (D). Sommer (P) sues for damages for rent due between the date Kridel (D) was to take possession and the date when the apartment was rented to the third party. Kridel (D) contends that there is no liability because Sommer (P) both failed to mitigate and accepted Kridel's (D) surrender of the premises. The companion case of *Riverview Realty Co. v. Perosio* has similar facts: Perosio (D) abandoned possession of a two-year lease after a one year occupancy.

Issue: Is a landlord under a duty to mitigate damages by making reasonable efforts to re-let an apartment wrongfully vacated by the tenant?

Decision and Rationale: (Pashman). Yes. The majority rule is that a landlord has no duty to mitigate. This is based on the property view of a lease. This view understands a lease to be a property interest which forecloses any control of the property by the landlord. For example, in *Muller v. Beck* [issue of whether landlord must mitigate when a tenant abandons] it was said that "the tenant has an estate with which the landlord cannot interfere." It was understood that when the tenant vacated, he could retake the premises when he wished. Since the landlord had no control, it would be silly to require him to mitigate. Modern social forces, however, have exerted pressure on the law of estates. The law of estates has responded by allowing specific clauses in contracts to deal with these forces. Since we now view a lease in large measure as a contract, we apply a contract principle: The landlord must mitigate damages. This rule derives from considerations of fairness. It would be unfair to allow a landlord to sit idly by and watch damages mount when he can prevent those damages. For example, in *Sommer v. Kridel*, Sommer (P) let over a year pass and allowed $4658.50 in damages to accrue before he made efforts to re-let. The landlord cannot argue that he will lose the opportunity to rent to another if he's required to first rent the apartment that has been abandoned. This is because each apartment has its unique characteristics, and there is no reason to believe that a tenant who wished to rent the apartment that has been abandoned also would have been willing to rent another vacant apartment. In fact, in *Sommer v. Kridel*, there was a specific request for the abandoned apartment. So the rule is: If the landlord has many vacant apartments, he must treat the abandoned apartment as one of his vacant stock and make reasonable efforts to re-let it. Since the landlord is in a better position to demonstrate that his efforts were reasonable, he shall have the burden of showing reasonable efforts to re-let. Judgment reversed.

Analysis:

This case illustrates the growing usage of contract law in the law of leaseholds. Note in particular that one of the goals of property law merges with a goal of contract law. That goal is the efficient use of land or resources. In contract law, a non-breacher must attempt to mitigate the damaging effects of a breach. Historically, however, a landlord did not have to mitigate the damages of an abandonment because he was not the possessor of the estate. To change this historical understanding of a leasehold, and to encourage the efficient use of property, the law of contracts was imported into the law of property. Using contract law in property law, however, is not without costs. Contract law has placed many burdens and duties on both the landlord and tenant that were not present at common law. Whether these new duties, such as the implied warranty of habitability, are desirable is in dispute. The next several cases take this issue up. The court can be criticized for discarding the argument that a landlord will lose the opportunity to rent another vacant apartment if he is required to first rent the apartment that has been abandoned (this is the familiar "lost volume seller" argument from contract law). The court says that since a lessee will chose an apartment for its unique characteristics, the landlord will not lose a tenant. However, though houses may have unique characteristics, most units in an apartment complex are usually very, very similar.

Reste Realty Corp. v. Cooper

(Landlord) v. (Tenant)

(1969) 53 N.J. 444; 251 A.2d 268

M E M O R Y   G R A P H I C

Instant Facts

Whenever it rained, the basement that Cooper (D) was leasing flooded.

Black Letter Rule

A tenant may vacate premises and terminate the lease if his quiet enjoyment is interfered with by the landlord.

Case Vocabulary

CAVEAT EMPTOR: "Let the Buyer Beware." Doctrine which asserts that a buyer takes what he buys as it is, and the buyer should be aware of defects.
CONSTRUCTIVE EVICTION: Eviction in the eyes of the law, though not actual eviction.
DEMISE: To transfer to another.
INDEPENDENT COVENANT: Mutual covenants in an agreement that remain enforceable even though the other has been breached.
LATENT DEFECT: A defect which is hidden.
NOTICE OF VACATION: A letter informing the landlord that the tenant will give up possession.
PATENT DEFECT: A defect which is apparent.
QUIET ENJOYMENT: That doctrine which asserts that a tenant is entitled to possession free of interference from the landlord.

Procedural Basis: Appeal from order of appellate court reversing judgment in action for damages for breach of lease.

Facts: In 1958, Cooper (D) leased the basement of a commercial office building from Reste's (P) predecessor in interest. Cooper (D) used the basement for meetings and training of sales personnel. Whenever it would rain, the basement would flood with water because the driveway and the surfacing was faulty. When the basement did flood, Donigan, an agent of the owner, promptly drained the water. After one year a new lease was negotiated for a term of 5 years. At this time, Donigan promised to remedy the flooding. The driveway was resurfaced, but the flooding continued. Donigan died in 1961. Whenever it rained thereafter, no one paid any attention to Cooper's (D) complaints. It became very difficult for Cooper (D) to hold her meetings there. In particular, the flooding was so severe one night that Cooper (D) was unable to hold her meetings there. Subsequently, she vacated the premises. Reste (P) sues for the balance of the lease. Reste (P) contends that abandonment by Cooper (D) was unjustified because the flooding was not permanent. Reste (P) also contends that abandonment was unjustified because Cooper (D) inspected the premises and accepted the premises in their condition at that time.

Issue: May a tenant vacate premises and terminate the lease if his quiet enjoyment is interfered with by the landlord?

Decision and Rationale: (Francis). Yes. Reste (P) first contends that abandonment was unjustified because Cooper (D) inspected the premises and accepted the premises in their condition at that time. This is unconvincing because the driveway and surfacing caused the flooding. This cannot be considered part of the premises. In any event, there is no reason to believe that Cooper (D) knew of the defect. Next, Reste (P) argues that Cooper (D) waived her right to quiet enjoyment because she signed the second lease knowing of the flood problem. This is unconvincing because Donigan promised to remedy the flooding. The crucial question is: Was Cooper (D) justified in vacating? A covenant of quiet enjoyment is implied in a lease. When an act or a failure to act renders the premises unsuitable for the purpose for which it was leased, this covenant is breached. If this occurs, the tenant may terminate the lease if she chooses; of course, she must vacate the premises. In this case, Cooper (D) could not use the basement for her sales meeting. This is the use for which the premises were rented. Thus, she was justified in vacating and canceling the lease. Reste (P) finally contends that Cooper (D) waived her right to cancel the lease because she remained in possession for an unreasonable time after learning of the defect. We must find that Cooper (D) vacated within a reasonable time since there was ample evidence for the trial court to find that she acted reasonably under the circumstances. Judgment reversed.

Analysis:

This case exemplifies the move away from property and towards contract in the law of leaseholds. In contract law, there is a doctrinal area called the implied warranty of suitability. This doctrine requires that sellers of some goods warrant their products to be fit for purposes for which it is sold. This doctrine has been incorporated into the law of property under the doctrinal heading of implied covenant of quiet enjoyment: the landlord warrants that the premises will be fit for the purposes for which it was leased. This doctrine protects tenants by ensuring that the premises are clean, safe, and "enjoyable." Whether this actually benefits tenants, however, is disputed. The argument is that since landlords must now guarantee that the premises are fit, they may increase the rent that they charge. Moreover, this increase in rent not only harms renters, but it may make it impossible for some to rent.

COURT MAKES LIFE EASIER FOR RENTERS: THERE IS AN IMPLIED COVENANT OF HABITABILITY IN EVERY LEASE

Hilder v. St. Peter

(Tenant) v. (Landlord)

(1984) 144 Vt. 150; 478 A.2d 202

MEMORY GRAPHIC

Instant Facts

St. Peter (D) leased an apartment unfit for habitability to Hilder (P). Though Hilder (P) informed St. Peter (D) of these defects, he failed to remedy them.

Black Letter Rule

There is an implied warranty of habitability in every residential lease.

Case Vocabulary

CAVEAT LESSEE: Literally, let the lessee beware; a doctrine which asserts that the lessee takes the premises as he finds it, whether fit for human habitation or not.
DE MINIMIS: A small amount not recognized by the law as significant.
IMPLIED WARRANTY OF HABITABILITY: A warranty implied in every contract for the lease of a residential dwelling to the effect that the landlord will maintain the premises fit for human habitability.
INTERDEPENDENT CONSIDERATIONS: Doctrine asserting that if landlord breaches a term of the lease, including the implied warranty of habitability, the tenant's duty to pay rent ceases.
PUNITIVE DAMAGES: Money awarded to plaintiff for the sole purpose of punishing defendant.
REFORMATION: The re-working of a contract.
RESCISSION: To voiding of a contract.

Procedural Basis: Appeal from judgment in action for damages for breach of implied covenant of habitability.

Facts: In 1974 Hilder (P) and her three children rented an apartment from St. Peter (D) for $140 per month. Hilder (P) has paid all rent due. Upon taking possession of the apartment, Hilder (P) discovered a broken kitchen window. St. Peter (D) promised to repair it but failed to do so. Eventually, Hilder (P) repaired the window at her own expense because she was concerned that one of her children might get cut. There was also no key to the door. St. Peter (D) promised to provide a key, but never did. The toilet was clogged and was filled with feces; it would only flush if water was poured down it. The bathroom light and wall outlet were inoperable. In order to have light in the bathroom, Hilder (P) attached an extension cord to an outlet in an adjoining room and ran it to the bathroom. Water leaked into the apartment from an apartment above. As a result, a large section of plaster fell onto Hilder's (P) bed and her grandson's crib. Also, there was a strong and offensive odor in the apartment. All of these things St. Peter (D) promised to remedy, but never did. The trial court ruled these faults breached the warranty of habitability and awarded Hilder (P) the total rent paid. St. Peter contends that it was error to award the full rent because Hilder (P) never vacated. Hilder (P) contends that abandoning the premises is not required.

Issue: Is there an implied warranty of habitability in every residential lease?

Decision and Rationale: (Billings). Yes. Historically the rule was that the lessee took possession in whatever state the premises were in. The landlord had no duty to make the premises habitable unless there was an express covenant in the lease. This is because a leasehold was viewed as an estate in land: The land was the essence of the conveyance, not the dwelling. The tenant was excused from paying rent only if the landlord ousted the tenant. In modern times, a tenant leases land for a safe, sanitary dwelling, not for arable land. Moreover, the characteristics of today's tenant has changed. The tenant of the middle ages was a farmer who was capable of making necessary repairs himself. In contrast, today's tenant is a city dweller who is unable to repair complex living units. On the other hand, landlords are in a much better position to repair residential units. Given these changes, we now hold that there exists in every residential lease an implied covenant of habitability. Moreover, this warranty cannot be waived by a tenant. In determining whether this warranty has been breached, the courts may look to the local municipal housing code or to the minimum state housing code standards, for example. These codes and standards need not be dispositive, however. These standards should be used to determine if the premises are safe. Once the warranty has been breached, the tenant must notify the landlord and allow him time to remedy the defect. If the defect is not remedied, the tenant may pursue rescission, reformation, and damages. Damages awarded shall be the difference between the value of the residence as warranted and the value of the residence as defective. The tenant may recover for discomfort and annoyance, and he may repair the defect and deduct the expense from the rent. The tenant may also withhold rent until damages are calculated. The burden of bringing suit will then be on the landlord, who can better afford to bring the action. Finally, the plaintiff may pursue punitive damages. Judgment affirmed in part and remanded for a calculation of damages.

Analysis:

The implied warranty is often hailed as a victory for renters. However, this is in dispute. First, as is the case with the doctrine of constructive eviction, landlords will increase rent since they must now warrant the premises. This will make housing less affordable. This is surely not a victory for tenants. Second, since the warranty is not waivable, it decreases renters' bargaining power. Why should an informed renter, willing to live in an unfit house for a reduction in rent, be denied the opportunity to live there? The answer often given is that the courts should not permit conduct that debases human dignity. Of course, this is no answer if the tenant's only other option is to live on the street.

Chicago Board of Realtors v. City of Chicago

(Land Owners) v. (City)

(1987) 819 F.2d 732

MEMORY GRAPHIC

Instant Facts

Chicago enacted a rent control ordinance which made minor re-allocations of rights between landlords and tenants.

Black Letter Rule

A rent control ordinance which makes minor re-allocations of rights between landlords and tenants is reasonably related to a legitimate public goal.

Case Vocabulary

CLASS LEGISLATION: Legislation designed for the sole purpose of aiding a particular class of individuals.

CONTRACTS CLAUSE: Constitution clause forbidding the government from interfering with contractual obligations.

PROCEDURAL DUE PROCESS: Clause of the constitution mandating that no life, liberty or property shall be taken without a fair chance for an individual to be heard.

REBUTTABLE PRESUMPTION: A presumption against a party which he may overcome by the introduction of evidence.

SUBSTANTIVE DUE PROCESS: Clause of the constitution (same clause as procedural due process) requiring that fundamental rights shall not be infringed upon unless the government has a compelling reason to do so.

TAKINGS CLAUSE: Clause of the constitution that requires that the government pay for land that it appropriates from private citizens.

VOID-FOR-VAGUENESS DOCTRINE: Doctrine which asserts that any law that is so vague that a reasonable person would not know how to avoid criminal behavior is void.

Procedural Basis: Appeal from denial of preliminary injunction in action to declare rent control ordinance unconstitutional.

Facts: In 1986, Chicago enacted a Residential Landlord and Tenant Ordinance which essentially codified the implied warranty of habitability. It also contained new landlord responsibilities and tenant rights, such as: (1) a tenant may withhold rent if the landlord violates a term of the lease; (2) the landlord must pay interest on security deposits; (3) the security deposit must be held in an Illinois bank; and (4) a landlord is forbidden from charging more than $10 for late rent. Chicago Board of Realtors contends that the ordinance violates the contracts clause of the Constitution, procedural and substantive due process, equal protection clause, and it is void for vagueness.

Issue: Is a rent control ordinance which makes minor re-allocations of rights between landlords and tenants reasonably related to a legitimate public goal?

Decision and Rationale: (Cudahy). Yes. [Judge Cudahy's constitutional analysis is omitted. Instead, the policy analysis of Judge Posner is included].

Concurrence: (Posner). We agree that the ordinance is reasonable. But a strong case can be made for its unreasonableness because it re-allocates rights between landlords and tenants. Though the stated purpose of the ordinance is to promote social welfare, this is probably not the true motivation. Moreover, it is not likely to be the actual result because, if landlords cannot charge more than $10 for late rent and if tenants can withhold rent, landlords will not improve housing as much, since it will no longer pay. In addition, landlords will try to raise rents. This will hurt tenants and force those who cannot pay the higher rent to go homeless. If the landlords can't raise rent, they will devote more resources to condominiums, reducing the stock of housing. The provision that requires that security deposits be placed in Illinois banks serves only to transfer wealth from landlords and out-of-state banks to tenants and local banks. This is class legislation and protectionism. This will really benefit the middle class, not the poor. This is because the middle class will get preferential treatment by the landlords because they are a better risk against late rent. Further, the middle class will benefit from over-supplied and lower priced condominiums. This ordinance transfers wealth from out-of-state banks and tenants to the middle class. This becomes clear when one realizes that out of state individuals can't vote in Chicago elections and that the poor rarely vote.

Analysis:

Judge Posner articulates the argument against rent control and doctrines such as the implied warranty of habitability. Though such attempts are noble, he says, they have the opposite effect of that intended. This illustrates an interesting element. Courts are reasonably free to develop doctrine to help the plight of the poor. The implied warranty of habitability is an example of such an attempt. However, the courts are almost powerless in striking down attempts by the legislature to help the poor, even when these attempts have the opposite effect of that intended. As the Supreme Court has said many times, it is not for the courts to judge the propriety of the legislature's actions.

Perspective
The Land Transaction

Chapter 7

There are two basic steps involved in the sale of land. The first involves the preparation of a contract of sale. After the sale is closed, the second step occurs as the seller delivers a deed to the land to the buyer. In exchange, the buyer gives the purchase price, almost always in the form of a check, to the seller.

This chapter covers the first step of the sale of land. First, an overview of a sale transaction is provided in a 1966 article, which breaks the process down into seven steps. After this introduction, more specifics of the actual contract of sale will be covered. The Statute of Frauds, and its effects on oral agreements, will be discussed with regard to the sale of property. Then, the concept of marketable title and its effects on a sales transaction will be studied. From there, the text will focus on the seller's duty to disclose defects to the buyer. Finally, the implied warranty of quality in the sale of property, whether with newly constructed or pre-existing structures, will be touched upon. After that, study will proceed to aspects of the deed and mortgage.

Next, the process after the closing of the contract of sale will be looked at. The first half of the reading will focus on the deed, the written instrument that proves that one person wishes to transfer his or her interest in land to another person. Specifically, the history behind the use of deeds will be explored, as well as the general types of deeds in use today. Also, there are six express warranties, or guarantees, of title that a typical deed contains. Examples from the legislatures and the courts will show how these warranties work, and how they can be maintained or violated by parties involved in a sale of land.

In addition, a deed will only be valid if it is properly "delivered" from one person to another. This does not mean merely handing the deed over; what does count as delivery will also be discussed.

The second half of the reading will cover the use of the mortgage in land sales. Basically, the mortgage is what a person wishing to borrow money to buy property gives a lender, like another person or a bank, in exchange for the desired money. This mortgage gives the lender the right to sell the property involved to pay off any debts the borrower does not pay for according to their agreement. Be aware that this is only a very basic explanation of how mortgages work. The various laws and exceptions to laws dealing with mortgages will fill much of the reading in the rest of the chapter.

Chapter Overview Outline The Land Transaction

Chapter 7

NOTE: THE PURPOSE OF THIS OUTLINE IS TO ORGANIZE THE CASES SO THAT ONE CAN QUICKLY UNDERSTAND THE RELEVANCE OF EACH CASE TO THE COURSE. NO ATTEMPT IS MADE IN THIS OVERVIEW TO ADDRESS EVERY CONCEPT THAT MUST BE STUDIED. BE SURE TO READ THE ENTIRE CASEBOOK AND/OR OTHER MATERIALS TO GAIN A FULL UNDERSTANDING OF ALL CONCEPTS.

I. Although U.S. law seeks to reduce burdens to the transfer of property, real estate transactions continue to be more burdensome than those for the transfer of personal property.

   A. Although somewhat variable from state to state, the standard real estate transaction in the U.S. involves seven steps. John C. Payne, *A Typical House Purchase Transaction in the United States.*

      1. First, the prospective buyer will consult a real estate agent from the locality in which the buyer is interested.
      2. Second, if prudent, the buyer will retain an attorney to write or review the contract for sale.
      3. Third, the buyer must finance the purchase, usually by obtaining a thirty-year mortgage, for which the mortgagee will require proof that the purchaser is receiving clear title to the land.
      4. Fourth, the real estate agent will work with the buyer and potential lenders to secure the financing.
      5. Fifth, the title to the land is investigated using three independent sources:
         a. An attorney may search the public records to establish the chain of title from the present owner back to the grant of the land from the sovereign and issue a *certificate of title* that no adverse interest has been created.
         b. An attorney may consult a certified abstract of the public records, prepared to make title searches easier.
         c. A title insurance company may issue a title insurance policy that the buyer and lender substitute for the attorney's *certificate of title*.
      6. Sixth, the sale *closing* brings all interested parties together for signature of relevant documents and buyer's payment of the purchase price.
      7. Seventh, the lender's attorney records the deed and mortgage, after which the attorney certifies that the buyer now has title to the property against which the mortgage is a valid first lien.

   B. The attorney's role in real estate transactions varies from state-to-state, but is generally greater in the transfer of commercial property than residential property, where the role of the broker has expanded.

   C. A standard real estate sales contract contains the following provisions:

      1. The Identities of the Parties
      2. The Earnest Money
      3. The Closing Date
      4. Possession
      5. The Deed
      6. Financing Conditions
      7. Prorations
      8. Disclosures
      9. Other Terms and Conditions
      10. Attorney's Modification
      11. Performance / Time Is Of The Essence Clause
      12. Inspections and Warranties
      13. Seller's Representations
      14. Title
      15. Affidavit of Title
      16. Clean Condition
      17. Escrow Closing
      18. Survey
      19. Risk of Loss
      20. Transfer Tax Compliance
      21. Well and Septic Test
      22. Statement of Assessments
      23. Statutory Compliance
      24. Merger of Agreements

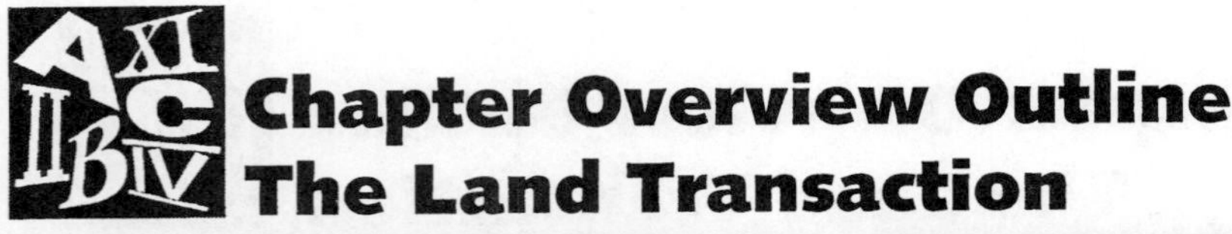

Chapter Overview Outline
The Land Transaction

II. The Contract of Sale for real estate transactions contains several unique provisions that must be met for a valid transfer.
  A. The real estate Contract of Sale must be in writing and state a price in order to comply with the *Statute of Frauds*.
    1. If the Contract for Sale does not state a price, a contract for sale at "fair market value" may be enforceable.
    2. Courts have carved out two common law exceptions to the Statute of Frauds.
      a. In most states, courts may enforce oral agreements where parties have made part performance pursuant to the agreement, (e.g., the buyer has taken possession of the property or paid the purchase price.)
      b. Courts may also use the doctrine of estoppel to enforce an oral agreement when one party would suffer unconscionable injury or to avoid unjust enrichment.
    3. The court will enforce a contract for sale of land despite its failure to satisfy the Statute of Frauds where there was a clear oral promise, partial payment, and actions in reliance on the contract. *Hickey v. Green.*
    4. Buyer's sale of another farm in reliance on oral contract for purchase of Seller's farm was not sufficient to overcome the Statute of Frauds where the Buyer's other sale was not foreseeable by Seller. *Walker v. Ireton.*
  B. The condition that seller's convey *marketable title* is implied in the Contract of Sale for real estate and the buyer may rescind if seller does not do so.
    1. Marketable title to real estate is title that does not expose the buyer to litigation. *Lohmeyer v. Bower.*
    2. In an action for specific performance by a seller or for rescission of contract by buyer, the seller will prevail if, at the conclusion of the suit, the court finds title to be marketable, even if it was proven marketable for the first time at trial. *Conklin v. Davi.*
    3. Courts in equity will usually grant specific performance in suits over real estate contracts on the grounds that the buyer sought to obtain a "unique" piece of land or that seller would have a hard time proving the difference between the contract price and market value of the property.
    4. Courts use the doctrine of *equitable conversion* (i.e., equity regards as done that which ought to be done) to determine whether buyer or seller bears risk of loss and whether the heirs of a deceased seller inherit the seller's real estate or personal property.
  C. The trend in real estate transactions has been away from *caveat emptor* and courts and statutory law increasingly require sellers to affirmatively disclose material defects.
    1. Where a seller has created a condition that materially alters the value of the contract for sale of real property, and the condition is uniquely within the knowledge of the seller and unlikely to be discovered by a careful buyer, failure to disclose that condition creates a basis for rescission as a matter of equity. *Stambovsky v. Ackley.*
    2. Sellers of real property have a duty to disclose to prospective buyers material facts affecting the value of the property, when those facts are not known or readily observable to the buyer. *Johnson v. Davis.*
    3. Many states have legislation that exempt the sellers from a duty to disclose facts that might affect market values for psychological or prejudicial factors (e.g., that a killing took place in the house or that a former resident was an AIDS patient.)
    4. Most states place a duty to disclose on real estate brokers equivalent to that placed on sellers.
    5. A federal environmental statute (CERCLA) requires disclosure of hazardous waste disposal on property being offered for sale.
    6. Courts will usually uphold "as is" clauses concerning easily discoverable defects.
    7. The old doctrine of *merger* that held that the Contract of Sale merged into the deed

and thereby discharged seller's duties is fading away; in modern land transactions, the seller's duties are considered collateral to the deed and may survive the closing.

D. Contracts of Sale in real estate carry an implied warranty of habitability upon which the buyer may sue after taking the deed.
   1. Buyer need not prove privity of contract to maintain a cause of action for builder's breach of implied warranty of workmanship and good quality for latent defects. *Lempke v. Dagenais.*
   2. Statutory law creates stricter warranties against vendor-builders than other sellers (e.g., the Uniform Land Transactions Act subjects those in "the business of selling" real estate to implied warranties of suitability and quality.)

III. In the U.S., the *deed* of land typically contains warranties of title and must be effectively delivered.

A. Although the language of deeds became quite cumbersome because of the historical developments of deeds (e.g., "By these presents grantor does give, grant, bargain, sell, remise, demise, release and convey unto the grantee. . . ."), many jurisdictions now permit short form deeds.

B. In the U.S. three types of deeds are common; from most comprehensive to least, they are:
   1. The *general warranty deed*, which warrants against any title defect, whether it arose while the grantor had title or before;
   2. The *special warranty deed*, which warrants only the acts of the grantor, not predecessors; and
   3. The *quitclaim deed*, which warrants nothing, but states that whatever title the grantor has (maybe none) is transferred.

C. Deeds also generally state that consideration was paid, describe the tract of land to be transferred, and in the past contained a seal or seal substitute.

D. Forged deeds are void.

E. General warranty deeds contain six express warranties.
   1. The first three, or "present" warranties are the *warranty of seisin*, the *covenant of the right to convey*, and the *covenant against encumbrances*; these can be breached only at the time of delivery of the deed but future successors may be assigned a chose in action against the grantor (see *Rockafellor v. Gray* below).
   2. The second three—"future" warranties—are the *covenant of general warranty*, *covenant of quiet enjoyment*, and *covenant of further assurances*; these "run with the land" to future successors in interest.
   3. A covenant of quiet enjoyment can be breached by interference with convenantee's right of possession creating a constructive eviction. *Brown v. Lober.*
   4. Seller's latent violation of a restrictive land use statute at the time of transfer does not constitute a violation of the warranty against encumbrances. *Frimberger v. Nazellotti.*
   5. The measures of damages for breaches of the present warranties are as follows:
      a. For breach of the warranty of seisin, return of some or all of the purchase price proportionate to the purchaser's loss;
      b. For breach of the covenant against encumbrances, the cost of removing the encumbrance or the difference in property value due to the encumbrance.
   6. The covenant of seisin runs with the land and is broken at the moment that the conveyance is delivered, becoming a chose in action held by the covenantee. *Rockafellor v. Gray.*
   7. In cases where a grantor conveys land that he does not own, but to which he later acquires title, the doctrine of *estoppel by deed* prevents the grantor from denying that he had title at the time of the conveyance.

F. For a deed to be effective, it must be *delivered* with the intent that it is to take effect immediately.

1. In most commercial land transactions, the deed is handed over when the seller receives the purchase price, or through an escrow agent at the closing; in donative transfers, however, delivery problems are more frequent.
2. Where a deed is handed over to the grantee, even where evidence shows that it was to take effect only upon the death of the grantor, the deed is considered properly delivered. *Sweeney, Administratrix v. Sweeney*.
3. Delivery does not require physical "handing over" of the deed, but may be achieved by any act that shows grantor's intent to be immediately bound to the transfer.
4. Where a grantor delivers a deed but retains a right of retrieval and states that the deed is operative only after the grantor's death, delivery is not legally sufficient. *Rosengrant v. Rosengrant*.
5. *Revocable trusts* serve to pass real property upon the grantor's death, but they avoid the hassles of probate because the trust document is a valid inter vivos instrument that establishes the beneficiary's title.

IV. Since most buyers cannot pay the purchase price in cash, financial institutions provide funds for real estate transactions.

A. Financial institutions lending money for real estate purchases require the borrower to execute a note and a mortgage, creating personal liability, but allowing the lender to reach the real property in the case of default.

B. The modern foreclosure sale developed as a way to avoid the cost and delay of judicial foreclosure.

C. Mortgagors seek deficiency judgments against borrowers for the difference between the outstanding debt and the price the property brings at the foreclosure sale; courts are more likely to award deficiency judgments following a judicial foreclosure than following a private foreclosure sale.

D. A mortgagee executing a power of sale has a duty to protect the interests of the mortgagor by exercising good faith and due diligence to obtain a fair price at the foreclosure sale of mortgagor's property. *Murphy v. Financial Development Corp*.

E. Absent wrongdoing or irregularity, the fact that the price obtained at a foreclosure sale was insufficient to cover the debt does not justify a court in setting aside or invalidating the sale. Grant S. Nelson & Dale A. Whitman, *Real Estate Finance Law*.

F. If a mortgagor transfers her land, the buyer takes either "subject to the mortgage" (with no personal liability for the loan, but a promise to the seller to settle the debt through sale of the land) or by "assuming the mortgage" (promising to settle the mortgage debt personally.)

G. Sellers attempt to avoid the hassles of foreclosure by using *installment land sale contracts* which allow buyers to take possession of land but transfer title only upon settlement of the purchase price through installments.

H. Because the buyer under an installment land sale contract acquires equitable title, which must be extinguished before the seller can retake possession, buyer's payments cannot be forfeited where there would be an inequitable disposition of property and exorbitant loss of money by buyer. *Bean v. Walker*.

I. Most states further protect buyers under installment land sale contracts with statutes that require sellers to give notice of potential forfeitures and barring seller's suit for the balance of the purchase price.

MASSACHUSETTS COURT HOLDS THAT PARTIAL PERFORMANCE OF AN ORAL LAND SALE AGREEMENT IS SUFFICIENT TO REMOVE THE TRANSACTION FROM THE STATUTE OF FRAUDS

Hickey v. Green

(Potential Buyer) v. (Seller)

Appeals Court of Massachusetts, 1982 14 Mass. App. Ct. 671, 442 N.E. 2d 37

M E M O R Y   G R A P H I C

Instant Facts

The Hickeys (P) sold their house in reliance on an oral agreement with the owner of Lot S, Mrs. Green (D). Mrs. Green rescinded the agreement.

Black Letter Rule

When there is a clear oral promise, partial payment, plus an act made in reliance, a land transfer is sufficient to overcome the Statute of Frauds requirement that contracts for the sale of land must be in writing.

Case Vocabulary

ESTOPPEL: A party is prevented by his own acts from asserting a right that will result in detriment to the other party.

RESCISSION OF A CONTRACT: To nullify or void a contract. The right of rescission is the right to cancel a contract upon default of some kind by the other party. Rescission may be effected by the mutual agreement of the parties.

SPECIFIC PERFORMANCE: Where money damages would be inadequate compensation, a court will compel a breaching party to perform specifically what he has agreed to do. These are considered appropriate remedies for buyers in land transfer cases, where each plot of land is considered "unique."

Procedural Basis: Appeal from an order granting specific performance to plaintiff.

Facts: The Hickeys (P) negotiated with Mrs. Green (D) to purchase Lot S from her. There were no lawyers involved in the negotiations. They orally agreed on a price of $15,000, and the Hickeys (P) put down a $500 deposit, which Mrs. Green (D) accepted. But, she did not cash the check. The Hickeys advised Mrs. Green that they intended to sell their home and build on Lot S. The Hickeys (P) sold their home very quickly. Two weeks after putting down the deposit with Mrs. Green (D), she (D) informed them that she no longer wished to sell, as she had another buyer willing to pay $ 16,000. Hickey (P) told Mrs. Green (D) that they had already sold their house and offered to pay $ 16,000, but Mrs. Green (D) refused to sell to him. The Hickeys (P) sued, seeking specific performance of the oral agreement.

Issue: In a land transfer where the Statute of Frauds is at issue, can a party be granted specific performance if they have substantially relied on the oral agreement?

Decision and Rationale: (Cutter) Yes. Restatement (Second) of Contracts, §129 sets forth the rule regarding specific performance. It requires that the party seeking specific enforcement must show reasonable reliance and that he or she has so changed his or her position that injustice can be avoided only by specific enforcement. The provisions of §129 have traditionally been enforced very strictly in Massachusetts. The comments to §129 illustrate that payment of the purchase price alone is not sufficient to constitute part performance. However, the requirement of part performance has been satisfied where the buyer makes payment and takes possession of the property. Here, there is evidence that both parties intended the sale of Lot S to be very quick. For that reason, the Hickeys (P) reasonably attempted to quickly sell their house, without seeking the assurance of a written document. The absence of a lawyer suggests that the parties did not intend to formalize their agreement. Additionally, the Hickeys' (P) acceptance and endorsement of a deposit for their house probably left them open to a suit if they had attempted to avoid transfer of their home. Mrs. Green (D) does not deny that there was an oral agreement. This is significant because it shows injustice, and it shows that the reliance by the Hickeys (P) was reasonable and appropriate. Judgment affirmed.

Analysis:

Comment b of Restatement (Second) of Contracts §129 articulates the two policy reasons for awarding specific performance based on reliance. First, such an award is justified based on the extent to which the parties' actions satisfy the evidentiary goals of the Statute of Frauds. In other words, the purpose of the Statute of Frauds is to provide concrete evidence that an agreement was made. If the parties' actions, through part performance, demonstrate good evidence of an agreement, courts are more likely to overlook the writing requirement. Second, the buyer's reliance may display the buyer's expectations as to what he thought the parties agreed upon. This provides to courts of equity more of a basis for enforcing the agreement than mere testimonial evidence.

Lohmeyer v. Bower

(Buyer) v. (Seller)

Supreme Court of Kansas, 1951 170 Kan. 442, 227 P. 2d 102

M E M O R Y   G R A P H I C

Instant Facts

Prior to transfer of property, a title search showed that the property in question had two encumbrances upon it, both of which were being violated.

Black Letter Rule

Marketable title to real estate is title that does not expose the buyer to litigation.

Case Vocabulary

EASEMENT: A right of use of a property by someone other than the owner, e.g., the right to use a waterway or path that extends over another's property; generally for the benefit of neighbors.

SPECIFIC PERFORMANCE: Where money damages would be inadequate compensation, a court will compel a breaching party to perform specifically what he has agreed to do. These are considered appropriate remedies for buyers in land transfer cases, where each plot of land is considered "unique."

Procedural Basis: Appeal from judgment awarding specific performance to defendant on cross-complaint.

Facts: Lohmeyer (P) entered into a contract whereby he was to purchase Lot 37, on which there was a house in a subdivision from Bower (D). The contract provided that the conveyance of the title was subject to Bower (D) producing a merchantable title, showing it was free and clear of all encumbrances. Restrictions and easements of record applying to the property, however, would not prevent the conveyance. Additionally, Bower (D) was to have reasonable time to correct any defects in the title. The abstract of title showed that there was a restrictive covenant on the property, requiring that all houses be two stories. Additionally, a municipal ordinance applying to the property provided that no house was to be less than three feet from a side or rear lot line. The house on Lot 37 violated both restrictions. Lohmeyer (P) sought to rescind the contract, not based on the existence of the restrictions, but on the fact that those restrictions were violated.

Issue: Does the violation of valid restrictions render a title unmerchantable?

Decision and Rationale: (Parker) Yes. The weight of the case law is clear that a buyer may not rescind a contract to purchase land where the encumbrance on the title is the result of a municipal ordinance. A buyer may ordinarily rescind a contract based on the existence of private covenants, but Lohmeyer (P) agreed to accept private covenants. Lohmeyer's (P) case is premised on the fact that the house on Lot 37 violates these restrictions, thus leaving him open to litigation. The case of *Peatling v. Baird* clarifies what constitutes merchantable title. *Peatling v. Baird* holds that "A marketable title to real estate is one which is free from unreasonable doubt, and a title is doubtful if it exposes the party holding it to the hazard of litigation." Property that is violating both a private covenant and a municipal requirement will expose Lohmeyer (P) to litigation. According to the contract, Bower (D) is entitled to have time to remedy the restrictions. While he may purchase more land to remedy the lot line problem, building a second floor onto the house would be too much to require.

Analysis:

The court points out that there is a different standard for marketable title in the case of ordinances than there is for private covenants. In other words, if a zoning ordinance required houses in a certain area to be of a certain type, a buyer, absent an agreement otherwise, cannot rescind the contract. On the other hand, if there is a private covenant running with the land that houses must be of that type, a buyer may rescind. The legal basis for this distinction is unclear. One reason might be that individuals may have greater notice of the existence of municipal ordinances before entering into the agreement. On the other hand, most citizens are not aware of the municipal ordinances in their city, especially as pertains to specified areas. A buyer might be more likely to notice that every house in a subdivision is two stories than that they are all equally distant from the lot line of the property.

STATE SUPREME COURT CLARIFIES THE ISSUE OF ADVERSE POSSESSION AND MARKETABLE TITLE.

Conklin v. Davi

(Seller) v. (Buyer)

Supreme Court of New Jersey, 1978 76 N.J. 468, 388 A.2d 598

M E M O R Y   G R A P H I C

Instant Facts

Buyers of a property refuse to consummate a sale, claiming that sellers have not proved marketable title, as sellers claim ownership of part of the property based on adverse possession.

Black Letter Rule

In an action for specific performance by a seller or for rescission of contract by a buyer, the seller will prevail if, at the conclusion of the suit, the court finds title to be marketable, even if it was proven marketable for the first time at trial.

Case Vocabulary

COUNTERCLAIM: A cause of action by a defendant in an action against a plaintiff.

QUIET TITLE: A proceeding to establish the plaintiff's title to land by bringing into court adverse claimants and compelling the adverse party to establish title or be estopped from ever asserting it.

Procedural Basis: Appeal from reversal of summary judgment and judgment entered by appellate court in favor of plaintiffs.

Facts: Conklin (D) contracted to sell residential property to Davi (P). Davi (P) refused to complete the sale, contending that Conklin (D) did not have marketable title, as Conklin (D) claimed to own part of the property by virtue of adverse possession. Conklin (D) sued for specific performance, and Davi (P) counterclaimed for rescission. Before trial, Conklin (D) dropped his claim for specific performance. Davi (P), in his claim for rescission, maintained that absent a deed or an action to quiet title, Conklin's (D) claim of ownership based on adverse possession rendered title unmarketable. After presentation of Davi's (P) case, the lower court granted Conklin's (D) motion for summary judgment. Davi (P) appealed, and the appellate court reversed the trial court judgment and, instead of remanding the case, entered a judgment in favor of Davi (P).

Issue: Where ownership by adverse possession has not been clearly established by a deed transfer or a quiet title action, may a seller establish marketable title?

Decision and Rationale: (Mountain) Yes. A contract for the sale of real property does not require a valid title of record, rather it requires that title be marketable or insurable. Here, an insurance company representative gave testimony at trial that they would have insured the property. Furthermore, a marketable title, all that is required by law, ensures that buyers are free from a reasonable doubt about their property. It does not require a guarantee that title is flawless. While summary judgment was not appropriate, the appellate court was clearly erroneous in denying Conklin (D) the opportunity for a de novo trial. Conklin (D) should have had an opportunity to demonstrate to the court that title was marketable. A title's marketability can be shown at trial, it does not have to have been proven to the buyer before trial. Additionally, in the case of adverse possession, an action to quiet title is not necessary to demonstrate marketability.

Analysis:

Note that marketable title is an implied term in real estate transfers. Buyers can contract for more protection ("good title") or less (e.g., by agreeing to accept any previous encumbrances on the land). However, if the contract or deed does not state the terms, a requirement of marketable title is construed.

IN SPITE OF THE DOCTRINE OF CAVEAT EMPTOR, NEW YORK COURT FINDS THAT SELLER HAD A DUTY TO INFORM BUYER THAT HOUSE WAS HAUNTED

Stambovsky v. Ackley

(Buyer) v. (Seller)

New York Supreme Court, Appellate Division, First Department, 1991 169 A.D.2d 254, 572 N.Y.S.2d 672

M E M O R Y   G R A P H I C

Instant Facts

Ackley (D) sells a house that she has widely publicized as a haunted house to Stambovsky (P), who is from a different city and does not know that it is haunted.

Black Letter Rule

Where a seller has created a condition that materially alters the value of the contract for sale of real property, and the condition is uniquely within the knowledge of the seller and unlikely to be discovered by a careful buyer, failure to disclose that condition creates a basis for rescission as a matter of equity.

Case Vocabulary

DOCTRINE OF CAVEAT EMPTOR: "Let the buyer beware." A maxim that a purchaser must judge, test and examine the quality of an item for himself.

Procedural Basis: Appeal from dismissal of a complaint.

Facts: Ackley (D) sold her house in the Village of Nyack to Stambovsky (P), a resident of New York City. Stambovsky (P) then discovered that the house was known in the area to be haunted. Ackley (D) had perpetuated that rumor by reporting the presence of ghosts in her local newspaper and to Reader's Digest, and by including the home in a walking tour of Nyack. She had not told Stambovsky (P) that the house was haunted. Stambovsky (P) sought to rescind the contract, but the trial court dismissed the cause of action because of the doctrine of caveat emptor.

Issue: Where the seller creates a condition that materially affects the value of land, and where the buyer has acted with reasonable prudence, can nondisclosure be the basis for rescission of the contract of sale?

Decision and Rationale: (Rubin) Yes. Preliminarily, the impact of the house's ghostly reputation goes to the very essence of the bargain. As Ackley (D) was responsible for circulating the folklore that the house was haunted, it is not for the court to decide whether there are, in fact, poltergeists in the house. Rather, Ackley (D) is estopped to deny the existence of ghosts, and the house is, as a matter of law, haunted. While the real estate broker, as agent for the seller, was under no duty to disclose the existence of poltergeists, equitable considerations suggest that the contract should be rescinded. It is difficult, and unusual, for a prospective buyer to order an inspection for ghosts. Additionally, we do not want to create a precedent that suggests that buyers should inspect for ghosts. Caveat emptor is appropriate where the buyer has equal opportunity to discover information about the house. A traditional means of refuting the doctrine was to show that the seller actively concealed a material fact. Here, while Ackley (D) did not actively conceal the existence of ghosts, she took unfair advantage of the Stambovsky's (P) ignorance of the folklore of the Village of Nyack. Enforcing this contract is offensive to the sense of equity. Judgment modified.

Dissent: (Smith) This court should not overturn the doctrine of caveat emptor because of the purported existence of poltergeists.

Analysis:

The court's decision rests upon the idea that the policy reasons for the doctrine of caveat emptor are not met in the case of a haunted house. The court finds that the existence of poltergeists is a material issue in the sale. And, the court implies that it would be undesirable to require all buyers to bring mediums or psychics to every house they purchase. For this reason, to best provide protection for the buyer and to avoid ridiculous consequences, the court is willing to make a substantial inroad into the destruction of the doctrine of caveat emptor. Did the court have to go as far as it did?

STATE SUPREME COURT FURTHER DESTROYS THE DOCTRINE OF CAVEAT EMPTOR IN LAND TRANSACTIONS

Johnson v. Davis

(Seller) v. (Buyer)

Supreme Court of Florida, 1985 480 So. 2d 625

M E M O R Y G R A P H I C

Instant Facts

Davis (P), with representation from Johnson (D) that a roof did not leak, buys home with a leaky roof.

Black Letter Rule

Sellers of real property have a duty to disclose to prospective buyers material facts affecting the value of the property, when those facts are not known or readily observable to the buyer.

Case Vocabulary

MATERIAL FACT: A fact which is significant enough to influence the bargain; if one of the parties had known this fact, there position in the land transfer would have changed.

MISFEASANCE: The improper performance of an act.

NONFEASANCE: Failure to perform an act that a person ought to do.

Procedural Basis: Appeal from a judgment for plaintiff for rescission of contract.

Facts: Johnson (D) contracted to sell his home to Davis (P). Although Johnson (D) knew that the roof leaked, he affirmatively represented to Davis (P) that it did not. Several days later, Davis (P) discovered water gushing in to the home, resulting from heavy rain. Davis (P) sued to rescind the contract.

Issue: Where a seller is aware of a material fact that is not known or readily observable to the buyer, does the seller have a duty to disclose that fact?

Decision and Rationale: Yes. (Adkins) The affirmative representation that the roof was sound was a material misrepresentation. Consequently, Davis (P) was entitled to rescission. Even if Johnson (D) had not affirmatively lied, Davis (P) should be entitled to recovery. Where the failure to disclose a material fact is calculated to induce a false belief, the distinction between concealment and affirmative representations is tenuous. The doctrine of caveat emptor, however, relieves a seller from liability for concealing material facts. This notion is out of date and undesirable. A seller should not take advantage of a buyer's ignorance. Therefore, where a seller of a home knows of facts that are material to the value of the property, and where these facts are not readily observable to the buyer, the seller has a duty to disclose these material facts. Judgment affirmed.

Analysis:

This case is one of many that carve away at the doctrine of caveat emptor. Many courts and legal scholars take the position that, in today's society, the doctrine is inappropriate. In today's society, most people have specialized skills and do not have a large amount of experience or knowledge about construction. Moreover, it is often impossible to discover defects until a period of time has elapsed and the buyer has experience with the property. For these reasons a majority of states impose a duty on the seller to disclose latent defects.

COURT FINDS THAT PRIVITY OF CONTRACT IS NOT NECESSARY FOR IMPLIED WARRANTIES IN SALE OF LAND

Lempke v. Dagenais

(Buyer) v. (Builder)

Supreme Court of New Hampshire, 1988 130 N.H. 782, 547 A.2d 290

M E M O R Y   G R A P H I C

Instant Facts

Lempke (P) purchases a house that has a garage that has been recently built, and later discovers the garage roof is defective.

Black Letter Rule

Privity of contract is not necessary to maintain a cause of action for the implied warranty of workmanship and good quality against a builder for latent defects.

Case Vocabulary

ECONOMIC HARM: Includes recovery for costs of repair and/or replacement of defective property, as opposed to simply decrease in value or personal injuries.

Procedural Basis: Appeal from dismissal of plaintiff's complaint.

Facts: Lempke's (P) predecessors in title contracted with Dagenais (D) to build a garage on their property. Lempke (P) bought the property six months later. After they purchased the home, the Lempkes (P) noticed structural defects in the garage's construction. They sued Dagenais (D) based on three grounds: 1) breach of the implied warranty of workmanlike quality, 2) negligence, and 3) breach of assigned contract rights.

Issue: Does a successor in title have a cause of action for the implied warranty of workmanship and quality against a prior builder?

Decision and Rationale: Yes. (Thayer) The lower court's decision relied on the opinion in *Ellis v. Morris,* which held that, absent privity of contract, a successor in interest could not recover for economic loss for the implied warranty of workmanship and good quality. Because privity was the major factor, we first consider that issue. The case *Norton v. Burleaud* established a cause of action for the implied warranty of quality. Courts and legal scholars have debated over which theory of liability the implied warranty of quality is based. Regardless of whether it is a tort, contract or hybrid, however, the implied warranty is a public policy doctrine that exists independently of any legal theory or of any agreement between the parties. The purposes of implied warranties are to protect purchasers from latent defects in their houses. To so protect purchasers, we hold that the privity requirement of the implied warranty of quality should be abandoned, where a subsequent purchaser suffers economic loss from a latent defect. To hold otherwise would leave innocent homeowners without a remedy. It would not be fair to relieve a contractor from liability for unsound workmanship simply because a house has changed hands. Finally, the builder is in a better position to prevent the damage from occurring. There are several overriding policy reasons behind implied warranties that support extension of the doctrine to successors in title. First, latent defects in a house often do not manifest themselves for a long period of time. Second, society is changing. People are less likely to stay in one place for long periods. Therefore, the ordinary buyer is not in a position to discover latent defects. Third, subsequent purchasers have little opportunity to inspect, and they have little knowledge about construction. In today's society, people rely on the craftsmanship of builders. Fourth, there is no unfairness to the builder, because he or she has a duty of workmanship to the first owner. Fifth and lastly, insulating only the first buyer might encourage "sham" first sales to protect contractors from liability. Finally, we address the issue of whether the extension of the implied warranty of workmanship and quality to successors in title should extend to purely economic loss. Most courts that have allowed recovery for economic loss have done so because of the difficulty in drawing the line between property damage and economic loss. We agree with these courts, finding the distinction between economic loss and personal injury or property damage is arbitrary. Note that there are limitations on our holding. We do not expect builders to act as insurers. The extension of the doctrine is limited to *latent* defects, where the buyer did not and, with an adequate inspection, should not have reasonably known of the defect. Additionally, the extension is limited to a reasonable period, and the plaintiff bears the burden of showing the defect was a result of the builder's poor workmanship. The duty to builders is to perform competently, according to acceptable standards.

Dissent: (Souter) I am not satisfied that there is adequate justification to overturn the rationale in *Ellis v. Robert C. Morris*.

Analysis:

Note that the policy justifications for extending implied warranties overlap the policy justifications for abrogating the doctrine of caveat emptor. In both instances, courts look to fairness and changing society as a basis for imposing liability. The court points out that these doctrines are being abrogated in the area of sales as well. This series of cases is as important for the trend they establish as they are for the actual holdings. Consider as well the court's reassurance that the warranty of quality will extend only for "a reasonable time." Doesn't this create more uncertainty on the part of the builders? Even if courts will be unwilling to impose liability for defects that are discovered several years after the home or structure has been built, allowing a cause of action for successors in interest may increase the number of actions brought against builders.

Brown v. Lober

(Land Buyer) v. (Bosts' Executor)
75 Ill. 2d 547, 389 N.E.2d 1188 (1979)

MEMORY GRAPHIC

Instant Facts

The Bosts sold land to the Browns, but conveyed only a one-third interest in the mineral rights to the Bosts.

Black Letter Rule

A covenant of quiet enjoyment can be breached by constructive eviction, but unless the covenantee's right of possession is interfered with, there is no constructive eviction, and, therefore, no breach of the covenant.

Procedural Basis: Appeal from judgment for damages in action for breach of the covenant of quiet enjoyment.

Facts: William and Faith Bost had eighty acres of land conveyed to them in 1947. The previous owner of this land had reserved a two-thirds interest in the mineral rights, thus conveying only a one-third mineral interest to the Bosts. In 1957, the Bosts conveyed this same land to James R. Brown and his wife (P) by a general warranty deed with no exceptions. In 1974, the Browns (P) contracted to sell their (P) mineral rights to Consolidated Coal Co. for $6,000. Consolidated Coal, however, renegotiated the contract to provide for payment of only $2,000 to the Browns (P) after learning the Browns (P) possessed only one-third of the mineral rights. The initial owner made no attempt whatsoever to exercise his mineral rights to the land. The Browns (P) sued Lober (D), the executor of the then-deceased Bosts, for $4,000 in damages for the breach of the covenant of quiet enjoyment. The trial court ruled for Lober (D), and the appellate court reversed.

Issue: Is the covenant of quiet enjoyment breached when a covenantee has not been prevented from enjoying possession of his or her interest in the given property?

Decision and Rationale: (Underwood) No. A covenant of quiet enjoyment can be breached by constructive eviction, but unless the covenantee's right of possession is interfered with, there is no constructive eviction, and, therefore, no breach of the covenant. This court's earlier decision in Scott v. Kirkendall [breach of covenant of quiet enjoyment of surface rights rejected because Scott could have taken possession at any time] is controlling in this case. There, Kirkendall granted title to Scott, even though others had paramount title. This was not a breach of the covenant of quiet enjoyment because the other parties never tried to assert the adverse title. The land in question had always been vacant, and Scott could have taken peaceable possession of it at any time. While that case dealt with surface rights, and not mineral rights, its reasoning is still applicable here. Here, no one tried to remove the minerals from the ground or do anything else to inform the community that the mineral interest was being exclusively used or enjoyed. The mineral estate of the land in this case was vacant, just as the surface land was in Scott. Likewise, the Browns (P) could have taken peaceable possession of it at any time, without any hindrance from anyone else. Until the Browns (P) meet such resistance in exercising this right of possession, there is no breach of the covenant of quiet enjoyment. Granted, there is a breach of the covenant of seisin involved here that results from the Bosts' deed to the Browns (P), but the Browns (P) did not raise a suit as to this issue within the ten years' statute of limitations. Moreover, the fact that Consolidated Coal modified the contract with the Browns (P) does not constitute a breach of the covenant of quiet enjoyment. Judgment of appellate court reversed.

Analysis:

A little more background should be given on the kind of covenants discussed in Brown and the way they can be breached. The covenants of warranty, quiet enjoyment, and further assurances are considered "future" covenants. These covenants can only be breached when someone with paramount title tries to disturb the current owner's possession. This opinion discusses the possibility of constructive eviction as a breach, but it does not really give an example of it. One way a person can be constructively evicted is by being forced to buy the superior title to keep from actually being physically evicted from the property. Another form of constructive eviction occurs when an owner is enjoined from using the property in a way that violates an earlier restrictive covenant on the property. If any of these situations were to arise, then the owner's right of possession would be considered "disturbed" and thus the "future" covenants would be breached. Because some form of eviction is needed for breach, even if not an actual "loss" of possession, the statute of limitations against bringing an action to challenge the breach would not run until the date of the eviction. Thus, there is little risk that a grantee would be barred from responding to a claim of paramount title in another person. Note that, in this case, there was no eviction, so the statute of limitations was never really an issue.

Frimberger v. Anzellotti

(Buyer) v. (Seller)

Appellate Court of Connecticut, 1991 25 Conn. App. 401, 594 A.2d 1029

M E M O R Y   G R A P H I C

Instant Facts

After purchasing property, Frimberger(P) discovered that the home on the property violated state environmental protection statutes.

Black Letter Rule

A latent violation of a restrictive land use statute does not constitute a violation of the warranty against encumbrances.

Case Vocabulary

ENCUMBRANCE: Every right or interest in the land which may exist in third persons, to the diminution of the value of the equity in the land, but consistent with the passing of the fee by the conveyance.

RESCISSION OF A CONTRACT: To nullify or void a contract; the right of rescission is the right to cancel a contract for cause. Rescission may be effected by the mutual agreement of the parties.

Procedural Basis: Appeal from trial court judgment awarding damages to plaintiff.

Facts: Anzellotti's (D) brother began to develop a property that, because it was adjacent to tidal wetlands, was subject to restrictive land use statutes. He then transferred the property to Anzellotti(D). Anzellotti (D) sold the property to Frimberger (P), free and clear of all encumbrances but subject to all building line and zoning restrictions. Frimberger (P) hired engineers to make improvements on the property. The engineers discovered that the improvements to the property made by the original owner violated the restrictive land use statutes. The Department of Environmental Protection ("DEP") informed Frimberger (P) that he could submit an application to the DEP, explaining the necessity of maintaining the improvements. The DEP did not fine Frimberger (P) or subject him to any sanctions for the violations. Nevertheless, Frimberger (P), without submitting the application to the DEP, sued Anzellotti (D) for breach of the warranty against encumbrances.

Issue: Can a latent violation of a land use statute, existing at the time a seller conveys a title, be considered an encumbrance violating the warranty against encumbrances?

Decision and Rationale: (Lavery) No. This is a case of first impression in Connecticut. However, a survey of other jurisdictions reveals that most jurisdictions find that statutes, ordinances or regulations do not affect marketability and should not be considered an encumbrance. The New Jersey case of *Fahmie v. Wulster* has a very similar fact pattern to this one. In *Fahmie*, a previous owner of a property had enclosed a stream in a manner that violated a New Jersey statute. The buyer of the property sued the seller for breach of the warranty against encumbrances. The New Jersey court held that to extend the warranty against encumbrances to land use violations would cause too much uncertainty in the law of conveyancing and title insurance. This uncertainty would result because neither a title search nor a physical examination of the premises would disclose the violation. The court decided that explicit contract provisions between private parties were the better method of protecting buyers. This case raises the same issues and concerns. Anzellotti (D) did not know of the defects in the property; they were discoverable only by consulting the DEP. Additionally, prior cases in Connecticut have held that for a title to be rendered unmarketable, the defect must subject the plaintiff to a real and substantial probability of litigation and loss. Here, the DEP, the entity charged with enforcement of the regulations, has taken no official action, and has even granted Frimberger (P) with a means to remedy his problem. Although the trial court awarded damages based on projected costs, there is no true means of awarding damages here, because Frimberger (P) has not yet been subjected to any real injury. Finally, Frimberger (P), an attorney and land developer, could have taken steps to protect himself before buying the property. He could have required a survey to ensure compliance, or he could have inserted protective provisions in the deed to protect him from liability for violations. The trial court further erred in finding Anzellotti (D) liable for innocent misrepresentation. The court's based its finding on its determination that Anzellotti (D) breached the warranty against encumbrances. Because we have found he did not breach the warranty against encumbrances, there was no innocent misrepresentation.

Analysis:

Recall the case of *Lohmeyer v. Bower*, where the court found that a prospective buyer could rescind his agreement upon a finding that the property violated a local zoning ordinance. These cases appear to be inapposite. In that case, the court allowed the buyer to rescind the contract because he was subject to a real and substantial probability of litigation or loss at the time of the conveyance. This case can be distinguished for two reasons. One, the state and municipal violations at issue here are latent; in other words, they do not show up on land records and are not known by the seller. Secondly, the agency charged with enforcement has taken no official action. Based on the facts of *Lohmeyer* and the language of the court's opinion here, it appears that both of these conditions must be met to be protected from rescission.

Rockafellor v. Gray

(Owner of Land) v. (Creditor)
194 Iowa 1280, 191 N.W. 107 (1922)

MEMORY GRAPHIC

Instant Facts

Rockafellor (P) purchases land and agrees to assume mortgage to Gray (D). Gray (D) forecloses on the mortgage.

Black Letter Rule

The covenant of seisin does run with the land, and is broken the moment the conveyance is delivered, becoming a chose in action held by the covenantee.

Case Vocabulary

CHOSE IN ACTION: A right of bringing an action or right to recover a debt or money.
COVENANT OF SEISIN: An assurance to the purchaser that the grantor has the very estate in quantity and quality which he purports to convey.
SEISIN: Possession of real property under claim of freehold estate.

Procedural Basis: Appeal by cross-defendant from a judgment in favor of cross-complainant.

Facts: Rockafellor (P) bought a parcel of property from Doffing and took over (assumed) a $500.00 mortgage to Gray (D). Subsequently, Gray (D) initiated foreclosure proceedings against Doffing, which culminated in a sheriff's deed, which was executed and delivered to Connelly. Connelly conveyed the property to Dixon. The deed contained the typical covenants of warranty, and Dixon paid $4000 consideration for the deed. Dixon conveyed the premises to Hansen & Gregerson for a consideration of $7000.00. Rockafellor (P) brought suit to vacate and set aside the foreclosure sale, on the grounds that the court did not obtain jurisdiction over Rockafellor (P). Hansen & Gregerson then cross-complained against Connelly on the ground that the covenant of seisin in his deed to Dixon also applied to Hansen & Gregerson.

Issue: Does the covenant of seisin run with the land, so that an action may be maintained by a remote grantee?

Decision and Rationale: Yes. (Faville) Although most American courts hold that the covenant of seisin does not run with the land, we adopt the English Rule. The English Rule states that the covenant of seisin does run with the land, and is broken the instant the conveyance is delivered, and then becomes a chose in action held by the covenantee in the deed. A deed by the covenantee operates as an assignment of such chose in action to a remote grantee. The remote grantee, on the basis of that assignment can then maintain an action against the grantor in the original deed. Connelly, however, contends that because he was never in possession of the land, the covenant cannot run with the land. Connelly's argument is that because seisin requires possession, he never had seisin of the land. Seisin is what gives rise to the idea that the covenant of seisin runs with the land. This argument is flawed, however, because we hold that the covenant of seisin exists as a chose in action. Connelly does not argue that Dixon was not protected by the covenant of seisin. Because Dixon himself was protected by the covenant of seisin, he could assign the covenant as a chose in action. Hansen & Gregerson are entitled to recovery of the consideration recited in the original grant from Connelly to Dixon. Judgment affirmed.

Analysis:

What is the significance of the court holding that the covenant of seisin is broken, but allowing it to be maintained as a chose in action? One reason is illustrated by this case -- to avoid issues of possession. For a covenant to "run with the land," the grantor must convey either title or possession, something to which a covenant can "attach" and "run." A chose in action is a personal right to sue that is not attached to property. Because a chose in action is not an interest in real property, calling the covenant a chose in action also may avoid issues raised by the Statute of Frauds.

A TRANSFER INTENDED ONLY TO TAKE EFFECT UPON THE TRANSFEROR'S DEATH IS VALID IF THE DEED IS DELIVERED DIRECTLY TO THE TRANSFEREE

Sweeney, Administratrix v. Sweeney

(Estranged Widow) v. (Brother)

Supreme Court of Errors of Connecticut, 1940 126 Conn. 391, 11 A.2d 806

MEMORY GRAPHIC

Instant Facts

Maurice Sweeney deeded his property to his brother John (D), and had the deed recorded. Simultaneously, John (D) deeded the property back to Maurice and did not record the deed.

Black Letter Rule

Where a deed is handed to grantee, but evidence shows it is to take effect only upon the death of the grantor, the deed is considered properly delivered.

Case Vocabulary

TESTAMENTARY: Made in lieu of a will; not to take effect until after death.

Procedural Basis: Appeal from a judgment for defendant.

Facts: Maurice deeded his property, which included a tavern, to his brother John (D) so that he would have it in case Maurice died. Maurice wanted to also protect himself in case John died, so he had John execute a deed transferring the property back to Maurice. The first deed was recorded; the second was not. The second deed [from John (D) back to Maurice] was ultimately burned in a fire. Maurice continued to run the tavern with only a little help from John (D). Upon Maurice's death, his estranged wife (P), claimed the property, by virtue of the second deed.

Issue: Where a deed is handed to a grantee, but the intention of the grantor is that it is to take effect only upon the grantor's death, will the court consider a valid delivery to have been made?

Decision and Rationale: Yes. (Jennings) Although Maurice intended the tavern to belong to John (D), the second deed, made by John (D) back to Maurice is valid. All of the elements of a good delivery were present: a deed had been executed and Maurice continued to possess the premises, pay fixed charges, receive rents and exercise full dominion over it until his death. Possession of the premises is not conclusive proof that the deed was delivered. John (D) may introduce evidence that the terms of the deed were not met. However, the evidence shows that John (D) intended to grant the property to Maurice. Additionally, The fact that the deed benefitted Maurice is prima facie evidence that he assented to it. These presumptions can be defeated only by evidence that John (D) did not intend to deliver the deed to Maurice. Maurice said that he requested the deed to protect himself, and this purpose would have been defeated had the deed not been delivered. This is conclusive proof that John (D) intended to deliver the deed. John's (D) final contention is that if there was a delivery, it was conditional on John's (D) death predating Maurice's. However, deliveries can only be conditional if the grantor delivers the deed into the hands of a third party. Here, the grantor delivered the deed into the hands of the grantee himself. Although the evidence suggests the intention of the parties was to make the deed conditional, we cannot bend the rules of property to fit this situation. To do so would open the doors of the court to fraud and fabrication of evidence. Judgment reversed and case remanded.

Analysis:

Does this case reflect too strict an adherence to formal rules? Maurice's clear intention was to ensure that his brother John received the property and not his wife. The court addresses this contention, deciding that, although the facts are compelling, "(t)he safety of real estate titles is considered more important than the unfortunate results which may follow the application of the rule in a few individual instances." Nevertheless, a number of courts have decided exactly the opposite of the court in *Sweeney*. The jurisdictions are split into three groups, some courts following the rule in *Sweeney,* some finding that these types of grants are testamentary and therefore invalid, and some ruling as to the intention of the parties. This latter group, illustrated by the Maryland case *Chillemi v. Chillemi,* reason that a deed can be held in escrow by the grantee as a conditional grant just as easily as by a third party. The court in *Chillemi* noted that decisions regarding traditional conditional grants are made by adhering to the intentions of the individual parties.

Rosengrant v. Rosengrant

(Deed Challenger) v. (Purported Grantee)
629 P.2d 800 (Okla. Ct. App. 1981)

MEMORY GRAPHIC

Instant Facts

An elderly couple attempted to deliver a deed to their nephew, but they stated that the deed would be effective only upon their deaths. After their deaths, an interested relative challenged the "delivery" because it was not a valid present transfer.

Black Letter Rule

Where a grantor delivers a deed but retains a right of retrieval and states that the deed is operative only after the grantor's death, the delivery is not legally sufficient.

Case Vocabulary

DE FACTO: As a matter of fact (as opposed to a matter of law).
IN PRAESENTI: At the present time.
PRO FORMA: As a matter of form or based upon assumed facts.

Procedural Basis: Appeal of verdict setting aside the transfer of a warranty deed to real property.

Facts: Mildred and Harold Rosengrant were an elderly couple who desired to transfer their farm to their nephew, Jay Rosengrant (D), upon their deaths. Jay (D) accompanied Harold and Mildred to the bank, where the couple signed the deed and handed it to Jay "to make this legal." They then instructed Jay (D) to return the deed to the banker, who put it in an envelope labeled "J.W. Rosengrant or Harold H. Rosengrant" in a safe deposit box. Harold and Mildred told Jay (D) that he could record the deed when they died. After Mildred died, Jay (D) consulted an attorney concerning the legality of the transaction. The attorney said the delivery should be sufficient but told Harold he could draw up a will. After Harold died (presumably without a will), Jay (D) obtained the deed from the bank and recorded it. Another Rosengrant (P) relative challenged the transfer, filing a petition to cancel and set aside the deed. Rosengrant (P) argued that the deed was void because it was never legally delivered and that the deed was really a testamentary instrument which was void for failure to comply with the Statute of Wills. The trial court agreed and found the deed null and void. Jay (D) appealed.

Issue: Where a grantor delivers a deed but retains a right of retrieval and states that the deed is operative only after the grantor's death, is the delivery legally sufficient?

Decision and Rationale: (Boydston, J.) No. Where a grantor delivers a deed but retains a right of retrieval and states that the deed is operative only after the grantor's death, the delivery is not legally sufficient. Harold and Mildred intended to comply with the legal aspects of delivery by handing the deed to Jay (D). However, after the "transfer" Harold continued to live on, farm, and pay taxes on the land. The words written on the envelope create an inescapable conclusion that the deed was retrievable by Harold any time before his death. There was an agreement that the deed was to take effect only upon the death of Harold and Mildred. Thus, the "transfer" to Jay (D) was only a pro forma attempt to comply with the legal aspects of delivery. The grantor clearly intended to exercise control over the land and had the power to revoke the transfer at any time. We agree with the trial court that the deed was not properly delivered. Affirmed.

Concurrence: (Brightmire, J.) A valid conveyance requires actual or constructive delivery of the deed, plus an intention by the grantor to divest himself of the conveyed interest. Here there was no valid delivery. If the grantors intended to convey the property prior to their deaths, they should have given Jay (D) the deed and told him to record it. The continued occupation and possession by the grantors indicates that they did not intend to create a present transfer. Moreover, Jay's testimony regarding the "delivery" is self-serving and suspicious. I agree that the deed failed as a valid conveyance. Affirmed.

Analysis:

The seemingly unjust result of this case underscores the importance of complying with the strict requirements of delivery. Harold and Mildred clearly intended for Jay (D) to take the property upon their deaths. Even though they attempted to legally deliver the deed, they failed to comply with the requirements for delivery. Harold and Mildred intended to pass title only upon their deaths. They could have handled the situation in at least two other ways in order to accomplish their goals. First, they could have simply created a will which transferred the property upon their deaths to Jay (D). The will would have had to comply with the Statute of Wills (i.e., in writing, signed, and witnessed appropriately). Second, if they wished to avoid probate associated with a will, they could have established a revocable trust on their farm. They would hold their farm in trust, retaining the right to possession and all rents and profits for their joint lives and the life of the survivor. A life estate would have been created in Harold ad Mildred for the life of the survivor, remainder to Jay (D) upon their deaths. They would have then been able to maintain the power to revoke the transfer at any time during their lives. This trust would have avoided probate and would be valid in all states. Note the important difference between a revocable deed and a revocable trust. The deed must strictly comply with the legal requirements for a present delivery, but delivery could be made without a written instrument. The trust, on the other hand, is an equitable instrument and the grantor need only manifest an intent to create the trust (plus sign a written instrument to satisfy the Statute of Frauds).

A MORTGAGEE CONDUCTING A FORECLOSURE SALE MUST EXERCISE GOOD FAITH AND DUE DILIGENCE IN OBTAINING A FAIR PRICE FOR A MORTGAGOR'S PROPERTY

Murphy v. Financial Development Corp.

(Unemployed Borrower) v. (Lending Institution)
126 N.H. 536, 495 A.2d 1245 (1985)

MEMORY GRAPHIC

Instant Facts

Financial Development Corporation foreclosed on Murphy's mortgage, but concluded the foreclosure sale after only one $27,000 bid was made on the $54,000 house.

Black Letter Rule

A mortgagee executing a power of sale has a duty to protect the interests of the mortgagor and exercise good faith and due diligence in obtaining a fair price for a mortgagor's property.

Procedural Basis: Appeal from judgment in action to set aside foreclosure sale or to obtain money damages.

Facts: In 1966, Richard Murphy and his wife (P) bought a house and financed it with a mortgage loan. In March 1980, the Murphys (P) refinanced the loan, executing a new promissory note and a power of sale mortgage, with Financial Development Corporation (FDC) (D) as the mortgagee. In February 1981, Richard Murphy (P) became unemployed, and the Murphys (P) went on to fall seven months behind on their (P) mortgage payments. FDC (D) discussed proposals to assist the Murphys (Ps) in making their payments, but none were implemented. On October 6, 1981, FDC (D) gave notice of its (D) intent to foreclose. The Murphys (P) soon paid the late mortgage payments, but not the costs and legal fees of the foreclosure proceedings. FDC (D) scheduled the foreclosure sale for November 10, 1981 at the property itself. FDC (D) fulfilled all the statutory requirements for notice. At the Murphys' (P) request, FDC (D) postponed the sale until December 15, 1981. Notice of this sale was posted at the property on November 10, and later at the local city hall and post office and for three weeks in the local newspaper. Further attempts to postpone the sale were unsuccessful. At the scheduled time of the sale at 10:00 a.m. on December 15, the roads were clear and the weather was warm. The only people present at the sale were the Murphys (P), an FDC (D) representative, and Morgan Hollis, an attorney filling in for the FDC (D) attorney who had been "apprehensive" about the snowy weather the night before. The FDC (D) representative made the only bid at the sale, which was for $27,00 owed on the mortgage and costs and fees. The sale ended with the acceptance of this bid. Later that day, one of Hollis' clients, a corporation represented by William Dube, offered to buy the property from FDC (D) for $27,000. FDC (D) countered with an offer of $40,000, and two days later, sold the property for $38,000. The Murphys (P) sued FDC (D) on February 5, 1982, and FDC (D) moved to dismiss. The master found that FDC (D) failed to exercise good faith and due diligence in obtaining a fair price for the property. Finding the fair market value to be $54,000, the master assessed damages at $27,000, and also legal fees on account of bad faith. FDC (D) appealed.

Issue: Is a mortgagee required to exercise good faith and due diligence to obtain a fair price when conducting a foreclosure sale of mortgaged property?

Decision and Rationale: (Douglas) Yes. The mortgagor's duty should be considered to be that of a fiduciary, as the trend has been to liberally define the term "fiduciary" in order to prevent unjust enrichment. Thus, a mortgagee executing a power of sale has a duty to protect the interests of the mortgagor and exercise good faith and due diligence in obtaining a fair price for a mortgagor's property. The question of what is a fair price, or whether a mortgagor must set a minimum price or make other similar efforts to assure a fair price, depends on the circumstances of each case. It is important to note that the duties of good faith and due diligence are distinct. There must be "an intentional disregard of duty or a purpose to injure" for there to be bad faith. Here, FDC (D) complied with the statutory requirements of notice and conducted the sale in compliance with similar provisions. FDC (D) also postponed the sale once, did nothing to discourage other buyers, and made its (D) bid without knowledge of any other immediate buyer. These facts demonstrate the lack of bad faith by FDC (D). FDC (D) clearly failed, however to exercise due diligence in obtaining a fair price. The test is whether a reasonable person in the lenders' place would have adjourned the sale. The house had been appraised at $46,000 in 1980. Even though FDC (D) did not have the house appraised again for the sale, a reasonable person would have known the Murphys' (P) equity in the home was at least $19,000. This considerable equity, FDC's (D) knowledge of the value of the property, and the Murphys' (P) efforts to pay the late installments all show that

FDC (D) had a duty to protect the Murphys' (P) equity by obtaining a fair price. The $27,000 bid did not provide for this, and instead was meant only to make FDC (D) "whole" with regard to the amount owed on the mortgage. In addition, FDC (D) did not give the same notice to the December 15 postponement that it gave to the November 10 sale. With only the postings at the house and the public buildings, and the resulting absence of bidders at the sale, FDC (D) was able to buy the house at a low price and make a quick profit. Granted, FDC (D) did not have an actual, specific buyer for the property at the time of the sale. Despite this, the fact that FDC (D) sold the house for so much more than it (D) had paid supports the view that FDC (D) had reason to know it (D) could make such a profit. This kind of knowledge is the most conclusive evidence that, in following the letter of the law, that FDC (D) violated its spirit. Further, damages should be assessed in the amount of the difference between a fair price for the property and the price obtained at the sale. Judgment reversed in part, affirmed in part, and remanded.

Analysis:

Judicial decisions following the *Murphy* rule of good faith and due diligence are but one means of protecting mortgagors in default. The courts have also paid more scrutiny than the *Murphy* court did to the amount of notice provided by a private individual conducting a foreclosure sale. In addition, some state legislatures have passed different laws to protect mortgagors. One type of statute enacts fair market value limitations in order to protect mortgagors from low foreclosure sale prices when the real estate market happens to be depressed. This statute enables a mortgagee to get a deficiency judgment only for the difference between the debt of the mortgagor and the fair market value of the property at the time of foreclosure, as determined by the court. Some other states have legislation which bars deficiency judgments by mortgagees on ordinary purchase money mortgages. These laws were the product of the Great Depression, after widespread promotion schemes caused people to engage in very shaky property investments throughout the 1920's. Further, many states provide for a statutory right of redemption, which may allow a mortgagor to stay in possession of the property until a set period of time has expired. In that extra time after foreclosure, the mortgagor can gather money and redeem from the purchaser at the foreclosure sale and get the property back.

WHEN A BUYER DEFAULTS ON AN INSTALLMENT LAND SALE CONTRACT, HIS OR HER PAYMENTS ARE NOT FORFEITED AS LONG AS HE OR SHE HAS ALREADY PAID A SUBSTANTIAL AMOUNT ON THE CONTRACT

Bean v. Walker

(Home Seller) v. (Home Buyer)
95 A.D.2d 70, 464 N.Y.S.2d 895 (1983)

M E M O R Y   G R A P H I C

Instant Facts

Walker defaulted on an installment land sale contract after paying Bean nearly half of the purchase price, and Bean sued to retake possession.

Black Letter Rule

The buyer under an installment land sale contract acquires equitable title which must be extinguished before the seller can retake possession, and so the buyer's payments cannot be forfeited where there would be an inequitable disposition of property and exorbitant money loss by the buyer.

Case Vocabulary

EJECTMENT: A cause of action raised by a person entitled to possession of property in order to retake such possession.
EQUITY OF REDEMPTION: A mortgagor's right to reclaim property after it has been forfeited.

Procedural Basis: Appeal from summary judgment in action fo ejectment.

Facts: In January 1973, the Beans (P) agreed to sell a house to the Walkers (D) for $15,000. The sale contract provided that the $15,000 was to be paid ove a 15-year period at 5% interest, in monthly installments of $118.62 each. The Beans (P) retained legal title and would convey it to the Walkers (D) upon ful payment of the purchase price according to the terms of the contract. The Walkers (D) were entitled to possession of the property. Under the contract, if the Walkers (D) defaulted in making payment and failed to cure that default within 3(days, the Beans (P) could demand the rest of the balance or terminate the contrac and repossess the premises. If this latter choice were made, then the Beans (P could retain all the money paid by the Walkers (D) to that point as "liquidatec damages" under a forfeiture clause. These payments would then be considere as going towards rent, and not as any kind of penalty. The Walkers (D) went intc possession of the house in January 1973. They (D) went on to make substantia improvements to the property. They (D) made all their (D) required payment under the contract until August 1981. Then, the Walkers (D) defaulted after Ca Walker (D) became injured. By that time, the Walkers (D) had paid the Beans (P $12,099.24, with $7,114.75 of it being applied to the $15,000 principal. Thus nearly half of the principal had been paid by the Walkers (D). The Beans (P waited 30 days and then filed this action, seeking a judgment granting them (P possession of the property. The court granted summary judgment to the Bean (P).

Issue: Does the buyer in an installment land sale contract automaticall forfeit his or her payments to the seller, and lose possession of the property to th seller, if he or she defaults in making payment?

Decision and Rationale: (Doerr) No. The buyer under a installment land sale contract acquires equitable title which must be extinguishe before the seller can retake possession, and so the buyer's payments cannot b forfeited where there would be an inequitable disposition of property an exorbitant money loss by the buyer. In the similar case of Skendzel v. Marsha [vendee in land sale contract acquires equitable title when contract i consummated], the Indiana Supreme Court found that the status of the parties i an installment land sale contract is like that of a mortgagor and mortgagee. Thi status strongly suggests that the concept that equity deems that which ought t be done as done should be applied here. Numerous cases of this state [New York have already demonstrated that parties to such an installment contract occupy th position of mortgagor and mortgagee at common law. The common la mortgagor also acquires equitable title. This form of title gives its owner the righ to any increase in the value of the property, and allows the owner's interest to b treated as real property. The seller's interest, by contrast, is personal property namely the right to receive money. Because the buyer possesses equitable title the seller must first extinguish the equitable owner's equity of redemption t resume possession. There is no reason why the Beans (P) and Walkers (D) shoul be treated differently than the mortgagee and mortgagor at common law. Th question that must be decided is whether the buyer in a land sale contract ha obtained the kind of property interest that must be extinguished before the selle may resume possession. The Walkers (D) do have such an interest as they (D acquired equitable title and the Beans (P) held the legal title in trust for them (D Thus, the Beans (P) had to foreclose the equitable title or bring an action at law fc the purchase price in order to resume possession. The Beans (P) sought neither c these remedies. The lower court judgment would allow the Beans (P) to retake th property, after improvements by the Walkers (D), along with over $11,000 i principal and interest payments. This result would clearly be inequitable; equity should be used when a forfeiture would lead to such an unfair disposition of property and an exorbitant loss of money would occur. Judgment reversed, motion denied, and matter remitted.

Analysis:

The law surrounding forfeitures in installment land contracts is not very clearly defined. In reality, the law has provided considerable flexibility while being incredibly vague and unpredictable. Some state courts require foreclosure by the seller, but there are often exceptions to this rule that are very difficult to apply. Generally, a proper analysis of the contract does not occur until after a breach has occurred, and only then are the rights and obligations of the parties determined. Most states currently require a seller to give notice of a possible forfeiture. This notice, however, must conform to either legislative or judicial standards for notice, depending on the particular state. In some states, a seller may waive future rights to forfeiture by accepting late payments, because this may lead a buyer to think that promptness is not necessary under the contract. Defaulting buyers may also have the right to specific performance in the event that all, or possibly a specified amount over fifty percent, of the purchase price is paid. In addition, a seller's declaration of forfeiture may bar any suit for the remainder of the purchase price. Indeed, a buyer, even one who willingly defaults on the contract, could get restitution of payments to cover his or her loss, even if such distribution is unfair to the seller.

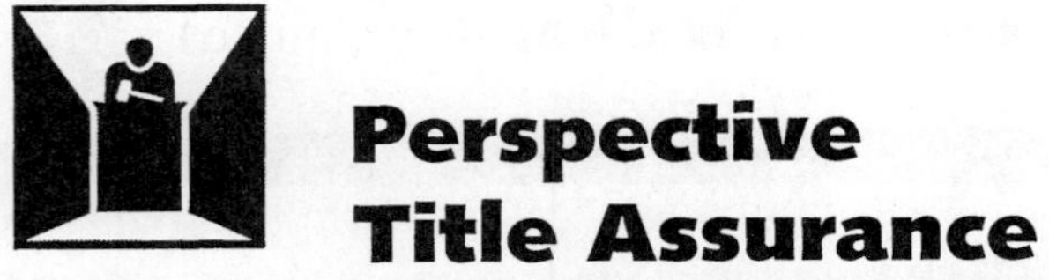

Perspective
Title Assurance

Chapter 8

This chapter discusses the importance of title assurance used in the United States. Title assurance does two important things. The first is to assure a landowner that he or she has good and clear title to the land he or she owns. The second reason is to assure a potential purchaser of land that he or she will be buying the land from someone who has the right to pass title, and also to guarantee to the buyer that no other person has a claim or an interest in the land.

There are three methods of title assurance. The first is the public recording system, which centers around the public records office. There, all instruments affecting land title like deeds, wills, and other documents, are to be recorded. Before buying, a purchaser must make, or have a professional make, a title search. This means he or she goes through the title records to determine who has the title to the land, and whether the land has a mortgage or agreement regarding use of the land attached to it. The results of this search affect the buyer's decision whether to obtain the land.

The second method is title registration. While public recording is available in all states, this registration system is only available in a small handful of them. Under this system, the state actually issues title certificates to the property owners, and these certificates are issued from owner to following owner.

The third method, title insurance, is a means to provide greater security of title for land purchasers. For a one-time premium, persons can keep records of title in an additional private storage system. The company will provide coverage for any loss or damage that results from a claim or defect (explained in the chapter) against the title.

The chapter will cover each of these methods in the order listed above, with the bulk of the materials focusing on the most common method, the public recording system.

When considering questions of title assurance, which typically arise when an owner decides to convey title to another person, three things should be considered. The first is the language of the conveyance or the recording statute. The second is whether the purchaser had any kind of notice whatsoever regarding the status of the property title. The third is the effect that any unrecorded instruments or errors in recording may have on the two parties, and also who must bear the costs of those effects.

Chapter Overview Outline
Title Assurance

Chapter 8

NOTE: THE PURPOSE OF THIS OUTLINE IS TO ORGANIZE THE CASES SO THAT ONE CAN QUICKLY UNDERSTAND THE RELEVANCE OF EACH CASE TO THE COURSE. NO ATTEMPT IS MADE IN THIS OVERVIEW TO ADDRESS EVERY CONCEPT THAT MUST BE STUDIED. BE SURE TO READ THE ENTIRE CASEBOOK AND/OR OTHER MATERIALS TO GAIN A FULL UNDERSTANDING OF ALL CONCEPTS.

I. The Recording System
  A. Introduction
    1. Public recording of deeds, mortgages, leases and other instruments affecting land title began in the United States around 1640. Today every state has statutes or recording acts that provide for land title records to be maintained by the county recorder or similar public official in each county, and which serve the function of:
      a. establishing a system of public recordation of land titles so that others may ascertain who owns land in the county;
      b. preserving in a secure place important documents that may be easily lost or misplaced by private individuals; and
      c. protecting purchasers for value and lien creditors against prior unrecorded interests.
    2. Generally any instrument creating or affecting interests in land can be recorded, such as deeds, mortgages, leases, and options.
      a. In most states, recorded copies of these documents can be admitted directly into evidence during a judicial proceeding, without producing or accounting for the original.
    3. While at common law, priority of title between successive grantees was determined by priority in time of conveyance, the recording acts in general have adopted and broadened the equitable doctrine bona fide purchaser (BFP), to protect BFP's against unrecorded interests.
  B. The Indexes
    1. The two types of indexes currently used in the U.S., which allow a buyer to search out and find all interests affecting a particular tract of land, are the "tract index" and the "grantor-grantee" indexes.
      a. The "public tract indexes," which indexes particular tracts of land through assigned identification numbers, do not exist in most states.
      b. In the "grantor-grantee indexing system," the most common method of indexing, separate indexes are kept for grantors, which index all instruments alphabetically under the grantor's surname, and grantees, which index all instruments under the grantee's surname.
        (1) Usually, many volumes compose the grantor and grantee index.
        (2) Sometimes they are separated into different grantor and grantee indexes for each type of instrument.
    2. Searching title
      a. In order to "search title," it is necessary to first trace backward in time to an acceptable source or "root of title," using the grantee index to discover each preceding source of title.
        (1) Then, it is necessary to search forward from that source using the grantor index.
        (2) This search is required in all jurisdictions, and produces a chain going back to a source deemed satisfactory.
      b. Determining what would be an acceptable source or "root title" will vary depending on local custom and the identity of the client.
        (1) In some jurisdictions, the practice is to go back to a sovereign, others 60 years or shorter, and for agencies of the federal government, custom requires a search back to the original source.
      c. A person is charged with constructive notice of whatever would be revealed by a proper search.
    3. In order to provide constructive notice to subsequent purchasers, an assigned interest must be sufficiently described on the re-

corded instruments that affect title to the particular tract of land.

a. Mother Hubbard Clauses, which describe the property to be conveyed through language such as "all of the grantor's property and interest in a certain county," will be upheld as between the parties to the instrument that contain it, but is an insufficient description for the purposes of giving constructive notice to subsequent purchasers without actual notice. *Luthi v. Evans*.

4. In some jurisdictions, the fact that a deed was not properly indexed by the register of deeds, will not prevent constructive notice of the record from being charged to a purchaser. *American Law Property § 17.25 (1952)*.

   a. While in most states, the recorder is protected from liability for negligently failing to properly index a deed by the doctrine of governmental immunity, some states provide a limited liability, though for far less than the land is worth. *Siefkes v. Waterton Title Co*.

5. Some courts following the modern trend, treat misindexed instruments as unrecorded, and hold that it would place an undue burden on the transfer of property to require a title searcher to examine title records under other possible spellings of a grantor's name. *Orr v. Byners*.

   a. Other courts may follow the doctrine of idem sonans (a Latin term meaning "having the same sound"), and hold that names similar to that of the record owner, spelled differently but pronounced alike, give constructive notice so long as they begin with the same letter. *American Law of Property § 17.18 (1952)*.

6. Indexing under hyphenated names is insufficient to provide constructive notice of claims against either of the unhyphenated version of the debtor's name. *Teschke v. Keller*.

7. Instruments indexed under nicknames or incorrect first names that are "sufficiently dissimilar" to the record name of an owner, are not valid against a subsequent BFP. *Frederick Ward Assoc., Inc. v. Venture, Inc.*

8. In recent years, to avoid being overwhelmed by growing amounts of paper, many urban counties with numerous daily real estate transactions have begun to record information onto a computer. In some localities, computer tract indexes have been established, giving each parcel of land a parcel identification number.

B. Recording Acts

1. In general, there are three types of recording acts: *race*, *notice*, and *race-notice*.

   a. Under a *race statute* type of recording act, the first to record will prevail over subsequent recorders, regardless of whether a subsequent purchaser has actual knowledge of a prior purchaser's claim.

   b. Under *notice* statutes, which are used by about half the states, a subsequent purchaser could not prevail over a prior grantee, if the subsequent purchaser had notice of the prior grantee's claim, regardless of whether the prior claim was recorded.

   c. Under *race-notice* statutes, which are used roughly by the other half of states, a subsequent purchaser is protected against prior unrecorded instruments only if he or she:

      (1) Is without notice of the prior instrument, and

      (2) Records before the prior instrument is recorded.

2. Lawyers or other agents in charge of closing a transaction may be liable in negligence for failing to record a deed promptly if the grantee suffers as a result. *Meerhoff v. Huntington Mortgage Co.*

   a. A lawyer may be liable for negligent title work to the buyer, even if he or she is the lawyer for the seller, since it is reasonably foreseeable that the buyer will detrimentally rely on the lawyer's title work. *Century 21 Deep South Properties, Ltd. v. Corson*.

3. Although a document may be actually copied by the recorder, it may not be "legally recorded" for purposes of constructive notice, if not authorized.

   a. In almost all jurisdictions, an instrument

must be acknowledged before notary public or other official. An instrument that is not properly acknowledged is not entitled to be recorded. *Messersmith v. Smith*.

C. Chain of Title
   1. While "chain of title" generally refers to the recorded sequence of transactions by which title has passed from a sovereign to the present claimant, the term is also used to describe the period of time in which records must be searched and the documents that must be examined within that time period.
      a. Since some jurisdiction require a more extended search than others, the meaning of the term will vary between different jurisdictions.
   2. A deed from a grantor outside the chain of title (a "wild deed"), even if recorded, is treated as though it were unrecorded and gives no constructive notice. *Board of Education v Hughes*.
   3. In about half of the jurisdictions, a subsequent purchaser from a common grantor in a subdivision has constructive notice of the restrictions on the rest of the subdivision, and thus acquires title subject to those restrictions. *Guillette v. Daly Dry Wall, Inc.*
      a. Other jurisdictions take the position that an easement or restrictive covenant on parcel A, that appears in a prior deed of parcel B from the common owner of A and B, is not in the purchaser's chain of title to Parcel A. *William B. Stoebuck & Dale A. Whitman, The Law of Property*.
   4. Older cases have held that a title searcher may have a duty to examine the records under the name of each owner prior to the date of the deed transferring title to the owner, in order to determine whether the owner deeded particular real estate to another before that real estate was actually or completely deeded to him or her. *Ayer v. Philadelphia & Boston Face Brick Co.*
      a. The majority of cases however, emphasize the cost of searching title under the name of every owner for many years prior to the date the owner received title, and will regard any possible prior deed given by the owner as outside the chain of title.
      b. *Tract index* jurisdictions do not have this chain of title problem, since any "prior deed" by an owner will be seen by a title searcher looking at the tract index.
   5. Cases are split with regards to the question of whether a prior deed from an owner, recorded after a later deed from the same owner, gives constructive notice of the prior deed to subsequent purchasers from the grantee of the later deed.
      a. About half the cases hold that a purchaser is not bound to examine the record after the date of a recorded conveyance, to discover whether the grantor made a prior conveyance recorded later. *Hartig v. Stratman*.
      b. The other half of cases hold that a deed recorded after a later deed from the same owner, gives constructive notice to subsequent purchasers. *Woods v. Garnett*.
      c. *Tract index* jurisdictions do no have the chain of title problem since any "late-recorded" deed can be found in the tract index.

D. Persons Protected by the Recording System
   1. Almost all recording statutes have been judicially construed as not protecting donees and devisees, making it necessary for the court to sometimes decide whether a person is protected as a *purchaser* who paid *valuable consideration* for an acquired interest.
      a. Most jurisdictions require that a grantee give or pay more than nominal consideration in order to be deemed a purchaser. For example, a "substantial amount" or an amount "not grossly inadequate." *William B. Stoebuck & Dale A. Whitman, The Law of Property*.
   2. Where a buyer receives notice of an outstanding interest subsequent to paying some, but not all, of the full purchase price, the buyer is not considered a bona fide purchaser. *Daniels v. Anderson*.
      a. The "payment of value" rule expressed above in *Daniels* and other cases ignores the modern realities of real property transaction. A seller need not be paid in full

before the buyer can be considered a bona fide purchaser. *Lewis v. Superior Court.*

3. To be protected against a prior unrecorded deed, a purchaser without notice must have paid reasonably adequate consideration in full before he or she has notice of the earlier deed. *Alexander v. Andrews.*
   a. However, where a subsequent grantee's payment is insufficient to constitute complete consideration and the prior grantee obtains legal title, the subsequent grantee is entitled to reimbursement from the prior grantee for the amount of consideration paid for the interest. *Alexander v. Andrews.*
4. In some jurisdictions, a purchaser by quitclaim deed will not be regarded as a bona fide purchaser without notice, because a refusal by the grantor to warrant title is considered to have raised a strong suspicion that the title is defective. *Polhemus v. Cobb.*
   a. Courts may even find that any quitclaim deed in the chain of title puts all subsequent purchasers on inquiry notice (notice that a further investigation about the deed is required). *Schwalm v. Deanhardt.*
   b. However, most jurisdictions treat quitclaim deeds the same as warranty deeds for the purposes of giving notice, holding that there are many other reasons why a grantor may use a quitclaim deed other than a questionable title.

E. Notice
1. There are three kinds of notice that a person may have or be deemed to have with respect to a prior claim:
   a. Actual notice (actual knowledge of a prior interest or claim);
   b. Record notice (constructive notice of any interest or claim that a reasonable search of the records would have revealed); and
   c. Inquiry notice (constructive notice of information that would have been attained by a reasonable investigation).
2. Subsequent grantees are held to have inquiry notice of the contents of prior recorded deed in the chain of title for purposes of a race-notice recording act. Thus for example, where a prior recorded deed expressly refer- ences an earlier unrecorded deed, the grante is imputed with constructive notice of th earlier unrecorded deed. *Harper v. Paradise*
   a. However, where a commercial lessor an lessee do not wish to place the entire leas into public record, and merely record memorandum of the lease instead, a sub sequent purchaser may not be impute with constructive notice of the contents o the entire lease, which may contain som restrictions or covenants. *Howard D Johnson v. Parkside Dev. Corp.*
3. A subsequent purchaser is charged wit constructive notice of an individual's posses sion of a given property and of whateve such an inquiry into the given property woul reveal. *Waldorff Insurance and Bonding, Inc v. Eglin National Bank.*

F. Marketable Title Acts
1. Marketable title acts are intended to limi required title searches to a reasonable period generally the last 30 or 40 years.
2. These acts are intended to operate in con junction with recording acts, and provide tha if a person has an unbroken chain of titl from the present to his or her "root of title," then he or she has the sort of title that extin guishes old title defects automatically. *Wal ter E. Barnett, Marketable Title Acts-Panace or Pandemonium.*
   a. The "root of title" is the most recent trans action in a chain of title that has been o record at least forty or thirty years depend ing upon the jurisdiction.
3. Generally, marketable title acts require claimant of interest in land, to file a notice o the claim every 30 to 40 years after th recording of his or her instrument of acquisi tion.

II. Registration of Title
A. According to some, major changes must b made in the outdated American system of lan transfer. *Myres S. McDougal & John W Brabner-Smith, Land Title Transfer: A Regres sion.*
1. Title to property cannot be easily acquired c

securely held because of the wild disorder and incompleteness of public record. Therefore, a change to the "Torrens system," which has prevailed in Europe, may be in order.

B. First, according to *Land Title Transfer: A Regression,* it would be necessary to either provide cheap and efficient procedures for quieting title or a short Statute of Limitations, in order remove any existing stale claims to land.

C. Second, a common-sense change in the method of keeping books would be required, most likely in the form of an improved "tract" index, giving all facts about title to any one piece of land.

D. Third, the doctrine of caveat emptor ("buyer beware") should be eliminated, and the bona fide purchaser protected, by making the public records as nearly conclusive and as nearly unimpeachable as is constitutionally permitted.

III. Title Insurance

A. Title insurance developed in response to the inadequacies and inefficiencies of the public record in protecting private titles, and generally insures the amount of the purchase price of property in an owner's policy, or the amount of a loan in a lender's policy.

1. Title insurance guarantees that the insurance company has searched the public records and insures against any defects in the public records, except as otherwise provided for in the particular policy.

2. This insurance creates liability only to the insured and will not run with the land to subsequent purchasers.

B. If a title company fails to conduct a reasonable title examination, or having conducted such an examination, fails to disclose the results to the insured, then it may run the risk of liability under the terms of the insurance policy and not under tort for negligence. *Walker Rogge, Inc. v. Chelsea Title & Guaranty Co.*

C. Title insurance policies are intended to protect the condition of an owner's title to land, and not provide coverage for the physical condition of the land itself. *Lick Mill Creek Apartments v. Chicago Title Insurance Co.*

1. Similarly, a title insurance company will not be held liable for a failure to disclose any land-use restrictions, since such restrictions are not considered encumbrances on title and do not make title unmarketable. *Somerset Savings Bank v. Chicago Title Insurance Company*.

2. However, an exculpatory clause against negligence in a policy may not, because unfair and unconscionable, bar a claim based on a breach of an assumed duty to search and disclose. *Somerset Savings Bank v. Chicago Title Insurance Company*.

INSTRUMENTS RECORDED WITH "MOTHER HUBBARD" CLAUSES ARE VALID WITH REGARD TO THE PARTIES TO IT, BUT DO NOT PROVIDE CONSTRUCTIVE NOTICE FOR SUBSEQUENT PURCHASERS

Luthi v. Evans

(Subsequent Assignee) v. ("Mother Hubbard" Assignee)
223 Kan. 622, 576 P.2d 1064 (1978)

M E M O R Y G R A P H I C

Instant Facts

Owens and others assigned all their oil and gas interests in the county to Tours, and Burris found no record of this when inspecting title.

Black Letter Rule

A Mother Hubbard clause is upheld as between the parties to the instrument that contains it, but is insufficient to give constructive notice to subsequent purchasers without actual notice of it.

Case Vocabulary

MOTHER HUBBARD CLAUSE: Language used in a conveyance which describes the property to be conveyed as all of the grantor's property in a certain county; reference is to a nursery rhyme describing Mother Hubbard going to her cupboard, "and when she got there, the cupboard was bare," the idea being a grantor's interests in a county are similarly cleared out by this clause.

Procedural Basis: Appeal from judgment to quiet title.

Facts: Grace V. Owens owned interests in several oil and gas leases in Coffey County, Kansas. On February 1, 1971, she assigned all of these oil and gas interests to International Tours, Inc. (Tours) through a written instrument. This document stated that the Owens and the other assignors intended to convey "all interest whatsoever of working nature in all working interests and overriding royalty interest in all Oil and Gas Leases in Coffey County, Kansas." This sort of clause, conveying all of a grantor'sfp property in a certain county, is commonly referred to as a "Mother Hubbard" clause. This assignment was recorded in the county office of the register of deeds on February 16, 1971. In addition to the seven leases specifically outlined in the agreement, Owens owned a working interest in an oil and gas lease known as the Kufahl lease. This lease was also located on land in Coffey County. Although it was not specifically described in the assignment, the Kufahl lease nonetheless fit the description in the Tours assignment. On January 30, 1975, Owens executed and delivered a second assignment of her interest in the Kufahl lease to J.R. Burris (P). Before this assignment took place, Burris (P) personally checked the records in the office of the register of deeds. After the assignment, he (P) obtained an abstract of title to the same property. Neither his inspection nor the abstract revealed the prior assignment to Tours. Tours contends that the 1971 assignment effectively conveyed Owens' interest in the Kufahl lease to Tours, and that its recordation with the county gave constructive notice to all subsequent purchasers, including Burris. Burris, however, asserts that the language of the assignment provided an inadequate description of the interests conveyed. Burris prevailed in district court. On appeal, the general description in the 1971 assignment was held to be sufficient, when recorded, to provide constructive notice.

Issue: Is an instrument using a Mother Hubbard clause to describe assigned interests sufficient to provide constructive notice to subsequent purchasers?

Decision and Rationale: (Prager) No. A Mother Hubbard clause is upheld as between the parties to the instrument that contains it, but is insufficient to give constructive notice to subsequent purchasers without actual notice of it. This court agrees with both parties that the 1971 assignment constituted a valid transfer of Owens' interest in the Kufahl lease to Tours, but only as between the two parties to that assignment. Likewise, a single instrument can convey separate tracts by specific description, and by general description which can be made specific. This can be done when the language of the assignment expresses that clear intent. The state statutes, however, require the register of deeds to keep a general index of title that records a description of each tract conveyed when appropriate. Further, county commissioners are required to record a numerical index of all deeds, complete with brief descriptions of the properties involved. It is clear that these statutes are intended to notify a subsequent purchaser regarding instruments which affect the title to a specific tract of land. Thus, the legislature likely intended that recorded instruments describe the conveyed land well enough so that it could be identified later on. An instrument using a Mother Hubbard clause is ineffective as to subsequent purchasers unless they have actual knowledge of the transfer. A Mother Hubbard clause can be used in the event of emergency, so long as the grantee takes steps to protect his or her title against subsequent purchasers. These steps could include taking possession of the property or filing an affidavit with the county containing a more appropriate description of the property. Here, because Burris had no actual notice of the 1971 assignment to Tours, the assignment to Burris prevails. Judgment of district court affirmed.

Analysis:

Mother Hubbard causes are but one means of description available for recorded deeds, and, as demonstrated here, it is certainly one of the least reliable and most difficult to locate in a title search. There are two systems for governmental description of "official" parcels of land. The first official method is the Government Survey System, which was devised by Thomas Jefferson and adopted by the Continental Congress in 1785. It is generally available throughout the country except along the East Coast and Kentucky, Tennessee, and West Virginia. The System is based on 36 sets of north-south Principal Meridians and east-west Base Lines. East-west lines running every six miles split the sections into Townships, while similar north-south lines divide the land into Ranges. With this System, lands can be described by citing an intersection number for the Meridian and Line, and then numbers for the Township and the Range. The other system, recognized in every state, is the plat. A plat is a map drawn to specific standards of form and accuracy. Though approved by and filed with an appropriate government body, it is drawn up by an engineer or surveyor hired by the landowner. The plat must contain references to recognized landmarks outside the property, so the land itself can be located. The plat can then serve as the basis for description of subdivisions of the land. A common yet risky method is to describe a quantitative or fractional part of a lot that has already been described; for example, "the North 100 feet of Lot 5," or "the North half of Lot 5." Obviously, this method is best suited to clearly geometrical parcels. Without a description of the shape of the land conveyed, however, such quantitative descriptions can be declared void for the courts on sheer vagueness.

Orr v. Byers

(Judgment Winner) v. (Property Buyer)
198 Cal. App. 3d 666, 244 Cal. Rptr. 13 (1988)

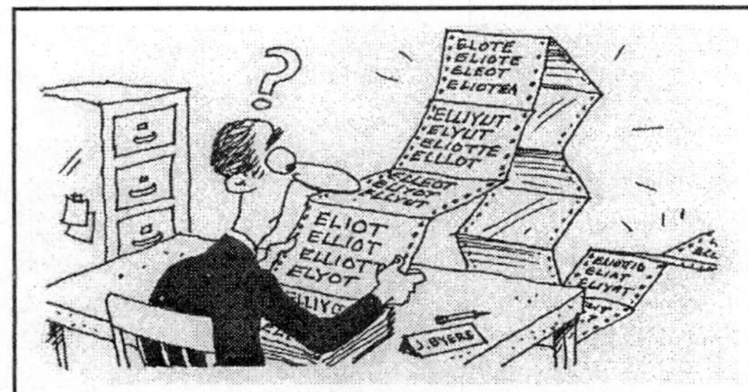

M E M O R Y   G R A P H I C

Instant Facts

Byers was unaware of Orr's lien on Elliott's property because Elliott's name was misspelled on the abstract of judgment, causing misspellings in the title index.

Black Letter Rule

Requiring a title searcher to examine title records for other spellings of the grantor's name would be an undue burden on the transfer of property.

Case Vocabulary

ABSTRACT: An abridged summary; less detailed than a transcript.

IDEM SONANS: "Having the same sound"; Latin term given to doctrine that states though a person's name has been inaccurately written, the person's identity will be presumed from the similarity of pronunciation between the correct and incorrect spellings of the person's name.

Procedural Basis: Appeal from judgment denying declaratory relief.

Facts: In October 1978, James Orr (P) obtained a judgment against William Elliott (D) in excess of $50,000. Orr's (P) attorney prepared a written judgment against Elliott (D), but misspelled his name with only one "t." That November, an abstract of the judgment was recorded in the Orange County Recorder's Office, with "Elliott" being misspelled as "Elliot" and "Eliot." This abstract was listed in the County's Grantor-Grantee Index under those names only. Elliott (D) later obtained title to a parcel of property. This property became subject to Orr's (P) lien. Elliott (D) sold that property to Rick Byers (D) in July 1979, but a title search failed to reveal the abstract of judgment. Thus, the preliminary title report did not disclose Orr's (P) judgment lien against Elliott (D), and the sale of Elliott's land to Byers (D) was not used to satisfy Orr's (P) judgment lien. In February 1981, Orr (P) filed suit against Byers, Elliott, and two local financial institutions (D), seeking a declaration of the rights and duties of all parties. In effect, Orr (P) sought judicial foreclosure of his (P) judgment lien. Orr (P) argued that the others (D) had constructive notice of the abstract of judgment through the doctrine of idem sonans. The trial judge ruled that the doctrine was inapplicable and denied Orr's (P) request for declaratory relief. A formal judgment was filed in February, 1986, and Orr (P) appealed.

Issue: Is a title searcher required to examine the records for alternative spellings of a grantor's name under the doctrine of idem sonans?

Decision and Rationale: (Sonenshine) No. Requiring a title searcher to examine title records for other spellings of the grantor's name would be an undue burden on the transfer of property. Under the doctrine of idem sonans, the identity of a person whose name has been inaccurately written will be presumed from the similarity of sounds between the pronunciations of the correctly and incorrectly spelled names. This doctrine, however, is inapplicable when it is the written, not the spoken, name that is material. Here, the written name is clearly material. Requiring Byers (D) or any title searcher to "comb the records" for alternative spellings of a given name would place an undue burden on the transfer of property. Indeed, adding that burden to the already potentially daunting task of searching title for all those who have identical names would be unjustifiable. Already, not every name uncovered by a search pertains to the person subject to a particular lien. Checking for liens against those with similarly spelled names, and checking to see if those liens affected the desired property, would make the problem worse. While new software and computer systems are now used in title searches, these measures could generate even more extraneous names, particularly if the name in question is a common one in a large county. The burden should rest with the judgment creditor, Orr (P), to take appropriate action to ensure the judgment will be satisfied. That action includes spelling the names of the debtor properly on official documents. Judgment affirmed.

Analysis:

The cases are divided on this issue of misrecorded instruments, and often depend on the specific language of the governing statutes, as was demonstrated by the Court here. The majority of states, notably Vermont and Virginia, regard the mere act of copying the deed or other instrument into the official record as a sufficient recording to uphold it. The modern trend, however, has been to decide along the line of Orr and treat misindexed instruments as unrecorded. This has been the rule in Alaska, California, Illinois, and North Carolina, to name a few states. Practically speaking, this is the more logical view, as there is no reasonable way to locate such an instrument until it has been properly filed and indexed. Although both the earlier and later grantees are innocent in this situation, the former grantee could have easily checked the index after the earlier transaction and made sure it was properly recorded. The latter grantee, by contrast, would have had no idea that anything was wrong with the recordation of the earlier grantee's transfer. Moreover, the latter grantee would have been unable to correct the error as he or she would still be a stranger to the title when the error occurred.

Messersmith v. Smith

(Title Grantor) v. (Title Grantee)
60 N.W. 2d 276 (1953)

M E M O R Y G R A P H I C

Instant Facts

After a first deed was found to be incorrect, Messersmith took a second deed to a notary public, who got Messersmith's acknowledgment over the telephone.

Black Letter Rule

An instrument that is not properly acknowledged is not entitled to be recorded.

Case Vocabulary

NOTARY PUBLIC: A public officer with the duty of authenticating and acknowledging certain documents, including deeds and other instruments of conveyance.
QUITCLAIM DEED: A conveyance of title without any warranties or guarantees for the title or that the grantor's title is even valid.

Procedural Basis: Appeal from finding in statutory action to quiet title.

Facts: Caroline Messersmith and her nephew, Frederick Messersmith (P), each owned an undivided one-half interest in three sections of land in Golden Valley County, North Dakota. On May 7, 1946, Caroline executed and delivered a quitclaim deed to the property to Frederick (P) which was not recorded until July 9, 1951. From January to April 1951, oil fever hit the County, as brokers, oil men, and speculators flocked to North Dakota. On April 23, 1951, she met with Herbert J. Smith, Jr. (D) to discuss a gas and oil lease to the properties. Caroline claimed that only royalties were negotiated, while Smith (D) claimed the matter of the mineral deed was discussed. On May 7, 1951, Caroline executed a mineral deed for an undivided one-half interest in the oil, gas and minerals under the three sections of land. Caroline claims that she thought she was signing a transfer of royalties only. Smith (D) paid a consideration of $1,400 for the deed. After leaving, Smith (D) discovered that the deed incorrectly stated the term "his heirs" instead of "her heirs." Smith (D) returned to Caroline's home the same day and explained the mistake to her. He (D) then tore up the deed and prepared another one in the same form and with the error corrected. Smith (D) then, according to his (D) testimony, took the deed to the same notary public to whom Caroline acknowledged the first deed. The notary called Caroline for her acknowledgment over the telephone, and then placed his seal and signature on the deed. Two days later, Smith (D) executed a mineral deed conveying the interest conveyed by Caroline to E.B. Seale. Both deeds were recorded May 26, 1951. Seale apparently relied on the second deed between Caroline and Smith (D) when making his purchase of the one-half interest. Frederick Messersmith (P) filed action to quiet title to the land. Seale (D) answered by claiming he (D) was a purchaser without actual or constructive notice of Frederick's (P) claim. Frederick (P) further answered by claiming Seale's (D) mineral deed was never acknowledged, not entitled to be recorded and was obtained by fraud, deceit and misrepresentation. Smith (D) defaulted.

Issue: Is a deed which is improperly acknowledged entitled to be recorded?

Decision and Rationale: (Morris) No. An instrument that is not properly acknowledged is not entitled to be recorded. The trial court found that the deeds were not executed through fraud or false representation, and there is no reason to disturb that finding. Caroline's mineral deed to Smith (D) however, was invalid, for she had already conveyed her interest to her nephew (P). Smith's (D) conveyance to Seale (D) was also invalid. The only way Seale (D) can assert title to any interest in the property is by citing the fact that Frederick's (P) deed was not recorded until July 1951. This reasoning is insufficient, however, to support Seale's (D) claim because Seale's (D) deed was nonetheless improperly executed. Under the governing state statutes, a deed to real property cannot be recorded without proper acknowledgment by the parties. Caroline did not appear before the notary and acknowledge she executed the deed that was recorded; she allegedly did so over the telephone. Because the deed was not entitled to be recorded, the record then did not constitute notice of its execution. Because the record did not constitute notice, the purchaser, Seale (D), did not become a subsequent purchaser in good faith within the meaning of the statutes. The right Seale (D) tries to claim is dependent on compliance with the recording statutes. It is likewise dependent on the deed that was actually recorded, not the one that was destroyed. Judgment reversed.

Analysis:

Most courts hold that an individual has notice of documents in his or her own chain of title even if they are not recorded. The idea behind this is simply that a purchaser can reasonably be expected to know, and usually does know, about the history of his or her title. Several holdings in states such as Alabama, Minnesota, and Wisconsin have gone beyond this rule. The position outlined in these states is that a subsequent purchaser is not protected under the recording acts if earlier links in his or her chain of title have gone unrecorded. While this position does give a strong incentive for ensuring that the public records are complete, it is somewhat illogical and impractical. A potential purchaser would have no notice of prior adverse claims or conveyances to the title if such were unrecorded, and there would be no place to begin following up on those claims. The Messersmith case is perhaps the most extreme example of this position, though it is by no means unanimously followed by the states.

A DEED FROM A GRANTOR WHO IS NOT PART OF THE CHAIN OF TITLE DOES NOT COUNT AS A RECORDED DEED AND ITS RECORDING DOES NOT GIVE CONSTRUCTIVE NOTICE

Board of Education of Minneapolis v. Hughes

(Third Deed Grantee) v. (First Deed Grantee)
118 Minn. 404, 136 N.W. 1095 (1912)

M E M O R Y   G R A P H I C

Instant Facts

Hughes obtained title first, but recorded second; Duryea and Wilson obtained title second, but recorded third; the Board obtained title third, but recorded first. (Got it?)

Black Letter Rule

A deed from a grantor outside the chain of title, even if recorded, is treated as though it were unrecorded and gives no constructive notice.

Case Vocabulary

WARRANTY DEED: A conveyance which explicitly lists covenants concerning the quality of title being conveyed; by this deed, the grantor conveys good, clear title.

Procedural Basis: Appeal from order denying new trial in action to determine adverse claim.

Facts: The facts are undisputed, but the order is a bit confusing. On May 16, 1906, L. A. Hughes (D) offered Carrie B. Hoerger $25 for a vacant lot. Ms. Hoerger accepted this offer, and Hughes (D) then sent a check for this amount to Ed. Hoerger, Carrie Hoerger's husband, along with a deed to be executed and returned. The space for the name of the grantee on this deed was left blank. The Hoergers executed and acknowledged this deed on May 17, 1906, and mailed it back to Hughes (D). The grantee space on the deed, however, was still blank. The Hoergers did cash Hughes' (D) check. On April 27, 1909, Duryea and Wilson, real estate dealers, paid Mrs. Hoerger $25 for a quitclaim deed to the same lot. This deed was executed and delivered. On November 19, 1909, Duryea and Wilson executed and delivered a warranty deed to the lot to the Board of Education of Minneapolis (The Board) (P). The Board (P) recorded this deed on January 27, 1910. Hughes (D) only found the time to fill in the his (D) own name on his (D) deed from them shortly before recording it on December 16, 1910. Duryea and Wilson finally recorded their deed from Hughes (D) on December 21, 1910. No explanation was given as to why none of these parties, with the arguable exception of the Board (P), failed to file their deeds any sooner than they did.

Issue: Does a deed granted by an individual outside the chain of title count as a properly recorded deed and give constructive notice to subsequent purchasers?

Decision and Rationale: (Bunn) No. A deed from a grantor outside the chain of title, even if recorded, is treated as though it were unrecorded and gives no constructive notice. First, a preliminary issue must be discussed. The initial deed to Hughes (D) did become operative when he (D) put his name on it before recording it. Before that name was filled in, the deed itself was a nullity. Hughes (D) had implied authority to fill in the blank. It is to be presumed that the grantee has the authority to do this when the grantor retains the consideration for the deed, and delivers the deed to the grantee, just as the Hoergers did here. Turning to the issue of the deed to the Board (P), the facts support Hughes' (D) claim to title. When Duryea and Wilson deeded the property to the Board (P) in November 1909, there was no record showing they had any title to convey. The Duryea and Wilson deed was not recorded until December 21, 1910. By contrast, Hughes (D) was a subsequent purchaser, and is protected by the fact that his (D) deed was recorded five days before the deed from the Hoergers to Duryea and Wilson. At the time Hughes (D) recorded his deed, Duryea and Wilson were still not a record owner anywhere in the chain of title. Hughes (D) was thus the rightful owner of the lot. Order reversed, and new trial granted.

Analysis:

The problem presented here is often referred to as the "wild deed." Generally, it is a deed to property which is recorded, but not within the chain of title because neither the grantor nor the grantee is known to the searcher of title in official records. Here, the term "wild deed" refers to the deed from Duryea and Wilson to the Board. There are three other similar, 'generic' problems of title recordation, and these will be discussed in other cases in this chapter. One occurs when title is recorded too late, as when a grantee in one deed fails to record it until after the grantor's deed to a second grantee is recorded. Another problem results when a grantee records a deed before the grantor actually obtains title to the property in question. Still another problem arises when the owner of two or more parcels includes, in a deed to one parcel, language which encumbers title to any other commonly owned parcel. In all four of these chain of title problems, the courts have favored title searchers by treating the given conveyances as if they were unrecorded and as giving no constructive notice. Almost invariably, the grantee is spared the burden of discovering all claims to the title in question, as the four recording problems mentioned above render the task of finding all adverse claims to title incredibly difficult.

Guillette v. Daly Dry Wall, Inc.

(Neighboring Lot Owner) v. (Would-Be Apartment Builder)

367 Mass. 355, 325 N.E.2d 572 (1975)

MEMORY GRAPHIC

Instant Facts

Daly Dry Wall, Inc. tried to build an apartment building on a lot in a subdivision which was restricted to single-family houses.

Black Letter Rule

A subsequent purchaser from a common grantor in a subdivision has constructive notice of the restrictions on the rest of the subdivision, and thus acquires title subject to those restrictions.

Procedural Basis: Appeal from final decree in action for injunctive relief.

Facts: Wallace L. Gilmore sold lots in a subdivision to Mr. and Mrs. Guillette (P) in May 1968, by a deed referring to a plan dated in March 1968. Earlier, the Walcotts (P) purchased a lot in August 1967, by a deed referring to a plan dated in July 1967. Both these plans are essentially the same and mention no restrictions. In June 1968, the Paraskivas (P) purchased a lot in the subdivision by a deed referring to the 1968 plan. These three deeds, along with five other deeds to lots in the subdivision, set out or refer to restrictions on the respective lots. Gilmore and at least the three sets of neighbors (P) intended to keep the subdivision limited to single-family residential use. In April 1972, Daly Dry Wall, Inc. (Daly) (D) purchased a lot from Gilmore. This deed contained no reference to any restrictions, but it did refer to the 1968 plan. Daly (D) made no inquiry regarding restrictions on the property and did not know of any development pattern in the subdivision. Daly (D) learned of the restrictions in August 1972 after a title examination was made. Daly (D) later obtained a building permit for thirty-six apartment-type units. Guillette (P), the Walcotts (P), and the Paraskivas (P) brought suit to enjoin Daly (D) from constructing the apartment building on its (D) lot. A final decree was entered enjoining Daly (D) from building any structures which did not conform to the restrictions contained in the deed from Gilmore to the Guillettes (P). Daly (D) appealed.

Issue: Is a subsequent purchaser of a lot in a subdivision bound by restrictions contained in deeds to neighboring landowners when the purchaser took title without knowledge of the restrictions?

Decision and Rationale: (Braucher) Yes. A subsequent purchaser from a common grantor in a subdivision has constructive notice of the restrictions on the rest of the subdivision, and thus acquires title subject to those restrictions. The deed from Gilmore to the Guillettes (P) conveyed more than just the described lot. It also conveyed an interest in the land then owned by Gilmore. That remaining land owned by Gilmore was subject to the same restrictions as the rest of the land. Thus, when Daly (D) purchased part of the land, it (D) took title subject to those restrictions. Daly (D) argues that charging it (D) with notice would impose a nearly impossible burden of searching each and every deed given in the subdivision. The Daly (D) deed, however, referred to the same plan mentioned in the Guillette (P) deed. A search for such deeds would not be impossible. Decree affirmed.

Analysis:

This case is an example of the fourth generic chain of title problem discussed in the previous brief. It is important to note the difficulty that a subsequent purchaser in a subdivision faces in learning of the restrictions on neighboring lots and how they affect his or her lot. In many states that rely on name indexes to record title, the index books include a column where a brief description can be included for each affected parcel. This method is not mandatory, however, and is often maintained only as a favor to title searchers. Even if this column is present in the record, there is no guarantee that those in the recording office will accurately summarize which properties are affected by a given set of restrictions. This is particularly true if the restriction's effect on other parcels is very complex or not very obvious. A title searcher may only be legally entitled to rely on the comments in this brief description column if it is legally required to be included in the index. If it is not, then a searcher would have to go through every conveyance by the grantor. Granted, that task seemed fairly easy here, but if the grantor is a large-scale developer or real estate dealer, the number of conveyances could go well into the hundreds, making the task an enormous one. The courts are pretty evenly split on this issue, with some holding that this burden of title searching is too excessive, and some imposing this burden on the searcher anyway.

Daniels v. Anderson

(Option Holder) v. (Not Stated)
162 Ill.2d 47, 642 N.E.2d 128 (Ill. 1994)

M E M O R Y G R A P H I C

Instant Facts

A person who possessed the right of first refusal on a piece of property sues a subsequent buyer who purchased the property and took possession without allowing the prior buyer to exercise his preemptive option.

Black Letter Rule

Bona fide purchaser status attaches only when the full purchase price has been paid.

Case Vocabulary

EQUITABLE CONVERSION: The doctrine that vests equitable title to property in the purchaser once a binding land sale contract is executed.
PRO TANTO: Partial payment made on a claim or purchase.
SPECIFIC PERFORMANCE: The remedy of requiring performance of a contract under the exact terms of the agreement.

Procedural Basis: Appeal from order affirming verdict of specific performance of preemptive option in land sale.

Facts: In 1977 William Daniels (P) bought two lots from Stephen Jacula (D). The contract of sale gave Daniels (P) the right of first refusal if Jacula (D) ever decided to sell an adjacent parcel (the "Contiguous Parcel") for the same price as any prospective buyer offered. Daniels (P) received and recorded the deed, which did not mention the right of first refusal. The contract of sale was not recorded. In 1985, Zografos (D) contracted with Jacula (D) to buy the Contiguous Parcel for $60,000. Daniels (P) was not notified of the offer. Zografos (D) paid Jacula (D) $10,000 and gave Jacula (D) a note for the balance. Zografos (D) paid $30,000 more in early 1986. In June 1986 Daniels' (P) wife gave Zografos (D) notice of the right of first refusal. In August 1986 Zografos (D) paid the remaining $20,000 to Jacula (D). Zografos (D) received and recorded the deed to the Contiguous Parcel. Daniels (P) sued Jacula (D) and Zografos (D) for specific performance of the preemptive option. Zografos (D) contended that he was a bona fide purchaser without notice of the option. The trial court held that Zografos (D) was not a subsequent bona fide purchaser because he had actual notice of the option at the time he took title. The court ordered Zografos (D) to convey the Contiguous Parcel to Daniels (P), and ordered Daniels (P) to pay Zografos (D) the full purchase price of $60,000 plus $11,000 in property taxes Zografos (D) had paid on the Contiguous Parcel. Zografos (D) appealed on grounds that he became a bona fide purchaser because he took equitable title prior to receiving actual notice of Daniels' (P) interest, even though he did not take legal title until after he had notice. The appellate court affirmed, holding that Zografos (D) waived this theory because he did not assert it at any time prior to the appeal. Zografos (D) appeals to the Supreme Court of Illinois.

Issue: Where a buyer receives notice of an outstanding interest subsequent to paying some, but not all, of the full purchase price, is the buyer considered a bona fide purchaser?

Decision and Rationale: (Freeman, J.) No. Where a buyer receives notice of an outstanding interest subsequent to paying some, but not all, of the full purchase price, the buyer is not considered a bona fide purchaser. A bona fide purchaser, by definition, takes title to real property without notice of the interests of others. Some appellate courts have held that partial payment of the consideration is insufficient to render the buyer a bona fide purchaser. A majority of jurisdictions have relaxed this harsh rule and have applied a pro tanto rule, which protects the buyer to the extent of the payments made prior to notice, but no further. Courts can exercise considerable latitude in reaching an equitable resolution. We hold that the trial court's disposition of the issue between Zografos (D) and Daniels (P) was fair and not an abuse of discretion. Affirmed.

Analysis:

This case tackles the difficult question of when a buyer becomes a bona fide purchaser. The question is very important. If a subsequent buyer is considered a bona fide purchaser, he can take title despite a previous hostile interest in the same property. Clearly, where a party pays full consideration and takes legal title without actual or constructive notice of prior interests, that party is a bona fide purchaser and is protected. Conversely, where the new buyer has notice of the prior interest, he commits fraud upon the holder of the prior interest by consummating the purchase. But should a bona fide status attach prior to taking actual legal title? Without stating any policy justification, the opinion concludes that it should not. The result is quite harsh to Zografos (D). He contracted to buy (and presumably took possession) of the Contiguous Parcel, and he paid the majority of the purchase price prior to having any notice of Daniels' (P) hostile interest. Should Zografos (D) be forced to abandon the property and convey it to Daniels (P) simply because Zografos (D) had not yet made his final payment? Daniels (P) could have protected himself by either recording the sale contract (which provided notice of the right of first refusal) or by making sure the deed mentioned this preemptive option. Daniels (P) did not take either of these steps, but he was protected merely because his wife mentioned the option at the right time (a few months before Zografos (D) made the final payment). The opinion notes that courts can choose from a variety of equitable resolutions. Some courts award the land to the prior holder and refund any payments the subsequent buyer made. Another option is to divide the land between the two purchasers. Perhaps this approach would have been more fair in this case, assuming the property could be subdivided.

Lewis v. Superior Court

(Purchaser) v. (Court)
30 Cal. App. 4th 1850 (Cal. Ct. App. 1994)

M E M O R Y G R A P H I C

Instant Facts

A couple purchased property by giving a note to the seller one day before the lis pendens of a party claiming a hostile interest was properly indexed.

Black Letter Rule

A seller need not be paid in full before the buyer can be considered a bona fide purchaser.

Case Vocabulary

EXPOSTULATING: Reasoning in an effort to dissuade or correct.
LIS PENDENS: A notice of lawsuit affecting title to property.

Procedural Basis: Appeal from denial of motion for summary judgment in action to quiet title and expunge lis pendens.

Facts: In February 1991, Robert and Josephine Lewis contracted to buy a residence for $2.3 million. On February 24, Fontana Films (D) recorded a lis pendens on the property. On February 25, the Lewises (P) paid $350,000. Escrow closed on February 28, 1991, when the Lewises (P) gave the seller a note for $1.95 million. The Lewises (P) had neither actual nor constructive notice of the lis pendens at this time. On February 29, 1991, the lis pendens was indexed. Within the next year, the Lewises (P) paid the note in full and spent over $1 million in renovating the property. In September 1993, the Lewises (P) were served with Fontana's (D) lawsuit and learned about the lis pendens. The Lewises (P) brought suit to remove the lis pendens and clear their title. Fontana (D) contends that even if the Lewises (D) took title before the indexing of the lis pendens, they nevertheless were not bona fide purchasers because they did not fully pay for the property until after indexing. The trial court denied the Lewises' (P) motion for summary judgment, and they appeal.

Issue: Must a seller be paid in full before the buyer can be considered a bona fide purchaser?

Decision and Rationale: (Woods, J.) No. A seller need not be paid in full before the buyer can be considered a bona fide purchaser. Fontana (D) relies on our antiquated holding in *Davis v. Ward* [a buyer becomes a bona fide purchaser only upon payment in full]. The *Davis* payment of value rule cannot be reconciled with modern real property law and practice. The *Davis* rule was premised in part on the assertion that a purchaser who loses his property is "not hurt" if he has not fully paid for the land. This claim is inconsistent with modern market considerations. Any purchaser without notice who makes a down payment and unequivocally obligates himself to pay the balance has every reason to believe that, if he makes the payments when due, his right to the property will be secure. Such a purchaser may drastically alter his position by, for example, selling his prior residence and making significant improvements to the property. The landowner cannot be adequately redressed by simply returning the money he paid so far. Real property is unique and its loss cannot be compensated in money. Furthermore, the *Davis* holding cannot rationally be applied to cases involving only constructive notice. A completely innocent purchaser who has only partially paid should not be punished for simply living up to his payment obligations. Moreover, he should not be required to undertake a title search before each and every payment (360 title searches for a typical 30-year note!). Finally, applying *Davis* would unfairly penalize the Lewises for paying cash for the property, rather than financing the purchase price. In *Davis*, the court recognized that if the buyer had taken out a mortgage and given a note to the bank, he could be a bona fide purchaser because the seller would have been fully paid. On the other hand, a buyer who gives a note to the seller would only be considered a bona fide purchaser when he made his final payment to the seller. This distinction makes no sense. It unfairly penalizes a buyer who arranges a cash transaction with the seller rather than taking out a mortgage. We therefore issue a peremptory writ of mandate directing the superior court to vacate its order denying the Lewises (P) motion for summary judgment, and thereafter issue a new order granting the motion and expunging the lis pendens.

Analysis:

This well-reasoned holding effectively overrules the "payment of value" rule expressed in *Davis* and *Daniels* [bona fide purchaser status attaches only when the full purchase price has been paid]. In modern real property transactions, few buyers can make a full cash payment at the time of the sale. Rather, buyers typically finance the purchase price, either through the seller or by taking out a mortgage with a bank. In either case, the buyer is entitled to take possession of the property even though he has not yet fully paid the price. While the buyer does not have legal title until he pays off the mortgage or the note, he is in every other way the true owner of the property. The buyer should not be punished for failing to pay in full at the time of contracting, and there should be no difference whether the seller takes a note or the buyer utilizes a mortgage. Indeed, where a mortgage is used, the seller receives the full purchase price immediately. However, when considering whether a buyer is a bona fide purchaser, it should make no difference when the seller is fully paid. The opinion raises some strong policy justifications for the court's holding. First, buyers who take possession under a note or mortgage often drastically alter their position based on the understanding that they own the property. Buyers sell their prior residences, move their families, and improve the new property even though they do not yet have legal title. Second, the unique nature of real property makes it impossible to compensate the buyer merely by refunding what he has already paid. The opinion can be questioned only for failing to take into account the equitable considerations involving Fontana Films' (D) interest. Apparently, Fontana (D) could not record its lis pendens until it knew that someone was trying to buy the property over which Fontana (D) purportedly held an interest. Fontana (D) recorded its lis pendens immediately, and it probably was not Fontana's (D) fault that the lis pendens was not indexed until after the Lewises (P) gave the seller their note.

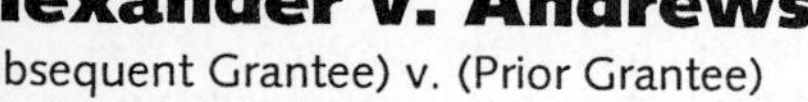

Alexander v. Andrews

(Subsequent Grantee) v. (Prior Grantee)
135 W. Va. 403, 645 S.E.2d 487 (W. Va. 1951)

MEMORY GRAPHIC

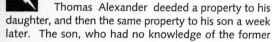

Instant Facts

Thomas Alexander deeded a property to his daughter, and then the same property to his son a week later. The son, who had no knowledge of the former deed, seeks the protection of the recording act because he recorded his deed first.

Black Letter Rule

Subsequent grantees must complete their transaction by paying valuable, reasonably adequate consideration in order to benefit from a recording act statute.

Case Vocabulary

PRIMA FACIE: On face value; evidence that in itself tends to prove a proposition.

Procedural Basis: Bill of relief to quiet title and clear cloud on property by utilizing a recording act statute.

Facts: Mary Alexander and Thomas Alexander each owned a one-half share in certain property as of June 1945. When Mary died in April 1946, she devised her one-half interest to Charles Alexander (P). On May 8, 1946, Thomas delivered a deed for his interest to Sarah Andrews (D), his daughter. The consideration for this deed was Sarah's "love and affection." On May 14, 1946, Thomas delivered a second deed for his interest to his son Charles (P), even though Thomas had already transferred his interest one week earlier. Charles (P) recorded the deed the same day. The consideration for the second deed was Charles's (P) $1000 payment made prior to May 14, plus his promise to care for Thomas until Thomas's death and to pay the burial costs for Thomas. Sarah (D) did not record her deed until July 8, 1946. Charles (P) had no notice of the deed to Sarah (D), and he seeks to utilize the West Virginia Recording Act to quiet the title to his property and to remove as a cloud upon his property the deed to Sarah (D). Sarah (D) claims that Charles (P) did not complete his transaction by rendering full consideration prior to the time Sarah (D) recorded her deed.

Issue: (1) In a race-notice jurisdiction, must the subsequent grantee have completed his purchase by providing the entire amount of reasonably adequate consideration before the original grantee records her deed? (2) Is a subsequent grantee entitled to reimbursement of the consideration paid if the prior grantee obtains legal title?

Decision and Rationale: (1) Yes. In a race-notice jurisdiction, the subsequent grantee must have completed his purchase by providing the entire amount of reasonably adequate consideration before the original grantee records her deed. The West Virginia Recording Act protects an innocent grantee who had no notice of a prior deed and who records his deed before the original grantee records. However, the subsequent grantee must have completed the transaction by rendering full consideration necessary to support the transfer. In the case at hand, Charles (P) had no notice of the prior deed to Sarah (D) when he obtained and recorded the deed from Thomas. In addition, Charles (P) recorded his deed before Sarah (D). However, Charles (P) did not complete his transaction. The record establishes that Charles (P) paid $1000, and that the reasonable value of the one-half interest was $3850. The $1000 payment was insufficient to constitute complete consideration. The remainder of the consideration was to be Charles's (P) actions in caring for Thomas until his death and Charles's (P) act of paying for Thomas's burial. Charles (P) did care for Thomas until July 8, 1946, the date Sarah (D) recorded her deed. Nevertheless, Charles (P) did not complete the transaction, since Charles (P) did not provide care until Thomas died (as Thomas had not yet died as of July 8) and Charles (P) did not pay the burial expenses prior to July 8. Therefore, after Sarah's (D) deed was recorded, it became effective for all purposes, and the grantee in the subsequent deed of May 14, not having completed his purchase, could obtain no rights based upon the payments thereunder made. (2) Yes. A subsequent grantee is entitled to reimbursement of the consideration paid if the prior grantee obtains legal title. Charles (P) did not get legal title to the property, as the transaction was not complete when Sarah (D) recorded her deed on July 8. However, Charles (P) paid $1000 and cared for Thomas in anticipation of obtaining the property. Charles (P) is entitled to reimbursement by Sarah (D) for the $1000 and for any sums expended in caring for his father until July 8, 1946. Remanded.

Analysis:

This case exemplifies the delicate balancing of equities involved in applying a recording act statute. Recording act statutes are designed to protect subsequent purchasers who have paid valuable consideration (1) without notice of a prior conveyance (a "notice" statute), or (2) who record their deed first (a "race" statute), or (3) who qualify for both (1) and (2) (a "race-notice" statute). At first glance, Charles (P) appears to have met the requirements for West Virginia's race-notice statute. However, the Supreme Court of Appeals focuses on the crucial prerequisite that the subsequent grantee must be a bona fide purchaser for value. In other words, the consideration paid must have been reasonably adequate to consider the transfer "complete." In the case at hand, the $1000 was not considered adequate for this purpose. But is it really fair to require Charles (P) to wait for the death of Thomas in order to gain title to the property? Couldn't Charles's (P) "promise" to care for and bury Thomas be sufficient? Apparently not, as far as this court is concerned. But in a typical equitable gesture, the court fashions a remedy for poor Charles (P). He was unlucky enough not to have Thomas die before Sarah (D) recorded her deed, but he at least deserves to be compensated for the consideration actually paid plus the sums expended in caring for Thomas. Note the awkward position that this holding places Sarah (D) in. She was granted the property on May 8, 1946 and her consideration was merely her prior acts of love and affection towards her father. However, by waiting two months to record her deed, Sarah (D) is stuck having to reimburse Charles (P) for his expenses. Thus, while the recording Act provides some solace for Sarah (D), the real lesson to be learned is that a grantee should record her deed immediately. If she chooses to wait, she must suffer the consequences.

Harper v. Paradise

(Remaindermen) v. (Subsequent Grantees)
233 Ga. 194, 210 S.E.2d 710 (Ga. 1974)

MEMORY GRAPHIC

Instant Facts

The Paradises, who claim title to property dating back to a 1928 deed, are challenged by Clyde Harper (P), who asserts that the Paradises had notice of a prior deed in which Clyde (P) was the remainderman.

Black Letter Rule

Subsequent grantees are held to inquiry notice of the contents of prior recorded deeds in the chain of title for purposes of a race-notice recording act.

Case Vocabulary

PLAT: A map of a parcel of property, showing boundaries and location.
REMAINDERMAN: The person who gains title to property once the prior tenancy ends, e.g., by death of a life tenant.

Procedural Basis: Appeal from directed verdict determining title to land.

Facts: In 1922, Susan Harper conveyed a deed for a farm to Maude Harper, for life with remainder in fee simple to Maude's named children, including Clyde (P). The deed was misplaced and not recorded until 1957, when Clyde (P) found the deed in a trunk and recorded it. Susan died in or about 1925 and was survived by her heirs. In 1928, all of the heirs except one (John Harper) executed a deed to Maude. The language of this deed, which was recorded in 1928, expressly noted that the prior deed from Susan to Maude had been lost. In 1933, Maude executed a deed which purported to convey the property to Ella Thornton as security for a loan. When Maude defaulted on the loan, Ella foreclosed. Ella received a sheriff's deed in 1936, which she recorded in 1936. An unbroken chain of title existed between Ella and the Paradises (D), who were grantees to a 1955 deed which was recorded in 1955. The Paradises (D) also assert title by adverse possession which began in 1940. The Paradises (D) claim their direct title from the 1928 deed from Susan's heirs to Maude. Clyde (P) alleges that the Paradises (D) do not hold valid title because the 1928 deed provided notice of the prior 1922 deed to Maude. Maude died in 1972. From a directed verdict in favor of the Paradises (D), Clyde (P) appeals.

Issue: Are subsequent grantees held to have inquiry notice of the contents of prior recorded deeds?

Decision and Rationale: (Ingram, J.) Yes. Subsequent grantees are held to have inquiry notice of the contents of prior recorded deeds. The 1928 deed, on which the Paradises (D) rely to establish their chain of title, expressly referenced the 1922 deed to Maude. Thus, Maude is bound to have taken the 1928 deed with knowledge of the 1922 deed. The recitals in the 1928 deed put any subsequent purchaser on notice of the earlier misplaced or lost deed. Thus, the 1928 deed is not entitled to priority, even though it was recorded years before the 1922 deed. Furthermore, the Paradises (D) cannot rely on the 1922 deed, because any interest they may have obtained under this deed would only be Maude's life estate, which terminated upon her death in 1972. We conclude that it was incumbent upon the Paradises (D) to ascertain through diligent inquiry the contents of the 1922 deed. The 1928 deed provides constructive notice of the 1922 deed. However, the Paradises (D) did not make any effort to inquire as to the interests conveyed in the 1922 deed when they purchased the property in 1955. Furthermore, the Paradises (D) cannot claim title by adverse possession from 1940 to 1955, because the adverse possession period would not have begun to run until Maude's death in 1972. Reversed and remanded with judgment to be entered in favor of Clyde (P).

Analysis:

Before even attempting to understand the intricate fact pattern of this case, it is essential to draw a chart showing the various entities, deeds, and dates involved. A chart indicates that the Paradises (D) must trace the chain of title back to Maude. The case is complicated by the fact that Maude received title under one of two possible deeds -- either the 1922 deed (which was lost) or the 1928 deed. If Maude had acquired the property by the 1928 deed and the effect of the recording act, then the Paradises (D) could have traced their title back to this deed and could claim valid title. However, the 1928 deed to Maude stated, on its face, that a prior deed existed. Thus, even though the 1928 deed was recorded first, it cannot take priority over the 1922 deed because there was not a lack of notice. Thus, at its most fundamental foundation, this case deals with the issue of notice. A subsequent purchaser for value is protected by a race-notice statute only if he acquires title without notice of the prior deed and if he records first. The notice need not be actual notice. Subsequent grantees must make some effort to determine if prior deeds existed. A simple analysis of the language of the 1928 deed would have revealed the prior 1922 deed, and thus the Paradises (D) do not meet the "notice" requirement of the recording statute.

Waldorff Ins. and Bonding, Inc. v. Eglin National Bank

(Condominium Owner) v. (Mortgagee)
453 So. 2d 1383 (Fl. Dist. Ct. App. 1984)

MEMORY GRAPHIC

Instant Facts

A bank attempts to foreclose on mortgages secured by condominiums, executed when one of the condo units subject to the mortgage was openly possessed and owned by another party.

Black Letter Rule

Actual possession gives constructive notice to the world of any right which the person in possession is able to establish.

Case Vocabulary

EQUIVOCAL: Ambiguous, doubtful, open to question.

Facts: Choctaw Partnership developed certain properties in Okaloosa County, Florida by constructing condominiums. In June 1972, Choctaw executed a promissory note and mortgage on the properties. The $1.1 million note and mortgage was eventually assigned to Eglin National Bank (Bank) (P) in January 1975, when less than $42,000 remained due on the note and mortgage. In April 1973, Waldorff Insurance and Bonding, Inc. (D) entered into a purchase agreement with Choctaw to buy Condo Unit 111. Waldorff (D) began occupancy of the unit immediately, continually occupying and maintaining the unit until the date of the hearing. In October 1973, Choctaw executed another note and mortgage for $600,000 in favor of the Bank (P). Unit 111 was included in this mortgage. In June 1974, Choctaw executed yet another note and mortgage in favor of the Bank for $95,000, securing a number of units including Unit 111. In March 1975, Choctaw, an insurance client of Waldorff (D), agreed to consider the purchase price of Unit 111 paid in full in exchange for a past due debt for insurance premiums owed by Choctaw to Waldorff (D). Waldorff (D) wrote off the debt on their taxes, and Choctaw executed a quitclaim deed in favor of Waldorff (D). In 1976, the Bank brought a foreclosure action against Choctaw. A final judgment of foreclosure was entered in September 1976, but this judgment explicitly retained jurisdiction to determine the ownership of Unit 111. Finally, in February 1983, a hearing on this issue was held. The trial court determined that the Bank's (P) ownership interest was superior to Waldorff's (D). The court held that Waldorff (D) did not have superior title, finding that Waldorff's (D) occupancy of Unit 111 was equivocal because Choctaw allowed several other condo units to be used for free, and finding that Waldorff (D) did not pay adequate consideration for Unit 111 so its quitclaim deed was void. Waldorff (D) appealed.

Issue: Does actual possession give constructive notice to all who claim an adverse ownership interest in a piece of property?

Decision and Rationale: (Shivers, J.) Yes. Actual possession gives constructive notice to all who claim an adverse ownership interest in a piece of property. In the situation at hand, Waldorff (D) openly and exclusively occupied and possessed Unit 111 at the time Choctaw executed the October 1973 and June 1974 mortgages to the Bank (P). Thus, the Bank (P) is held to have had constructive notice of Waldorff's (D) adverse title, so the Bank (P) cannot claim the benefit of the recording act. It is irrelevant that several other condo units were occupied by persons who possessed no legal or equitable title to the units. The units were intended to be conveyed as separate parcels, and thus the status of the other units is inconsequential. The Bank (P) contends that it would have been difficult to ascertain whether Waldorff (D) actually had a claim of ownership interest over Unit 111. Although it would be inconvenient for the Bank (P) to inquire as to the ownership of Unit 111, we follow the holding in *Phelan v. Brady* [actual possession of real estate is sufficient to a person proposing to take a mortgage on the property, and to all the world, of the existence of an right which the person in possession is able to establish]. In addition, we hold that the trial court erred in finding that the conveyance from Choctaw to Waldorff (D) was void due to lack of consideration. Although Waldorff (D) may have erred in taking a "bad debt" tax deduction for the cancellation of its debt, the fact that Choctaw was relieved from payment of the debt constituted valuable consideration. All in all, only the Bank's (P) 1972 mortgage lien is superior to Waldorff's (D) interest, and the satisfaction of this lien can come from the 1976 foreclosure sale of the other condo units. Waldorff's (D) title is superior to the other mortgages. Reversed and remanded.

Analysis:

Here is yet another factually complicated case that can be reduced to a relatively simple holding. In brief, this case involves three mortgages that the condo developer executed in favor of the Bank (P) (presumably in exchange for loans from the Bank (P) to the developer). As a security for the loans, the developer pledged the condo units. However, the developer did not own exclusive title to at least one of the units, Unit 111, when the second and third mortgages were executed. Waldorff (D), who held equitable title to Unit 111, should not have his interest taken away merely because the developer defaulted on his loans. Further, the holding is fair because the Bank (P) could have done a little research and determined that Waldorff (D) was openly possessing Unit 111 and held an equitable interest in the unit. The Bank (P) should have assumed that anyone occupying a condo had a legal interest therein until it could conclusively determine otherwise.

Walker Rogge, Inc. v. Chelsea Title and Guaranty Co.

(Property Owner) v. (Title Insurer)

116 N.J. 517, 562 A.2d 208 (1989)

M E M O R Y G R A P H I C

Instant Facts

Chelsea did not inform Walker Rogge when a prior deed indicated that the tract being insured was about seven acres smaller than what Walker Rogge believed.

Black Letter Rule

If a title company fails to conduct a reasonable title examination, or having conducted such an examination, fails to disclose the results to the insured, then it runs the risk of liability under the terms of the insurance policy and not under tort for negligence.

Procedural Basis: Appeal from judgment in action for damages.

Facts: Walker Rogge, Inc. (P) bought a tract of land from Alexander Kosa, who had acquired the land from Aiello. Before purchase, Kosa showed John Rogge, the company president, a 1975 survey by Price Walker which sized the tract at 18.33 acres. The sale contract referred to this Price Walker survey and indicated the tract was "19 acres more or less." The tract was priced at $16,000 per acre plus the cost of an existing house, with the total price being $363,000. The contract was signed on December 12, 1979, and closed on December 31. Rogge had the title work done by Chelsea Title and Guaranty Co. (D), which had issued two earlier title policies on the property. Chelsea's files contained the deed from Aiello to Kosa, which stated that the property contained only 12.486 acres. Both the deed from Kosa to Rogge and the title insurance policy by Chelsea referred to the Price Walker survey, but did not state the tract's acreage. The policy also stated, in part, that Chelsea (D) would insure against loss or damage which would result if the title were vested differently from what was stated in the policy; if any defect on the title existed, and if the title was unmarketable. An exception to this policy was that it would not insure against loss or damage which "could be disclosed by an accurate survey and inspection of the premises." In 1985, Walker Rogge (P) hired a surveyor to examine neighboring lots. This survey indicated the Walker Rogge (P) tract was 12.43 acres. Walker Rogge (P) then filed this action, saying the loss of acreage was insurable and that Chelsea (D) was negligent in failing to disclose the size of the property. The trial court found that the policy covered the shortage in acreage, that it was a defect in title, and that the title was unmarketable. It also found the survey exception to be meaningless, and awarded damages. The Appellate Division affirmed, but remanded for damages.

Issue: Can a title company be held liable under its policy for not disclosing the results of its title examination to the insured?

Decision and Rationale: (Pollock) Yes. If a title company fails to conduct a reasonable title examination, or having conducted such an examination, fails to disclose the results to the insured, then it runs the risk of liability under the terms of the insurance policy. As a preliminary issue, the survey exception outlined by Chelsea (D) is a pretty standard one, and not vague or meaningless. Like other insurance policies, title policies are liberally construed in favor of the insured, against the insurer. Title insurance policies are also inherently complex, however, and any buyer of real estate runs the risk of not receiving all the land he or she pays for without a surveyor's help. Title insurance is no substitute for a survey. A title insurance company does not insure the quantity of land if it makes no recitals of acreage. An insured should provide the title company with an acceptable survey. Here, such a survey would have revealed the shortage. With regard to liability, the rule in this state has been that a title company is only liable under the policy and not for negligence in searching records. The premise for that rule is that the duty of the title company depends on the agreement between insurer and insured. The evidence supports the trial court's finding that Chelsea (D) was only asked to prepare a title insurance policy. The title search performed by Chelsea was simply an internal procedure done for Chelsea's (D) own benefit. Courts and commentators have split over whether a title company should be liable under negligence and under its policy if it does not disclose information that would be of interest to the insured. This court believes the relationship between the two parties is essentially contractual, with the result being the insurance policy. An insured expects that, in exchange for its premium, it will be insured against certain risks subject to the terms of the policy. Thus, a title company that fails to make, or fails to disclose the results of, a reasonable title examination runs the risk of liability under the policy. Most states make such conduct a breach of the policy, as well. Chelsea (D) could be held liable if it assumed duties in addition to the mere insurance policy and damages resulted. The trial court did not determine whether Chelsea (D) assumed a duty to assure the acreage of the tract as a result of its earlier policies on the property. This court remands to the trial court on those issues. Judgment of Appellate Division affirmed in part, reversed in part, and remanded.

Analysis:

At first glance, it may seem foolish for a title insurance company to issue a policy without conducting a careful search of the records beforehand. Such a practice would obviously lead to larger claims down the road. The fact is that most title binders and policies do not explicitly state that a title search has been performed. Despite this, potential insurance buyers treat the policy as the practical result of a search, anyway, and consider it to be a report on the defects of title. The *Walker Rogge* case seems to suggest, and other cases more clearly state, that the insured has a right to be fully informed of any defects in title which the insurer finds in the official records of title. These defects are not limited to those which would be covered by the policy, but rather include all those that would be excepted from the policy or those that the insurer believes only present an inconsequential risk. *Walker* and other cases in Arizona, California, and New York, to name a few states, represent a clear and very recent trend to increase the rights of the insured. Still, there are some states holding out and finding no duty for a title company to search title at all.

Lick Mill Creek Apartments v. Chicago Title Insurance Co.

(Property Owner) v. (Title Insurance Company)
231 Cal App. 3d 1654, 283 Cal. Rptr. 231 (1991)

M E M O R Y G R A P H I C

Instant Facts

The apartment owners tried to have the title company indemnify them for the costs of cleaning up and removing the hazardous substances under their property.

Black Letter Rule

Title insurance policies are intended to protect the condition of an owner's title to land, and not provide coverage for the physical condition of the land itself.

Case Vocabulary

ENCUMBRANCES: Claims, liens, charges, or liabilities which are attached to and are binding on property.
GROUNDWATER: Water within the earth that is the source of wells and springs.
SUBSOIL: Weathered rock and earth beneath the surface soil.

Procedural Basis: Appeal from judgment of dismissal after demurrer.

Facts: Before 1979, various companies operated warehouses and chemical plants on the property in question. In addition, underground tanks, pumps, and pipelines were used in handling hazardous substances, which later contaminated the soil, subsoil and groundwater. In 1979, Kimball Small Investments (KSI) purchased the property. The California Department of Health Services ordered KSI to remedy the contamination problem, but KSI did not comply. In 1986, Lick Mill Creek Apartments (LMC) (P) bought lot 1 of the property from KSI, and also bought title insurance from Chicago Title Insurance Company (Chicago Title) (D). Before issuing the policy, Chicago Title (D) commissioned a survey and inspection of the property. LMC (P) then bought lots 2 and 3 from KSI and secured two additional policies from Chicago Title (D). The entire site was surveyed and inspected, and the inspection revealed the tanks, etc. on the property. When these policies were issued, the Department of Health Services and other state and county agencies kept records disclosing the presence of hazardous substances on the property. LMC (P) paid for the removal and cleanup of the materials after purchase, then sought indemnity from Chicago Title (D) for its (P) costs. LMC (P) claimed the hazardous substances impaired the property's marketability, and that their presence was an encumbrance on title because it would lead to cleanup costs. The policy would pay for loss sustained because of the marketability of title or any lien or encumbrance on the title. Chicago Title (D) denied coverage. The trial court sustained Chicago Title's (D) demurrer.

Issue: Does a title insurance policy provide coverage when physical conditions of the land result in a lowered market value and the possibility of added costs to the owner?

Decision and Rationale: (Agliano) No. Title insurance policies are intended to protect the condition of an owner's title to land, and not provide coverage for the physical condition of the land itself. LMC's (P) position on the marketability of their title is unsupported. There is a distinction between the marketability of title to land and the market value of the land. An owner's inability to make economic use of the land due to an owner's earlier violations of the law does not render the title defective or unmarketable under a standard insurance policy. Here, LMC (P) has only made complaints regarding conditions affecting the marketability of the land, and not the title. This distinction is recognized in other jurisdictions as well. LMC (P) thus cannot claim coverage under a title insurance policy for problems stemming from the physical condition of the property. Moreover, the fact that the property is contaminated, and as such will lead to added costs, does not constitute an encumbrance on the title. "Encumbrances" have traditionally been defined as liens, easements, restrictive covenants, and interests held by third persons. This court refuses to broaden the definition of encumbrances to include the presence of hazardous substances. The mere possibility that the government may impose a lien on the property at some future date is not enough to count as a defect in or lien or encumbrance on title. Judgment affirmed.

Analysis:

Title insurance policies are different from most other forms of insurance in that it covers only effects on title, which are often mere matters of recordation and documentation. Title policies do not come into play when the property itself suffers physical effects, either by hazardous substances as here, or by government regulations, natural changes in the land, etc. Title insurance also differs from other types of insurance in several other ways. Title insurance is, generally, paid for in a single premium. In addition, the policy coverage can last indefinitely, provided the owner or his or her heirs, devisees, or even corporate successors continue to hold the land. Moreover, defects which arise after the policy's date of issue cannot be the basis of a claim on the policy; the policy only covers the title as of the date it was issued.

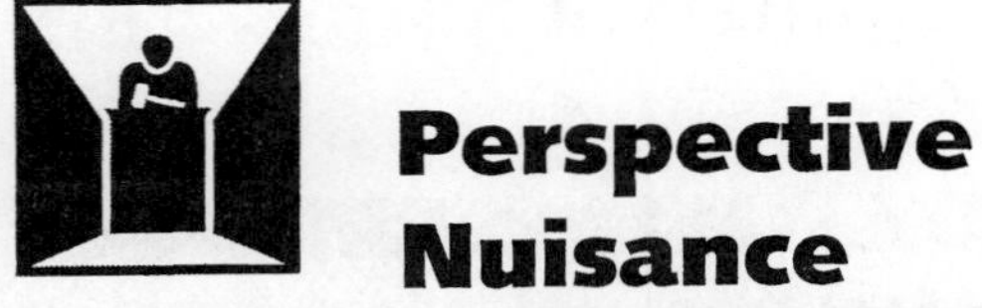

Perspective
Nuisance

Chapter 9

There are three main types of limitations on how owners can use their property. . In this chapter, the law of nuisance will be discussed. Chapter 10 discusses the various forms of servitudes. Chapter 11 will discuss the third type of limitation, zoning through the use of municipal laws and ordinances.

The law of nuisance can look very simple. Basically, it centers on the idea that an owner of land should not have to put up with another person's interference with the use and enjoyment of his or her land. More specifically, interference that is substantial, and either unreasonable or negligent, reckless, or abnormally dangerous is not allowed.

The details of nuisance, however, are complex. Figuring out when something counts as a nuisance is not much of a problem. The problem that courts have is trying to figure out what should be done about those nuisances. This problem is greatest when activities are done in the middle of nowhere and new landowners enter the area, or when a lawful activity is carried out too close to other people's homes. This chapter will cover the different remedies the courts have granted in these general types of situations.

Chapter 9

NOTE: THE PURPOSE OF THIS OUTLINE IS TO ORGANIZE THE CASES SO THAT ONE CAN QUICKLY UNDERSTAND THE RELEVANCE OF EACH CASE TO THE COURSE. NO ATTEMPT IS MADE IN THIS OVERVIEW TO ADDRESS EVERY CONCEPT THAT MUST BE STUDIED. BE SURE TO READ THE ENTIRE CASEBOOK AND/OR OTHER MATERIALS TO GAIN A FULL UNDERSTANDING OF ALL CONCEPTS.

I. An Introduction to the Substantive Law
 A. Rather than regulating any particular type of conduct, the law of nuisance seeks to protect a landowner's interest in using and enjoying his property. *Morgan v. High Penn Oil Co.*
  1. Thus, the character of the defendant's conduct – i.e. whether such conduct is forbidden by law, reckless, negligent or perfectly legal – does not determine the existence of a nuisance.
 B. Intentional vs. Unintentional Nuisance
  1. An unintentional nuisance arises when the defendant's conduct is negligent, reckless or ultra-hazardous. *Morgan v. High Penn Oil Co.*
   a. Thus, unintentional nuisances are usually not governed by the law of nuisance, but by the traditional tort principles of negligence and ultra-hazardous conduct.
  2. An intentional nuisance, on the other hand arises when the defendant acts for the purposes of causing the nuisance, or knows, or should know, that the nuisance is certain to arise as a result of his conduct. *Morgan v. High Penn Oil Co.*
  3. An intentional nuisance has two particular elements: the defendant's conduct must be "unreasonable," and it must have caused the plaintiff "substantial" harm.
   a. Unreasonableness: The term may carry a different meaning under the law of nuisance than it does under the law of negligence.
   b. Some courts hold that unreasonableness is determined by the level of interference with the plaintiff's use and enjoyment of his land. *Jost v. Dairyland Power Corp.*
    (1) The Restatement, however, applies a balancing approach which weighs the harm to the defendant against the utility of the plaintiff's conduct. *Restatement (Second) of Torts § 826.*
    (2) The Restatement has an alternate, more cryptic definition of unreasonableness, which makes a plaintiff liable if "the harm caused by the conduct is serious and the financial burden of compensating for this and similar harm to others would not make the continuation of the conduct not feasible." *Restatement (Second) of Torts § 826.*
 C. Other Nuisances
  1. Fear of Future Harm
   a. Courts are split as to whether the devaluation of property prices due to the fear of some future result caused by an undesirable enterprise, such as a toxic waste dump or halfway house, can be grounds for a nuisance suit. *Arkansas Release Guidance Found v. Needler*; *Nickolson v. Connecticut Halfway House*; *Adkins v. Thomas Solvent Co.*
  2. Aesthetic Nuisance
   a. While most courts hold that mere unattractiveness does not a nuisance make, when combined with the defendant's malicious intent, an eyesore can be grounds for damages.
 D. Note on Lateral and Subjacent Support
  1. The common law gives landowners the right of lateral support, support provided by neighboring parcels, by imposing upon landowners the duty to provide such support to adjacent parcels.
  2. Failure to provide such support gives rise to liability to the person who created the hazard, but only when subsidence actually occurs or is imminent.

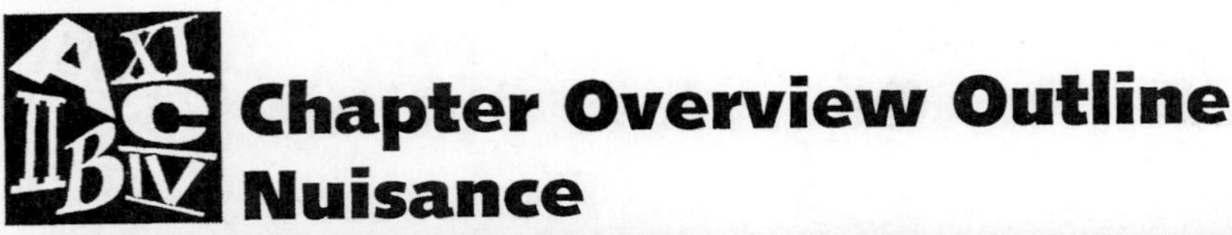

Chapter Overview Outline
Nuisance

II. Remedies (and More on the Substantive Law)
  A. Types of Remedies Afforded
    1. Injunctive Relief
      a. A plaintiff in a nuisance suit may be granted an injunction against the party causing the nuisance only after a "balancing of the equities," which requires the court to decide if denying the injunction causes greater harm to the plaintiff and the public than granting the injunction imposes on the defendant and the public. *Estancias Dallas Corp. v. Schultz.*
      b. Despite giving lip service to the common law notion that a plaintiff who proves the existence of a nuisance is entitled to an injunction, most courts undertake a balancing of the hardships to determine whether equitable relief is warranted. *Boomer v. Atlantic Cement Company.*
    2. Money Damages
      a. Where a court denies the plaintiff an injunction despite the finding of a nuisance, the court may undertake to determine all past, present and future damages – i.e. , *permanent damages* – which are to arise from the nuisance and order the defendant to pay the plaintiff that amount. *Boomer v. Atlantic Cement Company.*
    3. Paying for an Injunction
      a. One court has held that, under certain circumstances, the plaintiff in a nuisance suit may be granted an injunction only if the defendant is compensated for having to cease his activity. *Spur Industries, Inc. v. Del E. Webb Development Co.*
  B. Coming to the Nuisance
    1. Most courts hold that the plaintiff's decision to move near an existing nuisance is a factor relevant to a decision to grant injunctive relief or award money damages. *Restatement (Second) of Torts §840(D).*
  C. Note on Nuisance Law and Environmental Controls: While regulation is currently the most widespread method of environmental control and protection, the use of incentive systems, such as the trading of pollution rights, has become more significant in recent environmental legislation.

Morgan v. High Penn Oil Co.

Trailer Park Owner) v. (Refinery Operator)
953) 238 N.C. 185, 77 S.E.2d 682

ıEMORY GRAPHIC

Instant Facts

Trailer park owner sued for injunction against perator of a nearby oil refinery which produced ıauseating fumes.

Black Letter Rule

A private nuisance occurs when there is sub-antial interference with the use and enjoyment of land, ıd that interference is either intentional and ıreasonable, or unintentional and the result of ıegligence, recklessness, or abnormally dangerous :tivity.

Case Vocabulary

UISANCE *PER ACCIDENS*: Also nuisance in fact; an :herwise lawful act or structure which can become a ıisance by virtue of its location, surroundings, or the anner in which it is conducted or maintained.

UISANCE *PER SE*: Also nuisance at law; an act or ructure that is a nuisance at all times, regardless of its cation, surroundings, or the manner in which it is nducted or maintained.

C UTERE TUO ALIENUM NON LAEDAS: Latin phrase eaning, in essence, that one should not use his or her operty in a way that injures another.

:RMINUS: The end or finishing point of a transport ute.

Facts: Prior to August 1945, Morgan (P) acquired a composite tract of land which contained a dwelling-house. Immediately after purchasing the land, Morgan (P) built a restaurant and trailer park on it. Morgan (P) rented these improvements to third persons after their completion, and rented space in his (P's) home for additional income. Beginning in October 1950, High Penn Oil Company (D) operated an oil refinery approximately 1,000 feet from Morgan's (P's) property. In addition, a church, at least twenty-nine homes, a plant nursery, and various small businesses were located within a mile of the refinery. Two or three days a week, the refinery produced large amounts of nauseating gases and odors. People "of ordinary sensitiveness" within roughly two miles of the refinery were rendered uncomfortable or sick by these emissions, and thus substantially impaired the enjoyment and use of Morgan's (P's) land by himself (P) and his (P's) renters. Morgan (P) and others nearby demanded that High Penn (D) put an end to the pollution, but High Penn (D) failed to do so. High Penn (D) argued that because its (D's) use of an oil refinery is part of its (D's) occupation, it was a lawful enterprise and thus was not a nuisance at law. Also, High Penn (D) argued that the refinery can only be a nuisance if it is constructed or operated in a negligent manner. A jury found the refinery to be a nuisance, and awarded $2,500 in damages. The trial judge entered a judgment along those lines and also enjoined the High Penn Oil (D) from continuing to operate the refinery. High Penn (D) appealed.

Issue: Can an otherwise lawful enterprise constitute a nuisance *per accidens* or in fact if it is not constructed or operated in a negligent manner?

Decision and Rationale: (Ervin) Yes. A nuisance *per accidens* or in fact may be created or maintained even without the presence of negligence. A private nuisance occurs when there is substantial interference with the use and enjoyment of land, and that interference is either intentional and unreasonable, or unintentional and the result of negligence, recklessness, or abnormally dangerous activity. The refinery is a lawful enterprise, and thus is not a nuisance *per se* [act or structure which is a nuisance at all times, regardless of circumstances]. It is nonetheless a nuisance *per accidens* [act or structure which is a nuisance by virtue of location or manner of operation]. Courts have awarded damages for such nuisances even when negligence has not been proved or alleged. The key concept here is *sic utere tuo ut alienum non laedas* [every person should use his or her own property so as not to injure another]. Interference with a person's private use and enjoyment of land is intentional when the person whose conduct is in question acts for the purpose of causing the nuisance, knows the nuisance is a result of his or her conduct, or knows that a nuisance is substantially certain to result from his or her conduct. A person who intentionally creates or maintains a private nuisance is liable for the resulting injury to others regardless of the degree of skill exercised to avoid such injury. It is clear that High Penn (D) intentionally and unreasonably caused harmful gases and odors to escape and substantially impair Morgan's (P's) use and enjoyment of his (P's) land. Moreover, the evidence shows that High Penn (D) intends to continue operating the refinery in this same manner, and will continue to inflict irreparable injury on Morgan (P) and his (P's) use and enjoyment of his (P's) property. Morgan (P) is therefore entitled to temporary damages and injunctive relief. Judgment affirmed.

Analysis:

The phrases "*per se*" and "*per accidens*" have little analytic content to them. A nuisance per se is considered an "absolute" nuisance, one that renders a person liable no matter how reasonable his or her conduct may be. This label becomes problematic, however, with several situations, such as those involving facilities for highly flammable or explosive substances. Oil refineries, storage areas for explosives used in construction, chemical waste facilities, and other structures along these lines would seem to demand questions of reasonableness. Though these activities are abnormal and unduly hazardous, they still have legitimate purposes and fill important needs which may need to be addressed, perhaps when damages are set.

TEXAS COURT OF CIVIL APPEALS HOLDS THAT A PERMANENT INJUNCTION AGAINST THE OPERATOR OF AIR CONDITIONING EQUIPMENT WHICH CONSTITUTED A NUISANCE TO NEIGHBORING RESIDENTS WAS PROPER AFTER A BALANCING OF THE EQUITIES

Estancias Dallas Corp. v. Schultz

(Loud Equipment Operator) v. (Neighbors)

(1973) 500 S.W.2d 217

MEMORY GRAPHIC

Instant Facts

The Schultzes sued Estancias Dallas Corporation to permanently enjoin it from operating excessively loud equipment on a neighboring building.

Black Letter Rule

An injunction will be denied as a remedy for nuisance only if the necessity of others compels an injured party to seek damages in an action at law, and not because the party causing the nuisance has the right to work a hurt or injury to his or her neighbor.

Case Vocabulary

INJUNCTION: Judicial remedy requiring a party to refrain from doing or continuing to do a particular act or activity.

Facts: In March or April 1969, an eight-building apartment complex was completed next to the home of Thad Schultz and his wife (Ps) in the City of Houston. Shortly after this completion, Estancias Dallas Corporation (D) began operating a large, single air conditioning unit to serve the entire complex. The unit is located five and one-half feet from the Schultzes (Ps') property line, and roughly seventy feet from their (Ps') bedroom. This unit sounds very much like a jet engine or helicopter. This noise prevents the Schultzes (Ps) from carrying on normal conversations within their (Ps') home, and also interferes with their sleep at night. As a result of this noise, the value of the Schultzes' property went from $25,000 to $10,000. The original owner of the apartment complex claimed that this air conditioning system cost about $80,000 to construct. Separate units for each of the eight buildings would have cost $120,000, and changing to this latter system would cost between $150,000 to $200,000. According to the owner, these apartments could not be rented without air conditioning. At the time, there was no shortage of apartments in the city of Houston. The jury found that the noise from the air conditioning equipment constituted a permanent nuisance. The court granted the Schultzes (Ps) a permanent injunction against Estancias (D), as well as $10,000 in interim damages, considering material personal discomfort, inconvenience, annoyance, and impairment of health as elements of damages. Estancias (D) appealed, claiming in part that the court had erred in failing to balance the equities in their favor.

Issue: Can a court properly grant an injunction to a party complaining of a permanent nuisance if the harm the complaining party has suffered is less than the harm the party causing the nuisance would suffer from the injunction?

Decision and Rationale: (Stephenson) Yes. In determining whether to grant an injunction, a court, according to the doctrine of balancing of equities, will consider both the potential harm to the defendant and to the public if an injunction is granted, and the harm to the plaintiff if the injunction is denied. The rule of law was clearly established by the Texas Supreme Court in *Storey v. Central Hide and Rendering Co.*, 148 Tex. 509, 226 S.W.2d 615 (1950) [even though a jury finds facts constituting a nuisance, there should be a balancing of equities to determine whether an injunction should be granted]. If an injunction is not to be granted, it will not be because the party causing the nuisance has the right "to work a hurt, or injury to his neighbor." Instead, an injunction will only be denied, thereby allowing a nuisance to exist, if the necessity of others compels an injured party to seek relief in the form of damages. The Supreme Court of Texas, in deciding *Storey*, placed great emphasis on the public interest. It said that an injunction could be granted if it would cause only slight injury to the public and the nuisance-causing party compared to the injury suffered by the complaining party. Here, there is no evidence that there is a shortage of apartments in the City of Houston. Because of this, there is no indication that the public would suffer or have no place to live if the apartment complex had to go without this noisy air conditioning system. Further, there is no evidence that the 'necessity of others' compels the Schultzes (Ps) to seek relief through a suit for damages rather than one for an injunction. Judgment affirmed.

Analysis:

On the surface, this may seem to be a very unfair decision. The Schultzes (Ps) suffered, at most, $15,000 in loss of property value and $10,000 in various personal damages. Estancias (D) stands to lose up to $200,000 in dismantling the old air conditioning system and installing a new, quieter one in the eight separate units. There may be, however, other 'equities' the court considered in its balancing test. The Schultzes (Ps) possibly had only one major asset, their home, while Estancias (D) was, presumably, a larger corporation, with more resources at its disposal. In addition, emotional costs may have been a factor if the Schultzes (Ps) needed to move to a new home. Moreover, court costs should probably be balanced as well. The court seems to have placed weight on the fact that the Schultzes (Ps) were in that area first, mentioning that the area was "a quiet neighborhood before these apartments were constructed." Estancias (D), arguably, should have known that its equipment was going to be excessively noisy, like a jet engine. Because of this, Estancias (D) should have known that using this unit would have been like begging for litigation. Not only would it have consumed the time and resources of Estancias (D) and the Schultzes (Ps), it would have used up the court's valuable time and resources, as well.

COURT OF APPEALS OF NEW YORK HOLDS THAT AN INJUNCTION AGAINST THE OPERATOR OF A CEMENT PLANT WHICH CONSTITUTES A NUISANCE WILL REMAIN IN EFFECT UNLESS THE PLANT OPERATOR PAYS PERMANENT DAMAGES TO THE NEIGHBORING LANDOWNERS

Boomer v. Atlantic Cement Co.

(Neighbor) v. (Cement Plant Operator)

(1970) 26 N.Y.2d 219, 257 N.E.2d 870, 309 N.Y.S.2d 312

M E M O R Y   G R A P H I C

Instant Facts

A court found that a cement plant constituted a nuisance to neighbors, but denied an injunction.

Black Letter Rule

Courts can grant an injunction conditioned on the payment of permanent damages to a complaining party in order to compensate him or her for the impairment of property rights caused by a nuisance.

Case Vocabulary

METALLURGICAL: Having to do with the science of metals.

Procedural Basis: Appeal from judgment in actions for injunction and damages.

Facts: Atlantic Cement Company (D), or ACC (D), runs a large cement plant near Albany. Boomer (P) and other neighboring land owners (Ps) claimed that their property interests were injured because of the high levels of dirt, smoke, and vibration that the plant produced. The trial court found this constituted a nuisance, and temporary damages were allowed in various specific amounts up to the time of trial to the respective neighbors. An injunction, however, was denied on the grounds that the total damages to Boomer and the other neighbors (Ps) was small compared to the value of ACC's (D's) operations and the damage that an injunction would inflict upon ACC (D). Boomer and the other neighbors (Ps) were also awarded $185,000 in permanent damages.

Issue: Can the courts grant an injunction as a remedy for a nuisance when such an injunction would have greater economic consequences for the nuisance-causing party than the nuisance itself has for the complaining party?

Decision and Rationale: (Bergan) Yes. Courts can grant an injunction conditioned on the payment of permanent damages to a complaining party in order to compensate him or her for the harm caused by a nuisance. The trial court denied an injunction because of the large disparity in economic consequences between imposing the injunction and allowing the nuisance to continue. This reasoning, however, contradicts the longstanding doctrine that an injunction should be granted where a nuisance has been found and the complaining party has sustained substantial damage. Granted, following this rule literally would result in the closing of the plant. The trial court's awarding of damages, however, violates this longstanding rule. One option would be to grant the injunction, but postpone its effect until after a specified period of time. This way, technological advances would allow ACC (D) to eliminate the nuisance without shutting down its (D's) plant. There is no guarantee, however, that ACC could even make such advances on its own. Further, any such advances in eliminating dust and pollution by cement plants would likely result from industry-wide efforts, and the rate of research and development by the entire cement industry is clearly out of ACC's (D's) control. For these reasons, the best option is to grant the injunction on condition that ACC (D) pays Boomer and the other neighbors (Ps) a level of permanent damages as may be fixed by the court. This court undoubtedly has the power to grant such an injunction on these conditional grounds. Also, permanent damages are allowable when the loss a complaining party could recover would be smaller than the cost of completely removing the nuisance. In essence, ACC (D) would be purchasing a servitude on the neighbors' (Ps') land. This action would preclude future recovery by Boomer and the other neighbors (Ps) or their grantees. Judgment reversed.

Dissent: (Jasen) Though a reversal is required here, an award of permanent damages should not be allowed in place of an injunction where substantial property rights have been impaired by the creation of a nuisance. The majority essentially allows ACC (D) to continue causing harm to the surrounding community for a fee set by the court. Moreover, once all those who complain about the nuisance are paid off, there will no longer be any incentive to correct the nuisance, and the air pollution and blasting noise will simply continue.

Analysis:

This case reflects an almost classic conflict between environmental and economic interests. In addition to the dirt, smoke, and vibration mentioned by the court, there are even greater injuries to neighboring landowners that were not mentioned. ACC also owned a quarry less than a mile away. Blasting operations there had frightened the neighborhood children and cracked the walls and ceilings of many of the nearby homes. This practice also contributed heavily to the level of air pollution. Moreover, the blasting conducted by ACC was arguably unnecessary, as it only served to completely shatter the stones in the quarry. This step could have been easily bypassed in the production of cement in favor of less explosive and violent means. At the same time, however, ACC's plant undoubtedly provided hundreds of jobs to the local population. Those same employees certainly stimulated the local economy, and contributed to the property tax base of the community.

WHERE A COMPLAINING PARTY MOVES TO THE AREA OF A NUISANCE, AN INJUNCTION MAY BE ISSUED CONDITIONAL UPON THE COMPLAINING PARTY PAYING DAMAGES CAUSED BY ISSUANCE OF THE INJUNCTION

Spur Industries, Inc. v. Del E. Webb Development Co.

(Cattle Feeders) v. (Residential Developer)

(1972) 108 Ariz. 178, 494 P.2d 700

MEMORY GRAPHIC

Instant Facts

Spur owned a cattle feedlot well outside Phoenix for years, but when Webb's residential development grew to that area, Webb wanted the feedlot removed.

Black Letter Rule

An otherwise lawful activity can become a nuisance because others have entered the area of activity, and thus be enjoined; if the party requesting the injunction, however, is the one that creates the need for the injunction, that party can be required to provide compensation for the cost of moving or shutting down the activity.

Case Vocabulary

CONFLUENCE: The place where two rivers flow into each other and form one river.

Procedural Basis: Appeal from judgment in action for permanent injunction.

Facts: This case centers on an area of land located along Grand Avenue, roughly 15 miles west of the urban area of Phoenix. Roughly two miles of Grand Avenue, running east to west, is Olive Avenue. This area was first put to agricultural use in 1911, and was used primarily for that purpose until 1959. In 1954, Youngtown, a retirement community for senior citizens, was established in this area. In 1956, a separate company developed feedlots about one-half mile south of Olive Avenue. In April and May of 1959, between 7,500 and 8,500 head of cattle were being fed. In May 1959, Del E. Webb Development Company (P) began work on a residential development later known as Sun City. Webb (P) purchased about 20,000 acres of farmland, land that was less expensive than land closer to Phoenix, for this purpose. In 1960, Spur Industries, Inc. (D) bought the feedlots and began expanding them. In January 1960, Webb (P) began offering homes two and one-half miles north of the Spur lots. By May 1960, roughly 500 houses were completed or being built. At this time, Webb (P) did not consider odors from Spur's (D's) lots to be a problem and continued its southward expansion. By 1962, the feedlots had expanded from 35 to 114 acres. By December 1967, Webb's (P's) property reached Olive Avenue and Spur's (D's) lots were within 500 feet of Olive Avenue, on its southern side. Webb (P), but neither the citizens of Sun City nor Youngtown, filed an action to enjoin Spur's (D's) operation of the feedlots, claiming it was a public nuisance because of the flies and odor blown from the lots to Sun City. At the time of Webb's (P's) complaint, Spur (D) was feeding between 20,000 and 30,000 head of cattle. In addition, the cattle produced over a million pounds of wet manure per day. Although Spur (D) practiced good management of the lots, the odor and flies nonetheless created an annoying if not unhealthy situation. Citizens of Sun City expressed several complaints about this situation, and Webb (P) had difficulty in selling new homes in the area.

Issue: (1) Can an otherwise lawful activity become a nuisance because others have entered the area of the activity, and thus be subject to injunction? (2) If such an activity can be enjoined, should the party requesting the injunction be required to provide compensation for the cost of ending the activity?

Decision and Rationale: (Cameron) (1) Yes. An otherwise lawful activity can become a nuisance because others have entered the area of activity, and so the party causing the nuisance may be enjoined. A public nuisance affects the rights enjoyed by citizens as members of the general public. Here, it is clear that the feedlots amounted to both a public and a private nuisance as far as the southern residents of Sun City were concerned. Section 36-601 of Arizona state law lists public nuisances dangerous to public health, and includes "Any condition or place in populous areas which constitutes a breeding place for flies... which are capable of carrying and transmitting disease-causing organisms to any person or persons." The Sun City development satisfies the populous area requirement of the law. Moreover, as Webb (P) suffered an injury in the form of loss of sales, it (P) had standing to enjoin the nuisance. (2) Yes. The party requesting the injunction can be required to provide compensation for the cost of moving or shutting down the activity. Courts of equity must protect not only the public interest, but also the operators of lawful businesses whose activities become nuisances because of the encroachment of others. In such "coming to the nuisance cases," courts have held that parties may not obtain relief for injuries after they knowingly came into an area reserved for industrial or agricultural use. The law of nuisance, however, is elastic, not rigid. The goal should be to promote what is fair and reasonable under all the circumstances. Here, Spur (D) and its predecessors had no idea when they began their feedlot efforts that a new city would spring up and force their relocation. Spur (D) must move because of a proper regard for the public interest. Likewise, Webb (P) is entitled to relief because of the damage to people who bought homes in Sun City. Nonetheless, it would be unfair to allow a developer who has taken advantage of lower land prices in a rural area to develop a new city to use that city as a means of chasing a nuisance away without compensating the one who has to move. This kind of relief is limited to a case where a developer has introduced the very population which renders the lawful activity a nuisance. Judgment affirmed in part, reversed in part, and remanded.

Analysis:

The court calls Spur's (D's) operation of the feedlot both a public and a private nuisance. This kind of reasoning is typical of most courts. Courts usually hold that impairment of a person's use and enjoyment of his or her land, as was the case here, constitutes a private nuisance. This is true regardless of how many people are hurt by the nuisance, whether it is just a small group of people or a whole city. Such an action can also count as a public nuisance if it interferes with a more general public right, again as in Spur. Otherwise, this distinction between public and private nuisance can be important in at least two ways. One is that because a private nuisance is created when the use and enjoyment of land is interfered with, only an owner of land, or interest in land, can file a suit. Another is that, with a public nuisance, any member of the public can sue. Generally, though, only a person who can show he or she has sustained injury or damage that is different from that suffered by the rest of the public can actually file a claim.

Perspective Servitudes

Chapter 10

In the beginning of the text, the concept of "externalities" was introduced. Put simply, externalities are the costs and benefits that result for other people when an individual makes a decision as to how to use his or her resources. Clearly, decisions on land use create a wide variety of costs and benefits affecting people other than the decision-maker. In the next four chapters, these land-use decisions and the controls placed on them by private individuals and public bodies will be studied.

Note that there are other concerns, beyond economic ones of costs and benefits, which are involved in land-use decisions. It is important to understand the role history and politics have played in the development of land-use regulation. In addition, basic issues of justice and fairness are constantly raised in cases involving the control of land-use. While such controls are often distinguished as "private" and "public" actions, in reality, all land-use controls have varying degrees of public and private aspects to them.

This chapter will look at the two types of the most private sort of land-use controls, servitudes (“interests in *others'* land"). Part 1 will focus on “easements" (rights to enter another's land), and Part 2 will focus on “covenants" (private contracts to do/refrain from doing something on the land).

EASEMENTS: All of this chapter is devoted to land-use arrangements that come out of private agreements. Generally, these arrangements are made to increase the value of the two or more parcels of land involved. Most often, one parcel of land is given a certain burden, for the benefit of another parcel of land. Examples of this can include serving as the location of an access road for the land that is farther from the main highway, providing water from a well for both properties, and many other similar burdens. These arrangements do not bind the parties making the deal alone. They create interests in the land itself, and as such, will bind later owners of the properties involved. These interests are generally referred to as “servitudes.”

First, easements will be discussed. Basically, an easement is created when one property owner grants another the right to enter and use his or her land. The key questions surrounding easements deal with their creation and their termination. This chapter will discuss easements' historical background. Then, it will examine the different ways easements can be created. How far easements can be extended to other people and uses will then be discussed, followed by the ways easements can be terminated. Finally, some background on special agreements called negative easements will be provided.

The second type of agreement is called a “covenant." Covenants are basically promises by one landowner to another concerning use of the land. These promises are often in effect in condominiums and planned residential tracts, also known as subdivisions. There are two types of covenants. One is known as a “real covenant." The main question that must be asked is whether it will "run with the land." In other words, will the covenant pass on to a new owner when the land is transferred to that owner? A real covenant will run if there is privity of estate, which is a mutual or successive relationship between a property's earlier owner and its later owner. This is not an easy concept to grasp, but it is important to know in order to understand real covenants.

The other type of covenant is an equitable servitude. The main issue with an equitable servitude is whether it has even been created by a set of circumstances or not. Unlike real covenants, equitable servitudes can be implied by a development plan for property, also known as a scheme. Privity of estate is not required to establish an equitable servitude, but the covenant must touch and concern the land (in other words, have a direct effect on the legal rights of the owner of the land). The covenant must usually also give some kind of benefit to neighboring land. Also, if a person is unaware of the covenant when buying the land, that person is not responsible for the terms and restrictions of the covenant.

Chapter 10

NOTE: THE PURPOSE OF THIS OUTLINE IS TO ORGANIZE THE CASES SO THAT ONE CAN QUICKLY UNDERSTAND THE RELEVANCE OF EACH CASE TO THE COURSE. NO ATTEMPT IS MADE IN THIS OVERVIEW TO ADDRESS EVERY CONCEPT THAT MUST BE STUDIED. BE SURE TO READ THE ENTIRE CASEBOOK AND/OR OTHER MATERIALS TO GAIN A FULL UNDERSTANDING OF ALL CONCEPTS.

Easements

A. Definition
   1. An "easement" is the right to enter land to do something on it, e.g., the right to cross a neighbor's land, or take water from a pond there.
   2. Sometimes, it also includes a *restriction* on what a landowner can do on his land, to avoid harming neighbors' interests (a "negative" easement).

B. Historical Background
   1. In medieval England, most agricultural land was held in common, and anyone could enter/use it freely.
   2. Later in the 1800s, common land ownership was replaced by fenced private fields, creating the need for legal permission to enter.

C. Creation of Easements
   1. Statute of Frauds: Generally, easements are created by express written instrument. But they may also be created by implication, or by prescription.
   2. A land seller may retain an easement by deed.
      a. Also, most courts hold a grantor can reserve an easement in the property for third parties. *Willard v. First Church of Christ, Scientist* [when owner sells property intending churchgoers be allowed to park there, that intent binds the buyer]. *See Restatement (Third) of Property, Servitudes, §2.6(2) (2000).*
      b. But a few courts hold that easements benefitting third parties are invalid.
   3. Licenses
      a. A "license" is permission to enter land to do something that otherwise would be a trespass (e.g., permitting a guest to come in for dinner). It is not considered an interest in land.
      b. Generally, licenses are freely revocable. However, they may become irrevocable through estoppel. *Restatement (Third) of Property, Servitudes, §2.10.*
         (1) For example, a license cannot be revoked after the licensee has erected improvements on the land at considerable expense while relying on the license. *Holbrook v. Taylor* [landowner cannot block a road running through his land, after neighbors built a house in reliance on using it].
      c. An oral license can be just as binding as a written one. *Shepard v. Purvine* (Or. 1952) [neighbor may rely on other's oral promise, without insisting on written deed].
      d. But some courts hold that oral licenses can be revoked by the licensor, even if the licensee has spent money in reliance on the license, and even if the license was originally intended to be a continuous one. *Henry v. Dalton* (R.I. 1959) [oral licenses should be revocable to avoid burdening land with vague agreements].
   4. Easements by Implication
      a. Easements may be implied from a "prior existing use," (i.e., the land was being used for that purpose when it was conveyed, and this use was apparent to the buyer), or "by necessity" (the easement is "reasonably necessary" to let the buyer obtain value from the land). The definition of "necessary" is unclear, and often litigated.
      b. An implied easement's extent will depend on the circumstances under which the conveyance of land was made, including the extent to which the manner of prior use was known by the parties. *Van Sandt v. Royster* [sewer pipe connecting houses floods homeowner's basement].
         (1) Each party will be assumed to know about reasonably necessary uses which are apparent after reasonably prudent investigation.
      c. An easement can be created by implied reservation only when(see *Othen v. Rosier* (Tex.) [landowner cannot dig ditch which blocks other landowner's only access to highway]):

Chapter Overview Outline
Servitudes

(1) There was unity of ownership between the dominant and servient estates (i.e., a prior owner once owned both, but then sold them separately), and

(2) The necessity existed at the time the two estates were severed. An easement "by prescription" can only be acquired if the use of the easement was adverse.

5. Easements by Prescription
   a. Easements may be acquired "by prescription" in ways that are similar to adverse possession (basically, through long, continuous adverse use).
   b. Under the "public trust doctrine," the public's right to use the tidal lands and waters also includes the right to gain access through privately-owned dry sand areas, and to use these areas as reasonably necessary. *Matthews v. Bay Head Improvement Association* [landowner cannot block the public from access to public beach].

D. Assignability of Easements
   1. When two or more persons own an easement "in gross," (the right to enter/use land for *personal* benefit, rather than to improve one's *land*), any actions involving the easement must be made with the common consent of *all* the owners. *Miller v. Lutheran Conference and Camp Association* [artificial lake's co-owner cannot assign right to fish and swim in the lake without the other co-owner's consent].

E. Scope of Easements
   1. If an easement benefits its owner in the use of a particular parcel of land, any extension of the easement to other parcels is a misuse of the easement. *Brown v. Voss* [after landowners start building a house that straddles 2 parcels, owner of one parcel may revoke the road easement on it].

F. Termination of Estates
   1. An easement is terminated by abandonment when nonuse is coupled with an act manifesting either a present intent to relinquish the easement or a purpose inconsistent with its future existence. *Preseault v. United States* [government authorizes conversion of abandoned railroad easement running across private property into nature trail].
   2. Easements may also be terminated by prescription, where some person prevents the easement from being used for a certain period.

G. Negative Easements
   1. "Negative" easements authorize certain peopl to *prevent* adjoining landowners from doing something injurious on *their own* land, generally because it creates a nuisance for neighbors
   2. Old English courts recognized only 4 negativ easements; neighbors could not (a) block you windows, (b) block air flow to your land, (c undermine your buildings, or (d) block artificia streams. But British courts refused to recogniz any new types of negative easements.
   3. American courts usually resist creating nev negative easements, but occasionally recogniz new ones, e.g., rights to unobstructed views and rights to conserve historic landmarks an scenic spaces.

II. Covenants Running with the Land
   A. Definition: "Covenants" are private contract which require/restrict parties from doing specifie things on the land. They are said to "run with th land," meaning they are often enforceable agains people who *later* acquire either parcel.
   B. Equitable Servitudes -- Historical Approach
      1. After British courts refused to recognize mos negative easements, Englishmen used "cove nants" (contracts) to restrict uses of land usually to be free of nuisances from adjoinin parcels.
      2. Later in England, covenants became enforce able in equity (i.e., by injunction) against late buyers who had notice of the covenant. *Tul v. Moxhay* [land buyer, who purchased know ing previous owner covenanted to maintai existing garden, cannot build over it].
         a. But aggrieved persons could not sue at lav (i.e., for damages). This type of covenant - enforceable only in equity -- was called a "equitable servitude."
         b. Today, there is no difference between cove nants and equitable servitudes, since court of law and equity were merged.
      3. "Running with the Land": Covenants usuall "run with the land," meaning they bind futur owners of that land, even though they them selves were not parties to the original covenan
         a. Previously, if anyone acquired the land

through adverse possession rather than by contract, they could not enforce the covenant. Under the first *Restatement*, for the burdens and benefits of covenants to "run" to successors, courts required

(1) The original parties must have had a contract ("horizontal privity"), and

(2) Those successors must have obtained the land from prior owners through a string of contracts ("vertical privity").

b. Currently, under the *Restatement (Third) of Property*:

(1) For the burdens and benefits to "run" to successors, horizontal privity is not required. So, if the original land interest was acquired by adverse possession, it may still bind contractual successors.

(2) Vertical privity was modified. Negative covenants -- which prevent certain uses of the land -- no longer require "vertical privity." That is, they bind adverse possessors as well. Affirmative covenants -- promises to do something -- may also bind adverse possessors, but with some restrictions. *See Restatement (Third) of Property § 5.2 - 5.4.*

C. Creation of Covenants: Usually, real covenants must be created by written contract, and signed by the covenantor. Covenants are governed by the Statute of Frauds, so they cannot arise by estoppel, implication, or prescription.

1. An *equitable servitude* can be implied on a lot, even without any written instrument, if (i) there is a scheme for development of a residential subdivision, and (ii) the purchaser of the lot had notice of it. *Sanborn v. McLean* [lot buyer, who knew lots were originally intended for residences only, cannot build gas station on one, even though his deed contained no express restrictions].

2. The old judicial doctrine of "touch and concern" holds that covenants are binding against future landowners if the interest is closely tied to ownership of the land, rather than a personal promise between the original parties. It was applied to reject personal debts and agreements, which were deemed not sufficiently related to the land to bind successors. *Caullett v. Stanley Stilwell and Sons, Inc.* [real estate developer, which sold land for promise to develop it, cannot enforce the promise as a covenant].

3. An affirmative covenant to pay money for improvements or maintenance done in connection with (but not upon) the land which is to be subject to the burden of the covenant, does "touch and concern" the land, and binds future owners. A homeowners' association, as the agent of the actual owners of the property, has privity, and can rightfully enforce the covenant. *Neponsit Property Owners' Association, Inc. v. Emigrant Industrial Savings Bank* [after bank forecloses on a building whose deed provided for an annual maintenance fee, it is required to continue paying the fee to the homeowners' association].

4. Recently, *Restatement (Third) of Property, Servitudes, § 3.1 - 3.2* superseded the doctrine of "touch and concern," instead urging courts to void covenants which violate public policy, and articulate their reasons.

5. Defeasible Fees used to Control Land: Remember, a "defeasible fee" grants ownership of land, but subject to forfeiture if it is misused in specified ways. Defeasible fees can be used to control the use to which land is put, and were popular in the 1900s. But today, they are uncommon, since land purchasers object to contracts which create a risk of default.

D. Scope of Covenants

1. Ambiguous restrictive covenants should be construed in favor of the free use and enjoyment of property, and against restrictions. *Hill v. Community of Damien of Molokai* [covenant that land be used for "single family residence" cannot be used to enjoin group home for AIDS patients].

2. Restrictive covenants violate the *Federal Fair Housing Act* when they have a discriminatory intent, a discriminatory effect, or constitute a failure to make reasonable accommodations. *Hill v. Community of Damien of Molokai.*

3. Judicial enforcement of a restrictive covenant based on race constitutes discriminatory state action, and is thus forbidden by the *Fourteenth Amendment's Equal Protection Clause*. *Shelley v. Kraemer* [neighbors' covenant not to sell their houses to non-whites is unenforceable].

E. Termination of Covenants
   1. Older cases hold a restrictive covenant establishing a residential subdivision cannot be terminated as long as the residential character of the subdivision has not been adversely affected by the surrounding area, and it is of real and substantial value to the landowners within the subdivision. *Western Land Co. v. Truskolaski* [Reno, NV homeowners may block shopping center's construction, citing 31-year-old covenant].
   2. A single landowner in a subdivision under a restrictive covenant has the right to insist upon adherence to the covenant, even when the other owners consent to its release. *Rick v. West* [homeowner who covenanted for residential zoning may block construction of hospital].
   3. Under more recent law, courts are granted considerable leeway to terminate servitudes or modify them because of changed conditions, and to award or deny damages in such circumstances. *See Restatement (Third) of Property, Servitudes § 7.10.*
   4. A covenant running with the land cannot be terminated by abandonment so long as the owner still holds title in fee simple absolute. *Pocono Springs Civic Association, Inc., v. MacKenzie* [landowner finds he cannot get rid of useless lot to avoid paying association fees].
   5. Under the *Restatement (Third) of Property, Servitudes § 7.12*, covenants to pay money or provide [maintenance] services terminate after a "reasonable time."

F. Common Interest Communities
   1. As common interest communities (e.g., homeowners associations, condos, co-ops) have proliferated, states adopted statutes for organizing them.
      a. Some are based on the *Uniform Common Interest Ownership Act.*
      b. Under this *Act*, the governing body must disclose rules to all purchasers, may enact rules to maintain the community's character, and can even raise money through assessments and fines.
   2. Condominiums
      a. A condominium is like a privately-owned apartment complex, where each unit (apartment) is owned individually, but the common areas and the building itself are owned in common.
      b. Each resident is *individually* liable for his share of mortgage, taxes, and monthly maintenance. Residents' rights are set by state statute.
   3. The enforceability of condos' restrictions on the ownership and possession of pets may be appealed in court, which must decide whether the restriction was reasonable as applied to the particular case. *Nahrstedt v. Lakeside Village Condominium Association, Inc.* [after condo fines resident for owning cats in violation of regulations, resident may appeal in court].
   4. Cooperative Apartments:
      a. In a housing cooperative ("co-op"), residents of the building are shareholders of a corporation which owns the building.
         (1) The entire corporation (and all its shareholder-residents) are responsible for monthly mortgage payments, so if one resident cannot pay his share, the others must make up the difference.
         (2) Thus, residents have incentives to screen new applicants' ability to pay.
      b. (Coops are prevalent only in New York City.) New York case law holds that co-ops' boards can reject new applicants without cause, as long as they do not violate anti-discrimination laws. In practice, co-ops are notoriously selective.
      c. Gated Communities: "Gated communities" are private towns which restrict access to member-residents only. They protect residents against crime (and the poor). (*See Mulligan v. Panther Valley Property*.)
         (1) Many provide quasi-municipal services (e.g., police, local government).
         (2) Their rules tend to be very detailed and restrictive.
         (3) Critics charge that, if the rich retreat into their separate gated enclaves, society may become balkanized.
         (4) Also, they decry the community boards' intrusive regulation. *Owners Assn.* (N.J. Super. 2001) [gated community's ban on registered sex offenders may violate public policy].

Willard v. First Church of Christ, Scientist

Realtor) v. (Church)

Cal. 3d 473, 102 Cal. Rptr. 739, 498 P.2d 987 (1972)

Instant Facts

McGuigan sold Petersen a lot with an easement allowing nearby churchgoers to park on it, but Petersen sold it to Willard without mentioning the easement.

Black Letter Rule

A grantor can reserve an easement in property for a person other than the grantee.

Case Vocabulary

BUTTING: Bordering on; sharing a boundary.

SCROW: A legal document, money, or some other property of value delivered from one person to a third person and held by that person until some agreed upon condition or event occurs, at which point the third person then delivers the held property to the second person as intended.

Procedural Basis: Appeal from judgment in action to quiet title.

Facts: Genevieve McGuigan owned two lots, numbered 19 and 20, in Pacifica, California. These lots were located across the street from the First Church of Christ, Scientist (D). McGuigan was a member of this church (D), and she allowed lot 20, which was vacant, to be used as a parking lot during church (D) services. She sold lot 19 to Petersen, who used the building on that lot for office space. Wishing to resell the lot, Petersen listed it with Donald E. Willard (P), a Realtor. At the time, Petersen did not own lot 20. He did approach McGuigan with an offer to buy it. McGuigan would only sell the lot if the church (D) could continue to use it for parking space. She then had the church's (D) attorney draw up a provision for the deed to the lot stating that the change of ownership was "subject to an easement for automobile parking during church hours... such easement to run with the land only so long as the property for whose benefit the easement is given is used for church purposes." After this clause was inserted in the deed, McGuigan sold the property to Petersen, and he recorded the deed. Willard (P) paid Petersen the agreed purchase price and received Petersen's deed ten days later. Willard (P) recorded this deed, which did not mention an easement for parking by the church (D). Apparently, Petersen did mention that the church (D) would want to use lot 20 for parking, but did not tell him of the easement clause in his deed from McGuigan. Willard (P) became aware of this clause several months after he bought the lot, and then began an action to quiet title against the church (D). McGuigan testified in court that she had bought lot 20 to provide parking for the church (D). She also stated she would not have sold it unless she was sure the church (D) could use it for parking. While the trial court found that both McGuigan and Petersen intended to convey an easement for the church (D), the easement clause in the deed was invalid because a person cannot reserve an interest in property to a stranger to the title.

Issue: Can a property owner, in granting his or her property to a second person, reserve an easement in the property for a third person?

Decision and Rationale: (Peters) Yes. An owner who is granting property to a second person can reserve an easement in that property for a third person. The old common law rule stated that such a reservation of an interest was not possible. This rule was based on the feudal concept of reservation from a grant. In that time, a grantor could pass his whole interest in property to a grantee, but a new interest was created in the grantor. Early common law courts opposed the possibility of vesting an interest in a third party. While California used to follow this rule very closely, today's courts should not feel so restrained by feudal methods. The main objective should be carrying out the intent of the grantor. Thus, property grants are to be treated in the same way as contracts. Dealing with grants under the more rigid feudal approach would lead to unfair results. This is because the original grantee has likely paid a reduced price on the property in exchange for allowing a certain use of the property to continue. Willard (P) has not presented any evidence that he (P) or any others have relied on the common law rule when purchasing the property. Neither can Willard (P) claim he was prejudiced because the lot had not been used by the church (D) for an extended period of time. Indeed, the church (D) used lot 20 for parking throughout the period when Willard (P) was trying to buy it. Here, the interests of the grantors outweigh the interests the grantees may have if the old rule is followed. Looking at the clause as a whole, it is clear that McGuigan and Petersen intended to convey the easement for parking to the church (D). Judgment reversed.

Analysis:

here used to be serious questions in early English and American law as to whether a grantor, particularly one who owned a neighboring parcel land, could maintain an easement on the granted property after its conveyance. Over the years, these concerns have been eased, and it is enerally settled that such an easement can be reserved in the instrument of conveyance (e.g., a deed). Likewise, most jurisdictions today hold that an easement of this kind cannot be held in favor of a third person, as was done in *Willard*. This idea is usually justified by the fact that third party would have no interest in the land being conveyed from which the third party could reserve an easement in the first place. Thi decision in *Willard*, however, along with similar ones in Kentucky and Oregon, may represent a trend away from the earlier, more rigid rule Indeed, many legal writers are critical of the predominant ban on third party easements, which the Third Restatement of Property also refuse to adopt. While the question is by no means completely resolved, grantors may avoid this problem of reservation by simply making explici grants of the given property and of the desired easement in one deed. This way, the interest a third party requires for an easement is expressl given, and the *Willard* concern over parties' intent can also be addressed.

A LICENSE IS IRREVOCABLE ONCE THE LICENSEE HAS RELIED ON THE LICENSE TO HIS OR HER EXPENSE OR DETRIMENT

Holbrook v. Taylor

(Landowner) v. (House Builder)
532 S.W.2d 763 (1976)

M E M O R Y   G R A P H I C

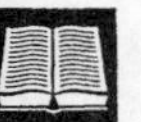

Instant Facts

Holbrook tried to block off a road on his property after Taylor used it extensively while building a tenant house for himself.

Black Letter Rule

A license cannot be revoked after the licensee has erected improvements on the land at considerable expense while relying on the license.

Case Vocabulary

EGRESS: Exit; the path for, or the act of, going out.
ESTOPPEL: Term which denotes that one person is prevented from claiming a particular right because another person was entitled to rely on such conduct and has acted on that reliance.
INGRESS: Entrance; the path for, or the act of, entering.
PROBATIVE: Tending or able to prove an issue or fact.
SERVIENT: Denotes that which is burdened with or subject to a servitude; the estate that benefits from an easement, by contrast, is called the "dominant" estate.

Procedural Basis: Appeal from judgment in action for declaratory and injunctive relief.

Facts: Mr. and Mrs. Holbrook (D) purchased the property in question in 1942. Two years later, they (D) allowed a mining road to be cut on the property. The road was used for that purpose until 1949, and the Holbrooks (D) received a royalty for use of the road during that period. In 1965, the Taylors (P) bought a three-acre building site next to the Holbrooks' (D) property. The Taylors (P) built a house on that site the following year. During the preparation for and the actual building of the house, the Taylors (P) were permitted to use the roadway for access for workmen, for transporting equipment and materials, and for the construction and improvement of the house. The Taylors' (P) home was completed at a cost of $25,000. After it was completed, the Taylors (P) continued to use the road on a regular basis. At trial, Mr. Holbrook (D) testified that he (D) allowed the Taylors (P) to use and repair the road so they (P) could reach their (P) home. This was the only location where a road could be created to provide an access route. The Taylors (P) widened the road and graveled part of it at a cost of roughly $100. The Holbrooks (D) and Taylors (P) had no disagreement over the use of the road until 1970. Then, according to Mr. Holbrook (D), he (D) wanted the Taylors (P) to give him (D) a writing which would relieve him (D) of any responsibility in case someone were injured or otherwise damaged on the old mining road. The Taylors (P) testified that the writing was an attempt to make them (P) buy the land the road was situated on for $500. The disagreement continued, and the Holbrooks (D) later raised a steel cable across the road to block passage, and set up "no trespassing" signs. The Taylors (P) then filed suit to remove the obstructions and to declare their (P) right to use the road without interference.

Issue: Can an easement be established by estoppel, or reliance?

Decision and Rationale: (Sternberg) Yes. An easement can be established by estoppel, even when the person making use of the property does not do so adversely, but with the permission of the property owner. It has long been recognized that a right to the use of a roadway over another person's land may be established by estoppel. The established rule in this state was set forth by this court in *Lashey Telephone Co. v. Durbin*, 190 Ky. 792, 228 S.W. 423 (1921). As stated in that case, a licensor may not revoke a license which includes the right to erect structures and acquire an interest in the land similar to an easement after the licensee has exercised the privilege of the license and erected improvements on the land at considerable expense. Here, it is clear that the Taylors (P) used the road with the consent, or at least the tacit approval, of the Holbrooks (D). Moreover, the Taylors (P) used the road to build and improve their $25,000 home, and widened and maintained the road at their own additional expense. These facts satisfy the requirements of the Lashey rule. Thus, the Taylors' (P) license to use the road may not be revoked, and their (P) right to use the road has been established by estoppel. Judgment affirmed.

Analysis:

Essentially, the Court here took a presumably oral agreement for a use of land out of the realm of the Statute of Frauds. There is no general, all-encompassing rule in equity to block the Statute. Instead, there are only two specific, recognized doctrines, and these, in turn, are limited to specific kinds of facts. The estoppel theory, as explained here, is the one most widely used. Some courts, particularly those in California and Illinois, have used even stronger terms to back estoppel in the past. These decisions have stated that allowing a grantor to revoke a license in such circumstances would work a "fraud" against the grantee. Several experts, most notably Judge Clark, have dismissed the use of the fraud theory as overkill, saying that the use of estoppel is sufficient to protect the license. The other doctrine, that of equitable part performance, is also demonstrated in this case. Basically, the idea is that the act of improving the property is tangible evidence that the license, or "oral easement," actually exists. Thus, one would not need to rely on the oral statements of the licensor and licensee alone, but rather could have the improvements themselves attest to the presence of the easement. Some courts, including those in Alabama and Virginia, have adopted this theory. Overall, however, both estoppel and part performance are recognized as means to justify protecting oral licenses, outside the reach of the Statute of Frauds.

ONE PERSON'S WORD TO ANOTHER PERSON IS ENOUGH TO CREATE A VALID LICENSE

Shepard v. Purvine

(One Friend/Neighbor) v. (Other Friend/Neighbor)
196 Or. 348, 248 P.2d 352 (1952)

M E M O R Y   G R A P H I C

Instant Facts

Two friends orally agreed upon a transfer of property rights and did not record it in a deed.

Black Letter Rule

An oral license can be just as binding as a written one.

Procedural Basis: Appeal.

Facts: Though the exact facts are unclear, apparently, Shepard (P) and Purvine (D) were neighbors and close friends. The two (P and D) agreed to a transfer of property rights that amounted to a license for a right of way. This agreement was done orally, without a written deed to establish the formal transfer of rights. Presumably, a disagreement over the license occurred and Shepard (P) filed suit.

Issue: Can a license be oral and still be valid?

Decision and Rationale: Yes. As far as these people (P and D) were concerned, one's word was as good as his bond. If Shepard (P) insisted on having a written deed to spell out their agreement, it would have been interpreted as an expression of doubt in Purvine's (D's) trustworthiness and integrity. Shepard (P) was not negligent in not insisting upon a formal transfer of the agreed-upon rights. An oral license, carried out promptly, is just as binding, valid, and irrevocable as a right of way conveyed by a deed.

Analysis:

Although the court here expressed its approval of oral licenses, a written license is still a more preferable device. Oral licenses could become significantly modified, intentionally or unintentionally, over the years, as property owners grow older and remember the context of the license differently. Also, conditions of the land may deteriorate or improve, which could lead to confusion over the original purpose and intent behind the initial license. Granted, an oral license may be inherently more flexible and amiable in nature, but even the best of friends can have a falling out. Just as married couples may not want to plan in case of divorce, detailed, written outlining of transferred property rights early on can help prevent drawn-out legal battles later.

RHODE ISLAND SUPREME COURT HOLDS THAT AN ORAL LICENSE CAN BE REVOKED EVEN IF THE LICENSEE HAS SPENT MONEY RELYING ON THE LICENSE OR IF THERE HAD BEEN AN INTENT TO CREATE A CONTINUOUS LICENSE

Henry v. Dalton

(Wall Remover) v. (Property Owner)
98 R.I. 150, 151 A.2d 362 (1959)

M E M O R Y   G R A P H I C

Instant Facts

No facts are given.

Black Letter Rule

An oral license to do an act on the land of the licensor can be revoked by the licensor, even if the licensee has spent money as a result of faith in the license and the license was originally intended to be a continuous one.

Case Vocabulary

PAROL: Oral or verbal.

Procedural Basis: Not stated.

Facts: No facts are given.

Issue: Can a property owner who gave another person an oral license to do an act on their property revoke the license, even if the licensee has spent money in carrying out the license?

Decision and Rationale: Yes. The rule was clearly stated in *Crosdale v. Lanigan*, 129 N.Y. 604, 29 N.E. 824, in which Lanigan had given Crosdale an oral license to remove a wall built on Lanigan's property. There, it was stated that while an oral license would justify any of the licensee's action before the license was revoked, the license is nonetheless revocable at the licensor's discretion. This is true even if the intent was to grant the license for a continuing right and the licensee had spent money in carrying out the actions permitted by the license. This rule is backed not only by statute, but by public policy. It prevents the burdening of lands with oral restrictions that can be easily misunderstood. The law of oral contracts for the sale of land is already well understood, but the law distinguishing licenses from irrevocable contracts is not as clear. Thus, it is better to establish a clear rule, rather than having a court balance the equities of a particular license and its revocation in every case. The statute of frauds does cover similar matters, but there is no evidence that the license at issue here is in any way fraudulent. The right being sought here is essentially an easement and should be the subject of a grant expressed in a written instrument.

Analysis:

Note that this case predates the decision in *Holbrook*. This case also seems to answer the concerns raised by *Shepard v. Purvine*, as the court addresses the problem of parties to a license confusing or forgetting terms over time. This reasoning casts light on how the term "irrevocable license," while useful in a simple description of the result, does not accurately describe what goes on in the granting of an easement. Changing "a license into an irrevocable right" to use land, as the Court here calls it, does not fully explain how an easement is actually created in the land. Similarly, terms like "oral contracts enforceable in equity" and "easements in equity" are similarly confusing. The use of the estoppel and part performance theories in *Holbrook* offer a stronger basis for the changing of an oral agreement into an easement. In 1959, however, courts had not fully articulated the theoretical bases needed to uphold such oral agreements in the face of the Statute of Frauds.

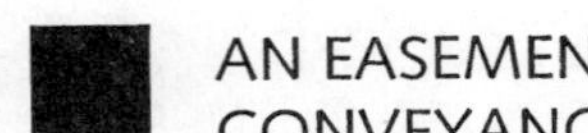

AN EASEMENT CAN BE IMPLIED FROM THE CIRCUMSTANCES SURROUNDING THE CONVEYANCE OF THE LAND, INCLUDING THE PRIOR USE OF THE LAND

Van Sandt v. Royster

(Flooded West Neighbor) v. (Center Neighbor)

148 Kan. 495, 83 P.2d 698 (1938)

MEMORY GRAPHIC

Instant Facts

Van Sandt claimed he never granted an easement for a sewer drain which connected his house to two others and flooded his basement.

Black Letter Rule

The implication of an easement will depend on the circumstances under which the conveyance of land was made, including the extent to which the manner of prior use was or might have been known by the parties; each party will be assumed to know about reasonably necessary uses which are apparent upon reasonably prudent investigation; an easement may be implied for a grantor or grantee on the basis of necessity alone.

Case Vocabulary

APPURTENANT: Essentially, connected to; an easement is appurtenant to a given parcel of land when the easement is used to the benefit of that parcel of land.

MESNE CONVEYANCES: Intermediate conveyances; those that occurred after the initial grantee and before the present holder in the whole chain of title.

Procedural Basis: Appeal from judgment in action for injunctive relief.

Facts: In 1904, Laura Bailey owned a plot of land lying directly south of Tenth Street and east of Highland Avenue in Chanute, Kansas. This plot was divided into three lots numbered, from east to west, as lots 19, 20, and 4. Bailey's home was on lot 4, the eastern part of her land. Early that year, the city of Chanute built a public sewer on Highland Avenue. At roughly the same time, a private, lateral drain was built, running from the Bailey home on lot 4, across lots 20 and 19, and to the public sewer. Also that year, Bailey conveyed lot 19 to John Jones by a general warranty deed with no exceptions or reservations, and conveyed lot 20 to Murphy by a similar deed. Each one built a home for himself on his respective lot. The title to lot 20 eventually passed to Louise Royster (D). Gray (D) succeeded to the title to lot 4 by the time Bailey sold lots 19 and 20. By 1924, lot 19 had been conveyed to Van Sandt (P), who continued to own and occupy the premises there. In March 1936, Van Sandt (P) discovered his basement had been flooded with several inches of sewage and filth. Upon investigation, he (P) discovered the sewer drain which extended across the property of Royster (D) and the property of Gray (D). This drain pipe was several feet under the surface of the ground. There was nothing visible on the ground behind the houses to indicate the existence of the drain or its link to the houses. Van Sandt (P) brought action to stop Royster and Gray (D) from using and maintaining the drain. Judgment was rendered in favor of Royster and Gray (D), and Van Sandt (P) appealed. Van Sandt (P) claimed that no easement was ever created in his (P) land, and that even if one was created, his (P) property could not be burdened with it because he (P) had no notice. Royster and Gray (D) argued that an easement was created by implied reservation when lot 19 was severed from Bailey's lot as a result of the sale to Jones.

Issue: Can an easement be created by implication when it was used by a previous owner, yet was not readily visible to a party to the conveyance of the property?

Decision and Rationale: (Allen) Yes. The implication of an easement will depend on the circumstances under which the conveyance of land was made, including the extent to which the manner of prior use was or might have been known by the parties; each party will be assumed to know about reasonably necessary uses which are apparent upon reasonably prudent investigation. An easement is an interest which a person has in another person's land. While this means an owner cannot have an easement in his or her own land, an owner can nonetheless use one part of his or her land to the benefit of another part of the land. This arrangement is generally known as a quasi-easement. Accordingly, the part of the land that benefits from this use is a quasi-dominant tenement, while the part of the land burdened with the particular use is a quasi-servient tenement. Early cases held that when the owner of the overall property transferred the quasi-servient tenement to a new owner, an implied reservation of an easement was made in favor of the conveyor of the property. Here, this factor, that the grantor of property is the one who claims the easement, is but one of many to consider in determining whether an easement can be implied. An implied easement arises as an inference of the intentions of the parties to a conveyance of land, and such an inference is to be drawn from the circumstances, not the language, of the conveyance. Under the Restatement, those circumstances should include the extent to which the manner or prior use was or might have been known by the parties. Thus, the parties will be assumed to know and to contemplate the continuance of reasonably necessary uses which would be apparent upon reasonably prudent investigation. When Jones bought lot 19, he was aware of the lateral sewer drain, and knew that it was built for the benefit of Bailey. The easement for the drain was necessary for the comfortable enjoyment of her property, and an easement can be implied on the basis of necessity alone. Moreover, Van Sandt (P) cannot claim that he (P) had no notice when he (P) bought the property. Van Sandt (P) and his (P) wife made a careful inspection of the property, and knew the house had modern plumbing and that the plumbing had to drain into a sewer. Thus, Van Sandt (P) had notice of the lateral sewer, and the easement was apparent. Judgment affirmed.

Analysis:

Note that there is no Statute of Frauds problem regarding the easement in this case, as opposed to the ones created through licenses in *Holbrook* and its accompanying cases. This is because the easement does not stem from any of the language of the conveyance, but rather the circumstances of the conveyance. Of course, the Statute could very well apply to the conveyance itself. Also, note the requirement that the easement implied from the prior use be "reasonably necessary." This part of the rule has led to much litigation. While some courts still believe that the prior use must be strictly necessary to the use and enjoyment of the dominant parcel of land, most courts follow the relaxed standard of *Van Sandt*. Then again, this rule of necessity has often been interpreted to mean whatever will be convenient to the enjoyment of the dominant land. Usually, the courts have found this rule is violated if the owner of the dominant land would be put to appreciable expense to provide an alternative to the claimed easement.

AN EASEMENT CAN BE IMPLIED FROM NECESSITY BASED ON THE CIRCUMSTANCES, OR BY PRESCRIPTION IF THE USE WAS ADVERSE

Othen v. Rosier

(Landlocked Neighbor) v. (Neighbor with Roadway)
148 Tex. 485, 226 S.W.2d 622

M E M O R Y G R A P H I C

Instant Facts

Othen used a roadway on Rosier's property to access the public highway, but Rosier later built a levee which made the road impassable for Othen.

Black Letter Rule

An easement can be created by implied reservation only when it is shown that there was unity of ownership between the alleged dominant and servient estates, that the easement is a necessity and not a convenience, and that the necessity existed at the time the two estates were severed; an easement by prescription can only be acquired if the use of the easement was adverse.

Case Vocabulary

CONTIGUOUS: Coming into contact with; adjacent.
LEVEE: A continuous ridge used to control irrigation and prevent flooding.

Procedural Basis: Appeal from judgment in action for injunctive relief and damages.

Facts: Hill once owned the entire 2493-acre Tone Survey. On August 26, 1896, Hill conveyed a 100-acre tract just west of Belt Line Road, a public highway running north and south. This tract was eventually conveyed to Estella Rosier (D) and others in 1924. In 1897, Hill conveyed a 60-acre tract just southeast of, and contiguous to, the 100-acre tract to others. Albert Othen (P) acquired this tract in 1904. By this point, Hill owned a 53-acre tract just east of the 100-acre tract, and a 16.31 acre tract just west of the 60-acre tract. On January 26, 1899, Hill conveyed the 53- and 16.31- acre tracts to separate buyers. These buyers later conveyed the larger tract to Othen (P) in 1913, and the smaller tract to Rosier (D) in 1924. Othen's (P) 113 acres are not contiguous with Belt Line Road or with either of the highways that border the Tone Survey to the north and south. Before this case, Othen (P) would reach the Belt Line Road by going through a gate on the west line of his 60-acre tract and the east line of Rosier's (D) 16.31-acre tract, then into a fenced lane which runs along the south side of Rosier's (D) 100 acres. This lane went to a gate which opened out onto the Belt Line Road. The south fence was built in 1895, while the north fence and the outside gate were built in 1906. Near this exit gate was the Rosiers' (D) home, orchard, and barns. They (D) used it to haul wood and to permit their livestock to go to the pasture on the 16.31-acre tract. The Rosiers' (D) tenants on the smaller tract have also used the roadway in the same way Othen (P) has. The Rosiers (D) made all necessary repairs to the lane, and no one else recognized any obligation to maintain it. Surface waters threatened to make the road impassable and erode the Rosiers' (D) farmland. To prevent this, the Rosiers (D) built a 300-foot-long levee along the southern fence of the road. This levee made the lane so muddy that the lane was impassable, except by horseback, for several weeks at a time. Othen (P) filed suit claiming this act of the Rosiers (D) deprived him of access between the highway and his (P) home. Othen (P) wanted a temporary writ of injunction to keep the Rosiers (D) from maintaining the levee and a mandatory writ of injunction to keep the Rosiers (D) from interfering with his (P) use of the roadway. The trial court found that Othen (P) had an easement of necessity along the roadway, and ordered the Rosiers (D) to ensure that it would be in a usable condition. The Court of Civil Appeals initially affirmed the judgment but reversed the injunction because it was too vague. On rehearing, the appellate court concluded that Othen (P) has no easement either of necessity or by prescription.

Issue:

Can an easement to use a roadway on a neighbor's property be implied when the owner seeking the easement has not proven the use of the roadway is a necessity, or that the use was not done with the permission of the neighboring property owner?

Decision and Rationale: (Brewster) No. This court has held previously that an easement can be created by implied reservation only when it is shown that there was unity of ownership between the alleged dominant and servient estates, that the easement is a necessity and not a convenience, and that the necessity existed at the time the two estates were severed. As previously stated, the entire Tone Survey had been owned by Hill. Unity of ownership is satisfied. There is no evidence, however, that the roadway was a necessity when Hill conveyed the 100-acre tract on August 26, 1896 and still retained the 60-acre tract which Othen (P) now owns. At the time, it appears the roadway was merely a convenience. Hill may easily have been able to cross the 53-acre tract and go around the 100-acre tract, or be able to go around the small 16.31-acre tract, to get to the Belt Line Road. Obviously, no such easement over the 16.31 acre tract existed, as Hill still held title to that land in 1896, and thus an easement could not be created over his own land. The mere fact that Othen's (P) land is completely surrounded by other people's land does not automatically mean that Othen (P) has a way of necessity over other property. No easement by necessity can be implied here. Moreover, an easement by prescription can only be acquired if the use of the easement was adverse. If one owner's property is put to use by another by virtue of permission or license, then the non-owner cannot claim he or she has a separate right to use the property. Here, the roadway has been fenced on both north and south sides since 1906. The Rosiers (D) and their (D) tenants have used it for general farm purposes as well as to haul wood and move livestock. In light of those facts, it appears that Othen's (P) use of the roadway has been merely with the permission of the Rosiers (D). Thus, his (P) use could not develop into a prescriptive right. Othen's (P) evidence of his (P) use of the roadway prior to 1906, when the fences and gate were completed, is also too vague to establish a prescriptive right to the road. Judgment affirmed.

Analysis:

As is the case with easements implied from prior use, most litigation involving easements implied from necessity stems from questions of what counts as "necessary." Undoubtedly, if a parcel of land is left without access to the public roads and highways -- in other words, landlocked -- the easement that would grant such access would meet the strictest definitions of "necessary." It would not be implausible to assume the necessity here must be more than what is required for prior use easements. Most courts, however, do recognize a degree of flexibility, allowing a claimant an easement if it is necessary to make effective use of his or her land. This does not mean that the necessity requirement for prior use easements and other implied easements is to be treated synonymously. Such a treatment would be extreme, as elements of pre-existing and apparent use would be essentially meaningless. In addition, it should be noted that the requirements for use by prescription, often known as adverse use, are not identical to those for adverse possession. While both require that the possession or use must be actual, open, notorious, and hostile (or non-permissive), the adverse possession requirements that the possession be "continuous" and "exclusive" are somewhat different for prescriptive uses. For easements, the particular use is treated as being "continuous" if the claimant engages in it as often as is normal for an easement of that kind; for instance, if a driveway used to reach a public road is used everyday to get to work, etc. Further, the definition of "exclusive" is also different for easements. For example, one rule states that an owner of land where an easement exists may only use the land in ways that do not interfere with the claimant's supposedly adverse use.

Matthews v. Bay Head Improvement Association

(Public Advocate) v. (Beach Improvement Association)
95 N.J. 306, 47 A.2d 355 (1984)

M E M O R Y G R A P H I C

Instant Facts

The Public Advocate claimed that the Association denied the public its rights of access to and use of the public beaches during the summer season.

Black Letter Rule

The public's right to use the tidal lands and waters under the public trust doctrine also includes the right to gain access through and to use privately-owned dry sand areas as reasonably necessary.

Case Vocabulary

FORESHORE: The wet sand area of a beach between the high and low tide levels.
WHILST: British term for "while."

Procedural Basis: Appeal from judgment.

Facts: The Borough of Bay Head is a fairly narrow strip of land, about one-and-a- quarter miles long. A beach runs along the entire length of Bay Head adjacent to the Atlantic Ocean. The beach is bordered by 76 separate parcels of land, six of which are owned by the Bay Head Improvement Association (D). The Association (D) was founded in 1910 and became a non-profit corporation in 1932. The Association's (D's) purpose was to promote the best interests of the Borough. Nine Borough streets run perpendicular to the beach and end at the dry sand. The Association (D) owns the land at the end of seven of these streets. These lands extended through the upper dry sand to the mean high water line. That point is the beginning of the foreshore, or wet sand area. Also, the Association owns six shore front properties. Three of these properties are contiguous and combine to create a 310-foot side facing the ocean. The Association (D) controls and supervises its beach property during the summer, employing about forty lifeguards, beach cleaners, and policemen. The policemen watch the beach entrances to ensure only association members and guests enter, and also patrol the beach to enforce membership rules. Membership is generally limited to Bay Head residents, and residents' applications are routinely accepted. During the summer, only Association (D) members and local fishermen are allowed to use the Association beach between 10:00 a.m. and 5:30 p.m. The public is only allowed to use that upper dry sand area from 5:30 p.m. to 10:00 a.m. during the summer. The public can access the foreshore by coming from the Borough of Point Pleasant Beach on the north or from the Borough of Mantlooking on the south. After several changes and amendments to the initial complaint, the Public Advocate argued that the Association (D) denied the general public its right of access to public trust lands along the beaches in Bay Head and its right to use private property along the ocean in exercising its rights under the public trust doctrine.

Issue: Does the public have a right to go through and use privately-owned lands as part of its right to use tidal lands and waters?

Decision and Rationale: (Schreiber) Yes. The public's right to use the tidal lands and waters also includes the right to gain access through and to use privately-owned dry sand areas as reasonably necessary. The public trust doctrine recognizes that "land covered by tidal waters belonged to the sovereign, but for the common use of all people." Such lands have generally been defined as that extending from the ocean to the mean high water level. Traditionally, the public's right to use these lands and waters has included navigation and fishing rights. In *Borough of Neptune City v. Borough of Avon-by-the-Sea*, 61 N.J. 296, 294 A.2d 47 (1972), the right was expanded to include recreational uses, like swimming and bathing. Extension of the public trust doctrine to include such recreational uses furthers the general welfare, and the public's right to enjoy these privileges must be respected. Exercise of this right, however, may depend upon a right to pass across the beach immediately upland from the foreshore areas. Without some form of access, the right to use the wet-sand part of the beach would be meaningless and unfeasible. The right of access is not an unrestricted one. As long as reasonable access to the sea is provided, the public interest is satisfied. Moreover, the right to upland, dry sand areas is not solely one of access. Reasonable enjoyment of the ocean cannot be experienced without being able to rest and relax on the dry sand area, as well. As long as the reasonably necessary use of these areas is also allowed, along with reasonably necessary access, then the public trust doctrine is satisfied. Here, the activities of the Association are akin to those of a municipality, from providing police to representing the interests of the Borough. The quasi-public nature of the Association is apparent, and thus

membership must be made open to the public at large. Accordingly, the general public will be able to use the beaches during the daylight hours in the summer months. This right of access and use should reasonably satisfy the public need at this time. Judgment entered against the Association (D).

Analysis:

The public trust doctrine is only one way that the public's interest in beaches is recognized. Some states, including California and North Carolina, have held that this kind of public easement can be acquired through long continuous use under a claim of right. The private owner must have notice, by virtue of the kind and extent of the use, that the general public, and not mere individuals, are claiming the adverse right. The prescriptive easement doctrine, however, is not particularly successful in its application to this area. This is mainly because most courts presume that the public use of private beaches occurs with the permission of the owners. Thus, adverse use cannot be proven in those situations. Courts in Florida, Oregon, and Texas, by contrast, have turned to the medieval doctrine of "customary rights." This term is used to describe uses which, essentially, have existed for as long as anyone can remember. Long usage of beaches has been held in these states to be protected as a customary right.

AN EASEMENT IN GROSS CAN ONLY BE USED OR TRANSFERRED AS "ONE STOCK," WITH THE CONSENT OF ALL COMMON OWNERS

Miller v. Lutheran Conference and Camp Association

(Surviving Brother) v. (Dead Brother's Executors Licensee)
331 Pa. 241, 200 A. 646, 130 A.L.R. 1245 (1938)

MEMORY GRAPHIC

Instant Facts

Rufus Miller's executors licensed the Association to use the lake without referring to Frank Miller, who owned three-fourths of the interests in such rights.

Black Letter Rule

When two or more persons own an easement in gross, the easement must be used as "one stock," meaning that any actions involving the easement must be made with common consent of all the owners.

Case Vocabulary

FI. FA.: An abbreviation for the Latin phrase 'fieri facias,' which means that you "cause it to be done"; in essence, denotes a writ of execution.
RIPARIAN: Relating to the bank of a river or stream.

Procedural Basis: Appeal from decree in action for injunctive relief.

Facts: Frank Miller (P), his brother, Rufus Miller, and others created the Pocono Spring Water Ice Company in September 1895 to create Lake Naomi. The Company would have "the exclusive use of the water and its privileges," and was created for the purpose of "erecting a dam..., for pleasure boating, skating, fishing, and the cutting, storing and selling of ice." This Company built a 14-foot dam across Tunkhannock Creek in Monroe County which formed Lake Naomi. This lake was about a mile long and one-third of a mile wide. The Company granted to Frank Miller (P) and "his heirs and assigns forever, the exclusive right to fish and boat in all the waters of [the Company]" by a deed dated March 20, 1899. On February 17, 1900, Frank Miller (P) granted to Rufus Miller, his heirs and assigns forever, "all the one-fourth interest in and to the fishing, boating, and bathing rights and privileges at, in, upon and about Lake Naomi..." that had been conferred to him (P) by the Company in March of 1899. On the same day, Frank (P) and Rufus entered a business partnership which operated and rented boats and houses on the lake. Three-fourths of all interests were allocated to Frank (P) and one-fourth were allocated to Rufus. They exercised their privileges without interruption until Rufus' death on October 11, 1925. On July 13, 1929, the executors of Rufus Miller's estate granted a year's license to the Lutheran Conference and Camp Association (D). This license allowed the Association (D) members to boat, bathe, and fish in the lake, with a percentage of their receipts to be paid to Rufus' estate. This led Frank Miller (P) to file a suit in equity, claiming that the Association (D) was threatening to license its own guests to bathe, boat, and fish in the lake. Frank Miller (P) requested an injunction to prevent the Association (D) from trespassing, and the trial court issued the injunction. He (P) claims that the Company never conveyed bathing rights to him (P) in its 1899 grant, and thus he (P) could not and did not vest them to Rufus. Moreover, if such bathing rights were vested in him (P), Frank (P) claims all of the bathing, boating and fishing privileges were easements in gross and as such were inalienable and indivisible. The Association (D) argues that the 1899 deed to Frank (P) transferred the bathing privileges along with the others, or alternatively that he (P) and Rufus acquired the bathing privileges by prescription, thus rendering the privileges alienable and divisible.

Issue:

Can one of two owners of an easement in gross grant a license to another party independently of the other owner?

Decision and Rationale: (Stern) No. When two or more persons own an easement in gross, the easement must be used as "one stock," meaning that any actions involving the easement must be made with the common consent of all the owners. The 1899 deed cannot be construed as conveying bathing privileges to Frank Miller (P). It clearly states the grant of exclusive rights to fish and boat; bathing rights are not mentioned at all. There is evidence, however, that Frank Miller (P) acquired these bathing rights by prescription. No principle of law forbids an adverse enjoyment of an easement in gross form becoming a title by prescription. Indeed, Lake Naomi has grown into a popular summer resort, with bathing and boating facilities having particular importance. Bathing uses are listed among the purposes for which the Company was chartered. From 1900 to at least 1925, both Frank (P) and Rufus Miller systematically exercised the bathing rights in pursuit of their business partnership. It would be highly unjust, therefore, to hold that the Miller brothers did not hold a title to the bathing rights by prescription that was just as valid as the boating and fishing rights conveyed by express grant. While there is disagreement over the assignability of easements in gross such as the fishing, boating and bathing privileges involved here, the important issue to consider is their divisibility. If these easements are to be divided between the owners, the easements must be used or exercised as an entirety. In other words, one user alone cannot convey a share in the common right; such action must occur with the consent of all the owners. Here, it appears clear that Frank (P) did not wish to grant Rufus a separate right to subdivide and sublicense their lake privileges. Instead, it is clear Frank (P) intended for them to use the rights together for their business, with one-fourth of the proceeds going to Rufus and three-fourths going to himself (P). This further demonstrates that these easements should be treated as "one stock," and not by two owners separately. Decree affirmed, and costs to be paid by defendant.

Analysis:

Once again, an easement in gross is an easement which gives a property owner the right to use a servient property, and does not benefit its owner in the use and enjoyment of his or her land. Transfers of these easements are different than those for easements appurtenant. As the latter kind are created to benefit a particular parcel, any transfer of title of that dominant parcel will carry the easement along with it. Of course, easements in gross for commercial purposes, as demonstrated by *Miller*, are transferable. By contrast, legal experts have speculated that "personal" easements in gross, namely those held for personal recreation and not for economic benefit, are probably not alienable. This distinction rests on the idea of grantor's intent. The belief is that a grantor would not intend the holder of an easement to transfer it when the easement was intended for the narrow purpose of benefiting the holder. Indeed, in helping shape much of this area of law, the Restatement has proposed making the alienability of easements in gross depend on "the manner or the terms if their creation."

AN EASEMENT WHICH IS APPURTENANT TO ONE PARCEL OF LAND CANNOT BE EXTENDED TO BENEFIT ANOTHER PARCEL

Brown v. Voss

(B and C Owners) v. (A Owners)

105 Wash. 2d 366, 715 P.2d 514 (1986)

M E M O R Y   G R A P H I C

Instant Facts

Voss (D) blocked off a private road easement for parcel B after Brown (P) started building a house that would sit on both parcels B and C.

Black Letter Rule

If an easement benefits its owner in the use of a particular parcel of land, any extension of the easement to other parcels is a misuse of the easement.

Case Vocabulary

SUMP: A pit or reservoir, often used for drainage.

Procedural Basis: Appeal from judgment in action for injunctive relief and damages.

Facts: In 1952, the then-owners of parcel A granted a private road easement across their property to the then-owners of parcel B for "ingress to and egress from" parcel B. The Vosses (D) acquired parcel A in 1973. The Browns (P) bought parcel B from one owner on April 1, 1977, and then parcel C from another owner on July 31, 1977. The previous owners of parcel C were not parties to the easement grant. The Browns (P) planned to build a single home that would straddle the boundary line between parcels B and C. The Browns (P) began clearing both parcels in November 1977. The Vosses (D) began trying to stop the Browns (P) from using the easement in April 1979, by which time the Browns (P) had spent over $11,000 in developing the properties. At this point, the Vosses (D) placed logs, a concrete pit, and a chain link fence within the easement. The Browns (P) sued for removal of the obstructions, an injunction against further interference with the use of the easement and damages. The Vosses (D) counterclaimed for damages and an injunction against the Browns (P) using the easement for parcel C. The trial court awarded each party $1 in damages, with the award against the Browns (P) being for a minor inadvertent trespass. The trial court also found that the Browns (P) made no unreasonable use of the easement while developing their (P) property, nor had they (P) acted unreasonably in making these developments. Also, if the Vosses' (D) injunction were granted, parcel C would be landlocked and the Browns (P) would not be able to make use of their property. The trial court also found that the Vosses (Ds) would suffer no appreciable hardship or damage their (D) requested injunction were denied. Moreover, the trial court held that framing and enforcing such an injunction would be impractical. Based on these and other findings of fact, the Vosses (D) were denied their injunction and the Browns (P) were allowed to use the easement as long as their properties were used solely for a single family residence.

Issue: Can the holder of a private easement use it to access a parcel of land that is not the dominant estate when there will be no increased burden on the servient estate?

Decision and Rationale: (Brachtenbach) No. The easement in this case resulted from an express grant made in 1952. Thus, the scope of this right acquired through the easement is to be determined from the terms of the grant and the way they give effect to the intention of the parties. By the express terms of the 1952 grant, the previous owners of parcel B acquired a private easement across parcel A and the right to use it to enter and exit parcel B. While the Browns (P) acquired these same rights to enter and exit parcel B, they (P) have no such easement rights with regard to parcel C. Parcel C was not a part of the original dominant estate under the terms of the 1952 grant. If an easement benefits its owner in the use of a particular parcel of land, any extension of the easement to other parcels is a misuse of the easement. Even though, as the Browns (P) contend, their (P) use of the easement to gain access to a home located partially on parcel B and partially on parcel C is at most a mere technical misuse of the easement, it is nonetheless a misuse. This does not automatically mean that the Vosses (D) are entitled to injunctive relief. As the proceeding for determining the validity of an injunction is an equitable one, deference should be paid to the findings of the trial court unless an abuse of discretion is shown. No such abuse is demonstrated in this case. Judgment of Court of Appeals is reversed and judgment of trial court is affirmed.

Dissent: (Dore) While the extension of this easement to nondominant property did constitute a misuse of the easement, the Vosses (D) should be entitled to injunctive relief. Misuse of an easement is a trespass. Consequently, the Browns' (P) continued misuse of the easement in building and residing in the home they (P) have proposed would result in a continuing trespass. Damages on such a prolonged trespass would be too difficult to measure; thus, injunctive relief would be the appropriate remedy under such circumstances. The Browns (P) should have known from public records that the easement was not connected to parcel C. If an injunction were granted for the Vosses (D), the Browns (P) could still acquire access to parcel C through other means, either by renegotiating the easement or some other statutory means.

Analysis:

While damages were awarded in this case, courts have also been ready to grant injunctive relief when easements are improperly extended to other properties. *Brown* demonstrates the courts' opposition to the use of an easement for inseparable activities situated on both dominant and nondominant property simultaneously. This rule, however, does not entirely block changes in the easement over the course of time. The permitted purposes behind an easement can change and expand to a certain degree. Specifically, changes in the dominant parcel that can be reasonably anticipated can be accommodated by the easement. Similar principles control the scope of easements stemming from prescription, implication, prior use or necessity.

Preseault v. United States

(Landowner) v. (Government)
100 F.3d 1525 (Fed. Cir. 1996)

MEMORY GRAPHIC

Instant Facts

Property owners sued the Government for an unauthorized taking after the Government authorized the conversion of an abandoned railroad easement into a nature trail across the owners' property.

Black Letter Rule

An easement is terminated by abandonment when nonuse is coupled with an act manifesting either a present intent to relinquish the easement or a purpose inconsistent with its future existence.

Case Vocabulary

HABENDUM CLAUSE: A clause in a deed which typically begins with "to have and to hold" and which defines the extent of ownership.

Procedural Basis: Appeal from judgment for defendant in action for damages for unauthorized taking of land by government.

Facts: The Preseaults (P) owned a fee simple interest in a tract of land along Lake Champlain in Burlington, Vermont. A right-of-way ran across the land. The right-of-way had been acquired in 1899 by a railroad company which laid rails and operated a railroad on the strip. In the 1960's the State of Vermont acquired all assets of the railroad and leased the right to use the right-of-way to the Vermont Railway. The Vermont Railway operated trains over the land until 1970. In 1975 the tracks and all railroad equipment were removed from the portion of the right-of-way running over the Preseaults' (P) tract. Eight years later, Congress approved the Rails-to-Trails Act in order to preserve discontinued railroad corridors for future railroad use and to permit public recreational use of the rights-of-way. The Act empowered the Interstate Commerce Commission ("ICC") to permit discontinuance of rail services and transfer the rights-of-way to public or private groups willing to maintain the strip as a public trail. In 1986 the ICC approved an agreement between the Virginia Railway and the state of Vermont and city of Burlington to discontinue rail service over the Preseaults' (P) land and to maintain the former railroad strip as a public trail. The Preseaults (P) sued the ICC, claiming the Rails-to-Trails Act was unconstitutional. The Supreme Court held that the Act was constitutional but that the Preseaults (P) may have a remedy under the Fifth Amendment Takings Clause. The Preseaults (P) then sued the United States (D), claiming that the Government (D), through the ICC, took the Preseaults' (P) property when it authorized the conversion of the former railroad right-of-way to public trail use. The Preseaults (P) argued that the right-of-way was originally an easement, that the use for public trail purposes was beyond the scope of the easement, and that the easement had terminated by abandonment in 1970. The trial court disagreed, ruling for the Government (D). The Preseaults (P) appeal.

Issue: (1) Does governmental use of land that goes beyond the scope of an easement constitute a "taking" of the servient estate? (2) Is an easement terminated by mere nonuse?

Decision and Rationale: (Plager, J.) (1) Yes. Governmental use of land that goes beyond the scope of an easement constitutes a "taking" of the servient tenement owner's property. In the instant action, we agree with the trial court that the right-of-way was (at least for a time) an easement. When a railroad acquires an estate in land for laying track and operating railroad equipment thereon, the estate acquired is no more than that needed for the purpose, and that typically means an easement, not a fee simple estate. Assuming for the sake of argument that the easement still existed in 1986, we find that the Government's (D) use of the land for a recreational trail is not within the scope of the easement. The scope of the original easement was specifically for the transportation of goods and persons via railroad. The scope of an easement may be adjusted over time only if the change is consistent with the terms of the original grant. We agree with the majority of courts in holding that the change to a public recreational trail is not consistent with the original terms of a railroad easement. There are significant differences in the degree of the burden imposed on the Preseaults' (P) servient estate between railroad and public usage. Although railroad usage is noisy, it is far less frequent and more controlled than public pedestrians and bicyclists. (2) No. An easement is not terminated by mere nonuse. In order to terminate an easement by abandonment, there must also be acts by the owner of the dominant tenement conclusively and unequivocally manifesting either a present intent to relinquish the easement or a purpose inconsistent with its future existence. In the case at hand, we agree with the trial court in holding that the removal of the rails and all railroad equipment in 1975 constituted an abandonment. It is inconsequential that it remains *possible* to restore the railway service over the right-of-way. In addition, the actions taken by the Vermont Railway in collecting various license and crossing fees from persons crossing the track is not persuasive evidence of a purpose or intent not to abandon the use of the right-of-way for actual railroad purposes. Furthermore, in the years since 1975, neither the State nor the Railroad has made any attempt to reinstate railroad service on the right-of-way. Our determination of abandonment provides an alternative ground for concluding that a governmental taking occurred. The Government has chosen to impose upon the Preseaults' (P) property interests, and the Fifth Amendment compels compensation. Reversed and remanded.

Dissent: (Justice Not Stated). We feel that the Railroad did not abandon its easement. Even though the tracks were removed, there was no clear and unequivocal signal of intent to abandon. To the contrary, the Railroad continued to enter into crossing and license agreements after 1975. On the issue of scope, a railroad easement can be used as a public trail. This merely shifts the use from one public use to another and imposes no greater burden on the servient tenement.

Analysis:

This case touches on a number of important topics related to easements, including the creation, scope, and termination of easements. The holdings are fundamental and straightforward. First, when railroads acquire estates in land for laying track and operating a railroad, the estates are typically easements. Second, the scope of easements may change over time; however, a railroad easement is limited to railroad (and possibly other transportation) uses. Third, the easements may terminate by abandonment where nonuse is coupled with an act evidencing an intent to abandon the property. In the railroad context, the act of removing all rails and equipment evidences an intent to abandon. Fourth, governmental use of an easement that goes beyond the scope of the easement, or that occurs after the easement is terminated, entitles the servient estate owner to compensation. The dissent raises some good points with respect to the scope and abandonment issues. Is it really inconsistent with the scope of a railroad easement to allow pedestrians and bicycles to use the land? This is a difficult question that depends on whether easements should be narrowly or broadly interpreted. Does the act of tearing up railroad tracks "conclusively and unequivocally" manifest an intent to abandon a railroad easement? Perhaps the Railroad was tearing up the tracks in order to install newer and better rails. Maybe the Railroad should have been given a certain amount of time to install new tracks before the easement was considered "abandoned." Note the difficult factual determination that courts must make when determining abandonment. In addition to abandonment, easements may be terminated by destruction of the servient estate, by attempts to sever the easement from the dominant estate, and by a written release. Easements also may be terminated by prescription, where some person prevents the easement from being used for a certain period; by estoppel, where the easement holder's conduct leads the servient owner to detrimentally rely on the reasonable belief that the easement has been terminated; and by the sale of the servient estate to a bona fide purchaser who has no notice of the easement (although recordation of the easement provides constructive notice which would prevent the buyer from being considered a bona fide purchaser).

ENGLAND COURT OF CHANCERY HOLDS THAT IT WOULD BE INEQUITABLE FOR A COVENANT THAT IS ENFORCEABLE AGAINST A SELLER OF LAND TO BE UNENFORCEABLE AGAINST A PERSON WHO PURCHASES THE LAND WITH NOTICE OF THE COVENANT

Tulk v. Moxhay

(Garden Seller) v. (Garden Buyer)
(1848) 2 Phillips 774, 41 Eng. Rep. 1143

M E M O R Y   G R A P H I C

Instant Facts

Tulk had a covenant which required maintenance of a garden on some land, but Moxhay later tried to put buildings on it after buying it.

Black Letter Rule

A covenant will be enforceable in equity against a person who purchases land with notice of the covenant.

Case Vocabulary

ASSIGNS: Another name for assignees.
ASSIGNEE: Person to whom one's property is transferred to.
DIVERS: Various.
MASTER OF THE ROLLS: An assistant judge of the English court of equity (known as court of chancery).
MESNE CONVEYANCE: A conveyance which is between the first grantee and the present holder in the chain of title.

Procedural Basis: Appeal from injunction granted by Master of the Rolls.

Facts: In 1808, Tulk (P) sold a vacant piece of land in Leicester Square to Elms. Tulk (P) also owned several of the houses that formed the Square. The deed of conveyance contained a covenant by which Elms, his heirs, and assigns would keep and maintain the property as a pleasure ground and square garden, enclosed by an iron railing. The covenant also stated that the property was to be "uncovered with any buildings." This property passed by various mesne conveyances [intermediate conveyances between the first grantee and the current holder of title] from Elms to Moxhay (D). Moxhay's (D) purchase deed contained no similar covenant against building on the Square. Moxhay (D) did admit, however, that he (D) purchased the land with notice of the original covenant in the 1808 deed. Moxhay (D) tried to assert the right to build structures on the garden as he (D) saw fit, and Tulk (P) filed for an injunction to prevent Moxhay (D) from using the pleasure ground and garden for any purpose other than as an open area, uncovered with buildings.

Issue: Is a covenant enforceable against a purchaser of land when that purchaser acquired the land with knowledge of the covenant?

Decision and Rationale: (Cottenham) Yes. Here, there was a clear contract between Tulk (P) and Elms, by which Elms promised not to use the land adjoining Tulk's (P) houses in the Square for anything other than a square garden. If Moxhay (D) were allowed to purchase this land from Elms and violate this contract, then any owner of land who tried to sell part of his land, like Tulk (P), would risk having his remaining land be rendered worthless. This is because the sale price of the land in question would be affected by the covenant. Moxhay (D) likely paid less for the land than he would have had to pay for land unburdened by such a covenant. If Moxhay (D) were allowed to build on the land, he (D) would have effectively received unburdened land for the lower price of burdened land. Nothing could be more inequitable than allowing this, for Moxhay (D) could then resell the unburdened land at a higher price, and thus would be unjustly enriched. If a covenant is attached to property by its original owner, no one with notice of that covenant can purchase that property and not be bound by the covenant. Decision affirmed.

Analysis:

This case created the equitable servitude. An equitable servitude is a covenant regarding the use of land which is enforceable against subsequent possessors in equity, even if the covenant itself is not enforceable at law. The traditional difference between this and a real covenant relates to the available remedies. When a real covenant is breached, the remedy is damages in a suit a law. When an equitable servitude is breached, however, the remedy is either an injunction or enforcement of a consensual lien, which secures a promise to pay money, in a suit in equity.

MICHIGAN SUPREME COURT HOLDS THAT WHERE A PROPERTY OWNER SELLS OFF LOTS BY DEEDS CONTAINING COVENANTS MEANT TO CARRY OUT A SCHEME OF A RESIDENTIAL DISTRICT, AND A LOT PURCHASER HAS NOTICE OF THOSE COVENANTS, THAT PURCHASER IS BARRED FROM BUILDING A GAS STATION ON HIS LOT BY AN IMPLIED COVENANT

Sanborn v. McLean

(Neighbor) v. (Gas Station Builder)

(1925) 233 Mich. 227, 206 N.W. 496, 60 A.L.R. 1212

MEMORY GRAPHIC

Instant Facts

The McLeans tried to build a gas station on their lot in a residential district, but were enjoined from doing so by their neighbors.

Black Letter Rule

An equitable servitude can be implied on a lot, even when the servitude is not created by a written instrument, if there is a scheme for development of a residential subdivision and the purchaser of the lot has notice of it.

Case Vocabulary

NUISANCE PER SE: An act that would produce public annoyance and inconvenience regardless of the circumstances surrounding it.

PLAT: A map of a specific area of land, such as a subdivision.

RECIPROCAL NEGATIVE EASEMENT: An easement created when the owner of two or more lots sells one with restrictions on it that benefit the land retained by the owner. This sale creates a mutual servitude, and while it is in effect, the original owner cannot use his or her retained land in any way that is forbidden to the buyer of the other lot.

Procedural Basis: Appeal from decree providing injunctive relief for violation of reciprocal negative easement.

Facts: In 1891, ninety-one lots were subdivided along Collingwood Avenue in Detroit. Each lot was designed for and sold solely for residence purposes. In December 1892 , Robert J. and Joseph R. McLaughlin, then the owners of the lots on Collingwood, deeded lots 37 to 41 and 58 to 62, inclusive, with restrictions that provided "No residence shall be erected ...which shall cost less than $2,500, and nothing but residences shall be erected upon said premises." In July 1893, they conveyed lots 17 to 21 and 78 to 82, both inclusive, and lot 98 with the same restrictions. On September 7, 1893, the McLaughlins sold lot 86 to the McLeans (D) by a deed which did not contain these restrictions. The McLeans (D) occupied a house on the lot. They (D) later started to erect a gasoline filling station at the rear of their (D) lot. Sanborn (P), who owned the neighboring lot, filed for an injunction. The McLeans (D) were enjoined by decree, and appealed.

Issue: Can a restriction on the use of property be implied on a lot purchased in a subdivision when the restriction is not contained in the deed, but is contained in the deeds of other lots in the subdivision that were previously sold?

Decision and Rationale: (Wiest) Yes. A negative servitude, such as a covenant restricting a lot to residential use, can be implied on a lot if a developer has set up a scheme for a residential subdivision and if the purchaser of the lot has notice of the covenants used to set up the scheme. Here, the McLaughlins imposed the restrictions on the Collingwood lots for the benefit of the lands they retained, namely to carry out the scheme of a residential district. Because they sold these lots with restrictions in order to benefit themselves, the servitude became a mutual one, and so the McLaughlins were bound by the same restrictions as their buyers. This restriction is thus considered a reciprocal negative easement, and this reciprocal negative easement attached to lot 86 before the McLeans (D) acquired the land. Such an easement was still attached to lot 86 after the sale to the McLeans (D) and can still be enforced by Sanborn (P) if the McLeans (D) had actual or constructive knowledge of it. Because the abstract of title to lot 86 showed that lot 86 was part of a much larger subdivision, and because the deeds resulting in reciprocal negative easements were on record, the McLeans (D) were bound by constructive notice to follow that easement. Furthermore, the general plan for the residential district had been observed by all lot purchasers, whether explicitly restricted or not, for over thirty years. The McLeans (D) could not have avoided noticing the strictly uniform residential use of the neighboring lots, and therefore were on inquiry notice to learn why all the lots conformed with each other. The least inquiry by the McLeans (D) would have revealed the easement on lot 86. Decree affirmed.

Analysis:

Most jurisdictions follow this case and imply negative restrictions from a common scheme. A few, however, closely follow to the Statute of Frauds [contracts for land sales must be in writing] in such matters. Courts in these jurisdictions say that an equitable servitude will not be implied from the presence of restrictions on other lots in a subdivision, from developer's oral promise to impose such restrictions, or from a general scheme not included in the deed to the lot in question.

NEW YORK COURT OF APPEALS HOLDS THAT A COVENANT REQUIRING MEMBERS OF A RESIDENTIAL COMMUNITY TO PAY A MAXIMUM FOUR-DOLLAR-PER-YEAR CHARGE FOR MAINTENANCE OF PUBLIC AREAS IS ONE THAT TOUCHES AND CONCERNS THE LAND, AND THEIR PROPERTY OWNERS' ASSOCIATION HAS THE RIGHT TO ENFORCE THE COVENANT

Neponsit Property Owners' Association, Inc. v. Emigrant Industrial Savings Bank

(Property Owners' Assn.) v. (Mortgage Bank)

(1938) 278 N.Y. 248, 15 N.E.2d 793

M E M O R Y   G R A P H I C

Instant Facts

Emigrant Bank took title to land previously deeded by Neponsit Realty, and the Neponsit Association tried to foreclose a lien contained in the earlier deed.

Black Letter Rule

An affirmative covenant to pay money for improvements or maintenance done in connection with, but not upon the land which is to be subject to the burden of the covenant does touch and concern the land, and a homeowners' association, as the agent of the actual owners of the property, can rightfully enforce the covenant.

Procedural Basis: Appeal from order denying motion for judgment on pleadings in action to foreclose lien on land.

Facts: In January 1911, Neponsit Realty Company, owner of a tract of land in Queens County, caused a map of the land to be filed in the office of the clerk of the county. This tract was developed for a strictly residential community. Neponsit Realty sold lots in the tract to purchasers. In 1917, Neponsit Realty deeded a lot to Mr. and Mrs. Deyer. The deed contained a covenant which provided that the property would be "subject to an annual charge ...(not) exceeding in any year the sum of four dollars," and the charge was to be used for the "maintenance of the roads, paths, parks, beach, sewers, and such other public purposes." The covenant also stated that the charges would be payable to a Neponsit Property Owners' Association (P), as an assignee of Neponsit Realty, and the Association (D) would be responsible for the use of the charges. In addition, the covenant stated that owners would be required to pay the charge on the first of May every year, and that failure to do so would result in a lien on the land until the fully paid. Emigrant Industrial Savings Bank (D) later acquired title to the Deyers' land at a judicial sale. The deed from the referee of the sale to Emigrant Bank (D) and every deed in the chain of title since the conveyance by Neponsit Realty claims to convey the property subject to the original covenant. The Association (P) brought this action to foreclose the lien and enforce the covenant for the annual maintenance charge. Emigrant Bank (D) filed a motion for judgment on the pleadings, and the motion was denied. Emigrant Bank (D) appealed.

Issue: Does a covenant to pay money for maintenance done in connection with, but not actually on, an area of land touch and concern the land and thus become enforceable against subsequent purchasers?

Decision and Rationale: (Lehman) Yes. The terms are not defined by statute, as they are meant to be determined by the court based on the facts of a given case. The key question to consider is to what degree the covenant substantially affects the legal rights of the parties to the covenant. This distinguishes a covenant that runs with the land from a mere agreement between a promisor and promisee. Here, by paying the annual charge, an owner in the tract acquired an easement, or right of common enjoyment, with other property owners in roads, beaches, public spaces and improvements in those areas. To fully enjoy these areas, the owners must help pay for their maintenance. Thus, the burden was inseparably attached to the land, held by the various owners, which enjoys the benefit, and so the covenant clearly touches and concerns the land. There was also concern over a possible lack of privity of estate between the Association (P) and Emigrant Bank (D). The Association (P) never owned the roads or other public places mentioned in the covenant, and was created solely as the assignee of the property owners. However, looking beyond the corporate nature of the Association (P), it is clear that the Association (P) was formed as a convenient means of advancing the common interests of the property owners. It would be almost impossible to separate the interests of the Association (P) and the individual owners. There is essentially privity of estate between the Association (P) and Emigrant Bank (D). An affirmative covenant to pay money for improvements or maintenance done in connection with, but not upon, the land does touch and concern the land, and a homeowners' association, as the agent of the property owners, can rightfully enforce the covenant.

Analysis:

Courts have almost always held that covenants that restrict the use of land do touch and concern the land, because such negative covenants substantially affect the value of the land. By contrast, courts have been hesitant to enforce affirmative covenants against successors for three reasons. First, courts do not like to compel parties to perform a series of acts that require long term supervision. Second, an affirmative obligation which requires a party to maintain property or pay money may leave a successor with a sizable personal liability. Finally, such a covenant, with an unlimited duration, is similar to perpetual rent or some other feudal device.

SUPERIOR COURT OF NEW JERSEY, APPELLATE DIVISION, HOLDS THAT WHERE A DEVELOPER AND A LOT PURCHASER ENTERED A COVENANT BY WHICH THE DEVELOPER RESERVED THE RIGHT TO BUILD THE ORIGINAL BUILDING ON THE PREMISES, THE COVENANT COULD NOT BE ENFORCED BECAUSE IT DID NOT RUN WITH THE LAND

Caullett v. Stanley Stilwell and Sons, Inc.

(Lot Purchaser) v. (Land Developer)

(1961) 67 N.J. Super. 111, 170 A.2d 52

M E M O R Y   G R A P H I C

Instant Facts

A developer deeded a lot to Caullett for $4,000, and the deed included a covenant giving the developer the right to build the first structure.

Black Letter Rule

A restrictive covenant does not run with the land at law or in equity when the benefit it creates would not touch and concern the land.

Procedural Basis: Appeal from summary judgment in action to quiet title.

Facts: Stanley Stilwell and Sons, Inc. (D) conveyed a one-acre lot to the Caulletts (P) by warranty deed. The deed was delivered on January 13, 1959. Negotiations collapsed over a covenant by which Stilwell and Sons (D) would have reserved "the right to build or construct the original dwelling or building on said premises." The item is designated in the deed as "running with the land ...[binding] the purchasers, their heirs, executors, administrators and assigns." The Caulletts (P) filed for summary judgment, claiming that no contract ever existed between them (P) and Stilwell and Sons (D) for the construction of any building on the lot. Stilwell and Sons (D) countered by saying that one of the main conditions of the sale was the understanding that it (D) would serve as the contractor for the Caulletts (P) after the sale. The trial court held that this covenant was unenforceable and should be stricken from the deed. Stilwell and Sons (D) appealed.

Issue: Can a covenant which imposes a burden on land, but creates a benefit personal to one of the parties, be enforced, either in equity or at law?

Decision and Rationale: (Freund) No. A covenant will not run at law or in equity if the benefit it creates is in gross (in other words, personal), because such a benefit would not touch and concern the property. The agreement would be a mere personal covenant, and not a real covenant that could run with the land. For a covenant to touch and concern the subject land, it must directly influence the occupation, use, or enjoyment of the land. Here, the promise between Stilwell and Sons (D) and the Caulletts (P) is, at best, a personal arrangement between them, designed to insure a profit for Stilwell and Sons (D) after allegedly selling the land for a relatively low price. This contract for a personal service has no effect on the title. The wording of the deed which described the covenant as one running with the land does not counter the personal nature of the promise. Even if this provision were seen as directly restricting the Caulletts' (P) use of their land, it would still not be enforced because the benefit is clearly personal to the grantor (D). If enforced, it would give the grantor (D) a commercial advantage only and would not affect the use or value of any land retained. A covenant which creates a burden on the land but only a personal benefit is generally held not to run at law. Public policy is strong against hindering the alienability of property when the act would not enhance surrounding lands. Moreover, the covenant could not be enforced as an equitable servitude, because the right to enforce such a servitude is mainly dependent on the covenant having been made for the benefit of other land, such as land in a subdivision or land retained by the grantor. Therefore, the clause cannot be held to impair the Caulletts' (P) title because of the indisputably personal nature of the benefit it confers.

Analysis:

The English courts have held that the burden of a restrictive covenant does not run in equity if the benefit is in gross (i.e., personal). This is because they believed an equitable servitude was merely an interest which was analogous to a negative easement. In England because an easement requires a dominant tenement, by analogy, an equitable servitude would also require a dominant tenement. The same reasoning, by way of analogy, could not support the rule in the United States. Here, the burden will run with the servient land when an easement in gross is created.

Hill v. Community of Damien of Molokai

(Neighbor) v. (Group Home Administrator)

121 N.M. 353 (N.M. 1996)

MEMORY GRAPHIC

Instant Facts

Residents of a planned community sued to enjoin an AIDS group home from occupying one of the houses, based on a "single family residence" clause in the restrictive covenant.

Black Letter Rule

Ambiguous restrictive covenants should be construed in favor of the free use and enjoyment of property and against restrictions; restrictive covenants with a discriminatory effect violate the Fair Housing Act.

Procedural Basis: Appeal of order enjoining use of property as group home for AIDS patients.

Facts: In a planned residential subdivision in Albuquerque, New Mexico, the Community of Damien of Molokai ("Community") (D) opened a group home for four individuals with AIDS. The individuals were unrelated and required varying degrees of home nursing care. William Hill III (P) lived on the same dead-end street where the group home was located. Hill (P) and other neighbors (collectively "the Neighbors") (P) noticed an increase in traffic once the group home was opened. The Neighbors (P) claimed that the use of the property as an AIDS group home violated a restrictive covenant, applicable to all homes in the area, which mandated that no lot be used for any purpose other than single family residence purposes. The Neighbors sued to enjoin the further use of the property as a group home. They argued that the term "single family residence" did not include group homes in which unrelated people lived together. The Community challenged this argument and contended that the restrictive covenant violated the Federal Fair Housing Act ("FHA"). The trial court granted the injunction. The Community (D) appeals on the ground that the group home is a permitted use under the covenant and, alternatively, that enforcing the covenant would violate the FHA.

Issue: (1) Should ambiguous restrictive covenants be construed in favor of the free use and enjoyment of property and against restrictions? (2) Do restrictive covenants violate the FHA when they have a discriminatory intent, a discriminatory effect, or constitute a failure to make reasonable accommodations?

Decision and Rationale: (Frost, J.) (1) Yes. Ambiguous restrictive covenants should be construed in favor of the free use and enjoyment of property and against restrictions. The restrictive covenant at issue requires homes in the area to be used for "single family residence purposes." Operating the AIDS group home constitutes the residential use of property. The individuals share communal meals, do their own shopping, and provide emotional, financial and spiritual support to each other. They contract with private health-care workers, none of whom reside at the home. The Community provides administrative assistance, collects rent from the residents, and enforces a no drinking and no drugs policy. The Community's activities do not render the home a nonresidential operation such as a group home or boarding house. Moreover the residents of the home meet the single family requirement. The word "family" is not defined in the restrictive covenant, and thus the use of the term is ambiguous. We must interpret any ambiguity in favor of the free enjoyment of the property. There are a number of other factors that lead us to define "family" as including unrelated individuals. First, the Albuquerque zoning ordinance includes within the definition of "family," "any group of not more than five [unrelated] persons living together in a dwelling." This is persuasive evidence for a proper interpretation of the ambiguous term. Second, a strong public policy exists in favor of removing barriers preventing disabled persons from living in residential settings. The FHA squarely sets out this important policy. Third, other courts have held that the controlling factor in considering whether a group of unrelated individuals constitutes a family is whether the residents bear the generic character of a relatively permanent functioning family unit. We conclude that the residents of the AIDS group home do have this character and should be considered a "family." Therefore, the Community's (D) use of the property as a group home does not violate the restrictive covenant. (2) Yes. Restrictive covenants violate the FHA when they have a discriminatory intent, a discriminatory effect, or constitute a failure to make reasonable accommodations. Even if we were to adopt the Neighbors' (P) proposed definition of "family" to include only individuals related by blood or by law, we would still find for the Community (D) because the estriction would violate the FHA. Although the Neighbors' (P) nforcement of the restrictive covenant was not intended to iscriminate against AIDS victims (a protected class according to the HA), the enforcement certainly had the *effect* of denying housing to e handicapped. We must balance the Neighbors' interest in voiding increased traffic against the Community's (D) interest in roviding housing to disabled individuals. We conclude that the FHA factors weigh in favor of the community, especially in light of the strong public policy favoring placement of disabled individuals in community living environments. Furthermore, we hold that the Neighbors (P) failed to make reasonable accommodations, as required by the FHA. A reasonable accommodation in this instance would have been not to seek enforcement of the covenant. Accordingly, the trial court's ruling is reversed and the injunction is vacated.

Analysis:

nis opinion presents a number of controversial legal and social issues in reaching an equitable result. Although couched in thorough legal scourse, the court essentially makes a fairness determination (the minor inconvenience of increased traffic on the street pales in comparison the benefits to AIDS patients in being able to live in a community environment). Nevertheless, the opinion can be questioned on several onts. First, the court's interpretation of the term "single family" renders the restrictive covenant essentially meaningless. If the drafters of the strictive covenant did not intend "single family" to mean a group of individuals related by law or blood, what was their intent? Based on the ourt's broad interpretation, "single family" could even mean several different families living under the same roof (surely a situation that the strictive covenant sought to avoid). The court seems all too willing to find that the term "single family" is ambiguous, simply because the term not defined in the covenant. Second, the purported benefits of living in this "community" are certainly open to debate. Arguably any such enefits would disappear after the Neighbors (P) sued to remove the patients from their dead-end street. Couldn't the Community (D) have osen a house that was not part of a master-planned community, providing the benefits of congregate living arrangements without the conflict th the neighbors? All in all, though, the opinion presents a compelling argument for a case-by-case analysis of whether restrictive covenants ould apply.

THE UNITED STATES SUPREME COURT HOLDS THAT WHERE MISSOURI SUPREME COURT ENFORCED A RESTRICTIVE COVENANT WHICH BARRED NON-WHITES FROM OCCUPYING PROPERTY, ITS ACT CONSTITUTED DISCRIMINATORY STATE ACTION AND WAS BARRED BY THE FOURTEENTH AMENDMENT OF THE CONSTITUTION

Shelley v. Kraemer

(Black Home Buyers) v. (White Homeowners)
(1948) 334 U.S. 1

M E M O R Y   G R A P H I C

Instant Facts

A black couple was buying a house while unaware of a racially based restrictive covenant on that street; the white homeowners tried to stop them.

Black Letter Rule

Judicial enforcement of a restrictive covenant based on race constitutes discriminatory state action, and is thus forbidden by the equal protection clause of the Fourteenth Amendment of the Constitution.

Case Vocabulary

IMPRIMATUR: "Let it be printed." License or permission.

Procedural Basis: Appeal from action to enforce covenant through divesting and revesting of title.

Facts: On February 16, 1911, thirty out of thirty-nine owners of property along both sides of Labadie Avenue between Cora and Taylor Avenues in St. Louis entered into an covenant relating to the use and occupancy of the property. This covenant provided that, for the next fifty years after the date of signing, no part of any of the property was to be used or occupied "by any person not of the Caucasian race, it being intended hereby to restrict the use of said property for said period of time against the occupancy ... by people of the Negro or Mongolian race." These thirty owners held title to forty-seven out of the total fifty-seven parcels of land in that district. On August 11, 1945, the Shelleys (P) (who were African-American) received a warranty deed to one of these forty-seven parcels from one Fitzgerald. The Shelleys (P) had no actual knowledge of the restrictive covenant at the time of purchase. On October 9, 1945, Kraemer and other owners of property subject to the covenant (Ds) brought suit to restrain the Shelleys (P) from taking possession of the parcel they bought. They (Ds) also requested that judgment be entered divesting title out of the Shelleys (P) and revesting title in Shackleford or some other person the court saw fit. The Missouri Supreme Court directed the trial court to grant relief for Kraemer (P) and the other owners (P).

Issue: Can a restrictive covenant based on race be judicially enforced?

Decision and Rationale: (Vinson) No. The equal protection clause of the Fourteenth Amendment prohibits judicial enforcement by state courts of restrictive covenants based on race. There is no question that the civil rights meant to be protected from discriminatory state action by the Fourteenth Amendment included the rights to acquire, own, enjoy, and dispose of property. These rights are essential to the enjoyment of other civil rights and liberties. If the restrictions imposed by the covenant on the Labadie Avenue property had been imposed by statue or ordinance, they would be clearly unconstitutional. Because it is the product of private, not state, action, however, the covenant by itself does not violate the Fourteenth Amendment. So long as the covenant is put into effect through voluntary action, it remains constitutional. Here, by contrast, the purposes of the covenant were secured through judicial enforcement by the state courts. It has long been established that the official action by state courts and judicial officers constitute action of the State, and this proposition applies to action regarding the Fourteenth Amendment as well. The undisputed facts clearly indicate that the Shelleys (P) were willing buyers of a parcel of property on Labadie Avenue, and that Fitzgerald was a willing seller. The Shelleys (P) would have been free to occupy the property if not for the intervention of the Missouri state courts. Though the racial restriction was initially defined by a private agreement, the State nonetheless has the responsibility of complying with the Fourteenth Amendment, and its action in judicially enforcing the covenant violated that Amendment. Judgment reversed.

Analysis:

In addition to the Fourteenth Amendment, a covenant that has a racially discriminatory effect may also violate the federal Fair Housing Act. This Act, passed as Title VIII of the Civil Rights Act of 1968, 42 U.S.C.A. §§3601-3631 (Supp. 1992) prohibits anyone from refusing to sell or rent, or otherwise make a dwelling unavailable, to another person on the basis of race, color, sex, religion, national origin, handicap, or familial status. In addition, §3604(c) of the Fair Housing Act. §3604(c) makes it unlawful to print or publish any statement, like a deed, which indicates a racial, religious, or ethnic preference with respect to the purchaser of a dwelling.

NEVADA SUPREME COURT HOLDS THAT WHERE A COMPANY WISHED TO BUILD A SHOPPING CENTER IN A RESIDENTIAL SUBDIVISION AFTER THE SURROUNDING AREA BECAME INCREASINGLY COMMERCIAL, THE RESIDENTIAL COVENANT COULD BE ENFORCED BECAUSE IT WAS STILL OF SUBSTANTIAL VALUE TO THE HOMEOWNERS

Western Land Co. v. Truskolaski

(Shopping Center Builder) v. (Homeowners in Subdivision)

(1972) 88 Nev. 200, 495 P.2d 624

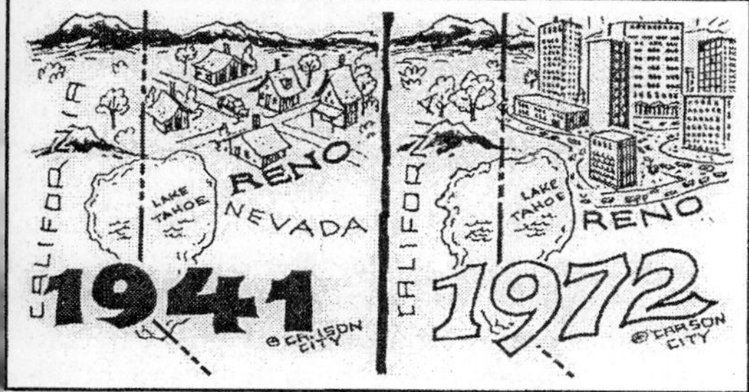

MEMORY GRAPHIC

Instant Facts

Homeowners want to prevent a shopping center from being built in their subdivision, even though the surrounding area has become more crowded and more commercialized.

Black Letter Rule

A restrictive covenant establishing a residential subdivision cannot be terminated as long as the residential character of the subdivision has not been adversely affected by the surrounding area, and it is of real and substantial value to the landowners within the subdivision.

Case Vocabulary

ARTERIAL: A street or highway where the traffic going through is given preference.
MERCANTILE: Relating to trade.
ZONING ORDINANCE: A municipal law dividing a city or town into districts with specific regulations regarding building use and construction.

Procedural Basis: Appeal from action seeking injunctive relief to enforce covenant.

Facts: In 1941, the Western Land Company (P) subdivided a forty-acre development southwest of Reno, outside the city limits. Western Land (P) subjected the lots to restrictive covenants which restricted them to single-family dwellings and prohibited any stores, butcher shops, grocery or mercantile business of any kind. The land around the subdivision was put to mainly residential and agricultural use, with very little commercial development. At the time, Plumb Lane, which bordered the subdivision to the south, went only as far east as one Arlington Avenue, and Reno had a population of about 20,000 people. By 1961, Plumb Lane had extended further east to one Virginia Street, and had been extended by the city of Reno into a four lane arterial boulevard. Plumb Lane had become the major east-west artery through the southern part of Reno. By 1969, Reno's population jumped up to roughly 95,100 people. In addition, a major shopping center had been built across from the east end of the subdivision, along with two more even further east. Despite these changes, the amount of traffic within the subdivision remained low. The homeowners (D) stated that this low level of traffic resulted in a safe living and playing environment for their (D) children. The homes in the subdivision were also very well maintained. The homeowners (D) brought an action in district court to enjoin Western Land (P) from building a shopping center on a 3.5 acre parcel in the subdivision. The court there held that the restrictive covenants were still enforceable, and Western Land (P) appealed.

Issue: Can a restrictive covenant for a residential subdivision be terminated when the nature of the surrounding area has changed and the homeowners within the subdivision still value the residential nature of the subdivision?

Decision and Rationale: (Batjer) No. A restrictive covenant establishing a residential subdivision cannot be terminated as long as the residential character of the subdivision has not been adversely affected by the surrounding area, and it is of real and substantial value to the landowners within the subdivision. There is enough evidence that the subdivision is still suitable for residential purposes despite the changed conditions of the area, and that the restrictions remain of substantial value to the landowners (D). The lower level of traffic has led to a safe environment for children which the landowners (D) value. This safety would likely be compromised if commercial traffic were allowed. Though Western Land (P) points to an intent by the Reno city council to rezone the area in question for commercial use, this intent does not prove that the property is more suited for commercial than residential use. A zoning ordinance does not override a private restriction, and a court cannot be forced to terminate a restrictive covenant merely because of a change in zoning. Even if the parcel in question would be more valuable if converted to commercial use, that does not permit Western Land (P) to escape its earlier restrictions. Other landowners (D) would still receive a substantial benefit from the enforcement of the restrictions. Moreover, though Western Land (P) points to violations by the landowners (Ds), including a nursery in one house and a contractor's office in another, the violations are too isolated to frustrate the purpose of the restrictions. Thus, they do not equal a waiver of the restrictions. Judgment affirmed.

Analysis:

Restatement (Third) Servitudes §7.10 adopts this change of conditions doctrine, allowing courts to terminate or modify servitudes based on changed circumstances. While the awarding of damages, instead of specific performance, as a remedy for breach of covenant has rarely been mentioned in cases denying an injunction, it does have the backing of several commentators. These persons support a damages remedy when multiple parties benefit from a covenant, making voluntary release impracticable, if not impossible.

NEW YORK SUPREME COURT HOLDS THAT WHERE NEIGHBORING LANDOWNERS ATTEMPTED TO SELL LAND IN THEIR RESIDENTIAL SUBDIVISION TO A HOSPITAL AND ONLY ONE LANDOWNER DID NOT WISH TO RELEASE THE RESTRICTIVE COVENANT, THE LOT OWNER HAS THE RIGHT TO INSIST UPON ADHERENCE TO THE COVENANT

Rick v. West

(Land Developer) v. (Uncompromising Landowner)
(1962) 34 Misc. 2d 1002, 228 N.Y.S.2d 195

M E M O R Y G R A P H I C

Instant Facts

West bought land from Rick under a restrictive covenant, and refused to release the covenant when Rick attempted to sell similar land to a hospital.

Black Letter Rule

A landowner in a subdivision under a restrictive covenant has the right to insist upon adherence to the covenant even when the other owners consent to its release.

Case Vocabulary

PECUNIARY DAMAGES: Any damages which can be compensated for with money.

Procedural Basis: Appeal from action to declare covenant unenforceable due to change of conditions.

Facts: Chester Rick (P) subdivided sixty-two acres of vacant land in 1946. Covenants that restricted the land to single-family dwellings were filed. In 1956, Rick (P) sold a half-acre lot to Catherine West (D), and there she (D) built a house. In 1957, the land was zoned for residential use. Rick (P) later contracted for the sale of forty-five acres to an industrialist, with the sale being conditioned upon the tract being rezoned for industrial use. The forty-five acres was rezoned, but the sale fell through after West (D) refused to release the covenant. After selling only a few more lots, Rick (P) conveyed the remaining land to the other lot owners (P). In 1961, they (P) contracted to sell fifteen acres from the tract to Peekskill Hospital, but again West (D) refused to consent to the release of the covenant. The other owners (P) sued, claiming the covenant was no longer enforceable because of a change in conditions. The trial court held for West (D) and the other owners (P) appealed.

Issue: Is a restrictive covenant still enforceable when only one landowner in a subdivision refuses to consent to the release of the covenant?

Decision and Rationale: (Hoyt) Yes. A landowner in a subdivision under a restrictive covenant has the right to insist upon adherence to the covenant even when the other owners consent to its release. In 1946, Rick (P) owned the land free and clear of all restrictions, and had the right to do what he felt was best for the property. Rick (P) chose to turn it into a residential development, and to encourage purchase of the resulting lots, he (P) imposed the residential restrictions. West (D) relied upon those restrictions when she (D) purchased the property and she (D) has the right to continue relying on them. The balancing of equities and the potential advantages of having a hospital on the property are irrelevant. The fact that West (D) is the only person opposed to releasing the covenant does not make her (D) right to have the covenant enforced any less deserving of this court's protection. She (D) has done nothing but insist upon adherence to a covenant which is just as binding as it was when she (D) and the other owners (P) entered it. Her (D) refusal to release the covenant, resulting from her satisfaction with the covenant as it stands, must be protected. Judgment affirmed.

Analysis:

Rick demonstrates the same issue as *Western Land*, only to a greater degree. In *Western Land*, a small minority blocked development; in *Rick*, a *single* holdout stands in the way of commercial progress. The argument against these decisions is utilitarian; allowing a few holdouts to prevent commercial efficiency seemingly violates the utilitarian ideal of "the greatest good for the greatest number." Economists might argue that the person resisting change should be forced to pay damages for the value that cannot be created because of him. But courts generally recognize holdouts' reliance interests. However, note that the latest *Restatement* gives courts considerable leeway to terminate servitudes or modify them because of changed conditions. *Restatement (Third) of Property, Servitudes § 7.10.* Still, it remains to be seen whether judges will exercise this discretion.

Pocono Springs Civic Association, Inc. v. MacKenzie

(Homeowner's Association) v. (Landowners)
446 Pa. Super. 445, 667 A.2d 233 (Penn. 1995)

MEMORY GRAPHIC

Instant Facts

The owners of a vacant lot in a housing development attempted to abandon the lot in order to avoid having to pay association fees.

Black Letter Rule

A covenant running with the land cannot be terminated by abandonment when the owner still holds title in fee simple absolute.

Case Vocabulary

PERFECT TITLE: Title representing absolute right of possession, as in a fee simple absolute, which is valid beyond all reasonable doubt.

Procedural Basis: Appeal of order granting summary judgment for plaintiffs in action to recover unpaid dues.

Facts: Joseph and Doris MacKenzie (D) had owned a vacant lot in a housing development since 1969. Tired of paying association fees on the vacant land, the MacKenzies (D) decided to sell their lot in 1987. However, they were unable to find a buyer because the property was not suitable for an on-lot sewage system. The MacKenzies (D) then made several attempts to abandon their property and avoid further association fees. First, the MacKenzies (D) attempted unsuccessfully to turn the lot over to the Pocono Springs Civic Association, Inc. (the "Association") (P). They then ceased paying property taxes. Although the Tax Claim Bureau offered the property for sale, there were no takers. Finally, the MacKenzies (D) mailed a notarized statement to "all interested parties" expressing their desire to abandon the lot, and the MacKenzies (D) ceased paying the association fees. The Association (P) sued the MacKenzies (D) for payment. At trial, the MacKenzies (D) defended on grounds that they had abandoned the lot. The trial court held that the abandonment defense was invalid and granted summary judgment in favor of the Association (P). The MacKenzies (D) appeal.

Issue: Can property be considered "abandoned" even though the owner still possesses perfect title?

Decision and Rationale: (Rowley, J.) No. Property cannot be considered "abandoned" when the owner still possesses perfect title. Pursuant to Pennsylvania law, abandoned property is that to which an owner has voluntarily relinquished all right, title, claim and possession with the intention of terminating his ownership, but without vesting it in any other person and with the intention of not reclaiming further possession or resuming ownership. The MacKenzies (D) have not relinquished their rights or title to their lot. They remain owners of real property in fee simple. Neither title nor deed has been sold or transferred. Thus, based upon our definition of "abandonment," the MacKenzies' (D) defense must fail. Despite their intent to the contrary, they have not abandoned their property. Affirmed.

Analysis:

Just what does it take for poor Mr. and Mrs. MacKenzie (D) to unload this burdensome piece of land? They tried to sell it, to give it away, and to have it foreclosed upon. They sent a letter to their neighbors expressing their intent to abandon. They never lived on the land, and probably had not set foot on it in years. Nevertheless, they were required to continue paying association fees simply because no one else wanted the land. Besides the obvious unfairness in the result, this opinion is logically inconsistent. After the opinion quotes the definition of "abandonment," it states that "perfect title . . . cannot be abandoned" and then later notes that "real property cannot be abandoned." Then what kind of property *can* be abandoned? Personal property only? If this is the case, why does the opinion quote the definition of "abandonment" at all? Indeed, if the definition were controlling, the MacKenzies (D) presumably could prevail in the action. It seems that the MacKenzies (D) did everything they could to voluntarily relinquish all right and title to the land, as required by the quoted definition. But if their perfect title cannot be abandoned, perhaps they are eternally out of luck. Something is wrong, however, with a ruling that imposes an eternal duty to continue to pay association fees on property that the owners do not want and cannot give away. Under the modern Restatement (Third), Property Servitudes §7.12, the result would be different; covenants to pay maintenance fees terminate after a reasonable time.

CALIFORNIA COURT OF APPEAL, SECOND DISTRICT, HOLDS THAT WHERE A CONDOMINIUM ASSOCIATION LEVIED FINES AGAINST A UNIT OWNER FOR VIOLATING A RESTRICTION AGAINST ANIMALS IN HER UNIT, SUCH A BLANKET PET RESTRICTION WAS OVERLY BROAD AND THUS WAS UNREASONABLE

Nahrstedt v. Lakeside Village Condominium Association, Inc.

(Cat Owner) v. (Condominium Association)

(1992) 11 Cal. Rptr. 2d 299, hearing granted by Calif. Sup. Ct

M E M O R Y   G R A P H I C

Instant Facts

Nahrstedt wants to continue living with her three cats in her condominium, in violation of the recorded covenants, conditions and restrictions governing the condominium.

Black Letter Rule

The enforceability of restrictions on the ownership and possession of pets should be decided in a trial court after evidence is heard as to whether the restriction was reasonable as applied to the particular facts of a case.

Case Vocabulary

DEMURRER: A claim by a defendant that, even if all the plaintiff's allegations in the complaint are true, the plaintiff has not successfully raised a cause of action to force the defendant to respond.

FIDUCIARY: Describes a person who has a special duty involving the good faith or trust of another.

Procedural Basis: Appeal from sustaining of demurrers without leav to amend in action for declaratory relief, invasion of privacy, negligent an intentional infliction of emotional distress, and invalidation of levied fines.

Facts: Natore Nahrstedt (P) lives in a condominium at the Lakeside Villag complex. Article VII, section 11 of the recorded covenants, conditions, an restrictions (CC & Rs) on the condominium provides that "no animals (which sha mean dogs and cats) ...shall be kept in any unit" and that "the Association (D shall have the right to prohibit maintenance of any pet which constitutes, in th opinion of the Board [of Directors of the homeowners association], a nuisance t any other owner." She (P) owns three pet cats, which she (P) claims make n noise and are not a nuisance. The Association (D) has allegedly harassed her (P by imposing increasingly large fines as a penalty for the cats. Nahrstedt (P) file this action to obtain, among other things, a declaration that she (P) is entitled t keep the cats, in spite of the CC & Rs, and that she (P) has no legal obligation t pay the fines. Nahrstedt (P) argues that the restriction was unreasonable unde Civil Code section 1354 [restrictions in the declaration of CC & Rs shall b enforceable equitable servitudes unless unreasonable]. The trial court sustained without leave to amend, demurrers on all five causes of action in Nahrstedt's (P original complaint.

Issue: Can a condominium association's enforcement of a restriction on pet be considered reasonable by a court without hearing evidence on th circumstances of the homeowner challenging the restriction?

Decision and Rationale: (Croskey) No. The enforceability o restrictions on the ownership and possession of pets should be decided in a tri court, after evidence is heard as to whether the restriction was reasonable a applied to the particular facts of the homeowner challenging them. Th Association (D) claims the pet restriction was reasonable and enforceable becaus it protects the Association (D) from always needing to litigate against homeowne whose pets are causing problems. This argument goes against the logic of th court in *Bernardo Villas Management Corp. v. Black* (1987) 190 Cal. App. 3d 153 235 Cal. Rptr. 509 [provision allowing parking of trucks only for loading an unloading held unreasonable when applied to clean noncommercial pickup trucks and the court in *Portola Hills Community Assn. v. James* (1992) 4 Cal. App. 4t 289, 5 Cal. Rptr. 2d 580 [ban on satellite dishes in planned community hel unreasonable when dish not visible to other community residents], which is t judge situations on their own specific facts. Nahrstedt's (P) home is her castl and she should enjoy it by the least restrictive means possible. The Association' (D) argument could be extended to support all-inclusive bans on anything fro stereo equipment to visitors under eighteen years of age. Blanket restriction against such things likely would not be reasonable, and it is certainly possible th a trial court would consider Nahrstedt's (P) three cats to be less of a threat to th peace and quiet in the complex. The trial court should hear evidence on th circumstances surrounding Nahrstedt's (P) ownership of the cats. Judgment c dismissal reversed, and cause remanded.

Dissent: (Hinz) Courts should have the power to rule on these matters the demurrer stage, because an association has a duty to its members to enfor restrictions. If an association were forced to litigate every matter, such litigatio paid for by the mandatory fees of each property owner, would become ve expensive. The majority's ruling only encourages prolonged litigation, whic would burden both the courts and the parties involved. Condominium livin involves increased density and intensified use of common areas, and so necessarily requires that individual unit owners relinquish some of the freedoms they would enjoy if they lived in separate property. The other residents at Lakeside Village apparently desired pet-free conditions, and Nahrstedt (P) consented to those conditions. The restriction is reasonable, and should be enforced. The demurrer should be sustained.

Analysis:

Recent cases involving homeowners associations demonstrate that there is far more litigation with condominium homeowners associations than there is for associations of owners of detached, single-family homes. Most cases involve faulty construction suits against the builder of the condominium, tort suits by an individual owner against the association, or suits by the association against a unit owner for improper activity. Such activity has included everything from unauthorized fences to repairing a car in the project's driveway.

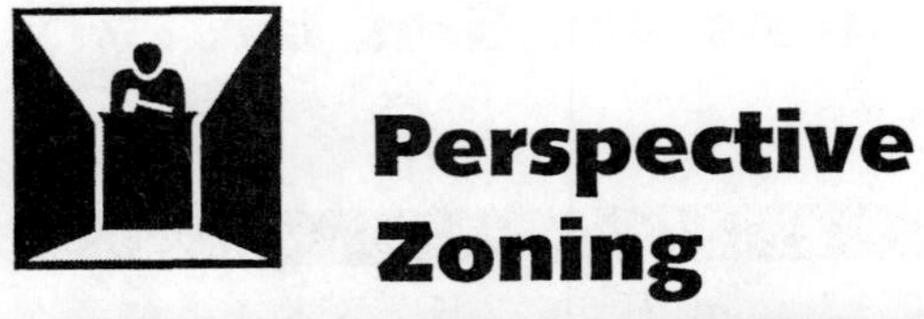

Perspective
Zoning

Chapter 11

In the previous chapter, nuisance law, otherwise known as "judicial zoning" was discussed. Here, the cases will focus on land use laws passed by local legislatures. These laws, known as zoning ordinances, attempt to confine different types of property uses and sizes of buildings and land lots to separate zones in one comprehensive plan. The cases will also discuss how these regulations are put into practice by various administrative and legislative bodies.

First, this chapter will discuss some of the fundamental concepts behind zoning, as well as how these concepts have developed over time. Then, the way zoning laws respond to property uses that do not conform to the overall zoning plan will be covered. A large part of the chapter will look at ways property owners and developers try to get around the more rigid aspects of zoning regulations. Such devices include variances, zoning amendments, floating zones, cluster zones, and planned unit developments. All these devices will be explained later.

This chapter will also help clarify how the government's zoning power has been expanded in recent years. This power now includes the ability to deny permits for buildings which do not conform in appearance to neighboring buildings and exclude people with unusual living arrangements from residing in a particular area. Finally, questions regarding the necessity of zoning will be considered. Particular attention will be paid to the example of Houston which grew and developed without a comprehensive zoning plan.

Chapter Overview Outline
Zoning

Chapter 11

NOTE: THE PURPOSE OF THIS OUTLINE IS TO ORGANIZE THE CASES SO THAT ONE CAN QUICKLY UNDERSTAND THE RELEVANCE OF EACH CASE TO THE COURSE. NO ATTEMPT IS MADE IN THIS OVERVIEW TO ADDRESS EVERY CONCEPT THAT MUST BE STUDIED. BE SURE TO READ THE ENTIRE CASEBOOK AND/OR OTHER MATERIALS TO GAIN A FULL UNDERSTANDING OF ALL CONCEPTS.

I. Introduction
- A. The Historical Development of "Zoning"
  - 1. In the beginning of the twentieth century, "zoning" was the preferable method used by so-called city planners to prevent harmful effects to neighborhoods.
    - a. Zoning and planning developed from the "City Beautiful" movement—derived from an architectural exhibition at the 1893 Chicago World's Fair—wherein cities would be beautified with huge civic monuments and public works.
    - b. Zoning ordinances were favored over "nuisance law" or "restrictive covenants" because:
      - (1) Courts were reluctant to declare something a "nuisance" unless it was extremely objectionable, and nuisance law did not allow for prevention, but rather only damages or an injunction after the fact; and,
      - (2) Restrictive covenants could not be used in connection with urban area neighborhoods, with multiple owners.
  - 2. As the use of "zoning ordinances" rapidly increased, so too did constitutional challenges to them. Common grounds for attack were that the ordinances amounted to a taking of property without compensation or deprivation of property without due process of law. The issue became ripe for the United States Supreme Court in 1926.
    - a. The Supreme Court held that zoning ordinances were a valid exercise of the police power and did not violate the constitutional protection of property rights under the Due Process Clause. *Village of Euclid v. Ambler Realty Co.* [upholding zoning ordinance that created "use" districts and restricted certain districts to that of industrial use.]
    - b. Similar zoning ordinances are now referred to as "Euclidean" zoning, where the districts are rated from highest to lowest, with single-family residences being at the top and the worst possible industry being at the bottom.
      - (1) Higher uses are allowed in the lower zoned areas, but lower uses are not allowed in the higher zoned areas.
- B. The Standard State Zoning Enabling Act
  - 1. In 1922, The Standard State Zoning Enabling Act was issued by a federal advisory committee on zoning, and has since been adopted by virtually all states in the country. A state's adoption of the Act authorizes local municipalities to engage in zoning. The Act gives power to:
    - a. Regulate and restrict the height, number of stories, and size of buildings and other structures, the percentage of lot that may be occupied, the size of yards, courts, and other open spaces, the density of population, and the location and use of buildings, structures, and land for trade, industry, residence, or other purposes.
    - b. Divide the municipality into districts of such number, shape, and area as is best suited, and regulate and restrict within such districts the erection, construction, reconstruction, alteration, repair, or use of buildings, structures, or land.
  - 2. The Act further provides that such regulations shall be made in accordance with a comprehensive plan and designed to lessen congestion in the streets; to secure safety from fire, panic, and other dangers; to promote health and the general welfare; to provide adequate light and air; to prevent the overcrowding of land; to avoid undue concentration of population; to facilitate

the adequate provision of transportation, water, sewerage, schools, parks, and other public requirements.

a. Only approximately fifty percent of the states require a "comprehensive plan," and even then, they are not strictly enforced.

C. Some states have recently enacted their own statutes that differ substantially from the Standard Act.

II. The Nonconforming Use

A. If a zoning law or regulation has the effect of depriving a property owner of the lawful pre-existing nonconforming use of his or her property, it amounts to a taking for which the owner must be justly compensated. *PA Northwestern Distributors, Inc. v. Zoning Hearing Board* [Zoning ordinance that gave pre-existing adult bookstore 90-days to comply declared unconstitutional under State Constitution that prohibits government interference with owner's use of his property without compensation to the owner.]

1. The protection of a nonconforming use "runs with the land," and not with the owner. Thus, as long as the use is maintained, it can survive a change of ownership.

2. Destruction or abandonment of a nonconforming use most often will terminate it.

B. "Amortization" refers to a provision in a zoning ordinance that requires the termination of nonconformities—usually nonconforming *use*, such as when the use of the land does not conform to the new zoning ordinance—within a certain specified time.

1. The amortization period is the subject of judicial uncertainty, with some courts favoring a short period and others favoring a much longer period.

C. The "vested rights" doctrine provides that a *proposed plan* to use the property in a particular manner may be protected if firm commitments have been made in reliance on existing laws, but subsequent changes will invalidate the proposed use.

III. Flexible Devices Used In Zoning

A. Variances and Special Exceptions

1. A zoning board shall have the power to grant a *variance* where because of some exceptional situation of the property, the strict application of a zoning ordinance would result in undue hardship upon the developer of the property, and the variance would not substantially impair the public good and the intent and purpose of the zone plan and ordinance. *Commons v. Westwood Zoning Board of Adjustment* [involving an area variance with respect to size of house in relation to size of lot.]

a. A "use" variance—relaxing restrictions on use—requires a greater showing of hardship than an "area" variance.

2. An *exception* is a use permitted by the ordinance, granted if certain criteria are met.

a. The power to regulate private property cannot be delegated from the legislature to a municipality or from a municipality to a local administrative body without a sufficiently detailed statement of policy to provide a guide to reasonably determine an owner's rights and prevent arbitrariness. *Cope v. Inhabitants of the Town of Brunswick* [Invalidating an ordinance that permitted apartment buildings only if granted as an exception by a local zoning board of appeals.]

b. Some jurisdictions, however, do permit the type of special exceptions approach set forth in *Cope*.

B. Amendments to Zoning Ordinances

1. A municipality's amendment of a zoning ordinance is a legislative act—under the municipality's delegated police powers—and the amendment will be upheld unless it is shown that it is unsupported by any rational basis related to promoting the public health, safety, morals or general

welfare, or that it amounts to a taking without compensation. *State v. City of Rochester.*

a. Some jurisdictions treat zoning amendments as quasi-judicial acts rather than legislative acts, which involve undeferential reviews. *Fasano v. Board of County Commissioners.* [Rejected by the majority in *State v. City of Rochester* and later overruled in part by the Oregon Supreme Court]

2. "Spot zoning" is an invalid zoning amendment, which creates a use classification inconsistent with surrounding uses and creates an island of nonconforming use within a larger zoned district, and which dramatically reduces the value for uses specified in the zoning ordinance of either the rezoned plot or abutting property.
3. "Conditional rezoning" occurs when the landowner agrees, unilaterally, to use the property in a certain way.
4. "Contract rezoning" occurs when the landowner and the zoning agency enter into a contract whereby they agree to specific terms concerning the property, such as where the owner agrees to a restricted use of the property and the zoning authority agrees to rezone.
5. "Floating zones" are used by some states to define a zone but yet determine its location in the future.
6. "Cluster zones" allow for development in a manner that is not strictly in compliance with the zoning ordinance, such as frontage and setback regulations. Because open spaces are maintained as part of the cluster, the population destiny is not increased even though there is not strict adherence to the regulations.
7. "Planned Unit Developments" or "PUDs" involve variations in both area and use, such as mixing residential, commercial, and sometimes industrial uses.

IV. Modern Day Zoning Aims

A. Zoning ordinances are now used as a means to regulate "aesthetics," to control household composition, and to control the nature and size of the local populations.

B. Aesthetics Zoning

1. Early judicial decisions held that zoning, as a function of the state's police power, could be used to further public health, safety, and general welfare, but not for solely aesthetic purposes.
   a. Public outrage concerning billboards caused courts to uphold ordinances outlawing them on public health and safety grounds—they could fall on someone or block sunlight and air—but the underlying reason was aesthetics.
   b. In the 1950s, many courts upheld zoning ordinances based solely on aesthetic considerations.
2. Some courts have upheld zoning ordinances that place restrictions on the design of houses based upon aesthetics and the fact that the unsuitable appearance would adversely affect the property values of the community. *State ex rel. Stoyanoff v. Berkeley.*
3. Even those courts that approve public building regulations purely upon aesthetic grounds still require them to provide clear standards and guidance to all interested parties. Ordinances that use subjective terms such as "appropriate proportions" and harmony with "the natural setting of the valley" and "monotony should be avoided" have been held unconstitutionally vague. *Anderson v. City of Issaquah.*
   a. However, specific standards are not required when *private,* as opposed to *public*, architectural restrictions are involved; rather, the committee is only required to act reasonably and in good faith.

b. Thus, it is possible to have a public zoning restriction that violates the Constitution, but is nevertheless valid as a private zoning restriction.

4. A city may not constitutionally adopt ordinances that prohibit all or almost all signs on residential property, even if such ordinances are intended solely to prevent visual clutter. Such ordinances impose too great of a restriction on free speech. *City of Ladue v. Gilleo.*

C. Zoning to Control Household Composition

1. The legislature may define what counts as a "family" for zoning purposes if the definition is rationally related to legitimate objectives, such as creating zones where family values, youth values, and the blessings of quiet seclusion and clean air are preserved. *Village of Belle Terre v. Boraas.*

   a. The Supreme Court invalidated a single-family zoning ordinance that limited the definition of "family" to no more than one set of grandchildren, distinguishing *Belle Terre* on the ground that the earlier case dealt with unrelated individuals only. *Moore v. City of East Cleveland.*

2. The Federal Fair Housing Act (FHA) allows cities to regulate the maximum number of individuals who can live in a house.

   a. A single-family zoning regulation is not automatically exempt from FHA scrutiny, even if it indirectly limits the maximum number of occupants in a house. *City of Edmonds v. Oxford House, Inc.*

D. Zoning To Exclude The Nature of the Local Population

1. A developing municipality must make, b its land use regulations, realistically possibl the opportunity for an appropriate variet and choice of housing for all categories c people who may desire to live there, includ ing those of low and moderate income Thus, it cannot establish regulations tha make it impossible for low and moderate income families to reside there. *Souther Burlington County NAACP v. Township c Mount Laurel.*

2. Communities have attempted to impos various requirements, which although nc blatantly discriminatory, have the effect c excluding certain segments of the popula tion.

   a. Minimum housing-cost requiremen have been invalidated by the courts.

   b. Minimum floor-area requirements, usu ally in connection with the number c residents in a dwelling, have been uphel by some courts, and invalidated by oth ers. Often, these requirements we superceded by housing codes that regu lated various aspects of housing design

   c. Minimum lot-size requirements usual are upheld.

   d. Minimum setback requirements are usu ally upheld.

   e. The barring of mobile or manufacture homes was almost always upheld, bu some recent decisions have rejected th ordinances.

E. Inclusionary Zoning

   a. Inclusionary zoning ordinances are de signed to require or encourage develope to provide communities with low- ar moderate-income housing.

UNITED STATES SUPREME COURT HOLDS THAT A MUNICIPAL ZONING ORDINANCE WHICH CREATES AND MAINTAINS DIFFERENT TYPES OF RESIDENTIAL DISTRICTS, WHILE EXCLUDING BUSINESSES FROM SUCH DISTRICTS, IS CONSTITUTIONAL

Village of Euclid v. Ambler Realty Co.

(Suburb) v. (Landowner)
(1926) 272 U.S. 365

M E M O R Y G R A P H I C

Instant Facts

A realty company challenged a municipal ordinance which established a zoning plan restricting the use and size of buildings in various districts.

Black Letter Rule

Zoning ordinances are a valid exercise of the police power and thus do not violate the constitutional protection of property rights.

Case Vocabulary

CLEW: Old English spelling of "clue."
DEROGATION: Act of discrediting or belittling.
MUNICIPALITY: A legally incorporated association of residents in a relatively small area for governmental or other public purposes; another term for town, village or city.
PARALLELOGRAM: A geometric figure with two pairs of parallel and equal sides, such as a rectangle or square.
SANITARIUM: A medical institution for the care of invalids or convalescing patients.

Procedural Basis: Appeal from order granting injunction against enforcement of ordinance.

Facts: The Village of Euclid (D) is essentially a suburb of the City of Cleveland. Most of this land is used for farms or undeveloped. Ambler Realty Co. (P) owns a 68-acre tract of land in the western end of the village. This tract is bordered by a principal highway, Euclid Avenue, to the south, and by a major railroad, the Nickel Plate, to the north. There are residential lots with buildings to the east and west of Ambler Realty's (P) land. In 1922, the Village Council (D) adopted a comprehensive zoning plan to regulate and restrict the use of land, as well as the size of the lots and the heights of buildings. This ordinance divided the village into six use districts, U-1 to U-6. Each higher-numbered district included the uses of the district below it. Thus, U-1 districts allowed only single-family dwellings, while U-2 districts were extended to include two-family dwellings along with U-1 uses; U-3 districts were extended to include public buildings like churches, schools, hospitals with U-2 uses, and so on. U-6 districts could be used for sewage plants and junkyards, as well as for all residential and industrial operations below this level. The ordinance also divides the village into three height districts, H-1 to H-3, and four area districts, A-1 to A-4. The zone map attached to this ordinance shows that the use, area, and height districts are all allowed to overlap one another. The ordinance is enforced by the inspector of buildings under the board of zoning appeals. This board is authorized to make rules in order to implement the ordinance, as well as impose penalties for violations. The board can also interpret the ordinance in harmony with its general purpose and intent, so that the public health, safety, and general welfare may be protected. Ambler Realty's (P) land itself falls under the U-2, U-3, and U-6 districts. Ambler Realty (P) claims this land is vacant and that it has been held in order to sell and develop it for industrial uses. If Ambler Realty's (P) land is used for industrial purposes, it is worth about $10,000 per acre, but if it is kept for residential use, it is only worth roughly $2,500 per acre. The records indicate the normal and reasonably expected use of the land facing Euclid Avenue is for industrial and trade purposes. Ambler Realty (P) claims the ordinance violates its (P) constitutional rights, at both the state and federal levels, against deprivation of property and liberty without due process of law and denies it (P) the equal protection of the law.

Issue: Is it unconstitutional to enact an ordinance which establishes a comprehensive zoning plan regulating the use of property?

Decision and Rationale: (Sutherland) No. Zoning ordinances are a valid exercise of the police power and thus do not violate the constitutional protection of property rights. It is not necessary to decide separately if this ordinance violates the Ohio Constitution, as the question is substantively the same. Building zone laws are relatively new, yet are clearly necessary and valid. The increasing urbanization of modern life has required the use of regulations which, fifty years ago, would have been considered arbitrary or oppressive. While the meaning behind constitutional guarantees is constant, they must be applied in ways to meet the new conditions of life. The ordinance under review, then, must be justified through some aspect of the police power. This line is not a clear one, but must vary with circumstances and conditions. As with the law of nuisances, the maxim *sic utere tuo ut alienum non laedas* can serve as a guide. The building of a structure should be considered after the building itself is looked at in connection with the circumstances and its surroundings. No one has doubted the validity of regulations regarding the height of buildings within reasonable limits, the materials used in construction, the exclusion of certain trades from residential areas, etc. The Village (D), though essentially a suburb of Cleveland, is nonetheless a separate political body. As such, it has the power to govern itself as it sees fit within the limits of the Ohio and Federal Constitutions. Here, the serious question is over the exclusion of apartment houses, stores and shops, and other similar establishments from residential areas. The state courts that deny or narrow this power are greatly outnumbered by the state courts that sustain it. Various commissions and experts have reported for the separation of residential, business, and industrial buildings. They have pointed to the ease of providing appropriate firefighting measures in each section; increased safety, especially for children, by reducing traffic in residential areas; and increased home security. Also, the distracting of apartment houses helps preserve the quiet, open character of single-family neighborhoods, while preventing heavy traffic, overcrowding, and excessive noise. If nothing else, these reasons are enough to counter any arguments that the ordinance is arbitrary, unreasonable, or not substantially related to the public health, safety, morals, or general welfare. Unless such arbitrariness and unreasonableness is proven, the ordinance cannot be declared unconstitutional. Granted, it is entirely possible that the provisions set forth in a zoning ordinance may be found to be clearly arbitrary or unreasonable in a specific situation. When an injunction is sought, however, because the mere existence or threat of enforcement of the ordinance may cause an injury, the court will not go over the ordinance, sentence by sentence, to find which parts are constitutional and which parts are not. Without a specific complaint of actual injury, a land owner cannot challenge the constitutionality of such an ordinance. Decree reversed.

Analysis:

The seeds of four dominant themes in legislative zoning are planted in this opinion. First, there is the idea that a city or municipality is allowed to exclude some uses of property in certain circumstances. Second, the court essentially allows the same government body to control the economic markets, in a way, by designating where areas of trade can be set up. Third, the court places emphasis on local control in zoning measures, particularly when it establishes early in its opinion that Euclid is a separate governing entity. Finally, the court places some emphasis on aesthetic values, and how these can be a valid basis for a zoning ordinance in the appropriate context. This concept can be found in the discussion on separating apartment buildings from other residences. These concepts are mentioned throughout various judicial opinions and treatises on legislative zoning.

PENNSYLVANIA SUPREME COURT HOLDS THAT A ZONING ORDINANCE THAT REGULATED ADULT BUSINESSES AND GAVE AN ADULT BOOKSTORE OWNER A NINETY-DAY AMORTIZATION PERIOD IN WHICH TO COMPLY WITH THE ORDINANCE WAS AN UNCONSTITUTIONAL TAKING OF PROPERTY WITHOUT JUST COMPENSATION

PA Northwestern Distributors, Inc. v. Zoning Hearing Board

(Adult Bookstore Owner) v. (Local Zoning Board)
(1991) 526 Pa. 186, 584 A.2d 1372

M E M O R Y   G R A P H I C

Instant Facts

After an adult bookstore was opened, a local zoning board enacted an adult business ordinance which gave the bookstore operator only ninety days to comply.

Black Letter Rule

If a zoning law or regulation has the effect of depriving a property owner of the lawful pre-existing nonconforming use of his or her property, it amounts to a taking for which the owner must be justly compensated.

Case Vocabulary

AMORTIZATION: As used in zoning matters, provisions in zoning ordinances that require the termination of nonconformities--where land does not conform to new zoning ordinances--within a certain specified time..
ATTRITION: Wearing away or erosion.

Procedural Basis: Appeal from order denying appeal to zoning board.

Facts: On May 4, 1985, PA Northwestern Distributors, Inc. (P), or PAND (P), opened an adult bookstore in Moon Township, Pennsylvania. Four days later, the local Board of Supervisors published a notice of its intention to amend the Moon Township Zoning Ordinance to regulate "adult commercial enterprises." A public hearing followed, and on May 23, 1985, the Board of Supervisors adopted Ordinance No. 243, effective May 28, 1985. This ordinance imposes extensive restrictions on the location and operation of adult commercial enterprises. It also includes an amortization provision which gave all those who operated pre-existing businesses in conflict with this ordinance a period of ninety days to comply. PAND's (P's) bookstore, by definition, is an adult commercial enterprise under Ordinance No. 243, and it does not fall into any of the areas designated for such businesses by the ordinance. The Zoning Officer of Moon Township informed PAND (P) that the bookstore did not comply with the ordinance. PAND (P) then filed an appeal to the Zoning Hearing Board of Moon Township (D), challenging the validity of this ninety-day provision. After a hearing, the Board (D) upheld the validity of the ordinance as applied. PAND (P) then filed an appeal to the Court of Common Pleas of Allegheny County. No further evidence was taken, and the appeal was dismissed. This decision was appealed, and the Commonwealth Court affirmed, citing *Sullivan v. Zoning Board of Adjustment*, 83 Pa. Commw. 228, 478 A.2d 912 (1984) [provisions for the amortization of nonconforming uses are constitutional exercises of the police power so long as they are reasonable.]. The Commonwealth Court held that the "real and substantial benefits to the Township of elimination of the nonconforming use from this location ... more than offset the losses to the affected landowner," and ruled against PAND (P). PAND (P) then appealed to the Pennsylvania Supreme Court.

Issue: Is an ordinance which has the effect of depriving a property owner of a nonconforming use of his or her property constitutional when such use was pre-existing and lawful?

Decision and Rationale: (Larsen) No. Sullivan is not a correct statement of the law regarding amortization provisions. Amortization is not a reasonable means of zoning regulation. In Pennsylvania, all property is held subject to the right of reasonable regulation by the government that is necessary to preserve the health, safety, morals, or general welfare of the people. A zoning ordinance is generally presumed to be valid. That presumption, however must be balanced by an individual's constitutionally guaranteed right to use property without government restrictions, except when his or her use creates a nuisance or violates a covenant, restriction, or easement. It has long been the law of this Commonwealth that local governments cannot compel a change in the nature of an existing lawful use of property. A lawful nonconforming use establishes a vested property right in its owner that cannot be infringed upon unless it is a nuisance, it is abandoned, or it is extinguished by eminent domain. If a zoning law or regulation has the effect of depriving a property owner of the lawful pre-existing nonconforming use of his or her property, it amounts to a taking for which the owner must be justly compensated. Here, the amortization provision deprives PAND (P) of the lawful use of its property by forcing it to cease its business operations there within ninety days. The Pennsylvania Constitution protects the right of a property owner to use his or her property in any lawful way that he or she chooses. This ordinance restricts future uses and extinguishes a present lawful nonconforming use against the owner's wishes. If municipalities were allowed to amortize nonconforming uses out of existence, economic development could be seriously compromised, with investors afraid of changes in the zoning laws. Further, any use could be subsequently amortized out of existence without just compensation to the property owner. No use and no property owner would be safe. Judgment reversed.

Concurrence: (Nix) The Sullivan decision should be upheld, because a reasonable amortization provision is valid if it reflects the consideration of several factors. Any blanket rule against amortization provisions would prevent effective zoning, unnecessarily restrict a state's police power, and prevent the elimination of nonconforming uses to further the public interest. Several factors have been used to determine the reasonableness of amortization, including the duration of the investment in the property use; the length of the amortization period in relation to the nonconforming use; and the degree of offensiveness of the nonconforming use to the character of the surrounding neighborhood. A community should have the right to change its character without being locked into outdated definitions of what is or is not offensive. Here, the amortization provision is not a reasonable one as it does not provide adequate time for the nonconforming use to be eliminated. Ninety days is not enough time to allow a merchant to close a business and settle contractual obligations. Moreover, such a period is not enough for PAND (P) to find an alternative means of income or obtain a reasonable return on its (P) investment. Commonwealth Court order reversed.

Analysis:

This protection of a nonconforming use "runs with the land," and not with the owner. Thus, as long as the use is maintained, it can survive a change of ownership. If, however, a landowner abandons that nonconforming use, the right to continue that use may be terminated. In addition, expanding the scope of the use (bigger stores, increased business, etc.) can also lead to a termination of the right. Occasionally, communities attempt to discourage undesirable businesses from entering their areas by enacting ordinances which set limits on expansion and renovation, or prevent owners from repairing nonconforming structures when damaged.

Commons v. Westwood Zoning Board of Adjustment

(Landowners) v. (Local Zoning Board)

(1980) 81 N.J. 597, 410 A.2d 1138

MEMORY GRAPHIC

Instant Facts

A builder trying to construct a home on a lot that was below the local zoning ordinance's minimum size requirements was denied a variance.

Black Letter Rule

A zoning board shall have the power to grant a variance where because of some exceptional situation of the property, the strict application of a zoning ordinance would result in undue hardship upon the developer of the property, and the variance would not substantially impair the public good and the intent and purpose of the zone plan and ordinance.

Case Vocabulary

BOROUGH: An incorporated, self-governing town.

FRONTAGE: The front side of a lot, or the side facing the street.

SETBACK: The distance between the front side of a lot or the street and the structure on that lot.

VARIANCE: Permission given to a landowner to use his or her property in a manner that is otherwise prohibited by a zoning ordinance.

Procedural Basis: Appeal from judgment affirming denial of zoning variance.

Facts: Gordon and Helen Commons (P) own a vacant lot in the Borough of Westwood. It is the only undeveloped property in an established neighborhood of one and two-family homes. The Commons (P) and their predecessors in title have owned this land since 1927. Leo Weingarten (P), a builder, contracted to buy the land on the condition that he (P) could construct a one-family residence on the lot. This lot has a frontage (side facing the street) of only 30 feet and a total area of 5,190 square feet. The original zoning ordinance, enacted in 1933, had no minimum frontage or area provisions. In 1947, however, the ordinance was amended to require a minimum frontage of 75 feet and a minimum area of 7,500 feet. At that time, most of the homes did not satisfy the frontage requirement. This situation has remained essentially unchanged since that time. Weingarten (P) proposed to build a single-family home on the lot. He (P) had no architectural design of the actual house, but proposed scaled-down version of larger designs. The home would be centered on the 30-foot lot in order to provide the minimum five-foot sideyards required by the ordinance. The home's distance from the street would also conform to the zoning ordinance. A local Realtor also testified that the proposed home would not impair the zoning plan because it would be new, its value would be comparable to that of neighboring homes, and the distances from the street and neighboring homes would be substantial. In 1974, Gordon Commons (P) offered to sell the lot to one neighbor for $7,500. Negotiations ended after that neighbor countered with a $1,600 offer. Weingarten (P), when contracting to buy the lot, also unsuccessfully attempted to purchase a 10-foot strip of land from another neighbor. Many neighbors opposed the Commons' and Weingarten's (P) application for a variance, citing aesthetic reasons, lowered property values, and the possibility of excessive noise and trespassing. The Westwood Zoning Board of Adjustment (D) denied the variance, finding "that the applicant failed to demonstrate any evidence to establish hardship" and only that the granting of the variance "would substantially impair the intent and purpose" of the Westwood zoning plan. The trial court affirmed this decision, because it felt the variance "would be detrimental to the entire area." The Appellate Division then affirmed in a brief per curiam opinion.

Issue: Can a variance be denied when the applicant has demonstrated the possibility of undue hardship because of the exceptional nature of the property and the zoning board has not explained how the variance would impair the intent or purpose of the zoning plan?

Decision and Rationale: (Schreiber) No. A zoning board shall have the power to grant a variance where because of some exceptional situation of the property, the strict application of a zoning ordinance would result in undue hardship upon the developer of the property, and the variance would not substantially impair the public good and the intent and purpose of the zone plan and ordinance. "Undue hardship" is based on the idea that an owner can make no effective use of his or her property if a variance is denied. An owner is not entitled to have his or her property zoned for its most profitable use. Nonetheless, when a regulation renders property unusable for any purpose, the presence of undue hardship is possible. If an owner or a predecessor in title created the nonconforming condition, though, the hardship may be considered self-imposed and thus would not merit a variance. Likewise, an owner's attempts to sell the property to neighboring landowners, the negotiations between such parties, and the reasonableness of the price offers by both sides are relevant factors. In addition to undue hardship, the possibility of substantial threat to the public good and to the intent and purpose of the existing zone plan must be considered. The applicant generally has the burden of proving the variance will not cause such harm. It is less likely that the restriction will be vital to valid public interests, however, if less of an impact occurs. In this case, the Board (D) concluded that Commons and Weingarten (P) "failed to demonstrate any evidence to establish hardship." The record indicates otherwise, as ownership began when no zoning ordinance was in effect. In addition, Weingarten (P) did attempt to acquire a 10-foot strip of neighboring land, and negotiations concerning the sale of the property to a neighbor. Moreover, it is possible that without a variance, the lot would be zoned into inutility. With all these factors in mind, it cannot be argued that there was no evidence of hardship. Further, the Board (D) did not explain its conclusion that the variance would substantially impair the intent and purpose of the zone plan and ordinance. The relation of the size of the house and the lot to the overall plan is not made clear. If the Board (D) was concerned with the effect of the house's appearance, then the purpose for zoning would be valid. However, the Board (D) does not address this issue. An explicit discussion of findings and reasoning must be made when making variance decisions. Likewise, an applicant for variance must submit a detailed plan of the proposed structure to insure a well-informed decision before the Board (D). Judgment reversed and remanded.

Analysis:

The Commons and Weingarten (P) would seem to have little chance of success, even on remand. Although there certainly is evidence supporting a claim of undue hardship, there is some evidence on the other side, as well. In particular, the notion that Weingarten (P) willingly contracted to buy the lot in order to build a house could be damaging. Weingarten (P) should reasonably have known that any house he (P) attempted to build would automatically violate the zoning ordinance, and thus any hardship he (P) would suffer would be self-imposed. In addition, although they were not mentioned in the Board's (D) initial decision, aesthetic concerns could bar the use of a variance here. The record shows that at least one neighbor testified that a house on the smaller lot would be "aesthetically displeasing," and as such would impair property values in the neighborhood. The court cited the proposed home's appearance as a potentially valid basis for zoning.

MAINE SUPREME COURT HOLDS THAT PARTS OF A BRUNSWICK ZONING ORDINANCE IMPROPERLY DELEGATE LEGISLATIVE AUTHORITY TO THE BRUNSWICK ZONING BOARD OF APPEALS AND THUS ARE UNCONSTITUTIONAL

Cope v. Inhabitants of the Town of Brunswick

(Apartment Builders) v. (Rest of Town)
(1983) 464 A.2d 223

MEMORY GRAPHIC

Instant Facts

Two apartment builders appealed a local zoning board's decision to deny them a zoning exception to construct multi-unit apartment buildings in town.

Black Letter Rule

The power to regulate private property cannot be delegated from the legislature to a municipality or from a municipality to a local administrative body without a sufficiently detailed statement of policy to provide a guide to reasonably determine an owner's rights and prevent arbitrariness.

Case Vocabulary

EXCEPTION: Permission given to a landowner to use his or her property in way which the local zoning ordinance expressly permits.
INIMICAL: Hostile; adverse.
INTER ALIA: "Among other things"; phrase used when entire statutes, cases, etc. are
not completely set forth.
SELECTMEN: In New England towns, term used for board of governing officers.

Procedural Basis: Appeal from decision affirming denial of zoning use exception.

Facts: On March 16, 1982, Mitchell and David Cope (P) filed an application requesting that the Brunswick Zoning Board of Appeals (the Board) grant them (P) an exception under the Brunswick zoning ordinance. The Copes (P) wished to build eight six-unit apartment buildings on an undeveloped parcel of land in the Town of Brunswick. This land is classified under the ordinance for "suburban A residential" use. Multi-unit apartment buildings are only permitted in these zones "as an exception granted by the Board of Appeals." Section 1107 of the ordinance lists the criteria that an applicant must fulfill to qualify for an exception. The applicant must prove, in part, that "the use requested will not adversely affect the health, safety, or general welfare of the public" and that "the use requested will not tend to devaluate or alter the essential characteristics of the surrounding property." This section also states that an applicant "shall submit to the Board diagrams or photographs... illustrating the proof required by this section." After a public hearing on March 30 and April 10, 1982, the Board found that the Copes' (P) proposed use would endanger public safety and seriously alter the basic characteristics of the surrounding neighborhood by dramatically increasing the amount of traffic. The Board denied the Copes' (P) application, and the Copes (P) appealed to Superior Court. They (P) claimed that the ordinance improperly delegates the authority to permit the constriction of apartment buildings to the Board and thus is unconstitutional. The Superior Court affirmed the Board's denial of the Copes' (P) application.

Issue: Can a zoning ordinance give a local zoning board the authority to determine whether a proposed use of private property will comply with general guidelines and thus merit an exception?

Decision and Rationale: (Wathen) No. Local zoning boards, like municipalities, have no inherent authority to regulate the use of private property. The power of a town, and therefore the power of its local zoning board, comes from the State. The power to regulate private property cannot be delegated from the legislature to a municipality or from a municipality to a local administrative body without a sufficiently detailed statement of policy to provide a guide to reasonably determine an owner's rights and prevent arbitrariness. In *Waterville Hotel Corp. v. Board of Zoning*, Appeals, 241 A.2d 50 (Me. 1968) [zoning ordinance provision that gave absolute power to zoning board to approve or disapprove "all major changes of uses of land, buildings, or structures" was struck down], this Court noted that the legislature could not give a zoning board the discretionary authority to approve or disapprove permits in order to serve the public interest without also giving standards to limit and guide it. Likewise, in *Town of Windham v. LaPointe*, 308 A.2d 286 (Me. 1973) [zoning ordinance vesting unguided authority in selectmen and planning board to approve or disapprove of trailer park locations] this Court noted that such "broad delegation of power breeds selectivity in the enforcement of the law." This rationale does not conflict with earlier decisions allowing zoning boards to determine who is to be granted zoning variances. While a variance extends authority to a landowner to use his or her property in a manner that is otherwise forbidden by the ordinance, an exception allows a landowner to use his or her property that the ordinance expressly permits. As such, the exception is a conditional use under a zoning ordinance and results from a legislative determination that the use will not be detrimental to the regulated neighborhood. Thus, the question of whether the use will generally interfere with the public interest and the essential character of the neighborhood is a legislative question. The power to decide that question cannot be delegated without specific guidelines. In essence, the voters of Brunswick determined that an apartment building was generally suitable for location in a residential zone by enacting the ordinance. Because the Board found that the Copes (P) had only failed to comply with the requirements for exception that this Court now finds invalid, they (P) should be granted exception. Judgment reversed.

Analysis:

There is more than one method of implementing special exceptions, also termed conditional uses. Under the *Cope* approach, special exceptions are used in a discretionary fashion, as listed uses will be allowed an exception if very general criteria are met. This approach gives significant amounts of leverage to zoning boards, and many courts agree with the opinion of the Maine Supreme Court in this case. Another approach points to detailed criteria which a proposed use must meet in order to receive an exception. These requirements can include hours of operation, location, and other similar characteristics. Such an approach tends to limit the amount of discretion involved. Still another way of granting exceptions places the burden on the zoning authorities to demonstrate why the use exception will have an adverse affect on the public welfare.

State v. City of Rochester

(Neighboring Owners) v. (City)
(1978) 268 N.W.2d 885

MEMORY GRAPHIC

Instant Facts

Third party neighbors (P) filed suit challenging the validity of a City Council (D) zoning ordinance amendment, which rezoned neighboring land from single-family and low-density residential use to high-density residential use.

Black Letter Rule

A municipality's amendment of a zoning ordinance is a legislative act—under the municipality's delegated police powers—and the amendment will be upheld unless it is shown that it is unsupported by any rational basis related to promoting the public health, safety, morals, or general welfare, or that it amounts to a taking without compensation.

Case Vocabulary

ADMINISTRATIVE ACT: Action taken by a board, commission, or agency, etc.
QUASI-JUDICIAL ACT: An act, judicial in nature, yet performed by one who is not a judge (such as an administrative agency), or by a judge who is not acting as a judicial officer.
SPOT ZONING: An invalid zoning amendment, which creates a use classification inconsistent with surrounding uses and creates an island of nonconforming use within a larger zoned district, and which dramatically reduces the value for uses specified in the zoning ordinance of either the rezoned plot or abutting property.
STANDARD OF REVIEW: The method of review used by a higher court or appellate court to review the decisions of lower courts or administrative agencies, such as *de novo* standard of review [reviewing the entire record without record to decision of lower court or tribunal], *abuse of discretion* standard of review [reviewing the record and reversing the decision only if there is a clearly erroneous decision by the lower court or tribunal], or *substantial evidence* standard of review [reviewing the record to determine if there is substantial evidence to support the decision].

Procedural Basis: Appeal to State Supreme Court from trial court's denial of declaratory judgment and injunctive relief in action challenging the validity of City rezoning ordinance.

Facts: The Rochester Association of Neighborhoods and individual owners (P) filed suit challenging the City Council's (D) decision to grant the rezoning application filed by the owner and prospective purchaser of a parcel of land. The rezoning application sought to have the property rezoned from single-family and low-density residential use to high-density residential use in order that condominiums could be developed on the land. The City Council (D) rejected the planning commission's recommendation to deny the application, and instead passed an ordinance rezoning the property to high-density residential use. The trial court denied the third party neighbors' (P) requested relief and they appealed contending that (1) the City Council's (D) action in rezoning should be subject to close judicial scrutiny as an administrative or quasi-judicial act; (2) that if the act of rezoning was nevertheless held to be a legislative act—as opposed to an administrative or quasi-judicial act—the ordinance is arbitrary and capricious and without reasonable relation to promoting public health, safety, morals, and general welfare; and (3) the ordinance is an invalid "spot zoning." [In other words, it just plain stinks!]

Issue: Is the rezoning of a single tract of land by a municipality a legislative act?

Decision and Rationale: (Rogosheske) Yes. With respect to whether the City Council's (D) action in rezoning is an administrative or quasi-judicial act, subject to close judicial scrutiny, or a legislative act, we have consistently held that when a municipality adopts or amends a zoning ordinance it acts in a legislative capacity under its delegated police powers. As such, the rezoning will be upheld unless it can be shown that the classification is unsupported by any rational basis related to promoting the public health, safety, morals, or general welfare, or that it amounts to a taking without compensation. We note that while a zoning amendment can permit particular property to be used in a manner formerly forbidden by the ordinance, a special use provision permits property within the discretion of the governing body, to be used in a manner expressly authorized by the ordinance. In passing a zoning or rezoning ordinance, a city council must make a legislative judgment that the classification will promote the public health, safety, morals, and general welfare. In granting or denying a special-use permit, a city council is not altering the legislative judgment as to the zoning classification. Rather, it has the function of applying specific use standards set by the zoning ordinance to a particular use, and must be held strictly to those standards. With respect third party neighbors' (P) contention that, should we hold the rezoning to be a legislative act, which we do, the ordinance is arbitrary and capricious and without reasonable relation to promoting public health, safety, morals, and general welfare, we reject such contention. There was evidence of the need for more high-density housing in the city of Rochester, and there was a rational basis for concluding that a six-story condominium would be compatible with existing uses in the neighborhood of the subject property. Given the use of the surrounding areas, it was reasonable for the City Council (D) to conclude that the development of the property for further low-density or single-family use would have been economically unlikely. In addition, the third parties' (P) generalized claims that their property may decline in value do not form a basis for invaliding the amendment. Finally, with respect to the contention that the ordinance should be invalidated as "spot zoning," [which is a bad thing] there is no proof of substantial diminution in the neighboring third parties' (P) property values due to the rezoning, nor have they shown that the rezoning would create an island of nonconforming use. Affirmed.

Dissent: (Kelly) I would urge the court to adopt the standard of review

placing upon the municipality the burden of supporting the ordinance as a valid exercise of the police power by findings of fact based upon substantial evidence. It is illogical to require municipalities to live up to a stricter standard of review in granting or denying a special-use permit than in rezoning a parcel of land. Thus, the standard of review should be a higher one for rezoning or at least the same as for securing a special-use permit.

Analysis:

This case is significant for a number of reasons. First, it is an example of how neighboring property owners can challenge an amendment to a zoning ordinance, which was obtained through another property owner making application to the local governing board for rezoning. Second, the court in this case declined to follow other jurisdictions that held the act of rezoning was a quasi-judicial act (thereby requiring a higher standard of review for justification of the ordinance). Instead, the court held that the act of rezoning is a legislative act, which is valid unless unsupported by any rational basis relating to public health, safety, morals, or general welfare, or it constitutes a taking without compensation. Third, the ability to challenge an ordinance based upon the concept of "spot zoning," whereby an ordinance creates a use classification inconsistent with surrounding uses and creates an island of nonconforming use within a larger zoned district, and which dramatically reduces the value for uses specified in the zoning ordinance of either the rezoned plot or abutting property.

State ex rel. Stoyanoff v. Berkeley

(Building Commissioner) v. (Architect)
(1970) 458 S.W.2d 305

MEMORY GRAPHIC

Instant Facts

Stoyanoff wanted to build a pyramid-shaped house in a neighborhood with more traditional-looking houses, but Stoyanoff refused to issue a building permit.

Black Letter Rule

An architectural review board may deny a permit for a structure if it would be unsuitable in appearance with reference to the character of the surrounding neighborhood and thus adversely affect the general welfare and property values of the community.

Case Vocabulary

AESTHETIC: Having to do with beauty and art.
COGENT: Compelling, convincing.
PEREMPTORY: Blocking or precluding a course of action.
PREAMBLE: An introduction.
RELATOR: One who is permitted to bring a suit on behalf of the People or the Attorney General.

Procedural Basis: Appeal from summary judgment for a peremptory writ of mandamus to compel the issuance of a residential building permit.

Facts: The City of Ladue is one of the finer residential suburbs of St. Louis, Missouri. There, the homes are considerably larger and more expensive than those in cities of comparable size. The average market value of these homes ranged from $60,000 to $85,000 each. Most of the residences were built in Colonial, French Provincial and English Tudor styles. Stoyanoff (P) and others (P) applied to Berkeley (D), the Ladue Building Commissioner, for a building permit that would allow them (P) to construct a single family residence in Ladue. This residence, however, would be of ultramodern design, with a pyramid shape, a flat top, and triangular shaped windows and doors at the corners. Stoyanoff (P) argued this design, though unusual, would nonetheless comply with all existing zoning regulations and ordinances. The permit application was not approved by the Architectural Board of the City of Ladue. A zoning ordinance was in effect in Ladue to promote a comprehensive plan "designed to promote the health and general welfare of the residents of the City of Ladue." The Architectural Board, established by Ordinance 131, as amended by Ordinance 281, is composed of three architects. It was created to ensure that new buildings would "conform to certain minimum architectural standards of appearance and conformity with surrounding structures." Those structures that were "detrimental to the stability of value and the welfare of surrounding property" were not permitted in Ladue under the Ordinances. According to another developer, a house built to Stoyanoff's (P) design would have a substantial adverse effect upon the market values of other residential property in the neighborhood. Stoyanoff (P) filed a motion for summary judgment to compel Berkeley (D) to issue a residential building permit for the proposed house. The trial court held that the ordinances deprived Stoyanoff (P) of the use of the property without due process of law.

Issue: Can a zoning ordinance be considered valid if it prohibits the building of property because it would not conform in appearance with neighboring structures?

Decision and Rationale: (Pritchard) Yes. An architectural review board may deny a permit for a structure if it would be unsuitable in appearance with reference to the character of the surrounding neighborhood and thus adversely affect the general welfare and property values of the community. There is an existing, comprehensive plan of zoning intended to maintain the general character of buildings in the City of Ladue. The concerns regarding architectural appearance and stability of value are directly related to the general welfare of the community. Indeed, the assured preservation of property values is one of the most pressing reasons to have zoning ordinances in the first place. Neighboring owners are not the only ones threatened by property uses which may offend others' sensibilities and debase market values. The public also suffers, as lowered property values also affect the tax base of the community as a whole. While Stoyanoff (P) may argue that these zoning restrictions are unreasonable and arbitrary because they are based solely on aesthetic concerns, in fact, the aesthetic factor is not the sole one considered. The effect on property values in the area must also be considered. The building permit for Stoyanoff (P) was denied for the basic purpose of serving the general welfare of the community. Judgment reversed.

Analysis:

Architectural design regulations, like Ordinances 131 and 281 here, rarely come up for review in appellate courts. When they do, they have always resulted from disputes in suburban communities. In a few of these cases regulations were invalidated because the promotion of aesthetic values was not considered a proper purpose of zoning. More recent cases, like *Stoyanoff* and some other cases in the Midwest, have relied on the protection of property values in their rationale rather than purely aesthetic justification. This property values rationale is applicable in most cases. Some states like California and Florida have accepted the use of purely aesthetic considerations in deciding cases involving the regulation of signs and billboards. Thus, it is possible that the property value rationale may not be needed in these and other states that would accept aesthetic considerations in other contexts. Still, there is the possibility that architects or other individuals may challenge these sorts of design regulations on First Amendment grounds in the future. Such regulations can often exclude whole styles of architecture (modern, industrial, etc.) from large neighborhoods, and thus, potentially anyway, amount to unconstitutional content-based prohibition of commercial speech.

Anderson v. City of Issaquah

(Architect) v. (Municipality)
(1993) 70 Wash. App. 64, 851 P.2d 744

MEMORY GRAPHIC

Instant Facts

An architect appealed the denial of a construction permit, arguing that the subjective aesthetic standards used by the city building commission were unconstitutionally vague.

Black Letter Rule

Local building ordinances that impose aesthetic conditions must provide sufficiently clear guidance to all interested parties.

Case Vocabulary

AD HOC: For a special purpose.

Procedural Basis: Appeal of verdict dismissing action seeking approval of certification of building plans.

Facts: In 1988, Bruce Anderson (P) applied to the City of Issaquah (D) for certification to build a 6800-square-foot commercial building to be used for retail space. The application stalled when it was reviewed by the Issaquah Development Commission. The Development Commission was required to enforce various provisions of the Issaquah Municipal Code regarding building design and the relationship between the proposed building and the adjoining area. Among other things, the Code required that buildings be interesting and harmonious with the surrounding valley and mountains. The Development Commission informed Anderson (P) that his proposed building did not fit with the concept of the surrounding area. Specifically, the Commission did not like the building color, the design of either the front or rear facade, or the full-length glass windows. On three separate occasions, Anderson (P) modified his designs and returned to the Commission for approval. After nine months of this, the Commission finally denied his application, noting that Anderson (P) was unwilling to make the required changes to protect and enhance the aesthetic values of the City (D). Anderson (P), who had spent approximately $250,000 by this point, appealed to the Issaquah City Council. When the City Council denied his appeal, Anderson (P) filed suit in state court, arguing that the Code provisions were unconstitutionally vague. The trial court dismissed Anderson's (P) complaint, and he appeals.

Issue: Must aesthetic building standards provide clear guidance to all concerned parties?

Decision and Rationale: (Kennedy, J.) Yes. Aesthetic building standards must provide clear guidance to all concerned parties. Aesthetic standards are an appropriate and important component of land use governance. However, the Issaquah Code sections do not give effective or meaningful guidance to applicants, to design professionals, or to the public officials of Issaquah who are responsible for enforcing the Code. The words employed are not technical words which are commonly understood within the professional building design industry. Rather, the Code uses such subjective terms as "appropriate proportions" and harmony with "the natural setting of the valley," and it states that "monotony should be avoided." As a result, the commissioners were left to their own individual, subjective feelings about the "image of Issaquah" in reviewing Anderson's (P) application. We hold that the Code sections at issue are unconstitutionally void, both on their face and as applied to Anderson (P). We order that Anderson's (P) land use certification be issued, provided that the changes to which Anderson agreed be imposed.

Analysis:

This case presents the interesting issue of local zoning ordinances designed to promote aesthetic values. The opinion demonstrates how difficult it is to effectively draft such an ordinance, which necessarily is based upon subjective evaluations. The City of Issaquah (D) certainly had a laudable goal in drafting the building design regulations. As anyone who has been to Issaquah (D) can attest, the natural and architectural beauty of the city are unrivaled by most areas of the country. The City (D) should be entitled to maintain its beautiful character by imposing reasonable restrictions. On the other hand, architects working on projects in Issaquah (D) must have a clear and understandable set of regulations to follow. Note that if the regulations had been imposed by a private architectural control committee, such as a homeowners association, Anderson would probably have lost. Specific standards are not required when private architectural restrictions are involved; rather, the committee is only required to act reasonably and in good faith. Thus, it is possible to have a public zoning restriction that violates the Constitution, but is nevertheless valid as a private zoning restriction.

SUPREME COURT INVALIDATES ORDINANCE THAT RESTRICTS SIGNS ON RESIDENTIAL PROPERTY

City of Ladue v. Gilleo

(Municipality) v. (Resident)
512 U.S. 43 (1994)

M E M O R Y G R A P H I C

Instant Facts

A resident challenges a city ordinance that prohibits the displaying of signs, such as an antiwar protest sign, on front yards.

Black Letter Rule

A city may not constitutionally adopt ordinances that prohibit nearly all signs on residential property.

Case Vocabulary

CONTENT-NEUTRAL: A regulation that restricts the time, place, or manner of some form of speech rather than restricting the content of the speech itself.

Procedural Basis: Writ of certiorari reviewing order affirming judgment holding city ordinance unconstitutional.

Facts: Margaret Gilleo (P) owned a home in the City of Ladue (D). A city ordinance prohibited homeowners from displaying any signs except residence identification signs, for sale signs, or signs warning of safety hazards. In December 1990, Gilleo (P) erected on her front lawn a 24- by 36-inch sign printed with the words "Say No to War in the Persian Gulf, Call Congress Now." Gilleo's (P) sign was removed, and when she reported it to the police they instructed her that such signs were prohibited in Ladue (D). After the City Council denied her petition for a variance, Gilleo (P) sued the City in federal court, arguing that Ladue's (D) sign ordinance violated her First Amendment right of free speech. The District Court issued a preliminary injunction against enforcement of the ordinance. Ladue (P) then placed a 8.5- by 11-inch sign in her window stating "For Peace in the Gulf." The City responded by amending its ordinance to include a Declaration of Findings, which stated that the ordinance was aimed at preventing ugliness, visual blight and clutter, among other things. The District Court held the new ordinance unconstitutional. The Court of Appeals affirmed, holding that the ordinance was a content-based regulation and that the City's (D) interests were not sufficiently compelling to support the restriction. The Supreme Court granted certiorari.

Issue: Is a city ordinance that prohibits homeowners from displaying virtually any signs on their property constitutional?

Decision and Rationale: (Stevens, J.) No. A city ordinance that prohibits homeowners from displaying virtually any signs on their property is not constitutional. Our past decisions identify two analytically distinct grounds for challenging the constitutionality of a municipal ordinance regulating the display of signs. First, the measure may restrict too little speech because its exemptions discriminate on the basis of the signs' messages. Second, the measure may prohibit too much protected speech. The City of Ladue (D) argues that its ordinance was content-neutral and that the City's (D) regulatory purposes justified the comprehensiveness of the sign regulation. We disagree. Ladue's (D) sign ordinance is based on the desire to minimize the visual clutter associated with signs. This is a valid interest, but it is not sufficient to overcome the ordinances chilling effects on free speech. Signs such as Gilleo's (P), protesting an imminent governmental decision to go to war, are absolutely pivotal in our society. Ladue (D) has almost completely foreclosed a venerable means of communication that is both unique and important. Indeed, Gilleo (P) could have communicated her message through other means, such as pamphlets or bumper stickers, but a much stronger statement is made by having the sign on your front lawn. Ladue's (D) restrictions foreclose an entire media (lawn signs) and thus suppress too much speech. We feel that more temperate measures could satisfy Ladue's (D) regulatory needs without harm to the First Amendment rights of its citizens. Affirmed.

Analysis:

This case, which centers more on constitutional law than property, nevertheless provides an interesting insight into zoning regulations. As we have seen, cities have certain leeway to enact zoning ordinances for purely aesthetic purposes. Cities have a legitimate interest in keeping their neighborhoods free from visual clutter. But does an 8.5- by 11-inch sign in a window really cause visual clutter? In all likelihood, the City (D) ordinance was in fact aimed at suppressing the content of speech. The City (D) and its police force may have selectively chosen to enforce the ordinance against Gilleo (P) only because they did not like her antiwar message. According to the Court, even if the City had a benign, content-neutral goal, the indirect suppression of free speech was unconstitutional. Indeed, as Justice Stevens notes, most Americans would be dismayed by an ordinance that prohibited a small window sign that expressed political views. However, Stevens' opinion goes overboard in discussing the "venerable means of communication" that is foreclosed by the ordinance. Does Ladue's (D) ordinance really foreclose an entire medium of expression? Even if it does, are residential signs really as important to free speech as Stevens' seems to think? Regardless, the opinion reaches a sensible conclusion, allowing reasonable zoning ordinances that restrict some speech while upholding the broad reach of the First Amendment.

Village of Belle Terre v. Boraas

(Long Island Village) v. (College Student)
(1974) 416 U.S. 1

M E M O R Y   G R A P H I C

Instant Facts

Boraas and five others challenged a Belle Terre ordinance which restricted land use to one-family dwellings and excluded households with over two unrelated persons.

Black Letter Rule

The legislature may define what counts as a "family" for zoning purposes if the definition is rationally related to legitimate objectives, such as creating zones where family values, youth values, and the blessings of quiet seclusion and clean air are preserved.

Case Vocabulary

ANIMOSITY: Resentment.
CAPRICE: A sudden, unmotivated impulse.
DOGMA: An established opinion, taken as authority.
PHILANTHROPIC: Characterized by goodwill and generosity.
TRANSIENT: One who passes through a place and stays only briefly.

Procedural Basis: Appeal from action for injunction and judgment declaring ordinance constitutional.

Facts: The Village of Belle Terre (D) is located on the north shore of Long Island. Though less than one square mile in area, it (D) is inhabited by 700 people in about 220 homes. Belle Terre (D) has restricted land use to single-family dwellings, excluding boarding houses, fraternity houses, and other multiple-dwelling houses. "Family" is defined as "[o]ne or more persons related by blood, adoption or marriage, living and cooking together as a single housekeeping unit." Households with more than two unrelated persons are explicitly excluded from the allowed definition of "family." Bruce Boraas (P), a student at nearby State University at Stony Brook, entered into a lease for a house in the village owned by the Dickmans (P). Another student was already leasing the house at this point. Later, four more students moved into the house. None of the students is related to the other by blood, adoption, or marriage. The Dickmans (Ps), Boraas (P), and two other tenants (P) filed suit for an injunction and a judgment to declare the Belle Terre ordinance unconstitutional. They (P) challenge the statute as arbitrary and unreasonable on several grounds, including that the restriction violates their right of privacy, that it is of no rightful concern to villagers whether the residents are married or not, and that having the neighborhood conform to one type of family is not a legitimate governmental interest. The District Court held the ordinance unconstitutional, but the Court of Appeals reversed.

Issue: Can a zoning ordinance which restricts land use according to what it defines as a family be constitutional?

Decision and Rationale: (Douglas) Yes. The legislature may define what counts as a "family" for zoning purposes if the definition is rationally related to legitimate objectives, such as creating zones where family values and the blessings of quiet seclusion and clean air are preserved. The concept of public welfare, which is usually the goal of zoning regulations, is a broad and inclusive one. The legislature may determine what is involved in maintaining standards to protect the public welfare. The reasons offered by Boraas (P) and the others (P) for challenging the ordinance are invalid in this case. No fundamental right of the Constitution, including the right of privacy, is at stake in this case. Numerous cases in the past have involved the drawing of lines by the legislature between two different classifications of people. The distinctions here are not made on lines that are inherently suspect, like those based on race. Economic and social legislation such as this should withstand charges of violating the Equal Protection Clause if it is reasonable, not arbitrary, and if it bears a rational relationship to a permissible state objective. Here, a line is drawn between two unrelated people and three or more unrelated people in the definition of "family." The discretion in setting this line belongs with the legislature, not the courts. Moreover, boarding houses, fraternity houses, and other similar living arrangements present legitimate concerns for the Village (D). Increased population density, higher traffic flow, higher numbers of cars parked at each property, and greater noise levels can all result without the single-family restriction. These are all legitimate guidelines in a land-use project directed at filling family needs. The police power includes the ability to establish zones where "family values, youth values, and the blessings of quiet seclusion and clean air make the area a sanctuary for people."

Dissent: (Marshall) The classification imposed by the Belle Terre (D) ordinance burdens the students' fundamental rights of association and privacy as guaranteed by the First and Fourteenth Amendments. Although deference should be given to legislatures in areas of zoning, this Court still has the duty of protecting fundamental rights. People have the freedom to choose their associates, not only in the political sense, but also in areas that are of economic and social benefit. This concept is tied to the individual's right to privacy in his or her home. Surely, the choice of one's household companions falls within this right. Here, the ordinance essentially singles out those people who choose to live their lives in a manner that differs from that of current residents. The concerns of population density and traffic are legitimate ones. The ordinance does not, however, impose any occupancy limitations whatsoever on people who are related by blood, adoption, or marriage. It is even more underinclusive in that it does not restrict the number of automobiles owned by members of one household. The ordinance is also overinclusive in that it can exclude a large number of unrelated persons who may live together even if they had only one income and no vehicles contributing to traffic and space problems. It goes beyond restricting land use and attempts to regulate the people's particular means of association. Because such fundamental rights are at stake, the ordinance should only pass constitutional scrutiny if the burden imposed is necessary to protect a compelling and substantial governmental interest.

Analysis:

Consider that this case took place in or near a college town in 1974. It appears that there may have been other concerns in addition to those of urban planning problems, like population density and traffic flow. The Court makes particular note of "family values... and clean air" in its listing of legitimate purposes for zoning ordinances. It is certainly possible that in addition to the more "urban" problems, the residents of Belle Terre (D) were afraid that their quiet little village would be overrun by "hippies" from the State University looking to establish co-ops and communes in the area. Since then, more and more state courts have invalidated the kind of restrictive definition of "family" that was sustained here. These courts have done so on either state statutory or constitutional grounds. For example, the New Jersey Supreme Court believes its state constitution prohibits zoning regulations that limit the number of people in a given household, saying that "such regulations are insufficiently related to the perceived social ills" that they are meant to address [*State v. Baker*, 81 N.J. 99, 405 A.2d 368 (1979)]. The highest courts in Michigan, New York and Pennsylvania have all made similar rulings. The California Supreme Court, as well, has held that a zoning ordinance which sets out a definition of a "family" violates its state constitutional protections of "privacy." The issue of group homes and such regulations will be discussed in the next case.

SINGLE-FAMILY ZONING RESTRICTION IS NOT EXEMPT FROM FEDERAL HOUSING ACT SCRUTINY

City of Edmonds v. Oxford House, Inc.

(Municipality) v. (Group Home)

(1995) 514 U.S. 725

M E M O R Y   G R A P H I C

Instant Facts

A city sued to enforce its residential single-family zoning restrictions against a group home for recovering alcoholics and drug addicts.

Black Letter Rule

A single-family zoning regulation is not automatically exempt from FHA scrutiny, even if it indirectly limits the maximum number of occupants in a house.

Case Vocabulary

EUCLIDEAN ZONING: A typical general zoning plan that separates a city into different districts based on use restrictions.

Procedural Basis: Writ of certiorari reviewing order reversing judgment exempting city housing ordinance from FHA.

Facts: The City of Edmonds' (P) zoning code restricted the composition of households in single-family areas, defining "family" as any number of persons related by genetics, adoption, or marriage, or a group of five or fewer unrelated persons. Oxford House (D) opened a group home in Edmonds (P) for 10 to 12 unrelated adults recovering from alcoholism and drug addiction in a neighborhood zoned for single-family residences. The City (P) issued criminal citations to the owner and a resident of the Oxford House (D) for violating the zoning code. The City (P) then sued Oxford House (D) in federal district court for a declaration that the Fair Housing Act ("FHA") did not prohibit Edmonds' (P) ordinance. Oxford House (D) counterclaimed based on the FHA, claiming that the City failed to make reasonable accommodations for handicapped persons. The City (P) conceded that the residents of Oxford House (D) were "handicapped" for purposes of the FHA, but the City (P) relied on an FHA exception which exempts any reasonable restrictions regarding the maximum number of occupants permitted to occupy a dwelling. The District Court held that the Edmonds' (P) ordinance was exempt from FHA scrutiny, but the Ninth Circuit reversed. The Supreme Court granted certiorari.

Issue: Does a city's single-family zoning ordinance, requiring households to be related or fewer than five people, qualify for an exemption to the FHA as a restriction of the maximum number of occupants permitted to occupy a dwelling?

Decision and Rationale: (Ginsburg, J.) No. A city's single-family zoning ordinance, requiring households to be related or house fewer than five people, does not qualify for an exemption to the FHA as a restriction of the maximum number of occupants permitted to occupy a dwelling. The broad purpose of the FHA is to provide, within constitutional limitations, for fair housing throughout the United States. We feel that the FHA's exception to this general policy statement should be read narrowly in order to preserve the primary purpose of achieving fair housing. In contrast to single-family restrictions, which are aimed at preserving the character of neighborhoods, maximum occupancy restrictions cap the number of occupants in relation to floor space in order to protect health and safety. Single-family restrictions do not fall within the FHA's maximum-occupancy exemption. The City of Edmonds' (P) restriction is a classic example of a use restriction and family composition rule. This rule does not cap the number of people who may live in a dwelling for health reasons. Rather, a separate provision in the city code provides for maximum occupancy limitations. The single-family restriction does not answer the question, "What is the maximum number of occupants permitted to occupy a house?" Any number of genetically-related individuals could live in a house and be in conformity with the single-family restriction. We thus hold that Edmonds' (P) single-family occupancy restriction does not qualify for the FHA exemption. It remains for the lower court to determine whether the restriction violates the FHA. Affirmed.

Analysis:

This case returns to a topic covered previously in the textbook regarding the conflict between single-family housing restrictions and the FHA. Unlike previous cases, this opinion focuses on whether a single-family housing restriction qualifies under a narrow FHA exemption. Taken at face value, the Edmonds' (P) ordinance is "regarding the maximum number of occupants permitted to occupy a dwelling." Specifically, more than five unrelated individuals cannot live together in a single-family housing zone. The Court's analysis, however, makes clear that the purpose of the FHA exemption was to allow maximum-occupancy restrictions for the purposes of health and safety. Health and safety is arguably a more important goal than preserving the single-family character of neighborhoods. Nevertheless, it is important to note that single-family restrictions are not necessarily invalid; they just are not automatically exempt from the FHA. On remand, what should be the result of this case? Is the City of Edmonds (P) liable for failing to make reasonable accommodations for the 10 to 12 recovering alcoholics and drug addicts? Oxford House (D) would probably stress the importance of allowing such people to live in a community environment, and it would argue that it would be financially prohibitive to limit the number of residents to five or fewer. The City (P) probably would cite the increased traffic and noise resulting from the occupants. But would this group of people create any more noise or traffic than a large family with lots of children? In all likelihood, Oxford House (D) would win and be allowed to remain in the neighborhood.

Southern Burlington County NAACP v. Township of Mount Laurel

(Minority and Poor Representatives) v. (Town)

(1975) 67 N.J. 151, 336 A.2d 713, appeal dismissed and cert. denied, 423 U.S. 808

M E M O R Y   G R A P H I C

Instant Facts

Mount Laurel enacted a general zoning ordinance which effectively prevented low and middle income persons from acquiring affordable homes within the township.

Black Letter Rule

A developing municipality must, by its land use regulations, make realistically possible the opportunity for an appropriate variety and choice of housing for all categories of people who may desire to live there, including those of low and moderate income.

Case Vocabulary

RATABLE: A proportional value; something that can be apportioned according to changing values.
TOWNSHIP: Essentially, a town or parish.

Procedural Basis: Appeal from judgment in action for declaratory and injunctive relief.

Facts: The Township of Mount Laurel (D) is roughly 22 square miles, or 14,000 acres, in area. In 1950, Mount Laurel had a population of only 2817. By 1970, the population had grown to 11,221. The general zoning ordinance for the township (D) was enacted in 1964. About 10,000 acres is divided into four residential zones, designated R-1, R-1D, R-2, and R-3. All of these zones allow only single-family, detached dwellings, with only one house per lot. While this development arrangement did result in the quadrupling of the population, it has also resulted in intensive development of only the R-1 and R-2 sections, and at a low density. These homes were worth a substantial $32,500 in 1971 and are worth more today. The general zoning ordinance also establishes large minimum lot areas (9,375 square feet) and large minimum floor areas for houses (1,100 to 1,300 square feet) in the R-1 and R-2 zones. The R-1D district was created by ordinance amendment in 1968 as a cluster zone, and contains dwellings that are comparable in character and cost to those in the R-1 and R-2 zones. Between 1967 and 1971, Mount Laurel approved four planned unit developments (PUDs). These projects involve at least 10,000 sale and rental housing units of various types to be built over several years. None of these units, however, will be within the financial reach of low and middle-income families, especially those with young children. Indeed, the number of apartments having more than one bedroom are limited, and the number of children that can live in each unit are more strictly regulated. Also, rents are pushed higher as a result of required amenities, such as central air conditioning, and developer contributions to the township, such as contributions to schools, fire departments, and other public services. Further, a 1972 supplement to the general zoning ordinance created a new zone, R-4, Planned Adult Retirement Community (PARC). The supplement restricted the number of occupants in each unit and ensured that they would be too costly for many retirees. While an official report in 1969 recognized the lack of decent housing for citizens living in substandard conditions, the government has responded by waiting for rundown buildings to be vacated and then forbidding people to occupy them. When a private non-profit group attempted to construct subsidized, multi-family housing in the R-3 zone in 1968, the township (D) held the corporation to the strict zoning requirements for single-family dwellings on 20,000 square foot lots. Such requirements blocked this attempt at low-cost housing. The Southern Burlington County NAACP (P) represent the minority group poor, predominantly black and Hispanic, who have sought low and moderate-cost housing in Mount Laurel (D).

Issue: Can a municipality validly, through its land use regulations, make it physically and economically impossible to provide low and moderate income housing in the municipality for the various categories of persons who may need it or want it?

Decision and Rationale: (Hall) No. A developing municipality must, by its land use regulations, make realistically possible the opportunity for an appropriate variety and choice of housing for all categories of people who may desire to live there, including those of low and moderate income. This obligation must be met unless the municipality in question can sustain the heavy burden of showing that particular circumstances prevent it from fulfilling the obligation. Land use regulation is part of the police power of the state, and any zoning provision that goes against the general welfare is invalid. Granted, determining what is valid or invalid in the area of land use regulation is not always easy to determine. Nonetheless, a fundamental concept to be aware of is that when regulation has a substantial impact outside its original municipality, the welfare of the citizens of the state as a whole cannot be disregarded and must be recognized and served. Proper provision for adequate housing for all categories of people is critical in promoting this general welfare required in all local land use regulation. In this case, while single-family dwellings are readily provided by Mount Laurel (D), this housing option is certainly the most expensive one possible. Such housing is out of the economic reach of low and middle income families, most young people and many retired persons. The minimum lot area and house area requirements also clearly increase the size and cost of housing in the township (D). The inescapable conclusion is that Mount Laurel (D) permits this zoning to continue in order to benefit from the high property taxes that will result from it. Thus, Mount Laurel's (D) zoning ordinance is facially invalid, and so the burden shifts to the township (D) to establish valid reasons for not fulfilling its obligation to provide a full range of housing. The township (D) argues that it has the right to encourage the presence of commerce and industry and their accompanying high rates of tax revenue. It (D) also argues for the right to limit the presence of school-age children, for such residents would then require costly services and facilities, yet would be unable to pay their own way taxwise. These arguments are invalid, and no municipality may exclude or limit categories of housing for such financial reasons or purposes. Relief from these tax burdens will have to be paid for by other branches of government, and not through the zoning process. There is no reason why growing areas like Mount Laurel (D) may not continue to be attractive and prosperous communities, providing good housing and services for all their different residents. The entire zoning ordinance should not be nullified, as the trial court has held. The township (D) is given 90 days to adopt amendments which will comply with the ruling of this court, and it (D) should first have the opportunity to act without judicial supervision. Judgment modified.

Analysis:

The New Jersey Supreme Court eventually decided a second Mount Laurel appeal, along with seven other cases. The Court clarified and extended the first Mount Laurel with four major holdings. First, all municipalities, developing and otherwise, must provide a realistic opportunity for low and middle income housing. Second, those challenging exclusionary zoning can establish a prima facie case that the zoning is invalid if they can prove the zoning substantially limits the building of low and middle income housing. Third, to counter this prima facie case, a municipality has to show "numerical" evidence of the number of units needed both immediately and within a reasonable time in the future, and do more than show a "bona fide effort" in eliminating exclusionary zoning. Fourth, if removal of the invalid zoning regulations was insufficient, a municipality would have to take affirmative steps to provide a reasonable opportunity for low and middle income housing. This can include helping developers obtain federal subsidies, giving bonuses to developers who voluntarily provide such housing, and other forms of inclusionary zoning. Most experts have looked favorably upon this second Mount Laurel decision, and several states have adopted rules against exclusionary zoning on their own. The New York courts have developed a rule by which an allegedly exclusionary zoning ordinance is presumed to be valid unless it was enacted for an impermissible purpose or "without proper regard to local and regional housing needs and has an exclusionary effect." The Pennsylvania Supreme Court seemed to adopt New Jersey's "fair share" rule, but later went for a substantive due process test and an exclusionary impact test in various situations. Also, California, Michigan and New Hampshire have all taken various steps in invalidating exclusionary zoning. Still, most state courts have yet to address this kind of zoning problem.

Perspective
Eminent Domain

Chapter 12

Local governments often control the use of land in their community in one of two ways. The first way is to leave a piece of property with its owner while regulating that owner's use of it. This method of regulating is usually done through zoning ordinances. The concepts and issues of zoning are covered in the previous chapter.

The second way local governments exercise control over land use is by taking. With its power of eminent domain, the government can take a piece of property from its owner and put it to a "public use." This concept of public use is mentioned, but not explained, in the Fifth Amendment. That Amendment places a limit on the government's ability to take private property. It states, among other things, "nor shall private property be taken for public use, without just compensation." This Amendment also places limits on the government's ability to regulate the use of property. In various circumstances, government rules on property use can be considered to have the same effect as a taking. Because of this, enforcement of those rules may not be allowed unless the government pays compensation to a property owner.

First, this chapter will discuss the history and reasoning behind the government's power of eminent domain. Then, the questions of what counts as a public use and what counts as just compensation will be covered. The last, and largest, part of this chapter will look at the types of situations in which a government regulation results in a taking.

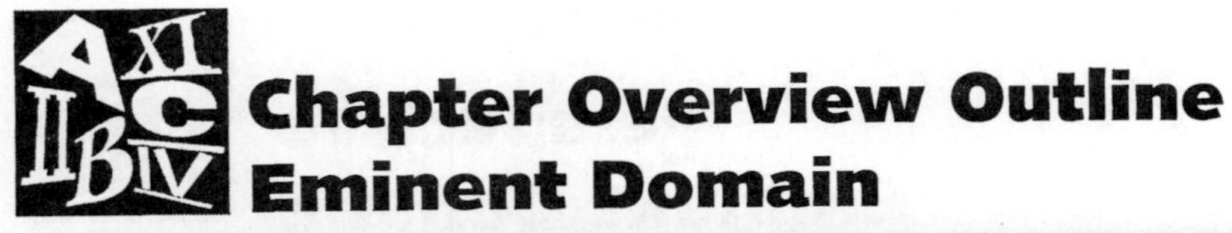

Chapter Overview Outline Eminent Domain

Chapter 12

NOTE: THE PURPOSE OF THIS OUTLINE IS TO ORGANIZE THE CASES SO THAT ONE CAN QUICKLY UNDERSTAND THE RELEVANCE OF EACH CASE TO THE COURSE. NO ATTEMPT IS MADE IN THIS OVERVIEW TO ADDRESS EVERY CONCEPT THAT MUST BE STUDIED. BE SURE TO READ THE ENTIRE CASEBOOK AND/OR OTHER MATERIALS TO GAIN A FULL UNDERSTANDING OF ALL CONCEPTS.

I. Eminent domain is the power of the government to force property owners to transfer their property to the government.
   A. Under the Fifth Amendment, when a government exercises this taking power it must provide just compensation to the property owner.
   B. The most common rationale for the taking power today is that it is an inherent attribute of sovereignty and is necessary for the existence of government.
      1. From an economic standpoint, the taking power can be important for ensuring that land is used efficiently, particularly in high-transaction cost settings. *Richard A. Posner, Economic Analysis of Law*.
      2. Similarly, efficiency and fairness rationales support the government's compensation obligation.

II. Under the Fifth Amendment, the government may only take property for "public use."
   A. A taking involving the transfer of property from one private person to another satisfies the Public Use Clause if it is rationally related to a conceivable public purpose. *Hawaii Housing Authority v. Midkiff*.
      1. There are two basic competing definitions of the term "public use": the broad view, focusing on public benefit or advantage, and the narrow view, emphasizing the public's actual use or right to use of the taken property. *Lawrence Berger, The Public Use Requirement in Eminent Domain*.
   B. When the condemnation of property benefits specific and identifiable private interests, a court must employ heightened scrutiny to determine if a clear and significant public interest is the predominant interest being advanced. *Poletown Neighborhood Council v. City of Detroit*.
      1. Some courts hold, however, that if a taking i for both public and private purposes, th public use requirement is not satisfied. *In r City of Seattle*.
   C. The promotion of the education, recreation, c pleasure of the public constitutes a legitimat public purpose. *City of Oakland v. Oaklan Raiders*.
   D. When the government does take property must pay the owner "just compensation, which is the fair market value of the con demned property. Just compensation does nc cover any additional, "personal" value a owner may place on the property. *Conisto Corp. v. Village of Hoffman Estates*.

III. While the key issues in straightforward condemna tion actions involve whether the taking is for public use and the amount of compensation, in th more difficult cases of physical occupations an regulatory takings the issue is whether a takin has occurred at all.
   A. The law of regulatory takings does [blessedly include some categorical rules.
      1. A permanent physical occupation of an owr er's property authorized by the governmer is always a taking of property which require just compensation. *Loretto v. Teleprompte Manhattan CATV Corp.*
         a. Courts never deny compensation in perma nent physical occupation cases, no matte how trifling the invasion. *Frank Miche man, Property, Utility, and Fairness: Con ments on the Ethical Foundations of "Ju Compensation" Law*.
         b. For temporary physical occupations, on th other hand, courts use a balancing proces
      2. A regulation that deprives an owner of pro erty for the purpose of prohibiting a nuisan is an exercise of the police power, and never a taking which requires compensatio *Hadacheck v. Sebastian*.
         a. Thus, the government exercises the takir power, which requires compensatio when land is useful for some public goo

and it exercises the police power, which does not require compensation, when land is causing some "public bad." *Ernst Freund, The Police Power § 511.*

b. However, it can be difficult to determine whether the government is trying to secure a public good or to control a public bad. For example, forbidding billboards along highways might be for the public good of beautiful highways, or to stop the public bad of distracting drivers. *Frank Michelman, Property, Utility, and Fairness: Comments on the Ethical Foundations of "Just Compensation" Law.*

B. Other regulatory takings rules require measuring and balancing.

1. While the government may regulate property to a certain extent, if a regulation goes too far in diminishing the economic value of the property, it effects a taking. *Pennsylvania Coal Co. v. Mahon.*

a. The diminution-in-value test of *Pennsylvania Coal* is important because most present-day takings cases stem from regulatory actions that involve neither permanent occupations nor nuisance controls.

b. The issue of conceptual severance also arose in *Pennsylvania Coal.* The Court viewed the land supporting the surface as a separate estate, while Justice Brandeis viewed it as only part of the whole property.

(1) More recently, the Court, though still divided, took Justice Brandeis' view and rejected conceptual severance, and consequently found that the diminution in value was not sufficient. *Keystone Bituminous Coal Association v. DeBenedictis.*

2. A law does not effect a taking if it does not interfere with an owner's primary expectation concerning the use of the property and allows him to receive a reasonable return on his investment. *Penn Central Transportation Co. v. City of New York.*

a. As *Penn Central* illustrates, the government eases the burden of some regulations by giving owners transferable development rights (TDRs), which allow them to use their land in ways the government would not otherwise allow.

(1) Although TDRs truly relate to the amount of compensation, the Court treats them as relating instead to the question of whether there is a taking, which does not occur if the land retains substantial value. The government can therefore use TDRs to pay owners less than full market value. *Suitum v. Tahoe Regional Planning Agency (Scalia, concurring).*

C. Another categorical rule is that a regulation that deprives an owner of all economically valuable use of property results in a taking, unless its prohibited uses are already prohibited by background principles of nuisance or property law. *Lucas v. South Carolina Coastal Council.*

1. However, the acquisition of title after the enactment of a regulation does not automatically bar a challenge to that regulation under the Takings Clause. *Palazzolo v. Rhode Island.*

D. A regulatory condition imposed on a development permit, or an exaction, is not a taking if it substantially advances the same governmental purpose that refusing the permit would serve. *Nollan v. California Coastal Commission.*

1. To be constitutional exactions must also be reasonably related and roughly proportional, both in nature and extent, to the impact of the proposed development. *Dolan v. City of Tigard.*

2. *Dolan's* rough proportionality test applies only to exactions and not to all land use regulations. Thus, the law not only gives governments broad power to regulate land use, but also limits landowners' ability to bargain for regulatory adjustments. *Lee Ann Fennell, Hard Bargains and Real Steals: Land Use Exactions Revisited.*

E. While courts typically granted compensation in inverse condemnation actions for physical occupations of land by the government, at first they only granted declaratory or injunctive relief for regulatory takings.

1. Now, a landowner who has suffered a regulatory taking is entitled to compensation for the period during which the regulation denied him all use of the land, and not just declaratory or injunctive relief invalidating the regulation. *First English Evangelical Lutheran Church of Glendale v. County of Los Angeles.*

F. There are several academic approaches to the law of takings.

1. Under one early approach, the government should have an obligation to compensate when it acquires property in carrying out entrepreneurial functions, but it should not owe compensation when it merely resolves disputes between private parties. *Joseph L. Sax, Takings and the Police Power.*
   a. A reformulation of this approach concludes that the government should not owe compensation when it acts to control spillover effects of private land use which harm neighboring landowners. *Joseph L. Sax, Takings, Private Property and Public Rights.*
2. An influential utilitarian approach states that compensation is due only when "demoralization costs" exceed "settlement costs." *Frank Michelman, Property, Utility, and Fairness: Comments on the Ethical Foundations of "Just Compensation" Law.*
   a. Applying this approach, some have concluded that efficiency and justice considerations suggest expanding takings law to sometimes award compensation when there is no taking and sometimes withhold it when there is a taking.
   b. For example, fairness might call for compensation even when efficiency does not, such as when it would be unjust to have the owners of regulated property bear the entire cost of a nuisance regulation. *Michael A. Heller & James E. Krier, Deterrence and Distribution in the Law of Takings.*
3. To an "Ordinary Observer," a person can us his property however he wants, except i ways that are unduly harmful to others, an others must ask him permission before usin his property unless they have a very compe ling reason. *Bruce A. Ackerman, Privat Property and the Constitution.*
   a. Thus, an Ordinary Observer would say taking results when the government tran fers his property to itself or someone el and when a regulation renders the prop erty virtually useless (unless he was usin the property in an unduly harmful way but not when the regulation merely re duces the property's value.
4. Under a libertarian approach, except f nuisance controls and some exercise of th police power, any governmental modificati of rights of possession, use, and disposition property is a taking. Under this view, pr gressive income taxation and welfare a unconstitutional. *Richard A. Epstein, Taking Private Property and the Power of Emine Domain.*
5. Another approach focuses on the public u requirement, and makes the government purpose the decisive factor in takings anal sis. *Jed Rubenfeld, Usings.*
   a. Under this approach, when the gover ment conscripts private property for sta use, then it must pay compensation;
   b. But when it does not put the property use (as when it destroys contaminat trees), or when its purpose would be qually well served by destroying the pro erty, it need not pay compensation.
6. Under a process-theory approach, since th legislative/political processes protect priva property well when they work right, the j of the courts is to police those processes, by protecting the powerless against exploit tion by insiders, rather than to evaluate th legislation they produce. *William A. Fisch Regulatory Takings: Law, Economics, a Politics.*

UNITED STATES SUPREME COURT HOLDS THAT A HAWAII STATUTE CONDEMNING RESIDENTIAL TRACTS AND TRANSFERRING THEM FROM THE OWNERS TO THE LESSEES IN ORDER TO REDUCE THE CONCENTRATION OF LAND OWNERSHIP SATISFIES THE PUBLIC USE CLAUSE OF THE FIFTH AMENDMENT

Hawaii Housing Authority v. Midkiff

(State Agency) v. (Landowner)
(1984) 467 U.S. 229

M E M O R Y   G R A P H I C

Instant Facts

Half of Hawaii's land was owned by only seventy-two people, and the State wanted them to break up their estates.

Black Letter Rule

A taking involving the transfer of property from one private person to another satisfies the Public Use Clause of the Fifth Amendment if it is rationally related to a conceivable public purpose.

Case Vocabulary

CONDEMNATION: The process by which private property is taken for public use, and with just compensation, through the power of eminent domain.
OLIGOPOLY: Market condition in which only a few parties own property; only a few competitors.

Procedural Basis: Appeal from action for declaratory and injunctive relief.

Facts: This case involves the history of land ownership in Hawaii. Originally, Polynesian settlers developed a feudal land system in which one island high chief held all the land and other lower chiefs were in charge of its development. There was no private ownership of land. Since the early 1800's, Hawaiian leaders and American settlers repeatedly tried to divide the lands. In the mid-1960's, the Hawaii Legislature learned that while the State and Federal government owned about 49% of the State's land, another 42% was owned by only 72 private landowners. Over 40% of this land was owned by 18 landowners with tracts of 21,000 acres or more. The legislature found this concentrated ownership distorted the land market and injured the public welfare. It then passed the Land Reform Act of 1967. Under this Act, when 25 tenants in a tract, or tenants on half the lots, whichever is less, file the appropriate applications, the Hawaii Housing Authority (P), or HHA can hold a public hearing to determine if State acquisition of the tract would "effectuate the public purposes" of the Act. If so, the HHA (P) can acquire, at prices set either by condemnation trial or by negotiation between lessors and lessees, the landowners' full "right, title, and interest" in the land. It (P) can then sell each land title to a tenant residing there, or sell it or lease the lot to someone else. No new purchaser or tenant is entitled to more than one lot. In April 1977, the HHA (P) held a public hearing on the proposed acquisition of Midkiff's (D's) lands. In October 1978, the HHA (P) directed Midkiff (D) to negotiate with lessees for the sale of the designated properties. When the negotiations failed, the HHA (P) ordered compulsory arbitration. Midkiff (D) refused, and instead filed suit in United States District Court, in February 1979, asking that the Act be declared unconstitutional and that its enforcement be enjoined. In May 1979, the Court held the compulsory arbitration and compensation provisions of the Act unconstitutional, but in December 1979, it held the rest of the Act constitutional under the Public Use Clause. The Ninth Circuit Court of Appeals reversed.

Issue: Does a taking involving the transfer of property from one private person to another satisfy the Public Use Clause of the Fifth Amendment?

Decision and Rationale: (O'Connor) Yes. A taking involving the transfer of property from one private person to another satisfies the Public Use Clause of the Fifth Amendment if it is rationally related to a conceivable public purpose. In *Berman v. Parker* 348 U.S. 26, 75 S. Ct. 98, 99 L. Ed. 27 (1954) [1945 Act providing for redevelopment of slum areas and sale or lease of condemned lands to private interests held constitutional], the Court stated that it is up to the legislature to determine what constitutes a public use. This principle does not change simply because the power of eminent domain is involved. While courts do have a role in reviewing a legislature's decisions in such matters, it is "an extremely narrow one," and they should defer to the legislature. The concentration of land ownership has altered the State residential land market and forced thousands of people to lease, rather than buy, the land underneath their homes. Because regulating oligopoly has been an exercise of a State's police powers since colonial times, Hawaii's exercise of this power should be allowed. Moreover, the Act is rationally connected to this problem. The Act authorizes the HHA (P) to condemn lots in a tract where a significant number of tenants wish to buy the land, and limits the number of lots each tenant can buy. Whether the Act is ultimately successful is not the issue. If the Hawaii Legislature rationally could have believed that the Act would promote the objective, then the Act is constitutional. The Court of Appeals reasoned that the Act created takings for private, not public, use because the lessees can retain the property throughout the condemnation process. This factor is irrelevant, as "it is only the taking's purpose, and not its mechanics, that must pass the scrutiny of the Public Use Clause." If the State can promote its objectives without taking actual possession of the land, it should be allowed to do so. The fact that this is a state legislature's decision as opposed to a congressional decision does not mean a higher level of scrutiny should be applied. District Court judgment affirmed.

Analysis:

Over the years, there have been two very different meanings of the "public use" requirement. As Lawrence Berger wrote in The Public Use Requirement in Eminent Domain, 57 Or. L. Rev. 203, 205, 209 (1978), there has been a "broad" view and a "narrow" view of public use. On one hand, the broad meaning of the term is that public use requires that there be an advantage or benefit to the public. The narrow meaning, on the other hand, requires the public actually use or have the right to use the condemned property. Although the narrow view has had its supporters, particularly during the latter half of the nineteenth century, it nonetheless competed with the broad view during that period. Under the narrow use definition, property could be condemned provided a structure which could serve a large number of people, like a hotel, restaurant, or theater could be allowed. Under the broader benefit definition, a major manufacturer can just as easily condemn property to build a factory that will employ substantial amounts of people in the surrounding area. To this day, the scope of public use is unclear.

MICHIGAN SUPREME COURT HOLDS THAT WHERE LAND WAS CONDEMNED SO THAT IT COULD BE RESOLD TO AN AUTO MANUFACTURER FOR A NEW ASSEMBLY PLANT, THE CONDEMNATION PROVIDED A CLEAR AND SIGNIFICANT BENEFIT TO THE COMMUNITY AND WAS THUS DONE FOR A PUBLIC USE

Poletown Neighborhood Council v. City of Detroit

(Neighborhood Residents) v. (City)

(1981) 410 Mich. 616, 304 N.W.2d 455

MEMORY GRAPHIC

Instant Facts

Detroit wanted to condemn some residential land so General Motors could build an assembly plant, and neighbors saw it as a taking for private use.

Black Letter Rule

When the condemnation of property benefits specific and identifiable private interests, a court must employ heightened scrutiny to determine if a clear and significant public interest is the predominant interest being advanced.

Case Vocabulary

BLIGHT: A rotting, deteriorated state; to suffer from such a condition.

FOUNDERING: Suffering from a disabled or weakened condition.

Procedural Basis: Appeal from action for injunctive relief.

Facts: In 1980, General Motors began discussions with the City of Detroit (D) in order to find a suitable site for an assembly plant in the city. General Motors conceived the project, imposed its own deadlines for property acquisition, and selected the site, a residential neighborhood. General Motors also demanded twelve years of tax concessions from the City (D). The City (D) agreed to condemn this residential neighborhood, clear the land, and convey it to General Motors. The land in question was not a slum or blighted area. At the time, unemployment was high throughout the nation, and was reaching "calamitous" levels in Detroit, Michigan. The domestic automobile industry was facing severe losses due to overseas competition. Unemployment in Michigan was at 14.2%. Furthermore, the City of Detroit (D) saw employment rise to 18%, and among its (D) black citizens the amount was nearly 30%. Many manufacturers had been taking their operations to the southern states. The removal of this assembly plant project would have resulted in the loss of at least 6,000 jobs, as well as business from design, manufacture, and sales companies associated with General Motors. In addition, millions of dollars would have been lost in real estate and income tax revenues. The Poletown Neighborhood Council (P), comprised of residents of the neighborhood in question, sued to enjoin the project. The Council (P) claimed that the City (D) was taking property for General Motors' private use, and not for a public use. The City (P) argued, however, that the controlling public purpose in taking this land was to deal with the problems of unemployment and economic distress.

Issue: Can a condemnation that clearly benefits a specific and identifiable private interest be authorized?

Decision and Rationale: Yes. Just as a condemnation for a public use or purpose is permitted, a condemnation for a private use or purpose is forbidden. If a private benefit is only incidental to a condemnation for public purpose, however, the condemnation cannot be forbidden. Here, the City (D) would clearly and significantly benefit from the thousands of jobs and vast revenues in taxes and local business that would result from the operation of the proposed assembly plant. As such, these benefits are sufficient to show that this condemnation project was of the type intended by the State Legislature when it allowed municipalities to condemn property, even when private parties may receive a benefit. The primary purpose of this project is the alleviation of unemployment and the revitalization of the local economy. Any benefit to General Motors is purely incidental. Judgment affirmed.

Dissent: The City relies on earlier cases in which condemnation for the purpose of slum renewal was upheld even though the property taken was eventually transferred to private parties. In those cases, unlike the situation here, resale of the properties to private parties was only incidental. The main purpose behind the condemnation was to protect the public health and welfare, which was threatened by the deteriorated conditions of the slums. By contrast, the transfer of property to General Motors is the primary objective of the condemnation. There is no evidence that the property in question here is similarly blighted. Any economic benefits for the community will only come about through General Motors' use of the property. Thus, the economic benefits are incidental to the private use of the property.

Dissent: The real issue here is the problem of condemning private property because another private party promises to use it to a greater public 'benefit' than the old use. When General Motors first proposed its new assembly plant site,

Detroit (D) was in the grips of a severe economic crisis. With such high rates of unemployment, the loss of so many manufacturers to neighboring states, and with the threat of 6,000 lost jobs, Detroit (D) had its economic back to the wall when General Motors pushed its deal. General Motors dictated all the terms of the project, and in allowing this, the City has seriously jeopardized the security of private property ownership in the state.

Analysis:

There are at least three other reasons why the authorization of this condemnation seems questionable. First, the majority states that the benefit to General Motors is merely incidental. This idea goes against the evidence of General Motors' involvement in the deal; General Motors set all the schedules, cost allocations, and deadlines, and even demanded twelve years of tax concessions from the City (D). General Motors did not benefit from this venture by chance; it orchestrated the deal to gain the maximum benefits and convenience for itself. Jobs are to be expected when a new factory is constructed; what General Motors did was structure the operation to gain benefits for itself as an inextricable part of the deal. Second, no consideration is offered as to the non-economic aspects of this decision. It is possible that construction of an assembly plant would destroy the cohesiveness of what may have been a close-knit community. Also, the loss of a 'green field' area in a city with almost none is significant; there is no evidence that this area, whether a park, playground, or other open 'green field' would be replaced elsewhere in the city. Finally, an argument could be made that this condemnation should have been subjected to heightened scrutiny. This decision directly affected the economic livelihood of the City (D), and possibly the State as well. This undoubtedly had deep political ramifications, and as such should have merited higher scrutiny.

CALIFORNIA SUPREME COURT HOLDS THAT WHERE A CITY TRIED TO TAKE AND OPERATE A PROFESSIONAL FOOTBALL FRANCHISE UNDER A CLAIM OF VALID PUBLIC USE, THE TRIAL COURT MUST DETERMINE IF OWNING THE TEAM, LIKE OWNING A FACILITY WHERE A TEAM MAY PLAY, CONSTITUTES A LEGITIMATE PUBLIC PURPOSE

City of Oakland v. Oakland Raiders

(City) v. (Football Team)

(1982) 32 Cal. 3d 60, 646 P.2d 835, 183 Cal. Rptr. 673

M E M O R Y   G R A P H I C

Instant Facts

The Oakland Raiders wanted to move down to Los Angeles, but their hometown fans did not want them to leave.

Black Letter Rule

The promotion of the education, recreation, or pleasure of the public constitutes a legitimate public purpose.

Case Vocabulary

GERMANE: Relevant, appropriate.

Procedural Basis: Appeal from action for taking through eminent domain.

Facts: In 1980, the owners of the Oakland Raiders (D), a professional football team, decided to move the franchise to Los Angeles. Oakland tried to keep the team in Oakland by acquiring it through eminent domain.

Issue: Does the taking of a professional sports franchise satisfy a legitimate public purpose?

Decision and Rationale: Yes. Granted, there is apparently no case that has held that a municipality can acquire and operate a professional football team. The City of Visalia, however, does own and operate a Class A baseball franchise in the minor leagues, and its right to do so has never been challenged in court. Also, in an earlier decision, the acquisition of a baseball field by the City of Los Angeles was described as "obviously for public purposes." The courts have also held that a county's acquisition by eminent domain of lands to be used for a county fair, and a city's power to build an opera house, all fall within the realm of legitimate public purposes. Generally, "anything calculated to promote the education, the recreation, or the pleasure of the public is to be included within the legitimate domain of public purposes." Candlestick Park in San Francisco and Anaheim Stadium in Anaheim are both owned and operated in municipalities. Also, the appellate court upheld the power of the City of Anaheim to condemn land for parking facilities at the latter stadium on the ground that the acquisition, building, and operation of such a stadium by a municipality represents a legitimate public purpose. The Raiders organization (D) has not presented a valid legal basis for concluding that the difference between owning and running a facility and owning and running a team is legally substantial. However, it is certainly possible that the trial court could decide with a fuller record that there is no substantial legal difference. Case remanded on public-use question. [The action was dismissed on other grounds without reaching that issue. The dismissal was then reversed by the appellate court and the case was again remanded. The court of appeal ruled that the taking would violate the commerce clause.]

Analysis:

There is a significant difference between owning a team and owning land for a playing facility or parking lot for a team. For ownership of a team to satisfy public use, questions of revenue would also seem to be accompanied by questions of civic pride in the team. Both would have to be measured by its ties to the community, through jobs, attendance, product sales, and the like. This sort of evaluation, however, could pose a problem when another city that has wanted a sports franchise, but has been without one, is pitted against a city that is trying to hold onto one of many. It can become a balancing question of public use in one city versus a possibly bigger public use in another. Ownership of a stadium, on the other hand, seems less complicated, particularly since it can be used for other, non-team purposes. Stadiums, arenas, and parking lots can generate revenue throughout the year through the staging of a wide variety of community events, sports and otherwise, and not just during the few months of a sports season. The ownership of a facility can be easier to characterize as a public use since it has wide-reaching financial effects which could include, but not be restricted to, a city's loyal or fickle pride in a team.

UNITED STATES SUPREME COURT HOLDS THAT A NEW YORK STATUTE ALLOWING A CABLE TELEVISION COMPANY TO PERMANENTLY ATTACH ITS COMPONENTS TO AN APARTMENT BUILDING WITHOUT INTERFERENCE AMOUNTED TO A TAKING

Loretto v. Teleprompter Manhattan CATV Corp.

(Building Owner) v. (Cable Company)
(1982) 458 U.S. 419

MEMORY GRAPHIC

Instant Facts

A new building owner sued a cable company over the cable it was allowed to install on the building by a state statute.

Black Letter Rule

A permanent physical occupation of an owner's property authorized by the government constitutes a taking of property which requires just compensation, regardless of the public interests it may serve.

Case Vocabulary

METAPHYSICAL: Pertaining to theories and philosophies on the reality of something beyond mere sensory perception.
TAP: An intermediate point in an electrical circuit which can support additional connections.

Procedural Basis: Appeal from summary judgment in class action for damages and injunctive relief.

Facts: On June 1, 1970, Teleprompter Manhattan CATV Corporation (D) installed a cable on an apartment building located at 303 West 105th Street, New York City. The owner gave Teleprompter (D) the exclusive right to provide cable television (CATV) services to the tenants. The cable was about one-half inch in diameter, and about 30 feet long. It ran along the roof of the building, and was attached to two small directional taps, which allowed for future connections. These and other components were attached directly to the masonry. This cable served as a "crossover" line, helping provide other buildings on the block with CATV. Jean Loretto (P) purchased the building in 1971. Teleprompter (D) connected a direct, "noncrossover" cable line to the building two years later. Earlier, the State enacted Executive Law §828, effective January 1, 1973, which provided that a landlord "may not interfere with the installation of cable facilities upon his property or premises." The State Commission on Cable Television said that a landlord is only entitled to a one-time $1 fee for installation. Loretto (P) was not aware of the cable until after she bought the building. Loretto (P) brought a class action against Teleprompter (D) on behalf of all owners of real property in the State on which Teleprompter (D) placed its components. She (P) claimed it was a trespass and, insofar as it relied on §828, a taking without just compensation. The City of New York intervened. The trial court granted summary judgment for Teleprompter and the city. The Court of Appeals, over dissent, upheld the statute.

Issue: Does a permanent physical occupation of an owner's property, authorized by government, constitute a taking of property which requires just compensation?

Decision and Rationale: (Marshall) Yes. A permanent physical occupation of an owner's property authorized by the government constitutes a taking of property which requires just compensation, regardless of the public interests it may serve. A permanent occupation has long been viewed as arguably the most serious invasion of an owner's property interests. A classic example of this is found in cases where a person constructs a dam which permanently floods another person's property. A permanent physical occupation prevents the owner from both possessing the occupied space and excluding the occupier from possession and use of it. This power to exclude is one of the most important elements in an owner's "bundle of property rights." The owner is denied any control over the use of the property. Though an owner may still have the right to sell the property, that right is seriously devalued, as a purchaser would also be unable to use the occupied space. While the size of an occupation should be considered in determining compensation, it should make no difference in finding whether a taking has occurred. Teleprompter (D) argues §828 only applies to rental property, and thus is a permissible regulation. An occupation of only one type of property, however, is nonetheless an occupation. This reasoning will not have adverse consequences on the state's ability to regulate housing conditions because such regulation imposes duties on landlords and tenants, not on outside third parties. Landlords can still install fire extinguishers and smoke alarms provided third parties are not involved. The State can still regulate an owner's use of property, but it cannot authorize a permanent physical occupation of the property. Judgment reversed. Case remanded on issue of compensation.

Dissent: (Blackmun) The permanent physical occupation formula is a very problematic standard. The exact meaning of "permanent" is unclear. Section 828 only requires that the cable equipment be allowed as long as the building "remains residential and the CATV company wishes to retain the installation." If this law results in a "permanent" occupation, other New York statutes that compe a landlord to make physical attachments (like smoke alarms) to his or her property must also constitute takings, "regardless of the public interests they may serve." The majority's "third party" problem would still exist even if Loretto (P) owned the cable herself (P). If Teleprompter (D) continued to transmit its signal through the cable, a host of conceptual arguments on whether such a signal is "physical" could result. The distinction between permanent occupation versus temporary invasion has no basis in Takings Clause precedent or economic logic. Takings claims should be evaluated under a multiple factor balancing test, and not by a set formula. Also, Loretto (P) would have had no other use for this space, and any determination of compensation should be made with this in mind. Moreover, the majority assumes that the tenants have no countervailing interest in allowing Teleprompter (D) to use the space. Finally, this decision suggests that the legislature cannot exercise its police power to grant Teleprompter (D) the rights to even one-eighth cubic foot of space.

Analysis:

The New York Court of Appeals heard the issue of just compensation on remand. The Court said the $1 sum was sufficient because cable service usually increases the value of a building, particularly in the eyes of potential renters. With this in mind, it would appear that Loretto brought this suit for nothing. Granted, Teleprompter's installments did constitute an occupation, but the Court of Appeals recognized it had increased the value of Loretto's property. The presence of cable television likely made the property more attractive to potential renters in a city where high-rise structures impair television reception. It was also a taking which the tenants who desired cable service presumably wanted. In addition, Teleprompter could have argued that their cable television service, authorized by the City, equaled a public use. In California, at least, the courts have declared that the promotion of public recreation and education is a legitimate public purpose. The provision of cable television could arguably fit this purpose. This idea, combined with the minimal space occupied and the obvious benefit to landlord and tenants, suggests that the majority decision was too rigid in its reasoning.

A BRICKYARD HAD TO BE SHUT DOWN ACCORDING TO A CITY ORDINANCE, EVEN THOUGH IT WAS BUILT LONG BEFORE THE CITY GREW; ITS OWNER WAS NOT ENTITLED TO COMPENSATION BECAUSE THE BRICKYARD WAS A NUISANCE

Hadacheck v. Sebastian

(Brickyard Owner) v. (Chief of Police)

(1915) 239 U.S. 394

M E M O R Y G R A P H I C

Instant Facts

Hadacheck built a brickyard outside city limits, but after the city grew and surrounded it, the city said Hadacheck violated an ordinance against brickyards.

Black Letter Rule

A regulation that deprives an owner of property for the purpose of prohibiting a nuisance is an exercise of the police power, and therefore does not result in a taking which requires compensation.

Case Vocabulary

HABEAS CORPUS: Writ which brings a party before a court, mainly to release that party from unlawful imprisonment.

KILN: An oven or furnace used for the firing and drying of bricks during their manufacturing process.

TRAVERSE: Denial of an allegation.

Facts: Hadacheck (P) is the owner of a tract which is now within the limits of the City of Los Angeles. An ordinance is in effect in the city which makes it unlawful for any person to establish or operate a brick yard or any other facility for the manufacture or burning of brick within city limits. At the time Hadacheck (P) purchased the land, it was outside city limits. He did not expect the city to annex the surrounding area. On this tract, there is a very valuable bed of clay, which can be used to make fine quality bricks. The entire tract, if used for brick-making purposes, is worth about $800,000; if the tract were used for any other purpose, it would be worth no more than $60,000. Hadacheck (P) has already made significant excavations over much of the tract; it cannot be used for residential purposes. He (P) has also set up expensive machinery for the manufacturing of bricks. The city has since grown and annexed the land adjoining the brick yard. Hadacheck (P) argues, among many other things, that his tract contains particularly fine clay, so that if the ordinance is declared valid he will be deprived of the use of his property without just compensation. Also, he (P) argues the brickyard is not a nuisance, and does not pose a danger to public health and safety. He (P) claims that no one has registered a complaint about it during the seven years he (P) has operated it. Affidavits were provided which counter Hadacheck's (P) allegations that the brick yard was not offensive to public health, claiming that fumes and dust from the yard have caused discomfort to those living nearby. Hadacheck (P) was convicted of a misdemeanor for his violation of the city ordinance.

Issue: Can a person's property be taken in the prohibition of a nuisance without compensation?

Decision and Rationale: (McKenna) Yes. A regulation that deprives an owner of property for the purpose of prohibiting a nuisance is an exercise of the police power, and therefore does not result in a taking which requires compensation. This is one of the most essential powers of government, and has few limitations. Though its particular use here may seem harsh, the general need for such power precludes any limitation, provided that the power is not used arbitrarily. A police power cannot be challenged by a person's interest in property because of conditions that were in effect when the property was obtained. To allow such opposition would hinder the growth and development of cities. To promote growth, private interests must yield to the good of the community. Granted, Hadacheck's (P's) business of brickmaking is lawful in and of itself. It is clearly, however, within the power of the State to regulate such a business and to declare that, in certain circumstances and certain areas, the business would constitute a nuisance. The affidavits provided, claiming the brickyard led to discomfort of nearby residents, further demonstrates that the adjoining area is now being used for residential purposes. Because of this situation, the brickyard does constitute a nuisance, and thus can be prohibited. Though Hadacheck (P) claims the enforcement of the ordinance will deprive him of the use of his (P's) property and his (P's) business, this is not entirely true. While Hadacheck (P) could not operate a brickyard on his (P's) tract, he (P) is not prohibited from removing the clay to be used at a brickyard outside the area bound by the ordinance. Though such operation of his business would be difficult from a financial standpoint, it is not impossible. Judgment affirmed.

Analysis:

Though it has not been overruled, the Court's categorical decision in Hadacheck has been heavily criticized. It appears that whenever a person engages in nuisance-like behavior on their property, the person must expect the government to regulate them, curbing his or her property rights if necessary. In Hadacheck's case, this belief requires that Hadacheck should have expected that Los Angeles would grow beyond its limits; that residents would move and build homes near his brickyard; that Los Angeles would annex the surrounding land; that the city would pass an ordinance against the business he would have been running for years up to that point; and that the city would have a valid claim to have him shut down his business or possibly move it off his property after several years. This chain of events seems to be a lot to hold Hadacheck responsible for. Still, this categorical ruling is markedly different from the categorical ruling in Loretto. There, the Court said that a permanent physical occupation by the government is always considered a taking; here, a nuisance-control action by the government is never considered by the Court to be a taking. The idea is that the exercise of police power is necessary because the property itself is detrimental to the public.. The exercise of eminent domain, by contrast, is necessary to take property which is useful to the public.

JNITED STATES SUPREME COURT HOLDS THAT WHERE A COAL COMPANY DEEDED 'HE SURFACE RIGHTS TO PROPERTY BUT RETAINED THE RIGHT TO MINE JNDERNEATH, A STATUTE WHICH BARRED SUCH MINING COULD NOT BE ;USTAINED BECAUSE IT DESTROYED THE COAL COMPANY'S MINERAL RIGHTS

'ennsylvania Coal Co. v. Mahon

Mineral Rights Owner) v. (Surface Rights Owner)
922) 260 U.S. 393

ΛEMORY GRAPHIC

Instant Facts

A company sold surface rights to some land to Λahon, but retained the right to mine underneath, and ıch mining was prohibited by statute.

Black Letter Rule

While property may be regulated to a certain xtent, if that regulation goes too far in diminishing the conomic value of the property, it will be recognized as taking.

Case Vocabulary

NTHRACITE: A hard natural coal which burns very eanly; also called hard coal.
ONFLAGRATION: A very large and dangerous fire.
XIGENCY: That which requires immediate action.
ECIPROCITY: A mutual transfer or exchange.
UBSIDENCE: A state of falling, sinking, or collapse.
VRIT OF ERROR: A writ issued by an appellate court in rder to compel the examination of errors alleged to ave occurred.

Procedural Basis: Writ of error after decree for bill in equity for injunctive relief.

Facts: In 1878, Pennsylvania Coal Company (D) executed a deed which conveyed property rights to the surface of some land to Mahon (P). The deed also states, however, in express terms, that the Coal Company (D) reserves the right to remove all the coal under that surface, and that Mahon (P) takes the premises with that risk. The deed also provides that Mahon (P) waives all claim for damages that may arise from mining out the coal. Mahon (P) claims that whatever rights the Coal Company (D) may have had, these rights were taken away by the Kohler Act, approved May 27, 1921. The Kohler Act forbids the mining of coal in such a way that would cause the sinking of, among other things, any structure used for human habitation. There are certain exceptions, including the mining of land where the surface is owned by the owner of the underlying coal and is more than 150 feet from anyone else's improved property. The Court of Common Pleas found that mining by the Coal Company would remove the supporting earth underneath the house and cause the house and surface to sink. Despite this finding, however, the Court denied Mahon's (P's) request for an injunction, holding that, if applied to this case, the Kohler Act would be unconstitutional. The Supreme Court of the State held the statute was a legitimate exercise of the police power and directed a decree for the plaintiffs. A writ of error was then granted.

Issue: Is a property regulation statute which eliminates a pre-existing property right the equivalent of a taking without compensation?

Decision and Rationale: (Holmes) Yes. While property may be regulated to a certain extent, if that regulation goes too far in diminishing the economic value of the property, it will be recognized as a taking. It has long been recognized that some property rights are enjoyed under an implied limitation and must yield to the government's police power. This implied limitation must also be limited, however, by the contract and due process clauses. At some point, eminent domain must be exercised and compensation must be given for interfering with a person's property rights. Where that point lies depends on the facts of each case. Here, while there is undoubtedly a public interest in protecting the owner of a single home, the potential damage is not common or public. Indeed, the Kohler Act demonstrates the limited extent of this public interest, with its exception for people who own both the surface and the coal beneath. Further, the Kohler Act is not justified as a protection of personal safety, as the Coal Company (D) here has given notice of its intent to mine under the house. To enforce this Act would eliminate the Coal Company's (D's) interest in the coal, which is viewed as an estate in land in Pennsylvania, and go against a valid contract between the Coal Company (D) and Mahon (D). The Act does not offer a public interest sufficient to warrant the taking of the coal. The right to coal must include the right to mine it. To make it commercially impracticable to mine coal has basically the same effect as appropriating it or destroying it. Some cases have allowed a statute which required that a pillar of coal be left standing between two adjacent mines to protect against flooding. That requirement, however, provides an average reciprocity of advantage to the owners of the two properties. Here, Mahon (P) took the risk of obtaining only the surface rights to the land. The fact that the risk is likely to occur does not warrant giving Mahon (D) greater rights than he (P) paid for. Decree reversed.

Dissent: (Brandeis) While coal is still in place, it is still part of the land, and the right of an owner to use his land is never absolute. No landowner can use land in a way that creates a public nuisance or threatens the public welfare. A restriction that is imposed to protect the public health, safety, or morals is not a taking. Also, such restrictions do not cease to be public just because some private persons, like Mahon (P) here, receive particular benefit from them. A restriction is lawful if it is an appropriate means to the public end; here, keeping the coal in place is one of the only ways of preventing the surface from sinking, and thus is appropriate. While the majority expresses its concern over the diminution in value of one part of the land, that value should be compared to the value of the property as a whole. Further, the mere presence of notice against danger or a mere contract cannot prevail against the exercise of the police power when the public safety is threatened. While the majority argues that the public interes affected by this Act is limited, in reality the Act includes provisior dealing with mining under streets and roads, churches, hospital schools, railroad stations, and many other places where man members of the public gather. Such prohibitions are obviously for public purpose. The majority states that an exercise of the polic power requires an average reciprocity [mutual transfer or exchange of advantage. Where the police power is exercised to protect th public from danger, however, there is no room for considerin reciprocity of advantage.

Analysis:

Holmes' test of whether a regulation has gone "too far" seems less rigid than the other tests for permanent physical occupation and measure prohibiting nuisances. This rule basically says that when a regulation of a use of property that is not a nuisance imposes too great a burden c property owners, it cannot be enforced without compensation. What is interesting about this test is that it allows questions of degree rath than questions of the type of taking involved. Also, in such cases the regulation in question may actually provide some compensation to th owner being regulated. This can occur through what Holmes called the average reciprocity of advantage. Persons who seem to be burdene by a government prohibition, say, against mining under certain structures, may not come away empty-handed, since these regulations a imposed for the benefit of the public, themselves included.

J. S. SUPREME COURT HOLDS THAT A NEW YORK LANDMARKS PRESERVATION LAW WHICH WAS THE BASIS FOR BARRING CONSTRUCTION OF AN OFFICE BUILDING OVER GRAND CENTRAL TERMINAL DID NOT EFFECT A TAKING BECAUSE IT DID NOT TRANSFER CONTROL OF THE PROPERTY, BUT ONLY RESTRICTED IT

Penn Central Transportation Co. v. City of New York

Landmark Owner) v. (City)

1978) 438 U.S. 104

MEMORY GRAPHIC

Instant Facts

Penn Central made plans to construct an office building over Grand Central Terminal, but was blocked by a Landmarks Preservation Law.

Black Letter Rule

A law which does not interfere with an owner's primary expectation concerning the use of the property, and allows the owners to receive a reasonable return on his or her investment, does not effect a taking which demands just compensation.

Case Vocabulary

ABROGATE: To end the effect of something through government action; to annul.

BEAUX ARTS: An artistic style which is known for its use of vivid decorative detail, historic elements, and a noticeable leaning toward grand, monumental forms in architecture.

Procedural Basis: Appeal from judgment in action for declaratory and injunctive relief.

Facts: In 1967, New York City's (D) Landmarks Preservation Commission (Commission) designated Grand Central Terminal a landmark under the city's (D) Landmarks Preservation Law. The Terminal, owned by Penn Central Transportation Co. (P) and its affiliates, has been described as "a magnificent example of the French beaux arts style." For at least 65 years, the property had been used as a railroad terminal with office space and concessions. The landmark law did not interfere with the Terminal's continued use in this capacity, but restricted any changes in the Terminal's exterior architectural features without the Commission's approval. In addition, landmark owners are allowed to transfer their development rights under zoning regulations to contiguous properties on the same block, or other properties they also own. At this time, Penn Central (P) owned several properties in downtown Manhattan. In 1968, in order to increase its income from the Terminal, Penn Central (P) entered into a long-term lease with UGP (P), a British corporation. UGP (P) was to build a 55-story office building above the Terminal, paying an annual rent of $1 million during construction and at least $3 million thereafter. Penn Central and UGP (P) submitted two plans to the Commission: one with a modern office tower over the French-style facade of the Terminal, and one with a completely redesigned Terminal. The Commission sternly rejected both plans, calling the first one "an aesthetic joke." It also said, however, that construction would be allowed depending on whether a proposed addition "would harmonize in scale, materials, and character" with the Terminal. Penn Central and UGP (P) brought suit in state court, alleging the landmarks law effected a taking of their (P) property. The trial court granted injunctive and declaratory relief, but the intermediate appellate court reversed. The New York Court of Appeals affirmed, finding no taking as the law only restricted, not transferred, control of the property.

Issue: Does the application of a law which restricts an owner's use of property, but does not interfere with the owner's primary use of the property or deny a reasonable economic return on it, constitute a taking?

Decision and Rationale: (Brennan) No. A law which does not interfere with an owner's primary expectation concerning the use of the property, and allows the owners to receive a reasonable return on his or her investment, does not effect a taking which demands just compensation. There is no set formula for deciding these cases, and so this Court must look at the particular facts here. The extent to which the law has interfered with distinct, investment-backed expectations is particularly relevant. Penn Central and UGP (P) claim that the airspace above the Terminal is a valuable property interest that has been taken through the landmark law. This claim is rejected because the rights in the property as a whole, not those in individual estates, must be considered. Also, Penn Central and UGP (P) argue that the law effects a taking by significantly diminishing the economic value of an individual landmark site, the Terminal property, unlike other laws which impose restrictions on entire historic districts. This argument is rejected because this landmark law, like others throughout the country, is part of a comprehensive plan to preserve landmarks all over the city. The interference with Penn Central's (P) property rights is not severe enough to equal a taking. The law does not interfere with Penn Central's (P) primary expectation concerning the use of the Terminal for railroad service, office space, and concessions. Thus, Penn Central (P) is permitted to obtain a "reasonable return" on its investment in the Terminal. Moreover, Penn Central and UGP (P) have not been barred from any construction over the Terminal; only the two plans in question have been rejected.

Because they (P) have not submitted plans for a smaller structure, it is not known whether they (P) will be denied permission to use any of the Terminal airspace. Finally, though Penn Central and UGP (P) claim their (P) airspace rights have been taken, they (P) have always had the right to transfer those rights to nearby properties. This situation may not be ideal for them (Ps), but those rights are still very valuable. Judgment affirmed.

Dissent: (Rehnquist) This landmark law is unlike typical zoning restrictions that usually provide benefits for, as well as impose burdens on, restricted properties. There is no reciprocity of advantage here. Only a few buildings are singled out with considerable burdens and no comparable benefits. Because there was no nuisance-control justification in restricting Penn Central's (P) airspace rights, the action resulted in a taking. Though the value of the transferable development rights may possibly be valuable enough to serve as just compensation, there is not enough evidence to prove this conclusively. The decision should be remanded to see if these transferable rights amount to "a full and perfect equivalent for the property taken."

Analysis:

The concept of "reasonable return on investment" is problematic. While prior to this decision, the New York Court of Appeals also relied on this idea, it noted that it was "an elusive concept, incapable of definition." The reasonableness of the return on the owner's investment must be based on the value of the property. However, the value of the property is inescapably dependent on the amount of return that is permitted or available. This circularity of reasoning is what makes the concept of reasonable return on investment a somewhat shaky one.

UNITED STATES SUPREME COURT HOLDS THAT THE ENFORCEMENT OF A SOUTH CAROLINA STATUTE WHICH RESTRICTED DEVELOPMENT IN COASTAL AREAS AMOUNTED TO A TAKING BECAUSE IT DEPRIVED AN OWNER OF ALL ECONOMICALLY PRODUCTIVE USE OF HIS PROPERTY

Lucas v. South Carolina Coastal Council

(Property Owner) v. (Government Body)
(1992) 112 S. Ct. 2886

M E M O R Y   G R A P H I C

Instant Facts

Lucas claimed that a South Carolina statute which barred him from building on his barrier island property resulted in a taking without just compensation.

Black Letter Rule

A land-use regulation that deprives an owner of all economically valuable use of property by prohibiting uses that are permitted under background principles of property and nuisance law results in a taking, and thus requires compensation.

Case Vocabulary

A FORTIORI: A term of logic which denotes that if one argument is held to be valid, another claim which is either part of that initial argument, or less improbable, or analogous to it must be a valid argument as well.
DISPOSITIVE: Persuasive; directed toward a certain point of view.
Ipse dixit: "He himself said it;" a positive statement that is based on an individual's authority.
SIC UTERE TUO UT ALIENUM NON LAEDAS: Common law principle that one should not use his or her property in a way that injures another.

Procedural Basis: Writ of certiorari after bench trial in action for taking without just compensation.

Facts: In 1977, the South Carolina Legislature enacted a Coastal Zone Management Act, after the earlier passage of a similar law in Congress. The South Carolina Act imposed restrictions on owners of coastal zone land that qualified as a "critical area," defined in the Act to include beaches and adjacent sand dunes. Owners of such land had to obtain a permit from the newly formed South Carolina Coastal Council (D) before putting the land to a "use other than the use the critical area was devoted to on [September 28, 1977]." This Act marked the beginning of South Carolina's expressed interest in managing the development of coastal areas. In the late 1970's, Lucas and others started extensive residential development on the Isle of Palms, a barrier island [island parallel to shore which protects it from the effects of the ocean] off the coast of Charleston, South Carolina. In 1986, Lucas (P) bought two lots on this island for $975,000, planning to build single-family homes on them. These lots did not fall within the "critical area" described in the 1977 Act, and thus were unaffected by it. The land adjacent to Lucas' (P's) lots already contained similar structures. In 1988, the Legislature enacted the Beachfront Management Act. This Act directed the Council (D) to establish a 'baseline' connecting the landward-most "point[s] of erosion ...during the past forty years" in the region of Isle of Palms where Lucas' lots were located. This 1988 Act prohibited the construction of occupiable improvements between the sea and a line drawn 20 feet landward of, and parallel to, this baseline. Lucas' (P's) land fell in this zone. Lucas (P) filed suit in the South Carolina Court of Common Appeals, contending this ban on construction effected a taking by completely extinguishing the value of his property. The trial court found that the 1988 Act "deprived Lucas of any reasonable economic use of his lots." Thus, the court concluded that Lucas' (P's) properties had been taken and ordered compensation in the amount of $1232,387.50. The Supreme Court of South Carolina reversed, saying when a regulation on the use of property is meant to prevent serious public harm no compensation is required, regardless of its effect on the property's value.

Issue:

Can the government enforce a land-use regulation regardless of its effects on the value of an owner's property?

Decision and Rationale: (Scalia) No. A land-use regulation that deprives an owner of all economically valuable use of property by prohibiting uses that are permitted under background principles of property and nuisance law results in a taking, and thus requires compensation. In the past, this Court has recognized that if the regulation of property goes "too far," it will be recognized as a taking. Though "too far" has never been exactly defined, a taking has been found when a land-use regulation denies an owner the economically viable use of his or her land. Though this rule has never been formally justified, it has been accepted because such a loss, in the landowner's point of view, is the equivalent of a physical taking. Though the government has been allowed, in certain cases, to affect property values without paying compensation, this should not occur when a landowner has been deprived of all economic beneficial uses of his or her land. Here, the South Carolina Supreme Court felt the 1988 Act involved a valid exercise of the State's police powers to mitigate the harm to the public interest that Lucas' proposed development would cause. Lucas (P) essentially conceded that the State's beach areas were a valuable resource, that new construction contributed to the erosion of these areas, and that discouraging such construction was necessary to prevent a great public harm. The distinction, however, between an act which prevents public harm and one which confers a public benefit often lies in the eye of the beholder. Such a distinction is almost impossible to make objectively. Thus, this sort of harmful-use logic should not be used to separate regulatory takings which require compensation from regulatory deprivations that do not. To adopt the South Carolina Supreme Court's approach to this problem would essentially wipe out the limitation on regulation which goes "too far." Therefore, a State should only be allowed to deprive a owner of all economically beneficial use of property, without needing to pay compensation, when the interest in the regulated use was not part of the title to begin with. In other words, a property owner necessarily expects the uses of his or her property to be restricted, on occasion, by newly enacted legislation. That owner, however, should not have to expect that his or her property will be rendered economically worthless by similarly new legislation against certain uses of land. Such a limitation must inhere in the title itself, in the background principles of the State's property and nuisance law. The source of such a sweeping limitation, then, must not be the legislative designation of something as a nuisance, but rather the common-law doctrine.Judgment reversed and cause remanded.

Concurrence: (Kennedy) The majority opinion, though establishing a framework for remand, did not decide the question of whether a temporary taking had indeed occurred. Also, the determination that Lucas' (P's) property was deprived of all economic value by a mere development restriction is a "curious" one. In addition, the finding that a parcel of property is left with no value must be based under the Takings Clause on the owner's reasonable, investment-backed expectations. Though this definition of value may seem circular in some aspects, it is not entirely so. The Constitution protects expectations that are based on objective rules and customs that are generally accepted as reasonable ones. Finally, "reasonable expectations must be understood in light of the whole of our legal tradition." The common law doctrine of nuisance is too narrow to rely on when considering issues of a government's regulatory power, particularly in the context of today's complex, modern society.

Dissent: (Blackmun) With this decision, "the Court launches a missile to kill a mouse." First, if the state legislature is correct that the construction ban in the zone outlined in the Beachfront Management Act prevents serious harm, then the Act is constitutional. Earlier decisions have consistently upheld regulations meant to protect the common welfare. Here, Lucas (P) never challenged the legislative findings as to the importance of the construction ban, so the South Carolina Supreme Court correctly found that no taking had occurred. Second, the trial court's finding that Lucas' (P's) property had lost all its economic value is "almost certainly erroneous." This property can still be used for swimming, picnicking, and camping; Lucas also retains the right to sell this valuable land. Third, the Court has based many decisions on the idea that the State has the full power to restrict an owner's use of property if it is harmful to the public. It would be ridiculous to suggest that, under this new theory, an owner can have the right to harm the public if the right amount of economic loss can be shown. Fourth, the Court's reliance on a "background principles" standard is questionable, as well. Though the Court claims the harm versus benefit question cannot be objectively answered by a legislative decision, state courts make exactly the same kind of decision that the Court refuses to accept when made by the state legislature. There is no reason to think that modern interpretations of historic common-law doctrines will be any more objective than a legislative decision. Finally, there is no historic or common-law evidence of any kind of any limit on a State's ability to regulate a harmful use of property to the point of eliminating its economic value.

Dissent: (Stevens) This new categorical rule is an entirely arbitrary one. A court could define property very broadly so total takings would only be rarely found. Likewise, an investor could purchase the right to build an apartment building on a particular lot, and later argue that a zoning restriction against such a use would deprive the owner's interest of value. This rule cannot be justified merely by an owner's perception of the regulation; a regulation which diminishes a lot's value by even a fraction would almost always appear to the owner as a condemnation. The Court belief in the relative rareness of total takings does nothing to explain why some regulations should be categorized as takings and some should not. Also, a total taking does not necessarily mean that a property owner is being arbitrarily singled out, even though such an occurrence is possible. Furthermore, the exception for uses of property that are permissible under background principles basically freezes the State's common law. This action denies the legislature its traditional power to revise and develop law. Also, with this rule and exception, the Court neglects to consider the character of the regulatory action. This has traditionally been the most important element to consider in taking analysis, yet it is disregarded by the Court's decision.

Analysis:

The South Carolina Supreme Court decided, on remand from the Supreme Court's decision, whether the right for Lucas to build homes on his two lots inhered in his title. The Court found that no common law basis existed for ruling that such a right was not part of the inherent bundle of rights. Thus, the trial court was ordered to make findings of damages to compensate Lucas for the temporary taking. Damages were to be paid for the period beginning with the 1988 enactment of the Beachfront Management Act and ending with the date of the court's order.

Palazzolo v. Rhode Island

(Landowner) v. (State)
121 S.Ct. 2448 (2001)

M E M O R Y G R A P H I C

Instant Facts

Rhode Island (D) found that regulations designating most of Palazzolo's (P) land as protected "coastal wetlands" did not effect a taking partly because the regulations predated Palazzolo's (P) title to the land.

Black Letter Rule

The acquisition of title after the enactment of a regulation does not bar a challenge to that regulation under the Takings Clause.

Case Vocabulary

QUIXOTIC: Capricious and impractical.

Procedural Basis: Certiorari granted after state supreme court rejected takings claim for damages.

Facts: Palazzolo (P) owns waterfront land in Rhode Island (D). His corporation, Shore Gardens, Inc. (SGI) purchased the property in 1959. In the 1960s SGI submitted three proposals to state agencies seeking to fill the property for development, but all were denied, two citing adverse environmental impacts. In 1971 Rhode Island (D) created the Rhode Island Coastal Resources Management Council (Council) (D). The Council (D) promulgated regulations which designated salt marshes like SGI's property as protected "coastal wetlands" and greatly limited development on them. SGI lost its charter in 1978 and the property passed to Palazzolo (P) as its sole shareholder. Palazzolo (P) tried again to develop the property and submitted proposals to the Council (D) for filling the land, but the Council (D) denied them. After unsuccessfully appealing the Council's (D) last decision, Palazzolo (P) filed an inverse condemnation action claiming the Council's (D) regulations took his property without compensation. Palazzolo (P) alleged that the Council (D) deprived him of "all economically beneficial use" of his property, resulting in a total taking under *Lucas v. South Carolina Coastal Council* [regulation that deprives an owner of all economically valuable use of property results in a taking]. The Rhode Island Supreme Court ruled against Palazzolo (P) because the regulations predated his succession to legal ownership of the property, and because the regulations did not deprive him of all economic use of the land since an upland parcel still had development value. The court also held that Palazzolo (P) could not recover under *Penn Central Transportation Co. v. City of New York* [law does not effect a taking if it does not affect the owner's "reasonable investment-backed expectations"] because the regulations predated his ownership.

Issue: Does the acquisition of title after the enactment of a regulation bar a challenge to that regulation under the Takings Clause?

Decision and Rationale: (Kennedy) No. Rhode Island's (D) position is essentially that purchasers and successive title holders are deemed to have notice of earlier-enacted restrictions and therefore cannot claim that those restrictions effect a taking. This position in effect allows a state to put an expiration date on the Takings Clause. Enactments which are so onerous or unreasonable as to effect a taking do not become less so through passage of time or title. Postenactment transfer of title does not absolve a state of its obligation to defend its actions restricting land use. Future generations too have a right to challenge unreasonable limitations on the use and value of their land, which is sometimes necessary since such challenges often take years to become ripe. Further, a rule that purchasers with notice have no compensation right would place different types of purchasers if different positions, depending, for example, on whether they wanted to hold onto their land or sell it. The Takings Clause is not so quixotic. The general rule in *Lucas* comes with an exception for limitations on land use that "inhere in the title itself" because the owner is constrained by restrictions that background principles of property law place on his land. Rhode Island (D) argues that *Lucas* stands for the proposition that a new regulation becomes one of those background principles, and those who acquire title after their enactment therefore cannot challenge them. Mere passage of title does not transform a regulation that would otherwise effect a taking into a background principle. A regulation cannot be a background principle for some owners and not for others, and it does not become a background principle for subsequent owners by enactment itself. Thus, the fact that Palazzolo (P) acquired title after the enactment of these regulations does not bar him from challenging them. However, these regulations did not deprive Palazzolo (P) of all economically beneficial use because he can still improve the uplands portion of his land.

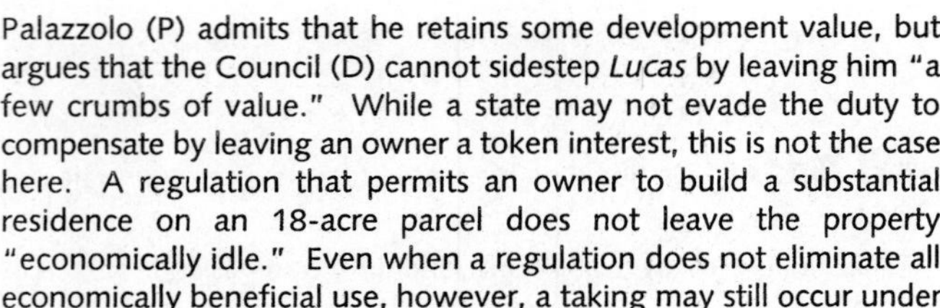

Palazzolo (P) admits that he retains some development value, but argues that the Council (D) cannot sidestep *Lucas* by leaving him "a few crumbs of value." While a state may not evade the duty to compensate by leaving an owner a token interest, this is not the case here. A regulation that permits an owner to build a substantial residence on an 18-acre parcel does not leave the property "economically idle." Even when a regulation does not eliminate all economically beneficial use, however, a taking may still occur under *Penn Central* based on factors including the regulation's economic effect on the landowner, the extent of its interference with reasonable investment-backed expectations, and the character of the government action. Since Palazzolo's (P) claim under *Penn Central* is not barred by the mere fact that he acquired title after these regulations became effective, we remand for consideration of the merits of that claim. Affirmed in part, reversed in part, and remanded.

Analysis:

In *Palazzolo* the Court explained that in cases involving direct condemnation or physical occupation, where the fact and extent of the taking are clear, compensation awards go only to the owner at the time of the taking and do not pass to subsequent purchasers. The Court explained that in regulatory takings cases, on the other hand, a landowner must wait for his claim to become ripe. This process, which may take years, may not culminate until after ownership has passed to another. Thus, the Court found that it would be illogical and unfair to bar postenactment owners from maintaining regulatory takings claims. The Court also relied upon *Nollan v. California Coastal Commission* [an exaction is not a taking if it substantially advances the same governmental purpose that refusing the permit would serve], the next case in this chapter. In *Nollan*, the dissent made the argument, similar to Rhode Island's (D) argument here, that since the Nollans purchased their home after the policy at issue went into effect, they were on notice of its restrictions. As the Court points out, the majority rejected this argument, reasoning that if the previous owners had a compensation right, they transferred it to the Nollans along with all their other property rights when they sold the property. Rejecting Rhode Island's (D) reading of *Lucas*, the Court stated that *Lucas* did not overrule *Nollan*.

U. S. SUPREME COURT HOLDS THAT WHERE A DEVELOPMENT PERMIT WOULD NOT BE ISSUED UNLESS PROPERTY OWNER AGREED TO BUILD AN EASEMENT TO A PUBLIC BEACH, THE CONDITION CONSTITUTED A TAKING BECAUSE THERE WAS NO NEXUS BETWEEN THE CONDITION AND THE PURPOSE BEHIND WITHHOLDING THE PERMIT

Nollan v. California Coastal Commission

(Beachhouse Builder) v. (State Commission)
(1987) 483 U.S. 825

M E M O R Y G R A P H I C

Instant Facts

The Commission granted Nollan a building permit on the condition that Nollan allow the public to pass across his property to access a public beach.

Black Letter Rule

If a regulatory condition is imposed on a development permit, that condition must substantially advance the same governmental purpose that refusing the permit would serve or else the action will constitute a taking and require just compensation.

Case Vocabulary

NEXUS: A link or connection.

Procedural Basis: Appeal from action to invalidate condition on development permit.

Facts: The Nollans (P) own a beachfront lot located between two public beach areas. Faria County Park is located a quarter-mile north of the Nollans' (P) lot, while "the Cove" is located 1,800 feet south of it. An eight-foot high concrete seawall separates the Nollans' (P) beach portion of their property from the rest of the lot. The historic mean high tide line forms the lot's other boundary. The Nollans (P) originally leased the lot for several years with an option to buy, and this option was conditioned on their (P) promise to demolish the pre-existing bungalow and replace it. To do this, the Nollans (P) were required under California law to obtain a coastal development permit from the California Coastal Commission (D). On February 25, 1982, they (P) submitted a permit application to the Commission (D). The Nollans (P) proposed to replace the bungalow with a three-bedroom house like others in the neighborhood. The Commission staff (D) informed the Nollans (P) that it (D) had recommended that the permit be granted, but subject to the condition that they (P) allow the public an easement across the beach portion of their (P) property. This was to allow the public easier access to Faria County Park and the Cove. The Nollans (P) opposed this condition but the Commission (D) nonetheless granted the permit as recommended. In June 1982, the Nollans (P) went to the Ventura County Superior Court to invalidate the condition, claiming that it could not be imposed without evidence that their (P) development would effect public access to the beach. The court then remanded to the Commission (D), which subsequently reaffirmed the condition. The Nollans (P) petitioned the Superior Court again and claimed the condition effected a taking. The Court ruled in their (P) favor on other grounds, and the Commission appealed (D). The Court of Appeal reversed, saying the imposition of the condition was not a taking. The Nollans (P) appealed.

Issue: Can the State's requiring of an easement on an owner's property as a condition for issuing a development permit serve as the equivalent of a taking?

Decision and Rationale: (Scalia) Yes. If the State imposes a condition on a development permit, that condition must substantially advance the same governmental purpose that refusing the permit would serve, or else the action will constitute a taking and require just compensation. The Commission (D) claims that the Nollans' (P) new house would interfere with the public's "visual access" to the beach, and thus create a "psychological barrier" to access. These burdens would supposedly be alleviated by requiring the Nollans (P) provide "lateral access" across their segment of the beach. Despite the Commission's (D) argument, it is impossible to understand how forcing the Nollans (P) to create an easement for people that are already on the public beaches reduces any visual obstacles that the new house creates in seeing the beach. In addition, it is impossible to understand how this requirement lowers any "psychological barrier" to using the public beaches. The use of the permit condition, thus, does not fulfill any of the stated "access" purposes. Justice Brennan argues that the easement should be granted because a person on the road would not be able to tell that a public beach is in the area unless the person can see people walking on the beach. This idea favoring the Commission's various access arguments is countered by the fact that a wall of houses would have completely blocked the view of the beach from the road, so no one there would see the beach at all. Property rights should only be abridged through the police power when such action results in a "substantial advanc[ing] of a legitimate state interest." This substantial requirement is needed due to the risk that the actual purpose of the use of police power may be to avoid compensation. Though the Commission (D) argues that the easement is part of a "comprehensive program" of public access to the beaches, if it (D) wishes to advance this purpose, it should use its power of eminent domain and pay for such an easement. Judgment reversed.

Dissent: (Brennan, Blackmun, Stevens) The majority has merely imposed a discredited standard in determining the validity of a state's exercise of police power. Despite this unwarranted, tight standard, the permit condition imposed against the Nollans (P) directly addressed the concerns over the burden on access that the Nollans' (P) new house would have caused.

Analysis:

The imposition of the lateral easement may seem like a valid means of achieving the average reciprocity of advantage Holmes' mentioned in Mahon. This may be particularly true for those who accept Brennan's arguments that the condition answered the Commission's concerns over all the different types of access. Although the granting of the permit with the easement condition would appear to fulfill the public's need for access and the Nollans' desire to build, it would also impose a burden solely on the Nollans. If the public were given free access to a walkway across the Nollans' personal beach, it is likely that trash and debris would end up in the Nollans' backyard. There would also likely be a problem with loud music or crowd noise, particularly in the summer months and holidays when young people are out of school and families go to the beach. Furthermore, the likelihood of such inconveniences may force the Nollans, if they choose to sell their property, to accept a lower purchase price.

Dolan v. City of Tigard

(Business Owner) v. (Municipality)
512 U.S. 374 (1994)

MEMORY GRAPHIC

Instant Facts

In exchange for the approval of a building permit, a city attempted to force a business owner to dedicate a portion of her property to the city for floodplain and recreational easements.

Black Letter Rule

Exactions are constitutional provided the benefits achieved are reasonably related and roughly proportional, both in nature and extent, to the impact of the proposed development.

Case Vocabulary

EXACTION: A local government measure that requires a developer to provide goods or services or pay fees as a condition to getting project approval.
NEXUS: A close connection.

Procedural Basis: Writ of certiorari reviewing state court orders affirming decision of land use board and city planning commission permitting imposition of exactions in exchange for building permit.

Facts: Florence Dolan (P) owned a plumbing and electric supply store in the Central Business District of the city of Tigard (D) in Oregon. Dolan (P) applied to the City (D) for a permit to redevelop the site. Dolan (P) desired to double the size of her store, build an additional structure on the property, and pave a parking lot. The City Planning Commission granted Dolan's (P) permit subject to certain conditions imposed by the City's (D) Community Development Code ("CDC"). The Commission required that Dolan (P) dedicate approximately 10% of her property for improvement of a storm drainage system and creation of a Greenway easement along Fanno Creek (which ran along a portion of Dolan's (P) property) and for a pedestrian/bicycle pathway. Dolan (P) requested variances from the CDC standards. She alleged that the Commission's exaction would cause an undue or unnecessary hardship. The Commission denied Dolan's (P) request. Dolan (P) appealed to the Land Use Board of Appeals ("LUBA") on the ground that the dedication requirements were not related to the proposed development as required by *Nollan v. California Coastal Comm'n* [an exaction is not a taking if it substantially advances the same governmental purpose that refusing the permit would serve]. LUBA concluded that there was a reasonable relationship between the proposed development and the requirement to dedicate land along the creek due to the increased amount of water runoff that the new development would create. LUBA also concluded that the pedestrian/bicycle pathway was reasonably related to the development, as the significantly larger retail sales building would attract more customers and employees who could use the pathway, thereby reducing motor vehicle traffic. The Oregon Court of Appeals and Oregon Supreme Court affirmed, rejecting Dolan's (P) contention that *Nollan* had abandoned the "reasonable relationship" test in favor of a stricter "essential nexus" test. The Court read *Nollan* to mean that an exaction is reasonably related to an impact if the exaction serves the same purpose that a denial of the permit would serve. The United States Supreme Court granted certiorari.

Issue: Must the benefits of an exaction be roughly proportional both in nature and extent to the impact of the proposed development?

Decision and Rationale: (Rehnquist, J.) Yes. The benefits of an exaction must be roughly proportional both in nature and extent to the impact of the proposed development. We adopt this "rough proportionality" test as a middle ground that is superior to the "reasonable relationship" test. Some states have required only very generalized conclusions as to the connection between the required dedication and the proposed development. Others have required a very exacting, specific and uniquely attributable connection. The majority of states have chosen an intermediate "reasonable relationship" test, but we find this confusing because of the similarity with the "rational basis" test under the Equal Protection Clause. Under the "rough proportionality" test, a city desiring to impose an exaction must make some sort of individualized determination that the required dedication is related both in nature and extent to the impact of the proposed development. If there is no "rough proportionality," then the conditioning of a permit on a forced dedication violates the Takings Clause of the Fifth Amendment. In the case at hand, it is difficult to see why recreational visitors trampling along Dolan's (P) floodplain easement is sufficiently related to the City's (D) legitimate interest in reducing flooding problems. Dedication of the Greenway easement to the City (D) would result in the loss of Dolan's (P) fundamental right to exclude others from her property. The City (D) has failed to make an individualized determination to support this part of its request. Likewise, with respect to the pedestrian/ bicycle pathway, the City (D) has not met its burden of demonstrating that the additional number of bicycle and vehicle trips generated by Dolan's (P) development reasonably relate to the city's requirement for a pedestrian/bicycle pathway. The City (D) merely found that the pathway could offset some traffic congestion, not that it was *likely* to do so. While the City's (D) goals of reducing flooding hazards and traffic congestion are laudable, they overly impose on Dolan's (P) constitutional rights. Reversed and remanded.

Analysis:

The Supreme Court, while purporting to establish a new "rough proportionality" test, essentially adopts the same "reasonable relationship" test that had been adopted by a majority of state courts. In brief, this test states that, in order for a city to condition a building permit on the dedication of land to the city, there must be a reasonable relationship between the dedication and the impact of the proposed development. The opinion clarifies the reasonable relationship test by requiring specific findings of fact; it thus supplements, rather than replaces, the *Nollan* rule. The City's (D) downfall resulted from failing to make specific findings. On remand, however, it is possible that the City (D) could still prevail. It could conduct studies and make more definite findings regarding the benefits of its proposed forced dedications. As the notes following the case indicate, exactions have become an important means of funding public improvements. Exactions allow a City (D) to relax zoning ordinances in exchange for goods, services, money, or the dedication of easements. Some commentators argued that the *Nollan* and *Dolan* decisions would significantly limit the ability of localities to impose exactions. Others disagree, based on the practical reality that many land developers (especially those who do a lot of work in a particular city) would not risk their goodwill with city regulators by suing to challenge exactions that the regulators impose.

U.S. SUPREME COURT HOLDS THAT A CHURCH WHICH CLAIMED ITS CAMPGROUND PROPERTY WAS TEMPORARILY TAKEN BY A LAND-USE REGULATION IS ENTITLED TO COMPENSATION BECAUSE INVALIDATION OF THE ORDINANCE WOULD NOT MAKE UP FOR THE LOSSES SUSTAINED WHILE THE REGULATION WAS IN EFFECT

First English Evangelical Lutheran Church of Glendale v. County of Los Angeles

(Campground Owner) v. (County)
(1987) 482 U.S. 304

M E M O R Y   G R A P H I C

Instant Facts

A county ordinance kept a church from re-building its campground for several years, and the church wanted to be compensated for that period of time.

Black Letter Rule

An owner whose property has been subjected to a regulatory taking is entitled to compensation for the period during which the regulation denied the owner all use of the land, and not just mere declaratory or injunctive relief invalidating the regulation.

Case Vocabulary

DENUDE: To strip land of trees; to make barren.
WATERSHED: An area, bounded on its extreme edge by a ridge, which drains into a body of water.

Procedural Basis: Appeal from motion to strike portion of complaint in inverse condemnation and tort action for damages.

Facts: In 1957, First English Evangelical Lutheran Church (P) bought a 21-acre piece of land in the Angeles National Forest. This land was located in a canyon, along the banks of Mill Creek. On this site, the church (P) ran a campground, called "Lutherglen," which was used as a retreat center and a recreational area for handicapped children. In July 1977, a forest fire in the canyon created a serious flood hazard. In February 1978, after a heavy storm hit the canyon, Lutherglen was flooded and its buildings were destroyed. In January 1979, the County of Los Angeles (D) enacted Interim Ordinance No. 11,855 in response to the flooding of the canyon. This ordinance stated, in part, that a "person shall not construct, reconstruct, place or enlarge any building or structure... located within the outer boundary lines of the interim flood protection area located in Mill Creek Canyon..." This interim flood protection area included the Lutherglen site. The ordinance went into immediate effect as the county (D) determined that it was "required for the immediate preservation of the public health and safety." Just over a month later, the church (P) filed a complaint against the county (D) in the Superior Court of California. The church (P) alleged, among other things, that the ordinance denied it (P) all use of Lutherglen, and sought damages for the loss of use of Lutherglen. The County relied on *Agins v. Tiburon* (1979) 24 Cal. 3d 266, 598 P.2d 25 [compensation not required for a regulatory taking until the regulation has been held to be excessive and the government allows it to remain in effect] in claiming the church's (P's) allegation was "irrelevant." The trial court granted a motion to strike this allegation. It also granted the county's (D's) motion for judgment on the pleadings and dismissed the complaint. On appeal, the Court of Appeal also relied on *Agins* in rejecting the cause of action. The California Supreme Court denied review on October 17, 1985. The merits of the case had yet to be determined at this time.

Issue:

Does the Just Compensation Clause require the government to provide compensation for the period of time during which a regulation denies an owner all use of his or her property?

Decision and Rationale: (Rehnquist) Yes. An owner whose property has been subjected to a regulatory taking is entitled to compensation for the period the regulation was in effect against the property, and not just mere declaratory or injunctive relief invalidating the ordinance. While the typical taking occurs when a government uses its power of eminent domain to condemn property, the doctrine of inverse condemnation is wholly based on the idea that a taking can occur by other means. The government cannot destroy the value of a piece of property and be exempt from the compensation requirement just because it did not convert the property to public use. This Court has noted that when the government abandons condemnation proceedings, the property is nonetheless subjected to temporary use and occupation. Compensation is thus required because an owner's use of property has been interfered with. Here, when the Supreme Court of California denied review, the ordinance had deprived First English (P) of the use of the property for over six years. The burden on First English (P) in having this case decided over that time is undoubtedly great. Because this burden is the result of a government ordinance, the Just Compensation Clause demands that the government provide compensation for the use of the land during this period. No subsequent action by the government, such as invalidation of the ordinance, would relieve it of the duty to provide compensation for that period. Though the county (D) relies on *Danforth v. United States* (1939) 308 U.S. 271 [changes in value caused by legislation for the beginning or completion of a project is not a taking in the constitutional sense] and *Agins v. Tiburon* in arguing against compensation, these cases only stand for the idea that the value of taken property is equal to its value at the time the taking occurred. This decision is based on the assumption that the ordinance did deprive First English (P) of all use of Lutherglen for several years. Judgment of California Court of Appeal reversed and case remanded.

Dissent: (Stevens) The Court has not found that a taking had occurred as a result of the flood control ordinance. Because this regulation was a valid safety measure, no compensation should be required. In addition, the duration of a restriction should be considered when determining whether a regulatory taking has occurred. There should be no constitutional distinction between a permanent restriction that reduces the value of a property by a fraction and a restriction that merely postpones the development of a property for a smaller fraction of its useful life. The former does not constitute a taking, but the majority has decided that the latter does and requires compensation. Moreover, property owners should have to explain why invalidation of a regulation would not provide an adequate remedy in order to challenge a temporary taking. Finally, this decision may lead local officials and land-use planners to refrain from enacting many forms of important health and safety regulation, out of fear of litigation.

Analysis:

The Court's decision that regulation of land could constitute a taking and require compensation was not an entirely new one. As Gene Rankin explains in "The First Bite at the Apple: State Supreme Court Takings Jurisprudence Antedating *First English*," at least eight states had already decided that their state constitutions required compensation for regulatory takings. These states, Arizona, New Hampshire, New Jersey, North Dakota, Oregon, Rhode Island, Texas, and Wisconsin, all have differing degrees of urban and rural development. What these decisions seem to indicate is that the courts in those states have a better grip on issues of local government and land regulation than their counterparts in Washington, D.C. The courts in these states, and later the Supreme Court, apparently understood that resources are limited. When a government ends up imposing land-use regulation which deprives owners of the use of their land, the owners cannot just pack up and find new land.